Haitian Revolutionary Studies

BLACKS IN THE DIASPORA
*Darlene Clark Hine, John McCluskey, Jr., and David Barry Gaspar,
General Editors*

DAVID PATRICK GEGGUS

Haitian
Revolutionary Studies

INDIANA
University Press
Bloomington & Indianapolis

This book is a publication of

Indiana University Press
601 North Morton Street
Bloomington, IN 47404-3797 USA

http://iupress.indiana.edu

Telephone orders   800-842-6796
Fax orders   812-855-7931
Orders by e-mail   iuporder@indiana.edu

The paper used in this publication meets the minimum requirements of American National Standard for Information Sciences—Permanence of Paper for Printed Library Materials, ANSI Z39.48-1984.

Manufactured in the United States of America

Library of Congress Cataloging-in-Publication Data

Geggus, David Patrick.
  Haitian revolutionary studies / David Patrick Geggus.
    p.   cm. — (Blacks in the diaspora)
Includes bibliographical references and index.
  ISBN 0-253-34104-3 (cloth : alk. paper)
  1. Haiti—History—Revolution, 1791–1804. I. Title. II. Series.
  F1923 .G34 2002
  972.94'03—dc21

                                   2001006201

1 2 3 4 5   07 06 05 04 03 02

Contents

Preface

The few hundred square miles around the modern town of Cap Haïtien have a special place in both the beginning and the beginning of the end of European imperialism. The first revolt against European colonization in the Americas took place there less than twelve months after Columbus's arrival in the Caribbean. Three hundred years later, long after the aboriginal Arawaks had vanished and French rulers, replacing Spanish, had repeopled the land with African slaves, the same region saw one of the most dramatic challenges ever mounted against a colonizing power in any age or continent. The 1791 slave insurrection was the largest in New World history, and in the course of twelve years of desolating warfare it led to the creation of Latin America's first independent state.

The destruction of la Navidad in 1493 and the slave uprising of 1791 took place in very different societies and were vastly different in magnitude and result. Some contemporaries of the Haitian Revolution, however, showed a fitting sense of history when they depicted the black slaves in poetry and prose as avenging the Amerindians who had died three centuries before. More important, the leaders of the ex-slaves themselves chose to underline the parallel by giving back to the land they reconquered from the Europeans the aboriginal name of "Haïti." Thus emphasizing the break with European colonialism, they gave their new state an American identity and expressed solidarity with the long-dead Amerindians whose patrimony they were then inheriting. It was in the northern plain of Haiti that non-Europeans made their first, and first successful, challenges to the European right to rule proclaimed at Tordesillas in 1494 and for five centuries thereafter.

The subject of this book is the revolution that grew out of that slave uprising and transformed French Saint Domingue, one of the most productive European colonies, into an independent state run by former slaves and the descendants of slaves. The Haitian Revolution of 1789–1803 produced the world's first examples of wholesale emancipation in a major slave-owning society, colonial representation in a metropolitan assembly, and full racial equality in a European colony. It occurred when the Atlantic slave trade was at its peak and when slavery was an accepted institution from Canada to Chile. The slave revolt that laid waste the immensely wealthy colony between 1791 and 1793 was probably the largest and only fully successful one there has ever been. Of all American struggles for colonial independence, the Haitian Revolution involved the greatest degree of mass mobilization and brought the greatest degree of social and economic change. In an age of tumultuous events and world war, it seized international attention with images of apocalyptic destruction and a new world in the making.

There has been no shortage of general studies of the revolution in English, but the quantity of primary research seems remarkably small seen against the prodigious output of dissertations by U.S. universities. The best recent scholarship (by John Garrigus, Stewart King, Mimi Sheller, and Laurent Dubois) has concentrated on Haiti before and after its revolution or on the revolutionary period in other French colonies. Most general histories of the Haitian Revolution are of a popular or superficial nature, and few are the work of specialists in the history of slavery or the French Caribbean. Even the very best tend to be their author's first publications on the subject—a situation scarcely imaginable in the historiographies of the French, Mexican, or Russian revolutions. However, Carolyn Fick's solidly researched *The Making of Haiti* (1990) points the way forward, and C. L. R. James's *The Black Jacobins* (1938) stands out as an unquestioned classic, although it was written nearly seventy years ago. Among French scholars, Pierre Pluchon's controversial biographies of Toussaint Louverture (1979, 1989) have been the outstanding works of recent years. Charles Frostin and the prolific Gabriel Debien, the leading historians of Saint Domingue, wrote relatively little about the revolution there. More recently, Yves Bénot and Florence Gauthier have restored the colonial question to French Revolution studies, but their research has been primarily on metropolitan matters.

This collection brings together thirteen essays that are mainly focused pieces of primary research. They are intended to widen and deepen knowledge of the revolution and construct a more accurate history than is currently available. Based on archival research conducted in a half-dozen countries, they marshal an unprecedented range of evidence that is used to explore some central issues and little-studied topics. The chapters are organized into six thematic sections. The first provides a narrative overview of the Haitian Revolution, its significance, and its international repercussions. Section II is devoted to recent historiography and to archival sources that have been little exploited in writing on the revolution. The following section, on the origins of rebellion, surveys debates regarding slave resistance in world history and then examines a long-running controversy in Haitian studies regarding the contribution to the revolution of the vodou religion and of fugitive slaves. The following chapter focuses on a seminal event known as the Bois Caïman ceremony. A vodou ceremony that preceded the slave uprising has often been viewed as the founding moment of the Haitian nation, but its nature, significance, and very existence have been sharply contested in recent years.

The book's fourth section is organized around the theme of the problematic relations between the enslaved and free nonwhite sectors of Saint Domingue society and their development during the years of revolution. The topic brings into fine focus the question of race, class, and color as competing categories of analysis. Chapter 7 is a study of the "Swiss," a group of slaves armed by free coloreds in their fight for racial equality who were later deported to Central America. The episode provides a window on the conflicted nature of free colored politics and has become a symbol of class relations in Haiti. The following chapter concerns the central figure of the slave revolution and one of its main turning points. The decision of the freedman Toussaint Louverture to abandon his Spanish allies in 1794 and lead the slave rebels over to the French Republic has been cloaked in obscurity and hotly debated ever since. The chapter examines materialist and idealist interpretations of this episode, which is critical for assessing the politics of the famous leader and the relationship between the French and Haitian Revolutions. Jean Kina, the subject of Chapter 9, was another black freedman and military leader whose career, however, followed a completely different trajectory to Toussaint Louverture's. An ally of the planter class, he fought against slave and free colored insurgents in Saint Domingue, but toward the end of his military service he staged an enigmatic revolt on Martinique, which led to imprisonment first in England, then in France in the same jail as the fallen Toussaint.

Section V groups three chapters that explore international ramifications of the Haitian Revolution. The first of these examines the impact of colonial developments on the French Revolution and the manner in which white colonists' pursuit of autonomy, free coloreds' campaigns for equality, and the slaves' desire for freedom interacted with one another and shaped metropolitan policy-making. Chapter 11 offers a unique comparative perspective on British, Spanish, and U.S. policy toward the unfolding revolution in Saint Domingue down to the achievement of Haitian independence. Particular attention is paid to Spain's involvement in the revolution, which has been very little researched. This is especially true of the Spanish government's extraordinary experiment in recruiting the slave rebels of 1791 as "auxiliary troops" in its attempted conquest of the colony. Chapter 12 deals with the resettlement of these men and their families after the experiment went awry. It traces their extraordinary odyssey and continuing struggles in Cuba, Central America, Mexico, Florida, and Spain.

By way of an epilogue, the final chapter investigates why the first modern black state was given an Amerindian name. The choice of name raises interesting questions about ethnicity and identity and historical knowledge among the former slaves and free coloreds who created Haiti. Surveying sources from the sixteenth to the twentieth century, the chapter traces use of the word "Haiti" and seeks to understand the meanings attached to it by different sections of Haitian society.

Chapters 7 and 12 are entirely new pieces of work; the other eleven have been previously published but have been extensively revised and updated. In all, a quarter of the text consists of new material. The published pieces appeared in specialist journals or books in the United States, France, Spain, Trinidad, Jamaica, India, and the Netherlands, several of which are not easily accessible even in research libraries. Assembling them in one volume offers an up-to-date collection that I hope will be useful for students and scholars in Latin American, African American, and Caribbean history who wish to explore beyond the basic narrative of the Haitian Revolution.

Acknowledgments

First I must thank Barry Gaspar of Duke University, general editor of this series, for originally suggesting the idea for this book and Joan Catapano of Indiana University Press for supporting the project. Kate Babbitt provided meticulous copyediting, and Linda Opper helped with retyping. Jim Sloan of the University of Florida geography department drew the maps. The comte de Chamski-Mandajors, Dr. Marcel Châtillon, Jean-Louis Clavière, Lord Colville of Culross, the late Gabriel Debien, and Mrs Phyllis Spencer Bernard gave permission to consult or loaned copies of documents in their possession. Marixa Lasso, Paul Lokken, and Douglas Tompson provided invaluable leads to sources for Chapter 12. I am extremely grateful to all of them for their help.

Research for these chapters stretches back to the early 1970s. It has received generous financial support from University of Florida research and travel grants and, in the form of fellowships, from the British Academy "Thank-Offering to Britain" fund, the John Simon Guggenheim Foundation, the National Endowment for the Humanities, the National Humanities Center, the Social Science Research Council, and the Woodrow Wilson Center for International Scholars. I am greatly indebted to these institutions and their staffs.

Earlier versions of eleven of the thirteen chapters previously have appeared in other publications. I am most grateful to their publishers for kind permission to reuse the material in this work. Original publication details are listed below.

Chapter 1, "The Haitian Revolution," is from *The Modern Caribbean,* ed. Franklin W. Knight and Colin Palmer, 21–50. Copyright © 1989 by the University of North Carolina Press. Used by permission of the publisher.

Chapter 2 was first published as "The Haitian Revolution: New Approaches and Old," *Proceedings of the 19th Meeting of the French Colonial Historical Society,* ed. James Pritchard (Cleveland: French Colonial Historical Society, 1994), 141–155.

Chapter 3 was first published as "Unexploited Sources for the History of the Haitian Revolution," in *Latin American Research Review* 18, no. 1 (1983): 95–103.

Chapter 4, "The Causation of Slave Rebellions: An Overview," is from *Indian Historical Review* 15 (1988): 116–129.

Chapter 5 was first published as "Marronage, Voodoo, and the Saint Domingue Slave Revolt," in *Proceedings of the 15th Meeting of the French Colonial Historical Society, Martinique and Guadeloupe, May 1989,* ed. Philip Boucher and Patricia Galloway (Lanham, Md.: University Press of America, 1992), 22–35.

Chapter 6, "The Bois Caïman Ceremony," is from *Journal of Caribbean History* 25 (1991): 41–57.

Chapter 8 was first published as "From His Most Catholic Majesty to the Godless République: The Volte-Face of Toussaint Louverture and the Ending of Slavery in Saint-Domingue," *Revue Française d'Histoire d'Outre-Mer* 65 (1978): 481–499.

Chapter 9, "Slave, Soldier, Rebel: The Strange Career of Jean Kina," is from *Jamaican Historical Review* 12 (1980): 33–51.

Chapter 10, "Racial Equality, Slavery, and Colonial Secession during the Constituent Assembly," is from the *American Historical Review* 94 (1989): 1290–1308. By permission of the American Historical Association.

Chapter 11, "The Great Powers and the Haitian Revolution," is from *Tordesillas y sus consecuencias: La política de las grandes potencias europeas respecto a América Latina (1494–1898)*, ed. Bernd Schröter and Karin Schüller (Madrid: Iberoamericana, and Frankfurt am Main: Vervuert Verlag, 1995), 113–125.

Chapter 13, "The Naming of Haiti," was first published in *New West Indian Guide* 71, no. 1/2 (1997): 43–68.

The map on page 4 is used by permission of Oxford University Press and first appeared in David Patrick Geggus, *Slavery, War and Revolution: The British Occupation of Saint Domingue, 1793–1798* (Oxford: Oxford University Press, 1982), © David Patrick Geggus 1982.

Part One.   *Overview*

*Sandwiched spatially and chronologically between the colonial
revolutions of North and South America, Haiti's revolution was
intimately bound up with the revolution in France of 1789–
1804, whose dates it shares. Just how much it owed to the French
Revolution is one of the major issues in its interpretation. French
scholars have generally preferred the term Saint Domingue Revolution to that of Haitian Revolution because the latter implies a
struggle for independence that the revolution became only during its final two years and because it obscures the conflicts
among the colony's white population with which the revolution
began. Like its metropolitan counterpart, the revolution in Saint
Domingue consisted of several separate struggles in one.*

*Perhaps the easiest way to get a grip on its complicated narra-
tive is to think of it as the pursuit of three political goals by three
social groups in a colony divided into three provinces. White
colonists, free people of African descent, and slaves constituted
the three legal divisions of colonial society. Despite their internal
class conflicts, most whites wanted from the revolution a greater
degree of self-government, free people of color wanted equality
with whites, and slaves wanted their freedom. White racism and
slave-holding by free persons made these goals incompatible.
Differences in social composition and history between Saint Domingue's north, west, and south provinces added an element of
regional variation to the revolution's development. Thus the civil
war of 1799–1800 can be seen as a clash between former slaves
and the colored middle class or as a struggle about greater
autonomy from France or as primarily a regional conflict.*

*The revolution's chronology fits less well into a tripartite struc-
ture. It is true that its last two years (War of Independence) and
first two years (before the slaves became political players) form
distinct units, leaving a long middle section. However, the period
1791–1801 was marked by a series of events that also count as
major turning points: the achievement of racial equality in
1792, the outbreak of war and the local abolition of slavery in
1793, the volte-face of Toussaint Louverture in 1794, and the ex-*

pulsion of foreign invaders in 1798. The outbreak of war with the colonial powers in 1793 was, along with the French Revolution, the main external influence that shaped the development of the Haitian Revolution. Historians tend to divide between those who stress these external influences and those whose explanations emphasize factors internal to colonial society.

The impact on the wider world of this 15-year struggle for racial equality, slave emancipation, and colonial independence was richly ambiguous. Although it aroused widespread fear among slave-owners, it stimulated the expansion of slavery elsewhere through its effect on prices and the refugee diaspora it spawned. It provided forceful arguments for abolitionists yet placed new barriers in their path. Its example encouraged slave resistance across the Americas but also increased controls by slave-holding regimes. The revolution lent material assistance to the independence struggle in Venezuela but proved a negative influence on decolonization in other places. For people of African descent, and for many radicals and romantics in general, it was a glorious symbol that in time became tarnished.

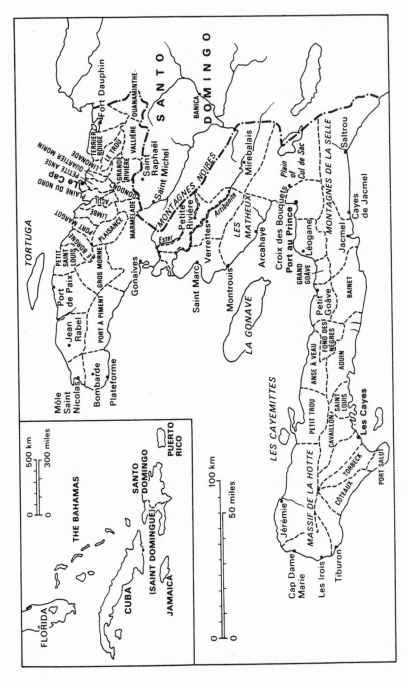

Map 1. Saint Domingue: parish boundaries and towns

1 The Haitian Revolution

Racial equality, the abolition of slavery, decolonization, and nationhood first came to the Caribbean with the Haitian Revolution.[1] Between 1791 and 1803, the opulent French colony of Saint Domingue was transformed by the largest and most successful of all slave revolts. After twelve years of desolating warfare, Haiti emerged in 1804 as the first modern independent state in the Americas after the United States. For slaves and slave-owners throughout the New World, the Haitian Revolution was an inspiration and a warning. The most productive colony of the day had been destroyed, its economy ruined, its ruling class eliminated. Few revolutions in world history have had such profound consequences.

Saint Domingue in the 1780s

In the period between the American and French revolutions, Saint Domingue produced close to one-half of all the sugar and coffee consumed in Europe and the Americas as well as substantial amounts of cotton, indigo, and ground provisions. Though scarcely larger than Maryland and little more than twice the size of Jamaica, it had long been the wealthiest colony in the Caribbean and was hailed by publicists as the "Pearl of the Antilles" or the "Eden of the Western World." Moreover, it was still expanding. In the long-settled coastal plains, the number of sugar plantations grew only slowly, but the mountainous interior was the scene of bustling pioneer activity where new coffee estates were being cut out of the mountain forests to meet a rising demand in Europe and North America.

By 1789, Saint Domingue had about 8,000 plantations producing crops for export. They generated some two-fifths of France's overseas trade, a proportion rarely equaled in any colonial empire. Saint Domingue's importance to France was not just economic but fiscal (in customs revenue) and strategic too, since the colonial trade provided both seamen for the national navy in wartime and foreign exchange to purchase vital naval stores from northern Europe (hemp, mast trees, saltpeter). In the Môle Saint Nicolas, the colony also contained the most secure naval base in the West Indies.

Although colonial statistics are not very reliable, Saint Domingue's population on the eve of the French Revolution consisted of approximately 500,000 slaves, 40,000 whites (including troops and transient seamen), and 30,000 free people of color, who constituted a sort of middle class. In broad outline, Saint Domingue society thus conformed to the three-tier structure common to all sugar colonies. However, there were some significant differences.

The tiny white community was united by racial solidarity but also divided to an unusual degree along class lines. The resulting tensions pitted sugar and coffee planters against each other as well as against merchants and lawyers and separated all of these groups from the turbulent *petits blancs,* or poor whites, an amorphous group that included plantation managers, artisans, clerks, shopkeepers, seamen, and peddlers. Such tensions reflected the wealth and diversity of Saint Domingue's economy. Also, because France was a much more populous country than Great Britain or Spain and possessed fewer colonies, Saint Domingue inevitably attracted uncommonly large numbers of indigent young men seeking employment. The richest planters, on the other hand, were able to reside in Europe and live off their revenues. This was typical of West Indian sugar colonies. At the same time, however, the extent of less profitable secondary economic enterprises such as coffee, indigo, and cotton meant that Saint Domingue also possessed a sizable resident planter class, like the southern United States or Cuba. Residence in the colony, the colony's competitive position in the world market, and its ability to produce much of its own food were factors that encouraged some planters to envisage Saint Domingue's eventual independence.

Saint Domingue's free nonwhite population was unusual for its size and, more particularly, its wealth. Except in the Iberian colonies, free people of color were generally a very small minority. Very rarely did they rise above the position of prosperous artisan. In Saint Domingue, however, the *gens de couleur libres* outnumbered the whites in two of the colony's three provinces, and they included in their number rich and cultivated planters who had been educated in France. In Saint Domingue, anyone with a black ancestor, no matter how remote, was subject to the humiliating legal discrimination typical of all slave colonies in the eighteenth century. Nonwhites were banned from public office and the professions and were forbidden to wear fine clothing, to carry weapons in town, or sit with whites in church, at the theatre, or when eating. They were not only unequal before the law but also suffered extralegal harassment, especially from poor whites with whom they competed for jobs.

The *gens de couleur* thus covered an extremely broad social range, from recently freed African slaves to rich landowners and tradesmen who were almost indistinguishable in appearance or culture from their white counterparts. They constituted merely a legal category (those who were neither slave nor white) rather than a class. Probably a majority of the men were artisans or smallholders. The women were usually petty traders or white men's mistresses. As most were of mixed racial descent, the term "mulatto" was sometimes applied to the entire free nonwhite community. Some had both whites and slaves for relatives. Their position in Saint Domingue society was therefore highly ambiguous. Many were slave-owners or hunted down fugitive slaves in the militia and rural police force. All were held in subjection by the whites.

Despite the spread of liberal ideas in Europe, the laws governing free nonwhites in France, as well as Saint Domingue, grew increasingly severe in the late eighteenth century—a paradox of the French Enlightenment. At the same time, the free coloreds grew rapidly in number and in wealth as they profited from the coffee boom. By the 1780s, they not only dominated the rural police force but in addition formed the backbone of the colonial militia.

Saint Domingue's slave population was easily the largest in the Caribbean. It was nearly twice the size of that of Jamaica, its closest rival. The imbalance between slave and free, black and white was not unusually extreme, but for most of the 1780s, the number of slaves grew at a faster rate than probably anywhere else. During the period 1785–1790, an average of more than 30,000 manacled Africans were imported each year. Despite the influx of white immigrants and the growing community of free coloreds, Saint Domingue was becoming increasingly African. Young men around 20 years old comprised a substantial proportion of the black population.

The slave community was not at all homogeneous; it was even more segmented than the white and free colored groups. Split up into small units, tied six days a week to plantation labor, the slaves constituted a random agglomeration of individuals from diverse cultures; they spoke different languages and were at different stages of assimilation into colonial society. On a typical sugar estate of 200 slaves there could be Africans from twenty or more different linguistic groups. Mountain plantations were much smaller and even more isolated. Everywhere in Saint Domingue, however, Bantu slaves known as "Congos" constituted the largest of the African groups; they formed a third of the African population in the plains and well over half in the mountains.

On the lowland sugar plantations about half the adults were Creoles—that is, individuals born locally and raised in slavery; they made up perhaps one-third of the total slave population. Accustomed to producing their own food and marketing the surplus, they tended to be better off than the Africans. Fluent in the local Creole tongue, superficially Christianized, and united by at least limited family ties, they constituted the slave upper class. From their ranks were chosen the domestics, artisans, and slave-drivers who formed the slave elite. Elite slaves would have some familiarity with French, the language of the master class, and a few could read and write.

Little is known about how these groups interrelated. Plantation labor, social interaction, and the common experience of slavery inevitably imposed some sort of solidarity, which was symbolized in songs of call and response, networks of fictive kin, and a strong sense of locality. Moreover, slaves from different estates could meet at weekly markets, at Saturday night dances, and in more secret assemblies associated with the religious practices colonists called *vaudou*. Vodou (the preferred modern spelling) apparently served to integrate different religious traditions—West African, West Central African, and Christian—and doubtless helped release anomic tensions. Nevertheless, the diversity of the slave community must be accounted as one reason why, in a comparative context, Saint Domingue's slaves seem to have been remarkably unrebellious. It is true that in the twenty years before the American Revolution, poisoning scares swept the colony, but these had as much to do with white paranoia as with real resistance; in the 1780s, little was said about poison. Compared to the British or Dutch colonies, organized, violent resistance in Saint Domingue was relatively slight.

The Haitian Revolution 7

This paradox underlying the greatest of all slave revolts has received little scholarly attention. The planters themselves tended to attribute the absence of slave revolts to Saint Domingue's military-style government, which precluded the democratic dissensions of the self-governing British colonies and which placed far more stress on militia training. Certainly the slaves there seem to have been no better treated than in any other sugar colony. Perhaps most important, the colony's size and low population density meant that slave discontent was most easily channeled into fleeing to the mountains and forests. Other slaves fled over the frontier into the even more sparsely populated Spanish colony of Santo Domingo as well as to towns such as Port-au-Prince and Cap Français. While some runaways formed armed bands which attacked travelers or isolated plantations, they were never very numerous, and the 1780s saw a definite downturn in such activities. Although this is a controversial area, it seems clear that desertions were usually short-term and offered little threat to the system. Moreover, in 1777, an extradition treaty was signed with Santo Domingo. As new settlements spread into the remaining frontier regions and as the colony's forests were felled, it was becoming increasingly hard to be a successful maroon. It may be, therefore, that by the 1780s, slave dissidents were coming to see revolt as a more viable alternative.

The Influence of the American Revolution

Vulnerability to slave rebellion and foreign invasion made all West Indian colonies especially dependent on their mother countries for military and naval protection. Nevertheless, the desire for self-government had a long history in Saint Domingue, and among a minority of radical planters it was notably strengthened after the North American colonists won their independence from England. Apart from its ideological impact, the American Revolution gave Saint Domingue a tempting taste of free trade. When France intervened in the conflict, it opened the colony's ports to Yankee traders, who supplied its needs more cheaply than could French merchants. These commercial contacts were sustained after the war through a new system of free ports, but the trade was heavily taxed and subject to frustrating prohibitions. Moreover, smuggling was severely curtailed by new measures reminiscent of British action in North America twenty years before. Such conflicts of interest encouraged planters to think of themselves as "Americans" rather than Frenchmen.

The War of Independence had perhaps its greatest impact on the free community of African descent. A special regiment of free coloreds was raised and sent to Georgia to fight alongside the rebel colonists. It included André Rigaud, Jean-Baptiste Chavannes, J.-B. Villatte, Henry Christophe, Jean-Pierre Lambert, and Louis-Jacques Bauvais; its muster roll read like a roll call of future revolutionaries. These men returned to Saint Domingue with military experience and a new sense of their own importance. Prominent free coloreds secretly drew up a report attacking the caste system and in 1784 sent a representative to France.

The government, however, for fear of offending the whites or exciting the slaves, dared not yield an inch.

The abolition of slavery in Massachusetts and other northern states in the 1780s must have been discussed in Saint Domingue by American seamen and local whites, but it is not known how this affected the slaves. By the end of the decade, news was arriving from France itself of a French antislavery society, the Amis des Noirs. At the same time, government reforms aimed at limiting abuses on the plantations outraged the planter class. Hitherto, whites had presented a solid front on the question of slavery. Now cracks were starting to appear in what had been a monolithic white power structure.

The Impact of the French Revolution, 1789–1792

Historians do not agree on just how close Saint Domingue came to having a revolution in the 1780s. Whether the whites' desires for autonomy, the free coloreds' desire for equality, or the slaves' desire for liberty would of themselves have led to violent conflict must remain a matter for speculation. No one doubts, however, that the French Revolution of 1789 precipitated the colony's destruction. If Saint Domingue was a dormant volcano, as contemporaries liked to say, it needed only the shock waves of the political earthquake in Paris to provoke its eruption.

The ideological impact of the French Revolution is not easy to distinguish from its political impact. The ideals of liberty, equality, and fraternity proclaimed by the revolutionaries in Paris were peculiarly dangerous for Caribbean societies, which represented their complete negation. But at the same time, the overthrow of the ancien régime in France also directly undermined the traditional sources of authority in France's colonies—governor, intendant, law courts, garrison, militia, police. The French Revolution thus enflamed social and political aspirations while weakening the institutions that held them in check.

The influence of the French Revolution was felt first at the peak of the social pyramid and thereafter worked its way downward. Although colonists were not invited when the States-General was summoned in 1788 to recommend sweeping changes in French government, wealthy planters in both Paris and Saint Domingue met in secret committees to elect deputies and ensure their representation. Their activities in fact merged with movements already underway to protest against recent government reforms in the colonies. It was the fall of the Bastille, however, and the creation of a National Assembly in the summer of 1789 that overturned the ancien régime in Saint Domingue as well as in France. While mobs of poor whites adopted the tricolor cockade and riotously celebrated the news from Paris, planters, merchants, and lawyers became politicians and elected assemblies in each of the colony's three provinces. In many parishes and towns, elected committees and municipalities emerged alongside or replaced local military commanders. The militia was converted into a National Guard dominated by the plantocracy. The intendant, former strongman of the administration, was driven out of the colony, and the governor, uncertain of support from France, was forced to accept what he could not prevent.

From April to August 1790, a Colonial Assembly met in the town of Saint Marc. It declared itself sovereign and boldly drew up a constitution severely restricting French control even over matters of trade. Its most radical deputies openly discussed the idea of independence. The extremism of these *Patriotes* (a.k.a. Côté ouest party, or Pompons Rouges) brought about a backlash which temporarily united the Assembly of the North with the governor and military. In 1789, the elegant northern capital of Cap Français (or Le Cap) had been in the forefront of the revolution. Thereafter its prominent merchants and establishment lawyers became a moderating influence, and sprawling and shabby Port-au-Prince took over as the center of colonial radicalism. Lower-class whites came to exercise increasing control over its politics, notably after its garrison mutinied in March 1791 and caused the governor to flee to Le Cap.

Colonial politics was an affair of factions and demagogues. Without previous political experience, Saint Domingue's whites threw up local leaders of ephemeral fame who maintained the Creoles' reputation for turbulence and impulsive egotism. Divided by regional, class, and political loyalties, colonists disagreed about what degree of autonomy Saint Domingue should seek, how much militancy they should employ, what classes of whites should vote and serve together in the militia, and whether the colony should be represented in the National Assembly or cooperate directly with the king's ministers. But the great majority agreed on two things—that no one should tamper with the institution of slavery, and that the system of white supremacy should be rigorously maintained. Increasingly, however, the revolution in France came to be seen as a threat to both these pillars of colonial society.

In 1789, the Société des Amis des Noirs gained new prominence as the revolution provided a platform for its leading members (Mirabeau, Brissot, Condorcet). It campaigned only for the abolition of the slave trade and for equal rights for free coloreds and disclaimed any desire to interfere with slavery. However, to the colonial mind, which saw racial discrimination as an essential bulwark of slavery, such action endangered white lives in the West Indies. Encouraged by the Amis des Noirs, free coloreds in Paris demanded that the National Assembly live up to its Declaration of the Rights of Man. Were they not men, too, and landowners and taxpayers? At the same time, the autumn of 1789, free colored property-owners in Saint Domingue also gathered to demand equal rights with whites. Some also seem to have called for the freeing of mixed-race slaves, and those in Paris spoke of an eventual, though distant, abolition of slavery. In general, however, free people of color acted like the slave-owners they usually were and were careful not to have their cause confused with that of the black masses.

In a few parts of the colony, the early days of the French Revolution saw people of African descent and whites attending meetings together and sitting on the same committees, but this was rare. The free coloreds' request to adopt the tricolor cockade created great unease among whites. Before long they and their few white allies became the victims of intimidatory acts of violence, including murder. Fears for the stability of the slave regime reinforced deep-seated prejudice, so that by 1790 it was clear that the colonists were determined to maintain the status quo and keep nonwhites out of politics. The Assembly of the West even demanded from them a humiliating oath of obedience. Faced by mounting persecution, some now fortified their plantations, but a small armed gathering in the spring in the Artibonite plain was easily dispersed. The free colored militia joined the governor's forces, which suppressed the Colonial Assembly, but the administration proved no more willing than the colonists to grant concessions.

Meanwhile, the men of color were acquiring leaders from among wealthy nonwhites now returning from France, men who had been accustomed to equal treatment. These included Villatte, J.-B. Lapointe, and Pierre Pinchinat, but it was the light-skinned Vincent Ogé (an unsuccessful small merchant) who decided to force the whites' hand. He had been a prominent spokesman of the free colored activists in Paris, where he had tried and failed to gain the cooperation of the absentee colonists. One of his brothers was killed in the skirmish in the Artibonite. In October, Ogé secretly returned to his home in the mountains of the north province. With Jean-Baptiste Chavannes, he rapidly raised an army of over 300 free coloreds and demanded that the governor put an end to racial discrimination. Despite the urging of Chavannes, Ogé refused to recruit any slaves. Free coloreds were not numerous in the north, and although they initially created great panic among the whites, Ogé's men were soon routed. Mass arrests and a lengthy trial followed. Twenty rebels were executed, Ogé and Chavannes suffering the excruciating punishment of being broken on the wheel. In the west and south, free coloreds had also taken up arms, but there they were peaceably persuaded to disperse by royalist officers. Military men were often more sympathetic to the mulattoes' cause, if only because they saw them as a counterweight to the colonial radicals. In the north, free coloreds were forcibly disarmed except for a few fugitives from Ogé's band who remained in hiding in the forests.

The National Assembly in Paris had maintained an ambiguous silence on the color question. France's revolutionary politicians were extremely embarrassed by events in the Caribbean and the issues that they raised. Colonial self-government, racial equality, and freedom for the slaves all posed serious threats to France's prosperity. The news of the barbarous execution of Ogé and Chavannes, however, shocked the National Assembly into making a compromise gesture. On May 15, 1791, free coloreds born of free parents were declared equal to whites in their political rights.[2] Although the measure concerned a very small proportion of free coloreds, news of the assembly's vote created a violent backlash in Saint Domingue. Whites, who were meeting to elect a second Colonial Assembly, seemed determined to resist the decree with force. Some talked of secession. When the governor announced he would not promulgate the decree, the patience of the free coloreds was exhausted. In August, those of the west and south began to gather in armed bands in the parishes where they were strongest. At the same time, news arrived from France that King Louis XVI had revealed his hostility to the revolution by attempting to flee from Paris.

It was in this rather complicated political situation, with civil war brewing between whites and free coloreds, with tensions rising between conservatives and radicals, with rumors circulating of secession and counterrevolution and a new assembly gathering in Cap Français, that the slaves took everyone by surprise. At the end of August 1791, an enormous revolt erupted in the plain around Le Cap. Beating drums, chanting, and yelling, slaves armed with machetes marched from plantation to plantation, killing, looting, and burning the cane fields. From the night it began, the uprising was the largest and bloodiest yet seen in an American slave society. Spreading swiftly across the plain and into the surrounding mountains, the revolt snowballed to overwhelming proportions. Whites fled pell-mell from the plain, and military sorties from Cap Français proved ineffective against the rebels' guerrilla tactics. By the end of September, over 1,000 plantations had been burned and hundreds of whites killed. The number of slaves slaughtered in indiscriminate reprisals was apparently much greater, but this only served to swell the ranks of the insurgents. Nevertheless, a cordon of military camps managed to confine the revolt to the central section of the north province.

Most slave conspiracies in the Americas were probably betrayed before reaching fruition, and most rebellions were quashed within a few days. The circumstances surrounding the August uprising are therefore of great interest. The divided and distracted state of the whites and the alienation of the free coloreds doubtless explain much of the rebels' success, both in gathering support and in overcoming opposition. Their aims, however, are less clear. The insurgents spoke with several voices, and many appear to have believed they were fighting to gain a freedom already granted them by the king of France but which the colonists were withholding. They tended to present themselves as defenders of church and king rather than demanding the rights of man. How far this was a deliberate ploy (perhaps designed to win aid from their conservative Spanish neighbors) is hard to say, but the influence of French revolutionary ideology on the revolt would seem slight. Since 1789, slaves had called the tricolor cockade the symbol of the whites' emancipation, but in revolt they adopted the white cockade of the royalists. Rumors of a royal emancipation decree had circulated in Saint Domingue in the autumn of 1789, along with news of an insurrection in Martinique, which was itself prompted by similar rumors that may have their roots in late ancien régime reforms. The Saint Domingue uprising was one of the first of a new type of slave revolt, soon to become typical, in which the insurgents claimed to be already officially emancipated. Apparently beginning with the Martinique rebellion of August 1789, this development probably owed more to the antislavery movement than to French revolutionary ideals.

Contemporary interrogations of captives revealed that the slave revolt was organized by elite slaves from some 100 sugar estates. Later sources connect their meetings with the vodou religion. Yet the colonists refused to believe that the slaves acted alone. Royalist counterrevolutionaries, the Amis des Noirs, secessionist planters, the remnants of Ogé's band, and the free coloreds in general were all accused by one group or another in the devastating aftermath of the rebellion. However, if any outside elements were involved, they soon found that the slaves were determined to decide their own fate. Their early leaders, Jean-François and Georges Biassou, imposed an iron discipline on the disparate groups they formed into armies. Yet when they attempted, fearing famine and defeat, to negotiate a sellout peace with the planters in December, their followers forced them back onto the offensive.

Free people of color from the parishes of Ogé and Chavannes certainly did join the slave rebels when the northern mountains were overrun, but in this they had little option. Elsewhere in the north, men of color fought against the slaves until they learned that the May 15 decree had been withdrawn. This was a fatal move by the wavering National Assembly. Although civil war between the whites and free coloreds had broken out in the western and southern provinces, the whites had been swiftly compelled to accept the latter's demands in these regions where free people of color predominated and showed exceptional military skill. Now, however, fighting began all over again. The towns of Port-au-Prince and Jacmel were burned and, as in the north, fearful atrocities were committed by all sides, making future reconciliation the more difficult. In parts of the west, white and colored planters combined to fight urban white radicals. In the south, they divided along color rather than class lines, while in the north many free coloreds joined the slave rebels. All sides began to arm slaves to fight for them, and plantation discipline slackened. Slave revolts broke out intermittently in the west and south, but the rebels were usually bought off with limited concessions, so that in general the slave regime remained intact, though shaken.

Beginning in December 1791, troop reinforcements started to arrive in small numbers from strife-torn France. The soldiers died rapidly from tropical diseases, and, needed everywhere in the colony, they had little impact on an enemy that avoided pitched battles. Not until France finally granted full citizenship to all free persons by the law of April 4, 1792 did the situation begin to stabilize. Prejudice and resentment remained strong, but in most areas outside the main towns, white and mulatto property-owners now grudgingly came to terms and turned their attention to the slaves. However, the civil commissioners who arrived in September to enforce the decree rapidly alienated most sections of the white population. Léger-Félicité Sonthonax and Étienne Polverel were dynamic and zealous radicals who scorned colonial opinion and who immediately adopted the cause of the Republic on learning that the French monarchy had been overthrown. After deporting the governor, they dissolved the Colonial Assembly, all municipalities, and political clubs. Royalist officers, autonomist planters, and racist poor whites were imprisoned and deported in large numbers, and free coloreds were promoted to public office in their stead.

Once separated from the race war, the slave rebellion assumed more manageable proportions. The 6,000 troops and national guards who came out with the civil commissioners were left inactive for months, but the northern plain was nonetheless easily retaken in November 1792. When a full offensive was eventually mounted in January 1793, Jean-François and Biassou were driven from one after another of their mountain camps, and thousands of slaves surrendered. By this time, however, the new French Republic was being propelled by its leaders into a world war that would leave Europe and Saint Domingue irrevocably changed.

War and the Rise of Toussaint Louverture, 1793–1798

By refuting the ideology of white supremacy and destroying the governmental structure that imposed it, the French Revolution thus brought the free coloreds to power in most parts of Saint Domingue in alliance with the republican officials from France. This transfer of power to the free coloreds also gained impetus from the outbreak of war with England and Spain in the spring of 1793. The colonists looked to foreign invasion to free them from the civil commissioners, who in turn grew intolerant of any white in a position of power. Port-au-Prince was bombarded into submission by Sonthonax, and its jails were filled with recalcitrant colonists. The southern coast was already a free colored stronghold, but, following a massacre of whites in Les Cayes in July, it became effectively autonomous under the mulatto goldsmith André Rigaud. In the plain of Arcahaye, the ruthless J.-B. Lapointe established himself as a local dictator, while in the plain of Cul de Sac behind Port-au-Prince, Pinchinat, Lambert, and Bauvais became the dominant influences. At Cap Français, Villatte would achieve a similar local dominance after the burning of the town in June and the flight of some 10,000 whites to North America.

With the white colonists eclipsed and the slave revolt close to suppression, the spring of 1793 represents the high point of mulatto control in Saint Domingue. The rest of the colony's history, indeed that of independent Haiti, may be viewed as a struggle between the emergent power of the black masses and the predominantly brown-skinned middle class. Whether the slave revolt in the north could actually have been suppressed and whether slavery on the plantations of the south and west would have continued as before, of course no one can say. However, the onset of war quite clearly transformed the situation not only of the veteran fighters in the northern mountains but also of all the blacks in Saint Domingue.

As soon as war was declared, both the republican French and the Spanish, preparing to invade from Santo Domingo, began competing to win over the black rebels. They offered them employment as mercenaries and personal freedom for themselves. Both in Europe and Saint Domingue, the fortunes of the new Republic were at their lowest ebb. Half of the soldiers sent to the colony in 1792 were already dead, and no more could be expected from a France racked by civil war and itself facing invasion. The civil commissioners' rhetoric about republican virtues therefore had little impact on Jean-François, Biassou, and the other black leaders. They preferred to take guns, uniforms, and money from the Spanish and continued to attack Frenchmen and free coloreds in the name of the king. Increasingly, Sonthonax and Polverel were compelled to turn to the masses in general to shore up republican rule. First they liberalized the plantation regime, then freed and formed into legions slaves who had fought in the civil wars. To forestall a counterrevolution by the new governor, they offered rebel bands the sack of Cap Français, and when an English invasion was imminent, they abolished slavery completely on August 29, 1793.

The decree of general emancipation was felt in the colony like an electric shock. It was greeted with hostility by white and colored planters and with some skepticism by the blacks; Sonthonax had acted unilaterally and might yet be overruled by the French government. Sonthonax's intention was to convert the slaves into profit-sharing serfs who were to be tied to their estates and subject to compulsory but remunerated labor. Almost nothing is known about how this system of forced labor functioned, either in 1793 or later years, but a disruption of plantation discipline and an increasing assertiveness on the part of the blacks were among the decree's initial effects. The hitherto powerless began to fully appreciate their latent power.

British and Spanish troops, sent from the surrounding colonies and welcomed by the planters, were to preserve slavery in most of the west and part of the south, but in some of the districts they occupied, their arrival itself provoked uprisings and the burning of plantations. Even without such militant action, a social revolution was quietly proceeding, for where planters abandoned the countryside, work in the fields ceased and the blacks adopted a peasant lifestyle centered on their provision grounds. Moreover, to supplement their scanty forces, the British, like the Spanish, were to recruit thousands of blacks as soldiers, further weakening the plantation regime. Above all, to repel the invaders, the republican forces would also, during five years of warfare, arm thousands of former slaves who until then had not left their plantations. As to the psychological effects of participating in a war of liberation, one can only guess, but in military terms the results were obvious. The civil commissioners in the north and west, André Rigaud in the south, the Spanish, and eventually the British all came to rely on armies predominantly made up of blacks.

One may argue, therefore, that although the Spanish and British occupations were intended to save the slave regime and the plantation economy, they had precisely the opposite effect. The outbreak of the European war greatly extended the effects of the slave revolt, breaking down the mental and physical shackles of slavery and plantation habit and enabling the ex-slaves to develop the military skills with which to defend their freedom. At the same time, it made the former free coloreds increasingly dependent on the martial ability of the blacks. More than this, foreign intervention completely divided the *anciens libres* (the "formerly free," as free nonwhites were now called) and isolated the large communities of the west from their cousins in the north and south. Slave emancipation was a fatal dilemma for the members of this classically unstable class. The Republic guaranteed their civil rights but then took away their property and offended their prejudices. Many, therefore, opted to support the Spanish and British, although a large number soon changed their minds. Rigaud and Villatte remained committed to the Republic, but friction between them and Sonthonax and the French general Laveaux mounted as the latter looked more and more to the blacks for support.

While this gradual shift in the internal balance of power lay in the logic of the political situation, it also came to acquire enormous impetus from the meteoric career of a single black general, Toussaint Bréda, who in August 1793 adopted the name Louverture.[3] A few months before, he had joined the Spaniards independently of Jean-François and Biassou, under whose command he had served. During the next ten years, he was to emerge as a military commander, diplomat, and political leader of consummate ability. He would achieve international renown and be acknowledged in some quarters as one of the great men of his day. Of the previous fifty years of his life little can be said with certainty.

Like the majority of slave leaders who achieved prominence, Toussaint was a Creole who had belonged to the slave elite. He had been a coachman and in charge of the livestock on the Bréda estate just outside of Cap Français, whose manager appears to have favored him. At some point he had become a pious Christian. Though his command of French would always remain fairly basic, he had learned to read and, late in life (between 1779 and 1791), to write his name. Despite his degree of acculturation, Toussaint did not lose touch with his African roots. He is said to have spoken fluently the language of his "Arada" (Ewe-Fon) father, who apparently was the son of a chief, and to have enjoyed speaking it with other slaves of his father's ethnic group. He seems also to have become skilled in the medicinal use of plants and herbs. Such slaves who lived at the interface between white and black society needed to know the ways of both worlds. To maintain their standing in both communities, they had to be shrewd observers of human nature and skilled performers of a number of roles. It is not so surprising, then, that among Toussaint's dominant characteristics in later life were his ability to manipulate and his virtuoso use of deception. In this respect, the plantation house was a good school.

This is perhaps one reason why it has only recently been discovered that Toussaint was no longer a slave at the time of the French Revolution. He had actually been freed around the age of 30. While he maintained a close connection with the Bréda estate and its manager, he also owned and rented both slaves and small properties at different times. He thus belonged to the class of free colored slave-holders, into whose lower ranks he and his children married. One gets a picture, then, of a man of diverse experience who was at home in various social milieus: among the white colonists, who thought well of him; among Creole slaves and free blacks; and among *bossales* newly arrived from Africa.

Two versions exist of Toussaint's behavior during the August 1791 insurrection, both shakily supported by contemporary documentation. Most historians suppose that Toussaint had nothing to do with the uprising and at first protected the Bréda plantation for several months until he threw in his lot with the rebels. Others suggest that Toussaint himself secretly organized the rebellion. They claim he acted as an intermediary for counterrevolutionary whites, using his contacts among leaders of the slave community but remaining shrewdly in the background. Similar puzzles exist with regard to many other events in his life. It is certain, however, that within three months of the August uprising he had

achieved prominence among the rebel blacks and was apparently one of Biassou's advisers. He interceded successfully for the lives of white prisoners, and,
as one of the free colored negotiators used by the slave leaders, he transmitted
their offer to the whites to help suppress the rebellion in return for the freedom
of a few score leaders. Despite the amnesty France offered to free coloreds in
rebellion, Toussaint stayed with the slave rebels through the dark days of 1792.
His relations with Jean-François, who called himself the "grand admiral," and
with Biassou, the self-styled "generalissimo," seem to have been stormy, but he
remained as one of their leading subordinates commanding a small force of his
own with the rank of brigadier (*maréchal de camp*).

After he joined the Spanish around June 1793, Toussaint's star rose rapidly.
In the great jumble of mountains of the north province, he immediately won a
series of startling military victories against the French and free coloreds. These
early campaigns reveal a leader of acute intelligence who was adept both at ambush and at totally confusing his opponents. They also reveal a man both ruthless and humane, capable of making barbarous threats but of sparing even those
who had double-crossed him. This policy reaped rewards. White and mulatto
property-owners surrendered to him, knowing his reputation for mercy. As
arms and ammunition fell into his hands, so his tiny army grew. Lances and
machetes were exchanged for muskets. Free colored and even French soldiers
joined its ranks and helped train its levies. If the essence of things Creole is
creative adaptation, this was a truly Creole army. In nine months, it grew from
a few hundred to several thousand men.

Meanwhile, the Spanish troops stayed cautiously on the Santo Domingo
frontier, paralyzed by a series of epidemics. The forces of Jean-François and
Biassou, for their part, gave up campaigning for quarreling among themselves
and for living it up outrageously at the expense of the king of Spain. The Spaniards soon realized that they had bitten off far more than they could chew. Such
successes as they had they owed almost entirely to Toussaint. They found the
handsome Jean-François vain and fickle and the impetuous Biassou gross and
overbearing. But in Toussaint, Spanish officers recognized a military commander
of ability and a man of honor and personal dignity. They were also much impressed by his piety and the hours he spent in church. Nonetheless, however
much the Spanish might respect piety, honor, and military ability, they found
themselves stuck with Jean-François and Biassou and compelled to recognize
them as principal commanders.

This raises the difficult question of Toussaint's volte-face—his sudden desertion of the Spanish in the spring of 1794 and his rallying to the French Republic.
According to one interpretation, it was frustrated ambition and increasing friction with Biassou that lead Toussaint to leave the Spanish and seek promotion
under the French. Others attribute the changeover to a desire to win freedom
for all the blacks in Saint Domingue. Specifically, they link his change of direction to the decree of February 4, 1794, by which the French government ratified
Sonthonax's actions and abolished slavery in all France's colonies. However, al-

though it would seem logical that these two great events were connected, the decree was not in fact known in the colony until long after Toussaint had turned on his Spanish allies and begun negotiating with the French general Laveaux.

Even so, Toussaint's volte-face was not simply a self-interested affair. His concern for the liberty of the blacks was genuine. Although in 1791 and 1792, he was prominent among the chiefs who offered to force their followers back into slavery on the plantations, this was at moments when defeat seemed certain. Unlike Jean-François and Biassou, Toussaint never rounded up plantation blacks for sale to the Spanish, and by mid-1793, he had become associated with the idea of general emancipation. His refusal to join the French thereafter was probably attributable to the Republic's precarious position. Anyway, having joined the Spanish, Toussaint played a double game, fighting to preserve the plantation regime but at the same time speaking to the blacks of liberty and equality. This doubtless helps explain why his army grew so rapidly. It was also at this time that he adopted the name Louverture ("the opening") with its cryptic connotation of a new beginning.

Matters came to a head early in 1794. After Spanish troops arrived from Cuba, Puerto Rico, and Venezuela, hundreds of French refugees began returning to the occupied districts. Only now, after almost a year of inaction, could the Spanish seriously contemplate restoring slavery on the plantations and launching an attack on Cap Français. Resistance came from various quarters: from plantation blacks who had not taken up arms but who refused to be coerced back into the fields, from free coloreds disenchanted with their treatment by the Spanish, and from some of the black mercenary troops as well. It was behind this movement that Toussaint decided to fling his weight as of the beginning of May 1794. For several months, nevertheless, he kept up his astonishing double game while he assessed the political situation. Although he told the French general Laveaux he was fighting hard for the Republic, he remained largely on the defensive, assuring the Spanish that such hostilities as occurred should be blamed on his disobedient subordinates. At the same time, he tried to allay the suspicions of Jean-François, and he also promised his allegiance to the British forces who were threatening him from the south. In the meantime, news trickled through from Europe of republican victories and of the abolition of slavery, while in Saint Domingue the spring rains brought fevers that decimated the Spanish and British troops. Cunningly choosing his moment, Toussaint then fell on each of his opponents in turn with devastating effect.

Whether motivated by idealism or ambition, Toussaint's volte-face was therefore tortuous, cautious, and protracted, and it was not a single-handed initiative. It was nonetheless the turning point of the Haitian Revolution. Now associated with the ideology of the French Revolution, black militancy became unequivocally directed toward the complete overthrow of slavery for perhaps the first time in the Americas. The balance of power tipped against the alliance of slaveowners and foreign invaders, and French rule in Saint Domingue would be saved for another decade, but after gaining a leader of genius, the movement for black self-liberation henceforth held center stage.

The next four years was a period of almost constant warfare. For much of this time, Toussaint's ragged soldiers, "as naked as earthworms," as he graphically described them, were perpetually short of food, clothing, and ammunition. They died by the hundred in their attacks on the well-entrenched positions of the British and Spanish, but in the process was forged a formidable army. The development should not be taken for granted. Unlike the freemen of color, who had a reputation as horsemen and sharpshooters, few slaves can have had much experience of firearms or artillery, even if they had been warriors in Africa. Since 1791, they had shown themselves skillful in their use of surprise and in exploiting terrain; they were capable of great endurance and difficult to pin down. To these qualities Toussaint added the ability to maneuver in large numbers, heightened esprit de corps, and a tactical brilliance few could equal. He gathered around him an experienced officer corps which was mainly black and (in its lower echelons) ex-slave but included many mulattoes and a few whites as well. Already prominent by the end of 1794 were the youthful Moïse, whom Toussaint called his nephew, and the vigorous and stern Jean-Jacques Dessalines.

By then, the Spanish and their black auxiliaries were almost a spent force in Saint Domingue. They had lost half of their conquests and even their own frontier towns of San Rafael and San Miguel on the grassy central savanna, which had been stormed by Toussaint in October. They held the strategic northeastern seaport of Fort Dauphin, but the massacre there of some 700 French colonists by Jean-François's soldiers, who were smarting from defeat, had ended all hopes of reviving the plantation regime. Instead, Spanish and black officers cooperated in stripping the sugar estates and sending their slaves and equipment to Cuba. Defeated in Europe and the Caribbean, Spain withdrew from the war in July 1795 and became an ally of the French Republic the following year. Santo Domingo, Spain's oldest colony, had become untenable and was surrendered to France, which for the time was too weak to occupy it. Jean-François and Biassou with 800 of their followers went into pensioned exile in different parts of the Spanish Empire. In the mountains of the northeast, however, many of their soldiers fought on in the name of the king until 1797.

Toussaint's forces occupied a cordon of some thirty camps stretching from the central mountains of the north province along the fringe of the Artibonite plain to the port of Gonaïves. He thus controlled access from the north to the west. Most of the northern littoral, however, was in the hands of Villatte and other semi-independent mulatto leaders. Laveaux, now governor, was confined with his few surviving white troops to the northwestern port of Port de Paix. The broad floodplain of the Artibonite became something of a no-man's-land, but the whole of the west province to the south of it eventually fell to the British and their planter allies, although independent bands of blacks continued to harry them from various mountain strongholds. The British also held the naval base of the Môle Saint Nicolas and, at the tip of the southern peninsula, the prosperous coffee-growing region of the Grand Anse. The rest of the southern peninsula was a mulatto fief ruled from Les Cayes by André Rigaud. Launching successive attacks against the Grand Anse and Port-au-Prince, Rigaud, like

Toussaint, built up an army mainly consisting of ex-slaves. By 1798, he commanded some 10,000 soldiers and Toussaint around 20,000.

Up to 1796, the British government had hoped to conquer Saint Domingue and add it to its tropical empire. Thereafter, it became resigned to failure but dared not withdraw for fear the black revolution would be exported to its own colonies. During their first two years in Saint Domingue (the only time they had any prospect of success), the British forces averaged barely 2,000 men. Although they were massively reinforced in 1796, British commanders continued with a mainly defensive strategy that condemned most of their troops to die of epidemic diseases in the seaports. Throughout these years of war, yellow fever flourished in the Caribbean, fueled by the huge influx of non-immune European troops and their concentration in the region's ports. During the 5-year occupation of Saint Domingue, the British lost 15,000 of the 25,000 soldiers they sent there. The British also gravely blundered early on by alienating the free coloreds, many of whom deserted them. Even so, the most valuable part of the occupied zone was the plain of Arcahaye, where the local commander, the *ancien libre* Lapointe, kept the plantations in full production. By 1798, the costs of occupation were found to be prohibitive, and under mounting pressure from Toussaint and Rigaud, the British staged a gradual evacuation. Only then did slavery come to an end for some 60,000 to 70,000 blacks.

During these years, Toussaint's position within the republican zone grew steadily more dominant. Early in 1796, Villatte and the *anciens libres* of the north province attempted to overthrow Governor Laveaux in an apparent bid for independence, which seems to have been secretly supported by André Rigaud in the south. According to some sources, Toussaint knew of the planned coup and with supreme cunning actually encouraged its instigators. But once it had broken out, he intervened in force and crushed it. The French government was left in no doubt on whom it depended for keeping Saint Domingue in French hands. Toussaint, the ex-slave, was proclaimed deputy-governor, and the following year he was named commander-in-chief.

For the time being, however, the republican position remained precarious. Not only were the British now pouring troops into the colony but also dissension was rife in the republican zone. Having fled to France in 1794, Sonthonax returned to Saint Domingue in May 1796 with four other civil commissioners and 900 white soldiers. Their attempts to centralize control of both the war effort and the economy of the republican parishes quickly made enemies. As Laveaux had found, mulatto leaders who had become accustomed to complete local autonomy resented attempts to take over abandoned property they themselves were exploiting. Efforts to raise the productivity of the surviving plantations also spread fears among the ex-slaves (now called "cultivators") of a restoration of slavery. This was especially true of the northwestern peninsula, where the plantations had suffered relatively little, and whose coffee was sold to American traders for food and munitions, as in the mulatto south. From the failure of Villatte's coup to the end of 1796, the northwest witnessed a succession of uprisings by black cultivators, in which were killed most of the few remaining white colonists in the region. Local *anciens libres* were probably behind at least some of these revolts. The revolts show, nevertheless, that even in these districts least affected by the slave revolution, a complete break with the past had by now occurred in the minds of the rural blacks. This did not mean, however, that such blacks were willing to defend their freedom by leaving their homes and becoming soldiers in Toussaint's army. Sonthonax had distributed guns to plantation workers, but when in a moment of crisis he tried to conscript all young males for military service, the extent of rebellion increased. At the same time, the mulatto south broke away from French rule, when the tactless commissioners sent to Les Cayes were expelled by André Rigaud and more whites were massacred.

The Republic was to weather these crises but only at the cost of seeing more and more power pass into the hands of Toussaint Louverture. It was his homespun diplomacy that finally pacified the blacks of the northwest. The African general Pierre Michel, hero of the northeastern campaigns and a favorite of Sonthonax, was then arrested. Earlier rivals of Toussaint had already disappeared. Toussaint had formed a remarkably close friendship with the aristocratic Governor Laveaux, referring to him in his correspondence as "Papa," although the two men were about the same age. Even so, by the autumn of 1796 Toussaint was intimating that Laveaux could best serve Saint Domingue if he were in Paris, where angry planters were demanding the restoration of Caribbean slavery; Laveaux was promptly elected a deputy for Saint Domingue and returned home to France. Next it was the turn of Commissioner Sonthonax. In the summer of 1797, Toussaint suddenly accused him of plotting to make Saint Domingue independent. Although still popular with the blacks, he also was forced to depart.

Smitten with life in the West Indies and threatened by political reaction in Paris, Sonthonax may indeed have wished to see Saint Domingue sever ties with France. Nevertheless, Toussaint's accusation suggests a neat sense of irony. While continuing to play the role of a loyal servant of the French Republic, he eliminated all his rivals within the colony one by one. The French government was becoming alarmed and in 1798 dispatched a new representative, General Hédouville. In six months, he, too, was deftly outmaneuvered, although with all due courtesy, and driven out of Saint Domingue by a supposedly spontaneous uprising. Whether or not Toussaint was aiming for independence, or even supreme power, at this time, historians will probably never agree. However, the growth of Toussaint's power was inexorable.

The Ascendancy of Toussaint Louverture, 1798–1802

Toussaint's expulsion of Sonthonax facilitated a rapprochement with Rigaud which enabled the two men to cooperate in driving out the British. Thereafter, only Rigaud himself stood between Toussaint and complete domination of Saint Domingue. Rigaud now controlled all the southern peninsula; Toussaint, all the north and west. Once their common enemy had been eliminated, relations between them rapidly deteriorated. Even today, the conflict between Toussaint and Rigaud is regarded by Haitians as one of the most sensitive topics in their history. It has become known as the War of Knives. Although it was in essence a regional power struggle, it tended to divide the light-skinned *anciens libres* from the new class of black military officers, although most of the troops on both sides were black ex-slaves. Many of Toussaint's light-skinned officers, although they had been with him for years, sided with Rigaud, and when Toussaint invaded the south, they staged rebellions against him. The fighting was desperate, and Toussaint's reprisals were brutal, although prudently delegated to subordinates. The details are disputed, but the black general Dessalines has been accused of waging something like a war of genocide against the southern mulattoes. Toussaint later reproved him: "I ordered you to prune the tree not to uproot it." Rigaud and most of the leaders fled to France.

By the middle of 1800, Toussaint ruled supreme in Saint Domingue and of necessity was recognized as its governor. A small, wiry man, very black, with mobile, penetrating eyes, he greatly impressed most who met him, even those who thought him ugly. He had lost his upper set of front teeth in battle and his ears were deformed by wearing heavy gold earrings, but his presence was commanding and suggested enormous self-control. Whether socializing with white planters or pacifying angry plantation workers, his manner was reserved but dignified. In private, the whites might mock his rusticity (his headscarf, his limited French) or his "pretensions" (his huge watch chains, his moralizing piety), but in his presence no one laughed. Though Toussaint maintained the external pomp of previous colonial governors and acquired much landed property, his private life was frugal. Wary of being poisoned, he ate little, and he slept only a few hours each night, invariably working late with his secretaries. His prodigious activity astonished people, as did the air of mystery he deliberately cultivated. He supposedly rode over 100 miles a day on horseback, making frequent changes of direction so that no one could be sure where he would appear next.

After the war ended in the south, Toussaint could set about rebuilding the colony and restoring its shattered economy. Although fiercely committed to the liberty of the blacks, he believed it essential that the plantation regime be revived in order to restore Saint Domingue's prosperity. With no export economy, there would be no revenue to maintain his army of 20,000 to 40,000 men. And without the army, the gains of the revolution would be at the mercy of France's unstable politics. Toussaint therefore continued with the schemes of Commissioner Sonthonax, whereby the ex-slaves were compelled to work on the plantations in return for a share of the produce. It was a difficult policy to implement, for increasingly the blacks preferred to establish smallholdings of their own and had little desire to work for wages. This was especially true of the sugar estates, which depended on regimented gang labor and where the working day was long and arduous. Already accustomed to marketing their own food crops, most blacks preferred to concentrate on extending their family provision grounds, cheerfully letting the fields of cane and coffee choke with weeds. Toussaint, however, refused to break up the great estates. He used the army to impose the regime of forced labor and sanctioned the use of corporal punishment; he even supported the reintroduction of the slave trade to make up the loss of manpower. As most estates had been abandoned by their owners, they were leased out, usually to army officers and other privileged figures in the new regime. In addition, Toussaint also encouraged the return from exile of the white planters to take charge of their properties and work toward the creation of a new Saint Domingue.

The return of the planters, of course, raised grave suspicions among the plantation blacks and among some of Toussaint's officers. They resented the white advisers he appointed and the pleasure he evidently took in inviting planters and merchants to his social gatherings. A naturally taciturn man, he seemed to be becoming increasingly remote. These tensions were given violent expression when the very popular General Moïse staged a revolt in the northern plain which caused the deaths of many of the returned planters. When Toussaint had him executed, many thought his policies were going awry. It is usually argued that Toussaint thought that the technical expertise of the whites and their social polish were necessary to the rebuilding of the colony and that he therefore was committed to a multiracial Saint Domingue. Recent work, however, has stressed that although Toussaint encouraged the whites to return, he rarely gave them back their estates. They tended to remain in the hands of his army officers, who constituted a new black landholding class. The return of the planters served to camouflage this development; it also provided hostages.

It is by no means clear how successful Toussaint was in reviving the plantation economy. Export figures for the twelve months following the war against Rigaud (1800–1801) show coffee production at two-thirds the 1789 level, raw sugar down by four-fifths, and semi-refined sugar, the most valuable item, almost nonexistent. On the other hand, it is likely that trade figures were deliberately understated to allow the amassing of secret funds and the stockpiling of munitions. The administrative confusion and the autonomy of local army commanders, of which white officials complained, probably fulfilled the same function. According to his critics, Toussaint kept his generals' loyalty by allowing them to amass personal fortunes. Their troops went unpaid, but the soldiers were allowed to exercise a petty tyranny over the cultivators, whose provision grounds were subject to army requisitions. Only on the generals' plantations were the labor laws effectively applied. Other commentators painted a more enthusiastic picture of the regime, insisting that a new spirit was abroad in the colony. Race prejudice was diminishing fast. Towns were being rebuilt. Justice was administered impartially. Even some schools were established (although this was a French initiative). All one can say with certainty is that the new regime was given very little time to prove itself.

Late in 1799, France, like Saint Domingue, acquired a military strongman for a ruler. Napoleon Bonaparte and Toussaint Louverture had much in common. Both were seen as defenders of basic revolutionary gains of the previous decade, particularly of new land settlements. Both were autocrats who extinguished all political liberty in their respective countries. Both were destroyed by their own ambition. In July 1801, shortly before Napoleon proclaimed himself consul for life, Toussaint promulgated a constitution for Saint Domingue which flagrantly concentrated all power in his hands and made him governor for life with the right to choose his successor. Drawn up by planters with a secessionist background, the document came within a hairsbreadth of a declaration of independence. Toussaint had anticipated by 160 years the concept of associated statehood. Napoleon was infuriated. Yet the first consul had already determined that French rule should be restored in what had been France's most valuable possession.

But there was nothing inevitable about the epic clash between Toussaint and Napoleon. Although he was constantly under pressure from vengeful planters, merchants, and colonial officials, Bonaparte had resisted for well over a year their clamor for a military expedition. His original policy was to leave Toussaint in control of Saint Domingue and to use the colony as a springboard for expanding French power in the Americas. Black troops would be sent to conquer the slave colonies of France's rivals. As part of the plan, Louisiana was purchased from Spain. However, by the spring of 1801 it was apparent that, under its black governor, Saint Domingue would be of little use to France; it was de facto already an independent state. Although France was at war with Great Britain and was unofficially at war with the United States (the Quasi-War of 1798–1800), Toussaint had made a secret commercial treaty and nonaggression pact with both these powers. This involved expelling French privateers from the colony. His purpose was to preserve the trade on which Saint Domingue, and his army, depended. The United States supplied vital foodstuffs, livestock, and munitions; the British navy controlled the sea-lanes, and would otherwise have blockaded Saint Domingue. This is why, when the French and *anciens libres* tried to foment a slave rebellion in Jamaica and sent agents there from Saint Domingue, Toussaint betrayed the plot to the Jamaican administration. Whatever his interest in black liberation, he needed to keep on good terms with his neighbors in order to preserve his autonomy.

In spite of Toussaint's independent foreign policy and his ambiguous behavior toward the planters, until March 1801, Napoleon's intention remained to work with the black leader, not against him. However, the last straw for Napoleon came when Toussaint suddenly annexed without reference to France the adjoining colony of Santo Domingo, which was then French territory. The ex-slave thereby became master of the entire island of Hispaniola. It was the high point of his career. Suspicious of French intentions, Toussaint aimed to deny a potential invasion force use of Santo Domingo's harbors. But it was precisely this event that persuaded Napoleon that an invasion was necessary. Toussaint's new constitution merely enraged him further. Nevertheless, the fatal decision to attempt to restore slavery in Saint Domingue was not taken for another year, long after the invasion force had landed. Although usually presented as an act of vicious megalomania, the Napoleonic invasion of Saint Domingue was more like a last-ditch attempt to keep the plantation regime in French hands.

Toussaint had grossly miscalculated. If he was willing to antagonize Napoleon to this degree, some say, he should have gone all out and declared complete independence, rallying the black masses behind him. Instead, he kept up the fiction of loyalty to France, sending envoys to Napoleon to explain each act of defiance. He continued to assure local whites of his goodwill and to admonish the blacks about the necessity of hard work. The ambivalence of his double game was to critically weaken black resistance to the coming invasion. Toussaint's failure to declare independence was doubtless due to a number of factors. Caution, the need for white administrative personnel, and the fear of alienating the slave-holding Americans and British were probably the most important. By stopping short of de jure independence, Toussaint evidently thought that Napoleon would negotiate rather than fight. Perhaps he overrated the military lessons he had taught the Spanish and British. Or perhaps he believed that the British navy would prevent a French fleet from crossing the Atlantic.

The British, however, would support the black governor's rule only so long as it weakened France's war effort, and the Anglo-French war was now drawing to a temporary close. The British government feared both Toussaint and Napoleon but regarded the latter as the lesser of two evils. To see the two embroiled in internecine conflict would be a perfect compromise solution to a threatening situation. In October 1801, as soon as peace preliminaries were signed, the British gave their assent to an invasion of Saint Domingue.

The War of Independence, 1802–1803

Napoleon's brother-in-law, General Leclerc, landed in Saint Domingue at the beginning of February 1802 with some 10,000 soldiers. By sending out a large force in the healthy winter months and deploying it rapidly, Napoleon avoided the worst mistakes of the British and Spanish. His troops were also far superior to those previously sent there, and their numbers were doubled within two months. Leclerc's orders were nevertheless to seize the colony by ruse, winning over the black generals where possible. Only later, once he had allayed their suspicions, was he to disarm their soldiers and deport all the black officers. The plantations would be returned to their owners. Slavery would be restored in Santo Domingo, where it had never been officially abolished, but in Saint Domingue the forced labor regime would be retained. Leclerc both said and thought he was reestablishing French rule but not slavery.

Uncertain of French intentions, the blacks failed to offer any concerted resistance, and Leclerc quickly occupied all the colony's ports. Cap Français, under the eye of Toussaint, was burned by its commander, Henry Christophe, as was Saint Marc by Dessalines, but several of the generals surrendered without a fight. They were now planters themselves and had property to protect. Toussaint, Christophe, and Dessalines, however, took to the mountains, fighting heroic rearguard actions and destroying all they left behind. Battle casualties were heavy, and from the beginning the war was marked by frightful atrocities on both sides. Fearing the return of slavery, the rural population rallied to the black army and produced guerrilla leaders of their own. However, as successive generals surrendered, their troops were turned against those who still held out.

Through the month of April, Toussaint kept up a vigorous guerrilla campaign with great persistence but dwindling resources. He surrendered early in May and retired to private life on one of his plantations. Christophe, Dessalines, and the other generals were maintained in their posts and used by the French to mop up remaining guerrilla resistance.

It may be that all three leaders were biding their time. Leclerc's army was already severely weakened, and the blacks well knew that during the summer it would be decimated by disease. Nevertheless, when within a month Toussaint was accused of plotting rebellion, it was Dessalines and Christophe who helped denounce him. The old leader was kidnapped and hastily deported; he died in a French dungeon in April 1803. Despite this devious maneuvering by the military leaders, small bands of insurgents fought on in the mountains in the tradition of the maroons. As Toussaint declared on leaving the colony, the French had felled only the trunk of the tree of liberty; it had strong roots and would grow again.

The situation changed dramatically in July 1802, when it was learned (by the blacks and Leclerc almost simultaneously) that the French government had decided to restore slavery in all French colonies. Attempts to disarm the rural population now met with massive resistance, just when hundreds of French soldiers each week were dying of yellow fever. The campaign of terror launched by Leclerc proved counterproductive. As thousands of black prisoners, men and women, went stoically to their deaths, a new sense of unity was forged based on racial solidarity. By the autumn, the French were fighting most of the nonwhite population of Saint Domingue. Even the *anciens libres* who had fled the south in 1800 and returned in Leclerc's army now combined with their former opponents. Led by Rigaud's protégé, Alexandre Pétion, they accepted the overall leadership of Jean-Jacques Dessalines, who finally deserted the French in late September. As Toussaint's inspector of agriculture, the conqueror of the mulatto south, and then Leclerc's chief collaborator, Dessalines had been responsible for the deaths of many blacks and *anciens libres*. However, he was the ideal person to lead the struggle to expel the French, and not only because he was the senior general. A menial slave under the old regime, he had none of the liking for the white society which Toussaint, and the former domestic Christophe, shared with the *anciens libres*. He spoke only *kreyol*, the language of the cultivators. And he was possessed of demonic energy; his battle cry was "Burn houses, cut off heads!"

After Leclerc himself died of yellow fever, the repugnant General Rochambeau openly waged a war of genocide against the black population, but to no avail. No one can say how far Napoleon would have gone in this hopeless venture, but once war was resumed with Great Britain in May 1803, he had to admit defeat. He had already sent 44,000 troops to Saint Domingue. Thereafter the British navy prevented any reinforcements from crossing the Atlantic. Napoleon's western design was at an end. Louisiana was sold to the United States. With British ships blockading the coast of Saint Domingue and Dessalines's forces besieging the coastal towns, the remains of the French army evacuated the colony in November. Since 1791, more than 70,000 European soldiers and seaman had died in the attempt to maintain slavery. Of the few thousand whites who optimistically stayed behind, most died in a series of massacres in the following months.

International Repercussions

On January 1, 1804, Dessalines declared Saint Domingue independent and gave it the aboriginal Amerindian name of "Haïti." "I have given the French cannibals blood for blood," he proclaimed. "I have avenged America."[4] During the war of independence, some of the blacks referred to themselves as "Incas," and some European writers also fancifully depicted the ex-slaves as avenging the Arawaks exterminated in the sixteenth century. While anchoring the new state to the American past, the country's new name meant above all a symbolic break with Europe. All whites were henceforth forbidden to own land in Haiti.

Having destroyed the wealthiest planter class in the New World and defeated the armies of France, Spain, and England, the former slaves and free coloreds now went about making laws for themselves and erecting a state apparatus. In a world dominated by Europeans and where slavery and the slave trade were at their height, the new state was a symbol of black freedom and a demonstration of black accomplishments. For both abolitionists and the proslavery lobby, Haiti was a great experiment, a crucial test case for ideas about race, slavery, and the future of the Caribbean. In Haiti itself, publicists and statesman spoke out against racism, colonialism, and enslavement.

Nevertheless, all the early Haitian statesmen took pains to disclaim any intention of intervening in neighboring colonies. Like Toussaint, they did not wish to provoke a maritime blockade or an invasion by the slave-holding powers. The exception to this policy was the annexation of Santo Domingo, which Dessalines attempted in 1805 and which was finally accomplished in 1822. As in the 1790s, rumors about the activity of Haitian "agents" continued to circulate; these rumors are given credence by some historians, but official involvement in any of the slave conspiracies or rebellions of the post-1804 period has yet to be proven. The only clear case we have of subversive proselytizing is by agents of the French Republic during the 1790s, most particularly by Victor Hugues, who from Guadeloupe helped foment rebellions among the French-speaking inhabitants of Grenada and Saint Vincent. Haiti nonetheless did make a major contribution to the abolition of slavery (and to decolonization) in the New World. In 1815, when Alexandre Pétion gave vital assistance to Simón Bolívar that enabled him to relaunch his campaign for South American independence, Pétion demanded as payment that the planter-aristocrat declare slavery in his homeland abolished, which he did on his return to South America.

From 1792 onward, laws were passed all around the Caribbean and in North America restricting immigration from strife-torn Saint Domingue. Even when the likelihood of direct interference was not considered strong, slave-owners feared the revolution's inflammatory example. Within a month of the August

1791 revolt, slaves in Jamaica were singing songs about the uprising, and before long whites in the West Indies and North America were complaining uneasily of a new "insolence" on the part of their slaves. Several plots and insurrections were partly inspired by events in Saint Domingue. Most notable of these were the conspiracies organized by free blacks in Venezuela (1795), Havana (1812), and Charleston (1822). However, many factors were at work in the slave rebellions of the period, and to suppose that mere inspiration from abroad was critical in provoking resistance would be to underestimate the difficulties confronting dissidents in this age of strong colonial garrisons.

Controversy remains about the extent to which the Haitian Revolution encouraged or delayed the progress of antislavery movements elsewhere. Some saw Haiti's example as a dire warning of what might happen if slavery was, or was not, abolished; others claimed it was irrelevant to circumstances in other places. One clearly paradoxical result of the revolution was the stimulation of slave-based agriculture elsewhere. By driving up the price of tropical products and creating a diaspora of skilled refugees, the destruction of Saint Domingue encouraged the spread of plantations along new frontiers in Louisiana, eastern Cuba, and Jamaica and increased production in already established export zones. Similarly, if Haitian assistance made a material contribution to the achievement of Venezuelan independence, its example proved to be an obstacle to decolonization in Cuba, and Haitian intervention in 1822 extinguished independence (as well as slavery) in the Dominican Republic.

France did not abandon its claims to its former colony until 1825, when the Haitian government agreed to pay a large indemnity to the expelled colonists. The debt the country thereby incurred was among the factors retarding its growth in the nineteenth century, and the concessions then given to French merchants further shifted the export economy into foreign hands. Britain and the United States had early established trade relations with the new state (which were briefly interrupted by Jefferson as a favor to Napoleon), but full diplomatic recognition was withheld by these countries until they had abolished slavery and no longer considered Haiti a threat.

The Legacy of Revolution

Created from a unique experience of slavery, war, and revolution, Haiti was to be like no other state. The fledgling black republic began life with its towns and plantations in ruins and under constant threat of another French invasion. Its population had been decimated; it was severely lacking in technical skills, and it was almost totally without experience in administration or government.

Despite the attempts to maintain production on the plantations, the ex-slaves had for a decade been building new lives for themselves as either soldiers or peasant cultivators. Fear of invasion and institutional self-interest were to burden Haiti with an exceptionally large army for the rest of the century. The earliest governments, particularly that of Henry Christophe (1806–1820), continued the struggle to revive the sugar plantations with forced labor. However, the desire of the masses for land and their hatred of estate work, together with falling sugar prices, forced the abandonment of the project by the 1830s. Haiti became a country of peasant smallholders who grew food crops and a little coffee on land distributed by the government or on which they squatted. The postwar population was presumably young and mainly female and therefore grew rapidly. The relative abundance of land meant that the peasants probably lived reasonably well in the nineteenth century. The vodou religion, although persecuted by all the early leaders as subversive to authority, became entrenched in the countryside.

Government revenues came primarily from taxing coffee exports. As in colonial times and during the revolution, the government remained military and authoritarian in character, although constitutional forms were to vary widely and regimes changed rapidly. After declaring himself emperor, Dessalines was assassinated in 1806, and for the next fourteen years Haiti was divided between a mulatto republic in the south and west and a northern state, ruled by Henry Christophe, which became a monarchy in 1811. Dessalines had made great efforts to preserve the fragile wartime alliance between blacks and *anciens libres,* but tensions continued to run deep, even after the reunification of the country in 1820. Haitian politics developed as a struggle between the uneducated black officer corps that controlled the army and the brown-skinned professional and business class which made up most of the country's elite.

This conflict was mirrored more broadly in the elaboration of two competing ideologies, one "black," the other "mulatto." In Haitian society, the color line was not at all absolute, but these two opposing camps, fronted by the Liberal and National Parties, tended to be divided by phenotype as well as by culture, religion, and attitude toward national development and toward the country's revolutionary past.

Part Two.   *Historiography and Sources*

By the time Haiti gained its independence in 1804, there already existed a burgeoning historiography devoted to its unique revolution. Angry colonists produced most of the output for a long time; other sources included government reports, military memoirs, and antislavery tracts, primarily in France and England. The first quasi-historical writings in Haiti, by Pompée de Vastey and Hérard Dumesle, were strongly marked by the propaganda needs of the Haitian state. Then, in the space of a decade, Haitian writers produced three monumental histories that remain indispensable sources today. These were Thomas Madiou, Histoire d'Haïti (1847–1848), Beaubrun Ardouin, Études sur l'histoire d'Haïti (1853–1860), and Joseph Saint-Rémy, Pétion et Haïti (1853–1857). In twentieth-century Haiti, a black nationalist approach gradually supplanted the elitist perspective associated with these figures and their successors. In France, the social history orientation of Gabriel Debien revolutionized Caribbean colonial history, while French Revolution scholars tended to ignore colonial matters until the 1980s. Specialized studies have multiplied since the 1950s, but primary research remains relatively limited compared to the topic's importance and the available source material. Thomas Ott, Carolyn Fick, and, most recently, Jacques de Cauna all produced solid histories of the Haitian Revolution in the last third of the twentieth century, but it seems fair to say that most books on the subject have been of a lightweight and popular nature. Easily the most influential general study has been C. L. R. James, The Black Jacobins (1938), an analytic tour de force of literary distinction and extraordinary staying power.

The source material for studying the revolution is widespread and very extensive, as befits a 15-year conflict to control the most important colony of the time. Even though the struggle destroyed most of the public and private archives in Saint Domingue with a large proportion of its buildings, much of the *most important documentation, as in any colony, was housed at metropolitan locations. Saint Domingue's major landowners, moreover, were all absentees. Despite losses in the two world wars, the main repositories of primary sources on the revolution are therefore in France. They are divided between national institutions, numerous municipal libraries and departmental archives, and private owners. National archives in Spain and national and local archives in Great Britain also contain substantial holdings, because of those countries' lengthy involvement in the revolution. U.S. archives contain more than thirty relevant collections that reflect refugee settlement and commercial contacts as well as government involvement. Further documentation can be found in Guatemala, Colombia, Canada, Jamaica, and the Dominican Republic. Notwithstanding the revolution's extensive historiography, much of these sources remains little or entirely unexploited by historians. Moreover, as material continues to pass from private hands into the public domain and finding aids multiply in number, opportunities for research continue to increase.*

2   New Approaches and Old

For sixty years a single work has dominated study of the Haitian Revolution in the English-speaking world. First published in 1938, Cyril James's *The Black Jacobins* clothed in brilliant prose a virtuoso analysis of the historical forces crisscrossing the Atlantic world in the age of the French Revolution. A black West Indian Marxist, James evinced a new feeling for the masses in history and for Caribbean slaves as people. Written halfway between the Russian Revolution and the Mau Mau uprising, *The Black Jacobins* displayed a novel awareness of blacks as political agents and a prescient sense of the Haitian Revolution as an anticolonial struggle. In 1963, the book was reissued in a second edition, its prestige enhanced by the wave of decolonization that it had predicted and by the onset of the new social history. Four decades later, its reputation is even stronger, enhanced by the apotheosis of James himself. *The Black Jacobins* is now firmly ensconced as a college text in Anglophone countries. A third edition appeared in 1980, an Italian edition in 1968, a German edition in 1984, and French editions in 1949 and 1983.[1]

The book has never been very popular with Francophone readers. When the colonial historian Gabriel Debien reviewed the work in 1946, he dismissed it as seeking to be controversial and made the cryptic comment that the author's ignorance might be wrongly mistaken for bad faith. Debien probably was referring to factual errors such as the claim that the black colonial deputy Jean-Baptiste Belley made the speech to the French Convention that led to the abolition of slavery, which was in fact made by his white counterpart, or presenting a colonial regiment decimated by Toussaint Louverture as a "famous corps of white creoles," although it consisted mainly of slaves.[2] Relying heavily on secondary sources, *The Black Jacobins* has its share of factual errors, but probably fewer than most of its competitors.[3] Compared to its strengths, its faults seem minor. For its portrait of Toussaint Louverture, it relied rather heavily on Victor Schoelcher's biography of 1889, and its picture of a French Revolution spearheaded by the mercantile bourgeoisie is now quite archaic. Although James warned against underestimating race as a factor, he accorded it less weight than a modern Marxian would, and in general he gave exaggerated primacy to material factors. Nevertheless, if the book is written with passion from a pronounced political viewpoint, James's judgements were in general remarkably sound. For well over half a century *The Black Jacobins* has remained a very hard act to follow.

In the last thirty or so years, however, a number of important studies have appeared that break new ground and extend our knowledge of the Haitian Revolution beyond the limits that obtained at the time C. L. R. James was writ-

ing. This is particularly true with regard to knowledge of pre-revolutionary society. The most influential writer on white society has been Charles Frostin. His
massive dissertation, "Histoire de l'autonomisme colon," abridged as *Les révoltes
blanches,* displays in a narrative of the entire pre-revolutionary period a more
holistic vision of white society than the fractured portrait presented in the
works of Gabriel Debien. Developing Debien's work on *l'esprit colon* (or white
colonial mentality), Frostin emphasizes secessionist and subversive tendencies
among Saint Domingue's planter class and *petits blancs.* In a provocative formulation, he presents the white population as the most rebellious sector of Saint
Domingue society. Frostin thus stresses continuity rather than change in the
colonists' turbulent reaction to the French Revolution.[4] What we now need are
histories of those planters and *petits blancs,* merchants, and lawyers, during the
revolution.[5]

Free people of African descent are invariably the least studied component of
slave societies, but knowledge of Saint Domingue's *gens de couleur* has been
greatly advanced in recent years, primarily by John Garrigus. Of particular relevance here is Garrigus's exploration of a growing sense of "American" identity
among this group and his radical reworking of the significance of their participation in the American Revolution. Stewart King's dissertation adds to the controversy surrounding the latter episode and sheds more light on the free colored
militia and police, but it is less successful in its attempt to distinguish "military"
and "civilian" castes within the free nonwhite sector.[6] Both King and Garrigus
mined long-neglected notarial records for their work; Garrigus looked at records
for three southern parishes, and King compared two northern and two western
ones. More such area studies are needed. A study of the politician Julien Raimond is forthcoming from Garrigus, and the career of the free colored leader
André Rigaud has been recounted in detail in a series of meticulously documented articles by Claude B. Auguste.[7]

In the study of slavery, Gabriel Debien's *Les esclaves aux Antilles françaises*
was a landmark when it appeared in 1974, in that it summed up much of that
prolific scholar's work of the previous forty years.[8] Whereas James relied for his
picture of plantation society on works of Vaissière and Peytraud that were published around the turn of the twentieth century, Debien argued that patient
analysis of plantation records was the best way to get beyond the propagandist
images bequeathed by the planters and abolitionists. Compared with the sophis-
ticated research done on slave societies elsewhere, the quantitative aspect of his
work looks a little antiquarian nowadays. However, one needs to remember the
enormous labor then required in seeking out and assembling primary sources.
There are no registration returns for Saint Domingue like those of the British
Caribbean, no detailed censuses or Parker-Gallman survey such as historians of
the United States have been able to use. Debien was very much a pioneer who
cleared new terrain, the sort of colonial personality he much admired.

The last, and most original, chapter of *Les esclaves aux Antilles françaises* examines the question of whether the conditions of slave life saw improvement in

the final years before the insurrection of 1791. Typical of the writings of this author, it reaches no firm conclusion. Debien's preferred genre was the case study, and he began his 1974 magnum opus by modestly warning that any attempt at synthesis would be premature. He also listed details of more than 100 manuscript collections to guide future work. Since then, the assembling and analysis of primary data on slave society that Debien began has accelerated, so that we now have a far more detailed and accurate picture of the population that made the Haitian Revolution than was available to its contemporaries.[9] Structural analysis does not hold the key to all questions of historical causation, but without this type of research it is difficult to talk with accuracy about the quality of slave life, and it is impossible to compare different slave societies or one part of Saint Domingue with another.

This seems important, as it is now apparent from both slave trade and plantation records that the composition of the slave population varied a good deal between Saint Domingue's three provinces and between its highland and lowland zones.[10] Can we find here some explanation of the rather different ways the slave revolution developed in the colony, say, between zones of coffee and sugar cultivation or between the plains of Cul de Sac, Les Cayes, and the north? It is clear at least that the great uprising of 1791 broke out in the part of the colony where locally born slaves were at their most numerous.[11] Moreover, the collation of estate inventories reveals an occupational hierarchy on the plantations, which by the 1780s was dominated by a Creole elite that monopolized the most prestigious posts. It should be no surprise, therefore, that almost all the major leaders of the slave revolution were also locally born Creoles—this includes figures sometimes identified as Africans, such as Biassou, Moïse, Dessalines, and (very probably) Boukman. At the same time, however, the massive compilations of slave trade data now available reveal that Africans, and particularly African males, had never been imported in such large numbers as in the final year before the revolt, particularly so in the area where it took place.[12]

This combination of an established Creole elite and huge numbers of recently enslaved African men may help explain both the success of the slave revolution and the internal stresses it experienced on the road to independence. At the very least, it invites a reading of the revolution that takes seriously differences between African and Creole slaves. This is not a popular approach with those who like to stress the solidarity of slave communities and the pervasiveness of African culture. However, it does fit with the analysis of Haiti's first major historian, Thomas Madiou, who argued that the triumph of the Creoles over the Africans was necessary to secure Haitian independence.[13] In three recent books, anthropologist Gérard Barthélemy builds the *bossale*/Creole contrast into a paradigm for understanding the whole of Haitian history.[14] The difficult relationship between leadership and masses in the Haitian Revolution forms an important theme in *The Black Jacobins*[15] and still more so in the recent studies of Carolyn Fick and Pierre Pluchon (discussed below). The full significance of this political cleavage, I think, only becomes apparent when situated in the context of the cultural, even class, divisions of slave plantation society. Further investigation of Creole and African identity in the plantation milieu should shed light on the dynamics of revolutionary politics.

Demographic research is also essential for understanding other basic features of slave life. At present, we have little scientific evidence regarding birth and death rates, but there are some suggestions that mortality was high in the colony even by Caribbean standards and that fertility was exceptionally low, especially in the northern plain.[16] C. L. R. James was certainly right to stress the "industrial" character of these northern plain sugar estates, where the 1791 revolt began.[17] Their slave workforces were in fact among the largest in the Americas. Yet, with an average size of fewer than 200 slaves per estate, they were a good deal smaller than many have imagined. Toussaint Louverture lived on a plantation with about 150 slaves, not the more than 1,000 slaves Ralph Korngold stated.[18] Similarly, with an average sex ratio of about 12 men to 10 women, the imbalance between the sexes was a lot less than usually supposed.[19]

The social history approach launched single-handedly by Debien has been particularly revealing with regard to the ethnic origins of Saint Domingue's African slaves. Although the extent of Aja-Fon and Yoruba influence on modern vodou has caused many to believe that these cultures supplied a majority of the colony's slaves, Debien and his collaborators discovered that peoples from Central Africa, known as "Congos," formed in fact the most important subgroup.[20] Subsequent research now shows they were even more numerous than Debien's data suggested and that their dominance in the slave trade goes back much earlier than formerly suspected.[21] On the eve of the revolution, West Central Bantu constituted more than two-fifths of the Africans in the northern plain, indeed one-quarter of all slaves in the north province.

These discoveries necessarily direct attention to the history of the disintegrating kingdom of Kongo during the eighteenth century. They have caused a reconsideration of the early evidence concerning vodou—by Carolyn Fick and myself—and they pose challenging questions regarding the evolution of Haitian culture.[22] Notably stimulating is the work of the Africanist John Thornton. His interpretation of Kongo culture as semi-Christian demands some rethinking of traditional notions of acculturation and syncretism in Saint Domingue, work that is now being pursued by Hein Vanhee.[23] Robin Law's study of the Bois Caïman ceremony, discussed in Chapter 6, offers further evidence that the entrance of Africanist scholars into the field of Haitian history will be an exciting development.[24] John Thornton has also put forward an interesting argument that captive African soldiers supplied the Haitian Revolution with military skills that Creole slaves lacked and thus explain much of its success. His portrayal of the ideologies the Kongolese brought with them strengthens the idea that the bizarre royalism displayed by many of the slave insurgents perhaps should be taken more seriously than it was by C. L. R. James or Victor Schoelcher.[25]

The ideological transformation of the Saint Domingue uprising, and of African-American resistance in general, is the striking theme of Eugene Genovese's *From Rebellion to Revolution*.[26] His thesis, discussed further in Chapter 4, is that the Haitian Revolution, under the leadership of Toussaint Louverture, marked a turning point in blacks' resistance to slavery. Influenced by the revolution in France, American slaves turned from "restorationist" rebellion to "bourgeois-democratic" revolution that sought for the first time to eradicate slavery as a system and to come to terms with the modern state and world economy. This bold formulation has encouraged further comparative work on slave resistance and on the international impact of the French and Haitian Revolutions.[27]

The Haitian Revolution clearly had an electrifying effect on slaves and free coloreds in other parts of the Americas and on whites in the New World and Europe. Various connections can be demonstrated between revolutionary Saint Domingue and black resistance elsewhere during the following decades. There is a danger, however, of exaggerating that impact, of overlooking local forces promoting resistance, and of reading into every plot and rebellion of these years the influence of Haiti. Also, the European antislavery movement was probably as important as the French Revolution in encouraging slave insurgents after 1789 to adopt a fully emancipationist program. Slave rebels rarely demanded freedom as a right; but in this period they often claimed that an emancipation decree had been passed in their favor. The Haitian Revolution was a high point in the black struggle against slavery but not exactly a turning point.[28] Robin Blackburn, who supports Genovese's argument, seems more convincing for not tying new trends in slave resistance narrowly to the French Revolution but situating them more generally amid the broader movement toward middle-class dominance in the West.[29]

French revolutionary ideology appears to have had less influence on slaves than on free people of African descent. Possibly the major recent discovery regarding the Haitian Revolution is that Toussaint Louverture, its principal protagonist, was not a slave at the time of its outbreak but a *nègre libre*. Research by Gabriel Debien and Marie-Antoinette Menier revealed, in a short article published in 1977, that he had been free at least since the mid-1770s, that he had rented land and slaves, and that he had owned at least one slave.[30] Thus he was not just a "privileged" Creole slave but a member of the lower ranks of the free colored community.

This finding makes certain aspects of Toussaint's career easier to understand. His literacy (albeit imperfect and belatedly acquired), his Christianity, and his sophistication when compared to the other early slave leaders all seem less surprising now we know he had spent at least half of his adult life as a freedman.[31] In fact, when we first encounter him during the early months of the slave uprising, it is in company with other freemen acting as intermediaries on behalf of the rebel slaves' leaders.[32] This was the first of two occasions when Toussaint favored offering a restoration of slavery in return for the freedom of only a handful of the rebels' leaders.[33] From the beginning, then, his interests were not exactly those of the rank-and-file insurgents; he was willing to seek compromise with the old regime. This helps explain why it took at least a year for him to emerge as a military chief and nearly three before he became the principal black leader.

On the other hand, he did stay with the slave insurgents when other free coloreds who had joined them took advantage of a government amnesty, and he was clearly never in the same camp as the main free colored leaders, who were predominantly freeborn and of mixed racial descent and who fought against the slave uprising. Toussaint's highly marginal status as a black freedman—no longer a slave but not the social equal of a Vincent Ogé or Jean-Baptiste Villatte—helps us make sense of this conduct.[34] It invites comparison, moreover, with other slave conspiracies or revolts of this period also led by free blacks—José Leonardo Chirino in Venezuela, José Antonio Aponte in Cuba, and Denmark Vesey in South Carolina.[35]

Two outstanding and controversial biographies of Toussaint Louverture have appeared in recent years, both authored by Pierre Pluchon.[36] In a field characterized by hagiography and romantic enthusiasm, Pluchon's work stands out for its hard-nosed lack of idealism. It displays little admiration for either Toussaint Louverture or the Haitian or the French Revolution. Pluchon is a former director of the Institut Français in Haiti, and such sympathy as he shows goes to the hapless French officials sent out to the colony that was slipping irrevocably beyond European control. In both biographies, Pluchon somewhat neglects the early period of Toussaint's career but makes full use of the discovery of his free status when explaining his later authoritarianism and, especially, his determination to maintain the system of export agriculture using forced labor. For Pluchon, Toussaint was "a man of the Ancien Régime" whose conception of Saint Domingue's economy was that of the white colonists he sought to replace. Thus, he revived the slave trade, outlawed vodou, and used corporal punishment to prevent workers from leaving the plantations to become peasant farmers.[37] Toussaint's growing distance from the masses, which James was forced to treat as a character flaw, the hubris of a tragic hero moving toward his downfall, was in Pluchon's view rooted in his pre-revolutionary past as a man of property, a slave-owner.

What is particularly original in Pluchon's interpretation, however, is his claim that Toussaint's support for the plantation economy did not extend to the white owners of plantations. He indeed invited them back to the colony, but few in fact regained possession of their estates. They were to be hostages to discourage a future French invasion. Most historians presume the black general envisaged a multiracial Saint Domingue, if only because he valued the technical and managerial skills of the whites. In Pluchon's version, however, Toussaint was a black nationalist who represented the interests of a new black landowning class of military officers. His government, like its predecessors, was *raciste*. It was not faith in republican France that prevented Toussaint from declaring independence but his reliance on U.S. trade and fear of a retaliatory embargo imposed by Washington.

The Napoleonic invasion of Saint Domingue in 1802 thus becomes a last-ditch attempt to restore French rule rather than an exercise in vengeful mega-lomania. Pluchon's Napoleon is a pragmatist. Far from being one with the co-lonial lobby, he initially planned to cooperate with Toussaint but was forced by the black governor's independence to overthrow him. Above all, Napoleon had no commitment to restore slavery, and he decided to do so only belatedly, months after the Leclerc expedition had sailed. This radical piece of revisionism has been vigorously challenged by the Haitians Claude and Marcel Auguste, and it remains a hotly controversial topic.[38]

Certainly Pluchon seems to go too far in his systematically cynical interpre-tation of all the key events in Toussaint's career. With regard to his commitment to the abolition of slavery, for example, he ignores the well-known letters of mid-1793 that show the black leader's identification with general emancipation long before he joined the republicans.[39] Nevertheless, Pierre Pluchon has pro-duced a refreshingly unsentimental portrait that is solidly researched and ele-gantly written.

Apart from Hubert Cole's fine study of Henry Christophe, published in 1967, few other figures in the Haitian Revolution have found a modern biographer. The appearance in 1985 of Robert Stein's *Léger Félicité Sonthonax* was therefore especially welcome.[40] The civil commissioner who wrote the emancipation proc-lamation of 1793 did more to shape the revolution than almost any individual except Louverture and Bonaparte. In Stein's book, the corpulent and aggressive young lawyer comes alive as a personality who became smitten with West In-dian society. Most important, Stein revealed that Sonthonax had been an abo-litionist for at least two years before his arrival in Saint Domingue. The colo-nists' hostility to him thus proves to be less irrational than it formerly appeared, and the commissioner's movement to abolish slavery in the summer of 1793 becomes much less a desperate act of realpolitik. This gives new weight to met-ropolitan and idealist factors in overall interpretations of the revolution as op-posed to local and materialist ones. The long-neglected Sonthonax has also attracted renewed attention from scholars in France. The proceedings of a col-loquium held in his honor have been published with contributions from Yves Bénot, Jacques de Cauna, and others.[41]

Another welcome event in this area was the recent appearance of a short bi-ography of Étienne Mentor, which has the added interest of drawing on several private manuscript collections in Haiti.[42] Best known for being murdered in prison alongside Boisrond-Tonnerre and for the striking portrait made when he was a colonial deputy in Paris, Mentor is just one of numerous characters thrown up by the Haitian Revolution who merit further study. Available sources are probably insufficient for a biography of Dessalines or Jean-François, but Martial Besse, Jean-Baptiste Lapointe, and the Chanlatte family could prove to be prom-ising subjects, and among the French, studies of de Blanchelande, Roume, and Laveaux could be fruitful.

The most recent scholar to produce a major history of the Haitian Revolution is Carolyn Fick. She approached the subject from a very different angle than Pierre Pluchon or any other biographer—explicitly "from below."[43] Her *Making of Haiti* seeks to recapture the viewpoint of the mass of ordinary men and women who made the revolution and to put them at the center of the political narrative. Here she goes much further than C. L. R. James, who, while acknowledging the political agency of common folk, devoted most of his attention to their main leaders and to wider economic and political forces. In Fick's study, Toussaint, Dessalines, and Rigaud are demoted and the people they sought to represent or dominate are brought to the fore. Making vivid use of the American newspaper accounts first exploited by Thomas Ott, Fick does more than any previous historian to unravel the confused chronology of the early days of the great insurrection in the northern plain. I would argue, however, that she overlooks the full scope of the rebels' plan out of a desire to emphasize its degree of organization.[44] Moreover, like early Haitian historians and, more recently, Gérard Laurent and Torcuato di Tella, she accepts somewhat uncritically contemporary claims that white counterrevolutionaries were mixed up in the insurrection.[45]

The great originality of *The Making of Haiti* is its concentration on events in Saint Domingue's neglected south province. The south is particularly interesting because during the revolution it quickly became a bastion of free colored power and because there the forced labor regime that followed slavery functioned longest. Neither slave–free colored relations or the revolutionary plantation regime have received much scholarly attention, so this study is especially valuable. Although Dr. Fick found few source materials for the late 1790s, she illuminates most effectively the interplay between free colored rule, plantation labor, and a grassroots militancy that rejected but had to come to terms with both.

Grassroots resistance is the central theme of *The Making of Haiti.* The book lies not only in the Marxian tradition of *The Black Jacobins* but also extends the tradition of Haitian nationalist historians such as Jean Fouchard, who stressed the continuity of slave resistance in Saint Domingue between the colonial and revolutionary periods.[46] The main argument here is that the black revolution that began in 1791 was a direct continuation of the age-old activities of fugitive slaves (known as marronage), which grew steadily more threatening in the later eighteenth century. The growth of the vodou religion, invariably presented by Haitian writers as an intrinsically revolutionary vehicle, is frequently made part of the argument.[47] In the hands of some of its exponents, such as Emmanuel Paul or Willy Appollon, the French Revolution becomes almost irrelevant to the Haitian Revolution; indigenous factors explain all.[48] For C. L. R. James, on the other hand, the French Revolution was an essential part of Haiti's Revolution. Carolyn Fick's book may be read as an attempt to combine James's respect for the *conjoncture* of the French revolutionary crisis with the Haitian emphasis on the *longue durée.*

Carolyn Fick gives us a much-better-documented but significantly scaled-down version of this *thèse haïtienne,* or Haitian nationalist argument. She notes in passing that before 1791, armed revolts had been rare or nonexistent in Saint Domingue,[49] and she accepts that the leaders of the slave revolution were not, as has often been claimed, leaders of maroon bands. She also obliquely acknowledges that large maroon communities were more prevalent in other colonies, and in general she avoids untenable claims about their increasing activism or participation in the revolution.[50] Instead, she directs attention toward the individual, short-term cases of slave absenteeism usually called *petit marronage*. Fick's novel contention is that such clandestine movements played an important role in the organization of the 1791 insurrection.[51] No proof is presented, but the argument carries some weight, especially because the leader Jean-François was already a fugitive at the time of the revolt. Nevertheless, as I argue in Chapter 5, the slaves did not lack opportunities *within* the system to meet and organize: at Sunday markets, on the way to provision grounds, at weekend festivities. The Lenormand plantation meeting, at which the uprising was planned, was in fact a large-scale feast held with the whites' knowledge. Moreover, several of the main conspirators were coachmen, who routinely would have traveled widely.

It thus remains highly uncertain that marronage contributed in any direct way to launching the black revolution. To state that in 1791 marronage "turned into" a revolutionary force simply begs the question.[52] It was large numbers of enslaved people that turned into a revolutionary force, but only one of them (admittedly an important figure) is known to have been a maroon. It seems to me that Dr. Fick has conducted a maroon-like rearguard action; having harried the positions of the oppressive Europeans, she stealthily withdraws from the main positions of the Haitian resistance school, using plenty of camouflage. Describing the rebels' military tactics as "maroon tactics" (when they might simply be called African) is, I think, obfuscation; if one accepts John Thornton's argument, they would not have fought any differently if marronage had never existed. Obfuscatory, too, is the practice, followed by Fouchard and Fick, of simply labeling the rebels of the 1790s as "maroons."

I agree with Michel-Rolph Trouillot's comment in *Ti dife boule sou istoua Ayiti*, the first history written in Haitian Creole, that "in 1791, especially in the north, the slaves reached a crossroads; instead of escaping in search of freedom, they preferred to fight for it."[53] The essence of marronage was the temporary, sometimes permanent, withdrawal of labor by a slave; it could be collective, though was usually individual; it could be passive or accompanied by acts of theft or (much more rarely) revenge. To confuse it with the violent and collective enterprise of openly risking one's life in an attempt to change the system, to my mind, greatly underestimates what the slaves of Saint Domingue took on in 1791.

Problems of *conjoncture* and *longue durée* confront all historians, but this is a peculiarly sensitive one, because it is usually assumed that at issue here is the slave's attitude toward slavery. To question the prevalence or political significance of marronage is easily read as an assertion that slaves "accepted slavery," or, as Trouillot argues, "forgot the taste for freedom."[54] This is not necessarily the case. Freedom is relative and dependent on context. Many slaves in Saint Domingue not previously tempted by the life of a fugitive were evidently willing to take up arms when the circumstances seemed right.[55]

What was it in the circumstances of 1791 that brought about this change? How should we weigh the significance of questions of ideology against perceived shifts in the balance of power? Did the French Revolution transform *mentalités* in the slave quarters, or did it merely facilitate the realization of existing aspirations? Something changed in 1791, but should we look for it in the apparatus of social control, in levels of discontent, or in changes of consciousness?

Avoiding the twin perils of exoticizing or occidentalizing the slaves, how are we to imagine the attitudes and beliefs of those Africans and children of Africans of two centuries ago: those who called their white enemies "the monkeys" or "the citizens"; those who in their native languages had no word for "liberty" even though thousands of them died in its pursuit?[56] This, in my opinion, remains the most intractable question facing historians of the Haitian Revolution.

3 Underexploited Sources

One of the greatest servile rebellions in world history, the Haitian Revolution has been the subject of a great deal of writing and controversy but relatively little archival research. For 200 years, the destruction of Saint Domingue and the career of the black leader Toussaint Louverture have inspired numerous general works that have tended to rely heavily on the same dozen or so secondary sources. The most prolific and influential historians of the colony in the second half of the twentieth century all chose to concentrate on the pre-revolutionary period.[1] The result is that modern scholars still do not know a great deal more about the revolution than did Thomas Madiou and Beaubrun Ardouin when they wrote their magisterial studies in the 1840s and 1850s.[2]

Great strides forward have certainly been made in recent years with the appearance of two solidly documented studies, Carolyn Fick's *Making of Haiti* and Pierre Pluchon's biographies of Toussaint Louverture.[3] Between them, and with little overlap, these two scholars mined the two main series of documents dealing with Saint Domingue in the French national archives. Pluchon's conservative biographies relied almost solely on the main series of government records, Colonies CC9, which he systematically exploited.[4] These materials are very sparingly cited in Dr. Fick's radical history, whose principal source, which was completely ignored by Pluchon, was the enormous Dxxv series of papers collected by the colonial committee of France's revolutionary assemblies. Extraordinary for a biographer of Toussaint Louverture, Pluchon also ignored the latter's letters in the series AA and AE of the Archives Nationales, and in his first biography, he ignored the well-known Bibliothèque Nationale collections of Sonthonax and Laveaux correspondence, as did Fick, although they contain a large part of Toussaint's surviving letters. These excellent modern histories of the revolution thus provide a rather unbalanced coverage even of the source material in Paris.

All this material, along with the invaluable collection of miscellanea left by Moreau de Saint-Méry (Colonies F3), has been dipped into frequently by writers on the revolution and is the primary source of most scholarly work on the subject. The purpose of this chapter is to draw attention to some of the more neglected material found not only in France but also in Spain, Great Britain, the Caribbean, and the United States that might illuminate further the period in which Saint Domingue was transformed into Haiti.

France

Among the most important and underused sources for the history of the entire revolution in Saint Domingue is a little-known manuscript of some

275,000 words entitled the "Précis historique des annales de la colonie françoise de Saint-Domingue depuis 1789." Its anonymous author was probably a colonial magistrate named Pélage-Marie Duboys.[5] The manuscript was formerly owned by the late historian Gabriel Debien, who presented typescript copies to the University of Florida Library and the Bibliothèque Nationale, Paris.[6] It is in many respects an essential counterpart to the "official history" published by the left-of-center deputy Jean-Philippe Garran-Coulon, the 4-volume *Rapport sur les troubles de Saint-Domingue,* which itself has been more ignored than read by writers on the revolution. Duboys's manuscript presents the subject from the standpoint of a colonist unsympathetic to the French Revolution, and yet, like Garran-Coulon's *Rapport,* it maintains a degree of objectivity that distinguishes it from many other merely polemical works. While Garran-Coulon's study ends in 1794, the Précis Historique continues up to the surrender of Toussaint Louverture in floréal year ten (May 1802). Rich in quotations from documents, the Précis Historique is above all an eyewitness account by someone who lived in the colony throughout the course of the revolution. Moreover, while most firsthand accounts from these years were written in Cap Français, the author of the Précis Historique lived in Port-au-Prince. All these factors produced a unique work well worthy of careful scrutiny.

Duboys, the putative author, arrived in Saint Domingue in 1785 at age 35. He had practiced as an *avocat* (trial attorney) before the Parlement of Paris and had occupied several minor judicial posts in the colony before 1787 when he became assistant public prosecutor in the controversial new appeal court the government established in Port-au-Prince. This earned him the enmity of northern lawyers, whose regional appeal court in Cap Français was closed. They took revenge at the beginning of the revolution, when they had him arrested for opposing the emergent democratic movement. They also accused him of favoring political rights for free coloreds and of criticizing colonists who attributed livestock epidemics to poisoning or sorcery by slaves. Like many west province conservatives, Duboys supported the local free coloreds' bid for equality after they took up arms in 1791. He had to flee mob rule in the capital for several months, first to the south, then to Santo Domingo. He sought but failed to obtain public office under the British occupation of 1793–1798 and practiced as a plantation and trial attorney during much of the revolution.[7] A series of detailed letters Duboys wrote between May and October 1803 that have recently come to light provide a continuation of his narrative. They are privately owned but accessible through the Internet.[8]

A manuscript comparable in length and scope to the Précis Historique, but less useful, is the "Histoire de la Révolution" that belongs to the Médiathèque of Nantes. It is attributed to an *avocat* named Listré, who practiced before the Conseil Supérieur (appeal court) of Cap Français.[9] Unlike his legal colleague P. M. Duboys, Listré gives his prejudices full rein; consequently, his reliability becomes suspect in parts. Writing a decade later than Duboys, he had also had more opportunity to incorporate material from published sources, which may explain the derivative appearance of some passages. Even so, while his Histoire lacks the acuity, originality, and balanced judgment of the Précis Histori-que, it contains much valuable information on events in the north province and is itself vivid evidence of the blinkered and violent self-righteousness of the *esprit colon*. An earlier, shorter, version of this history, although attributed to another author, can be found some 230 miles away in the municipal library of Auxerre.[10]

Yet another neglected manuscript history of the revolution, written in 1800, is owned by the Bibliothèque Municipale de Rouen.[11] Its author was probably from the northeast region of the colony, and certainly its most interesting pages concern the Fort Dauphin massacre of July 7, 1794. This library's collection also contains a key document devoted entirely to the subject of the massacre.[12] It combines an eyewitness description with a list of the victims, an analytic attempt to deduce the role of the Spanish in the affair, and an account of life in the town during the following eight months. This document contains much information about the black army of insurgent leader Jean-François and about the relations existing between *nouveaux* and *anciens libres* (as ex-slaves and free coloreds were called after emancipation). It forms a major addition to the material on the massacre in the Spanish archives and England's Public Record Office.

Provincial French libraries and archives contain many collections of Saint Domingue documents that include small amounts of correspondence from the revolutionary period. Sometimes it is only an occasional letter that nonetheless provides valuable detail, as in Belin de Villeneuve's papers in the Lot et Garonne departmental archives (on the beginnings of political mobilization in 1788), or the château de Ribaute papers in Marseille (on the Cul de Sac plain in 1792). Sometimes a brief run of correspondence allows us to watch how events unfolded for a particular individual, as in the Duplaa papers in Pau and the Boutin papers at La Rochelle.[13] The 130 letters of military commandant Loppinot de Beauport in the archives des Yvelines offer a critical point of entry to the milieu of the royalist Pompons Blancs.[14] Locating such sources has been made enormously easier by the Archives Nationales's publication of its *Guide des sources de l'histoire de l'Amérique latine et des Antilles dans les archives françaises*. For locating material in private hands, the twenty or so articles Gabriel Debien devoted to bibliography and source materials are the best place to start.[15]

Although it is a printed work, the *Débats entre les accusateurs et les accusés dans l'affaire des colonies* deserves mention here because it is an exceptionally rich source of evidence regarding the early revolution and has been very little used. It is a bibliographic rarity, and few historians have worked their way through all of its nine volumes.[16] The *Débats* are the result of a government inquiry into the momentous mission to Saint Domingue in 1792–1794 of the civil commissioners Sonthonax and Polverel. The work provides a verbatim transcription of the confrontation between the commissioners and their colonial critics, who made charges and countercharges, citing and quoting from documents for days on end. The intimate setting offers a unique view of the truculent Sonthonax and the shrill and scurrilous Patriots. The record of the proceedings contains information not available anywhere else.

Spain and Hispanic America

The large body of material on the Haitian Revolution in Spanish archives mostly derives from Saint Domingue's neighboring colony, Santo Domingo. The Spanish authorities there closely observed the revolution that threatened to engulf them, particularly the slave rebels with whom they traded across their common frontier. When war broke out in Europe, the governor of Santo Domingo enlisted thousands of rebel blacks into his army, and the Spaniards thus became major participants in the revolution. The documentation they left behind is substantial, is in excellent condition, and has been accessible for decades.[17] For any study of the slave revolt of 1791 and of its development, this material is vital. Although it is not quite as neglected as it was two decades ago, it remains remarkably underused.

This is especially true of the ten lengthy documents housed in the national archives in Madrid that concern the deportation from Saint Domingue to Cuba and later repatriation of nonwhite prisoners of war.[18] Most of the Spanish documentation, however, is divided between the Archivo General de Indias in Seville and the Archivo General de Simancas near Valladolid. The two collections overlap considerably, but for the war years 1793–1795, Simancas has the more important holding (Guerra Moderna, 7157–7161). The Seville holding is the larger; it is distributed between Estado 11, 13, 14 and Audiencia de Santo Domingo 1027–1035, 1089, 1102, 1110, with duplicates in 954–957.[19]

These papers are unique in several respects. They provide a firsthand account of Saint Domingue's revolution by observers who, at least initially, were not involved in it. They register the shock waves of that revolution in the colony where they were felt most severely. They describe the extraordinary experiment of recruiting rebel slaves to defend a slave society, and they also cast light on the early career of Toussaint Louverture, both before and after he joined the Spaniards. Although they include no letters by the black leader, the two collections contain a large number by other rebel leaders, in particular Jean-François and Georges Biassou. Most are translated copies, but there are some signed originals as well. They reveal much about the structure of the rebel forces and the identity of their leaders, the relations between the Spanish church and the slave rebels, and the mysterious Fort Dauphin massacre, in which hundreds of French colonists were killed by Jean-François's soldiers under the eyes of an immobile Spanish garrison. There are also among the Simancas and Seville material many letters relating to the famous maroon band of the Maniel, about whom little is known following the treaty they made with the colonial authorities in 1785. The connection between marronage and revolution in Saint Domingue has been hotly debated; here we have an important test case.

The exile of Jean-François's and Biassou's soldiers in different parts of Spain's empire after 1795 is no longer, as Chapter 12 shows, the unresearched topic it was until recently. The documentation in Hispanic archives produced by that diaspora nevertheless remains useful for studying the Haitian Revolution. This is because of the personal data generated by the exile process. We learn far more about the slave insurgents of 1791 as individuals and family members when they were in Honduras or Panama or Spain than we do for the period when they were in Hispaniola.[20]

The Caribbean

Scholars working in the Caribbean might like to know that many of the most important items from the Seville and Simancas collections can be found in typescript copies in the Dominican Republic. Made by historian J. M. Incháustegui, they are kept at the Universidad Católica de Madre y Maestra at Santiago de los Caballeros.[21] Apart from a few proclamations by the governor of Santo Domingo and some other, largely financial, material, little has survived of the original colonial archives in Santo Domingo.[22] They were removed to Cuba in 1800 and were repatriated in 1905 but suffered greatly from hurricane and theft. All the colonial archive cannot have been moved, however. Haitian historian Beaubrun Ardouin wrote of finding letters by Toussaint Louverture in the local archives in the 1820s.[23] As the letters he cited are very important, it is unfortunate that nothing of the sort can nowadays be found in the Archivo General de la Nación.[24] To judge from José Luciano Franco's *Documentos para la historia de Haití en el Archivo Nacional,* no Dominican material remains in Havana.[25] Fortunately, we have in Antonio del Monte y Tejada's *Historia de Santo Domingo* some compensation for the loss of this material, as well as presumptive evidence of its existence up to the end of the nineteenth century.[26] The very rare Volume 4 of this little-known work and an appendix to its Volume 3 consist of letters passed between local military commanders and the governor during the revolutionary period. They admirably complement the documents in Spain by introducing a broader range of opinion and providing a finer focus on day-to-day events.

In Jamaica can be found a number of small collections directly relevant to the Haitian revolution. The papers of Governor Nugent, which are kept in the Institute of Jamaica in Kingston, contain over twenty reports by British agents who resided in Saint Domingue during the ascendancy of Toussaint Louverture (1799–1801), as well as some seven letters by Toussaint and eleven by Jean-Jacques Dessalines.[27] These are contemporary duplicates of originals in the Public Record Office in London or in the National Library of Scotland, Edinburgh. The Institute of Jamaica more recently acquired the Fischer Collection (MS 36F) of some hundred small dossiers, many of which concern the southern region of the Grand Anse. They include wills, legislative acts, records of property transactions, and political correspondence. The Fischer and the Haitian manuscript (MS 36) collections together include about half a dozen letters by Toussaint or Dessalines. The Jamaica Archives at Spanish Town contain, among the papers of the Vice-Admiralty Court, captured correspondence from Saint Domingue and the trial papers of ships seized after March 1793. These documents shed light on U.S. commercial activity in the colony and could be combined usefully with North American sources.

Paradoxically, but understandably enough, few primary sources have survived in Haiti itself concerning the revolution that destroyed so much. According to a former director, the Archives Nationales in Port-au-Prince contain no documents from the colonial period. The Institut Saint Louis de Gonzague is an invaluable storehouse for Haitian studies, but the strength of its collection is not revolutionary-era manuscripts. The private collection of Edmond Mangonès, now belonging to the Fathers of the Holy Ghost, was formerly deposited at the Institut, but it has been transferred to the order's parent house in Europe. Copies of part of this collection can be found on nineteen reels of microfilm in the University of Florida's Special Collections Department; most of the material dates from before or after the revolution. On the positive side, the reopening in the 1990s after two decades of the Petit Séminaire Saint-Martial makes its holdings again accessible. Its small miscellany of manuscripts include two letters from Toussaint Louverture to his sister. The citation of a half-dozen private collections in Gaétan Mentor's recent book also gives substance to old rumors about the holdings in private hands and hope that more new sources will come to light in Haiti.[28]

Great Britain

One of the major finds of recent years occurred when twenty-seven letters signed by Toussaint Louverture surfaced in Scotland. They date from the summer of 1798 and concern the black leader's negotiations with General Thomas Maitland to have the British forces of occupation evacuate Saint Domingue. Although duplicates of these items exist in Paris, they occasionally differ from the text of the originals, and herein lies the great interest of the new find. While Toussaint was pretending to the French government that he was acting as a loyal vassal, he was negotiating with the British as an independent ruler. Descendants of General Maitland deposited the collection in the Scottish Record Office. It also contains a considerable quantity of the general's papers from the years 1797–1798 not found in the Public Record Office that provide much valuable information unavailable elsewhere.[29]

Three other collections concerning the period 1797–1798 also deserve note, particularly because none of them appears in Walne's *Guide to Manuscript Sources*.[30] The Devon Record Office at Exeter holds numerous papers of John Simcoe, Maitland's predecessor as commander of the British-occupied zone. Like the Steel-Maitland papers, these form a valuable supplement to the material in the Public Record Office and throw much light on the later stages of the war between the forces of Toussaint Louverture and the British.[31] Of similar extent and nature are the papers of Edward Littlehales, General Simcoe's aide-de-camp. Part of the Spencer Bernard private collection, they illuminate the everyday life of the European troops fighting the ex-slaves.[32] The same is also true of the smaller collection left by Captain James Guthrie, who served as acting quartermaster.[33] His accounts yield much information about price levels in the colony, but their importance derives from their data on casualties, which fill many lacunae in the Public Record Office statistics. All these collections contain plenty of French material, and their interest extends far beyond purely military matters.

Britain's 5-year attempt to conquer Saint Domingue generated enormous documentation on the revolution, which can be found in the Public Record Office; it is the second most important repository in this respect after the Archives Nationales.[34] All the series relating to the occupation have now been researched, but some material lying outside this subject might be noted. The records of the High Court of Admiralty include a rich holding of captured correspondence from Saint Domingue that is much larger than the holding in the Jamaica Archives.[35] It comes from mailbags, and it should provide detailed pictures of particular regions at specific moments. For instance, it contains nearly 400 letters mailed in the Port-au-Prince region around January 1793, when political divisions were sharpening and the vodou priest Hyacinthe was gaining prominence in the surrounding countryside. Bernard Foubert's analysis of soldiers' letters from the Cayes region exemplifies what excellent use can be made of such materials.[36]

Rhodes House Library at Oxford possesses two volumes of correspondence on the Caribbean by British War Minister Henry Dundas.[37] These include a section on Saint Domingue that supplements the existing Dundas material in the Public Record Office, British Library, National Library of Scotland, and the collection of the late Gabriel Debien. The British Library also contains a brief miscellany of official correspondence from Santo Domingo dating from 1792–1793. All the items, which largely concern relations between the Spanish and the black insurgents, duplicate others in either Simancas or Seville. They include letters by the governor and archbishop of Santo Domingo and by Jean-François.[38]

The United States

More than thirty manuscript collections in North American archives have a significant focus on the Haitian Revolution.[39] Some, like Lieutenant Howard's journal in the Boston Public Library, or the scattering of letters by prominent leaders, have attracted historians' attention; most have not. Other archival holdings, notably several dealing with international commerce and refugees' papers such as those of Grand Dutreuilh in Atlanta, also contain a few valuable items from the revolutionary period.

Of outstanding interest among the several relevant collections in New York Public Library are the papers of Jean-Baptiste de Cressac, a Creole coffee and indigo planter of Gros Morne parish in northwest Saint Domingue.[40] Dispersed through nine folders in the West Indies Collection, the documents unevenly span the period 1784–1801 and include a handful of earlier and later date. They contain rare correspondence and accounts from the post-slavery period, when

Saint Domingue's plantations were worked under a forced labor scheme that shared revenue between owners and workers. De Cressac, the former slave-owner, had then become a local magistrate in a colony where power had shifted into the hands of the ex-slave army. Of greatest interest, however, are the hundred or so letters from the years 1791–1792 that form the heart of the collection. They deal with the early development of the slave uprising seen from the northwest parishes, where planters kept precarious control of their slaves. They are primarily letters sent to him when he was parish commandant by other local colonists struggling to form and hold a cordon of military camps against the burgeoning insurrection. Recurrent themes are the constant patrolling of plantations, the difficulty of preventing desertion by citizen soldiers, and the tense relations between whites and free coloreds, who were allies in the war against the slaves but divided by the latter's aspirations for racial equality.

White–free colored relations in combating the slave insurgents is also the main theme in the letterbook of Anne-Louis de Tousard, held by the Hagley Museum in Wilmington.[41] De Tousard, who was a lieutenant-colonel of the Cap Français regiment, played a leading role in the early attempts to combat the slave insurrection in the north. The letterbook covers the period November 1791–March 1792, when de Tousard was posted to the northeast region, where, as in the northwest, the insurrection took hold slowly. The letterbook thus complements the de Cressac papers. Yet it is a richer source; it includes about 300 letters detailing the complex political world in which the royalist commander sought to maneuver. Caught between slave and free colored insurgents and others teetering on the verge of rebellion, the radical *corps populaires* in the towns, and the conservative Spanish across the frontier, de Tousard could make little headway. These were the months he lost his reputation as a popular and successful commander.

The Hagley Museum also contains several collections concerning U.S. trade with revolutionary Saint Domingue. It is not surprising that several of the holdings of this institution, which is best known for its connection with the DuPont family, shed light on the French family's role in supplying munitions, food, and financing to different parties in the Haitian Revolution.[42]

Around 1960, two very substantial and contrasting collections passed from private hands to the library of the University of Florida at Gainesville. One consists of the papers of General Rochambeau, who commanded the French army during the bloodiest stage of Haiti's war of independence (1802–1803). They exceed 2,300 manuscript items and consist primarily of letters sent to the commander-in-chief. An excellent calendar of them has been published.[43] The core of the collection is constituted by twenty-four lots from the auction of Rochambeau papers conducted by Sotheby & Co. in 1958. Indispensable for the history of the Napoleonic invasion of Saint Domingue, the collection has been exploited in the work of Thomas Ott, Carolyn Fick, and the Auguste brothers.[44] However, a microfilm supplement to the collection remains entirely unused. Contained on five reels of film, it is of comparable size and derives from the twenty-three lots purchased at the 1958 auction by the Haitian government. As these documents were never made available to the public and have since disappeared, the film is of considerable historical value.[45] The Rochambeau collection is completed by a collection of maps, which consists of a dozen very detailed, large format maps of the northern mountains and Artibonite plain and photographs of the other maps purchased by the Archives de France at the Sotheby's auction.

A less eye-catching collection, but potentially rather exciting, are the Jérémie Papers, notarial records from the southern region of the Grand Anse. Wills, inventories, marriage contracts, records of property transactions, and similar documents fill thirty-one boxes and number more than 4,000 items. They are supplemented by microform copies of other notaries' records from the same region held by the Centre des Archives d'Outre-mer, Aix-en-Provence. On the eve of the revolution, the Grand Anse was Saint Domingue's frontier, the scene of frantic pioneer activity riding on the coffee boom of the 1780s. An isolated region with a distinct personality, it experienced the impact of the revolution in a unique way. The plantation regime survived there, embattled but largely intact, until 1802. Notarial records go back to the 1770s but are clustered in rare abundance from the 1780s and 1790s. Similar documentation from these years is contained in the university's Mangonès Collection (reel A71), and in the Fis[c]her collections deposited at the New York Public Library's Department of Rare Books, Howard University, and the Institute of Jamaica. The Grand Anse is also well represented in the inventories of the Administration des Biens des Absents of the mid-1790s and in the Recensements des Biens Domaniaux of the late 1790s, both held by the Centre des Archives d'Outre-mer. These documents and others from the early national period offer an opportunity for a fascinating area study.[46]

The most recent collection to come to light consists of the papers of an obscure young merchant, Michel Marsaudon, that have been acquired by Georgetown University. Primarily letters written by or to individuals in Port-au-Prince, Le Cap, and Saint Marc, most date from the period 1790–1794. Alongside discussion of commercial matters, they make occasional reference to political developments, but much space is also given over to sexual and romantic matters. They include notes sent by free women of color, very rare voices in the documentation of the times. The collection serves as a reminder that in the midst of momentous events, everyday life went on.[47]

Part Three.   *The Seeds of Revolt*

*Why do people become willing to risk their lives, at a certain mo-
ment but not before, in order to change the society in which they
live? Despite an abundance of theoretical work on the subject in
the social sciences and a mountain of historical studies of revolutions, we have no clear answer. Where some see the threat of violence as the cement of social systems, others see shared values or
hegemonic mystification. Change might thus depend on new
ways of seeing the world or merely on enhanced prospects for successful resistance. Scholarly fashions change, and scholars are
drawn toward materialist or idealist explanations according to
their personal proclivities. One of the attractions to studying
slavery, the most extreme form of social control, is its potential
to shed light on this issue. The Saint Domingue slave insurrection, easily the largest in the Americas and one of very few to suc-
ceed, is obviously a key test case.*

*Chapter 4 briefly surveys debates about slave rebellion in
world history, which usefully helps distance the topic from its inevitable association with race in the American context. A wide
variety of factors have been posited as encouraging or preventing
slave resistance, but few scholars have developed typologies of
slave rebellions. Those of Eugene Genovese and Michael Craton
are examined here. In explaining the 1791 uprising in Saint
Domingue, historians tend to emphasize either the external
influence of the French Revolution or a range of internal factors.
Chapter 5 discusses the controversy regarding two of those internal factors, the vodou religion and the activities of fugitive slaves
known as marronage. Although interest in their historical importance seems to have begun with French historians around 1900,
they later became associated with a black nationalist viewpoint
in Haiti. This chapter reviews the evidence that underpins this
thesis and the variant forms it has taken.*

*The following chapter focuses on the central element in the
linkage between vodou and revolution, the so-called Bois
Caïman ceremony that was held on the eve of the slave uprising.*

Long part of the national mythology and the subject of lively debate, its very existence has recently been denied in the most searching study of its historiography yet published. The argument in Chapter 6 seeks to establish its historicity and to examine claims about the role it played by reviewing all the extant sources, archival, oral, and published.

4 The Causation of Slave Rebellions: An Overview

Slavery has existed in probably every century of recorded history and for much of that time in most parts of the globe. In all the diverse forms it has assumed, slavery has been synonymous with extreme degradation, and often with brutality, wherever it has appeared.[1] Yet slave revolts have been comparatively infrequent.[2] Violent resistance seems to have been more typical of ancient Greek helots and free urban workers, the Roman plebs, European serfs, Chinese peasants, and American Indians or Africans under colonial rule.

The Incidence of Slave Revolts

In the Ancient World, large-scale slave revolts were confined to the 70-year period 140–70 B.C., and the institution's demise half a millennium later was not, most historians agree, a product of slave resistance.[3] Only three rebellions in world history involved close to 100,000 slaves: two occurred in Sicily in the second century B.C. and the other in French Saint Domingue in the 1790s. Although each of these lasted for several years, as did the Zanj revolt of African slaves in southern Iraq (A.D. 868–883),[4] most slave insurrections were suppressed within a few days and involved far fewer participants.

The United States experienced many conspiracies during two centuries of slave-holding but only one revolt of more than 100 slaves and, according to John W. Blassingame, fewer than ten in all that claimed victims, although its slave population numbered 1 million in 1800 and 4 million in 1860.[5] The propensity of Brazilian slaves to rebel is usually held up in contrast, but there, too, revolts appear to have been fairly few during the 250 years prior to 1800, when the colony probably contained about 1.6 million slaves. The Brazilian reputation rests on the twenty or so insurrections of the period 1807–1835, many of which included several hundred participants.[6] Violent resistance in Cuba was concentrated in a similar period, corresponding to slavery's rapid expansion after 1790; apart from two startlingly ambitious conspiracies, it usually consisted of revolts on single plantations.[7] In the Americas, the peak of organized violent resistance to slavery was found probably in Jamaica, where the Baptist Rebellion of 1831 mobilized up to 20,000 slaves (6 percent of the slave population) and where in the previous 150 years there were eight other uprisings involving usually hundreds of slaves as well as several conspiracies. Most of the small islands, however—Antigua, Curaçao, St. Croix, St. John's, St. Kitt's, Barbados—witnessed only one or two revolts during two centuries of slavery.[8] More remarkable, the largest slave society in the Caribbean, Saint Domingue, whose slave population in 1790 numbered about half a million, also experienced only a few small uprisings before the great rebellion of 1791.[9]

Perhaps none of this is surprising. Slavery represented, after all, an extreme form not only of degradation but also of dominance and powerlessness. Significantly, conspiracies that failed to reach fruition were probably more common than rebellions. As slave revolts that enjoyed success were truly few in number, one may wonder that any bondsmen ever rebelled at all.[10] Yet, while not underrating either the institution's ability to repress, or its oppressiveness, one must remember that in many slave societies, slaves constituted a majority of the population; slaves typically accounted for 80 or 90 percent in the Caribbean, and in rural areas they were even more preponderant. Unlike prisoners, slaves in the Americas commonly worked with machetes, axes, and knives, and individuals occasionally possessed firearms (for hunting). In the Middle East, Africa, and the New World, slaves were sometimes recruited as soldiers, even as armed defenders of the slave regime itself (as in the Caribbean in the 1790s).[11] Should we, then, be more surprised that in the long history of slavery some bondsmen rebelled or that most did not?

Force and False Consciousness

Toward the end of the revolution that created Haiti, two leading antislavery writers debated in print how this dramatic transformation could have come about and how it would affect other American slave societies, which then stretched from Rhode Island to Buenos Aires. James Stephen, a profoundly religious conservative who had lived in the West Indies, thought that white authority rested primarily on the slaves' irrational fears, "fostered by ignorance and habit." Somewhat like a belief in ghosts, this "instinctive dread" was deeply ingrained, but once dispelled it vanished forever. The more secular and liberal Henry Brougham believed that the slaves' subordination derived simply from a rational appraisal of the costs of resistance.[12] Slave-owners similarly disagreed about the nature of the power they wielded. Some said that the system functioned by force alone. Others claimed that slaves accepted their status as inevitable, if not legitimate, in a world that had always been divided between slaves and slave-owners.

Assessment of the degree of coercion and consensus that respectively hold any society together is an intractable problem whose resolution seems to depend less on analysis than on acts of faith.[13] Yet it is difficult to avoid, lying as it does at the heart of all questions of social subordination. In the study of slavery, it is a particularly sensitive topic. Where some see symbiosis, others see constant conflict. It has engendered fierce dissension regarding the supposed personality of slaves (dependent, stoic, or defensively deceptive), their culture (impoverished and imitative or resiliently creative), and the system of social control that contained them (its degree of efficiency and inhumanity). One may readily accept that slave societies, more than any other, depended on force. But to what extent did whips, bayonets, and warships create attitudes of submission that themselves took on a life of their own? Underlying all discussion of the causes of slave rebellion is this conundrum of consciousness versus objective conditions.

It could be said that attempts to overthrow a social order are generated by two types of change. One is a shift in the internal balance of power, brought about either by a weakening of the forces of control or some other development that makes resistance more likely to meet with success. The other variety of change leads to increased discontent on the part of the oppressed and increased willingness to resist. Both types of change may be of an idealist or material nature. Social control might be weakened by damage to its physical apparatus or the undermining of hegemonic values or by religious beliefs promising rebels invulnerability or supernatural rewards. Discontent can be increased by an actual worsening of material conditions or by a perceived worsening (relative deprivation) or by the same sort of ideas that undermine hegemonic values. In trying to understand why slave rebellions occurred, the stress one gives to these different types of explanation will depend on one's orientation to materialism and idealism and their influence on one's perception of how slave societies functioned.

Factors Hindering Rebellion

Moses Finley, one of the leading historians of the Ancient World, singled out two main factors as the essential strengths of slave systems in all periods.[14] These were

i) *Atomization.* Slave classes were peculiarly lacking in cohesion, tending to be random agglomerations of kinless individuals, often from different cultures. (Thus, the great slave revolts of the first and second centuries B.C. may partly be attributed to the wholesale enslavement of people of common culture.)

ii) *Self-debasement.* Slaves inevitably internalized their masters' view of them as inferior and acted accordingly, thereby "proving" their inferiority.

Objections may be raised to both these points. To the first, there is one outstanding exception: the United States. This was the only slave society in the Americas with a high natural growth rate (births outnumbering deaths). Combined with a low rate of manumission, this produced a slave population that even by 1800 was predominantly made up of locally born slaves with one or more generations of locally born ancestors. Atomization therefore does little to explain the notable paucity of slave rebellions in the United States, even if, as Peter Kolchin argues, its slave population was never able to recreate the strong community bonds of traditional societies.[15] Nevertheless, ethnic divisions remained important throughout the history of Caribbean and Brazilian slavery. To these should be added sectoral divisions (some say "class divisions") between unskilled slaves and the slave elite of artisans, domestics, and supervisors. The sexual divide, too, requires mention, since revolts were overwhelmingly planned by men and quite often betrayed by women.[16]

The influence of ruling-class values on slaves is particularly elusive and controversial. In a universal study of slavery, Orlando Patterson follows Hegel in arguing that slaves never accepted their masters' view of them as inferiors.[17] Other writers take refuge in a "some did; some didn't" formula, which is sensible but not exactly satisfying.[18] "Inferior," of course, is not a very precise concept, and self-image did not necessarily determine willingness to resist. Eugene Genovese perhaps comes closest to resolving the dilemma with his fluid and dialectical model of paternalism in the U.S. south, where he sees respect for the master's power but not his person, a coexistence of deference and resistance in the same individual, the same act.[19]

Other stabilizing factors, beyond the slaveholders' deployment of force, that might be considered are:

iii) *The ethic of obedience in Christianity,* which became the majority religion of slaves in the Roman Empire, where it was formed, and in mainland North and South America. Orlando Patterson stresses the theological similarity in this respect between the Roman Catholicism of Latin America and the Protestant fundamentalism of the U.S. south, implying a contrast with the mainstream Protestant (and belatedly Christianized) British Caribbean.[20] Contrarily, church organization and other aspects of the Christian message also provided a vehicle and an inspiration for some of the most prominent insurrections in both the British Caribbean and North America.[21]

iv) *The more advanced material culture* that buttressed the slave-owning class in the New World and perhaps lent it sanction as well as ability to repress. The great expansion of American slavery after 1650 occurred in an age of cheap iron shackles and the flintlock musket. Although African slaves came from societies that differed widely in their acquaintance with the West, it seems that nowhere in the history of slavery was the technological gap between master and slave greater than in the Americas during the eighteenth and nineteenth centuries.

v) *Material and psychological rewards* that any slave system had to offer to work effectively. Chief among these was the prospect of being freed, which was extremely low in the Americas, particularly in the United States. The right to accumulate property (under Roman law) and to change masters (under Islamic law) and progressive assimilation to the status of kin (in Africa) also deserve mention. In addition, some slave occupations, notwithstanding their degraded status, must have brought certain rewards. Here one might include slaves who acted as soldiers, administrators, and political advisers, especially in the Roman and Islamic worlds. The slave elite of the New World presents a less clear picture, not least because most leaders of rebellions were drawn from its ranks. Still more controversial is the self-serving claim of American planters that Africans were "better off" being their slaves. Modern quantitative research shows that by about 1800, slaves born in the Americas were frequently taller than their African counterparts, which suggests they had been better fed, at least in childhood.[22] It is also possible that American plantations, although vulnerable to the vagaries of both the climate and the world market, may even have provided for those who survived the brutal transition to the New World a more secure environment than those parts of Africa worst affected by slave-raiding, famine, and kidnapping.[23] Nevertheless, such hypothetical improvements may have offered small solace for a dehumanized life of hard labor in a kinless and alien world.

vi) *The fact of having been born into slavery,* which, according to Orlando Patterson, was the fate of most slaves.[24] In the Ancient World, the enslavement of free peoples appears to correlate with the incidence of revolt.[25] In the Americas, too, the higher incidence of resistance among slaves transported from Africa than among locally born Creoles seems to point to the same conclusion. The incidence of slavery among some African ethnic groups also seems crudely related to their reputed ability to adapt to slavery in the Americas. Apart from the use of slaves in ritual sacrifice, and perhaps a higher incidence of castration, slavery was in many ways less harsh in Africa than on American plantations and was thus not an adequate preparation for bondage in the Americas. However, one can hardly expect those born slaves and those born free to have experienced captivity and sale in the same way, even in societies where personal autonomy, still less individualism, were unknown concepts.[26]

vii) *Witchcraft beliefs.* A magico-religious view of the world diverts energies into magico-religious instead of political activities.[27] For Africans who attributed misfortune to witchcraft, it may be that resignation or resort to counter-witchcraft seemed a more appropriate response than rebellion.[28]

Factors Facilitating Rebellion

Among various influences thought by scholars to have been conducive to slave rebellion, two obvious ones appear to have been of general significance.

a) *Grouping in large units.* Just as the 70-year period of intense slave rebellion in the ancient Mediterranean corresponded with the growth of the Roman latifundium, so too in Africa the rare use of slaves in commercial plantation agriculture provided the few known instances on that continent of either slave revolt (in Futa Jallon) or frequent desertion (in Zanzibar).[29] The geographical distribution of rebellions in the New World similarly coincides with the average number of slaves per estate—low in the United States, higher in Brazil, much higher in the Caribbean. This coincidence (which parallels a contrast Barrington Moore noted between the size of Russian and German factories in 1917),[30] may be attributable to organizational factors (ease of communication and of recruiting trustworthy conspirators) or to the degree of cultural or psychological autonomy resulting from the slaves' spatial distance from the master class or to the harsh and impersonal regimes associated with large estates, which tended to be run not by a resident owner but by a manager paid on a commission basis. In the Americas, large plantations were usually sugar plantations, whose "industrial" regimes notoriously produced the harshest known labor conditions. In North America, the major slave rebellions and conspiracies took place in sugar-growing Louisiana and in rice-growing South Carolina, where plantations were larger than in the regions of cotton and tobacco cultivation.

b) *A high ratio of slave to free* and, in the Americas, of black to white. Related to the previous point, this factor similarly serves to differentiate the Caribbean, Brazil, and the United States from each other and to differentiate South Carolina and Louisiana from the rest of the U.S. south. It also applies to Sicily and southern Italy in the first and second centuries B.C. In addition, shifts in the demographic balance within these areas sometimes corresponded to upsurges of slave resistance.

Other factors that supposedly facilitated rebellion present a more ambiguous appearance.

c) *The involvement of the ruling class in war or internal struggles.* War clearly did on occasion lead to insurrections among slaves who hoped for foreign assistance or who were encouraged by the departure of troops and militia. However, it has rarely received notice that many such conflicts actually saw a decrease in the incidence of revolt and conspiracy. This applies to the entire British Caribbean during the revolutionary wars with France of 1778–1783 and 1793–1815; to Brazil's secession struggle of 1821–1823; to the thirteen colonies during the War of Independence; and to much of Spanish America during its own war for independence. Sometimes these conflicts brought slaves new opportunities for flight and for manumission through military service, thus reducing the need for revolt. But it may also have been merely the mobilization of military forces, or their increase, that prevented potential rebels from reacting. In the Caribbean, the correspondence between slave rebellion and a declining local garrison is quite remarkable, while cases to the contrary are hard to find.[31]

d) *A "closed frontier."* Although Orlando Patterson suggested that the proximity of forest or mountain terrain encouraged rebellions,[32] one might also argue that, by facilitating the escape of slaves, it actually reduced the likelihood of uprisings. As Barrington Moore observes, an important determinant of revolution is an absence of alternatives.[33] In the islands of the West Indies, the possibility of becoming a fugitive was steadily circumscribed by the growth of settlement and sometimes also by the signing of treaties with former fugitives (maroons) who thereafter policed the interior as bounty hunters. This development can be related to a simultaneous shift in the dominant mode of slave resistance in some areas from flight or escapist rebellions to attempts to overthrow the slave regime.[34] A similar explanation might tentatively be applied to the coastal regions of nineteenth-century Brazil. It is more difficult, however, to see its relevance to the United States. Perhaps the Underground Railroad,[35] for an important few, kept the frontier always open. More likely, the balance of power was simply too unfavorable to organized resistance.

e) *Economic depression.* This has been put forward as a major cause of slave revolts in the United States and the Caribbean, particularly with regard to the 1730s and the three major nineteenth-century rebellions in Barbados (1816), Demerara (1823), and Jamaica (1831), which occurred at a time of sharply falling sugar prices.[36] On the other hand, the history of Brazil suggests quite the opposite scenario; the incidence of revolts coincides with economic expansion —in Minas Gerais in the early eighteenth century, Maranhão later in the century, and the revived northeast after 1800.[37] Elsewhere no obvious pattern appears at all. This is not too surprising. Low prices for staple crops brought bankruptcies, the sale or leasing of slaves, and no doubt cost-cutting and frayed tempers as well. But boom conditions brought an influx of unassimilated bondsmen, added intensity to the work regime, and made slave lives expendable. In any case, one cannot deduce the conditions of slave life from the state of planters' profits. Brazilian and Caribbean slaves, who often were responsible for growing their own food, were less vulnerable than U.S. slaves to market conditions but were more exposed to climatic hazards such as drought and hurricane. U.S. slaves were dependent on their masters for much of their food but were better fed than slaves elsewhere.

f) *Urbanization.* City-dwelling slaves enjoyed more independence than those on farms and plantations. They had more opportunity to meet and organize; they were more exposed to news and ideas from the outside world; and they were less likely to be restrained by family ties. In the United States, urban slaves were viewed as more insubordinate and dangerous than plantation slaves.[38] Although towns were not common venues for conspiracies, several of the most important occurred in New York (1741), Richmond (1800), and Charleston (1797 and 1822).[39] On the other hand, the high concentration of whites and free persons in towns and the presence of urban garrisons constituted a formidable barrier to mobilization of insurgents. Rebellions in towns were extremely few. New York in 1712 and Bahia in 1830 and 1835 are the best-known cases. Rural rebellions around Cap Français in 1791 and Puerto Príncipe, Cuba, in 1798 seem to have been linked to urban plots that were stifled before reaching fruition. The aborted uprisings at St. Pierre, Martinique, in 1789 and 1811 were incubated in the town but launched on its outskirts.[40] The urban environment, one might argue, facilitated conspiracy but hindered insurrection.

Urban slave conspiracies were perhaps less common in the Caribbean than on the American mainland. The important Aponte conspiracy of 1812 in Havana was mainly the work of free blacks.[41] As slaves made up a larger proportion of the urban population in the British and French West Indies than anywhere else in the Americas, this contrast between islands and mainland is difficult to explain. It is possible that urban slaves in the British and French Caribbean were more likely to be domestics living under the eye and roof of the master than independent craftsmen and laborers.

g) *High concentrations of the recently enslaved.* The slaves most prone to running away in the New World were almost everywhere Africans, especially newly arrived Africans, rather than the locally born slaves known as Creoles. Many early rebellions, and the nineteenth-century revolts in Brazil, were staged by Africans and organized along ethnic lines. The case of the United States similarly suggests that socialization within the system and a reduced cultural distance between master and slave were powerful antidotes to insurrection.[42] Nevertheless, it is not entirely clear that Africans rebelled more frequently than Creoles. The largest insurrections in the British Caribbean (the three major nineteenth-century revolts) occurred in colonies where Creoles made up most of the population. The great Saint Domingue uprising, too, was led almost exclusively by Creoles and broke out in the most creolized part of the colony.[43]

h) *Maroon activity.* It is sometimes stated that the existence of communities of fugitive slaves encouraged insurrections, and many have argued that maroons played a special role in the Haitian Revolution.[44] Yet the relationship between the two types of resistance was complex and ambiguous. Not only can marronage be seen as an alternative to rebellion, a safety valve, but in becoming maroons, slaves also took on new identities and interests that often set them apart from the slave population in general. Successful maroon communities maneuvered as third parties between the mass of the slaves and the planters and colonial authorities. The maroons of Jamaica, once granted free status in the treaties of 1739 and 1740, turned out to support the colonial administration in every slave uprising until emancipation and even afterward in the Morant Bay Rebellion of 1865. On the other hand, successful maroons were certainly a symbol of resistance, and even in Jamaica, rebels continued to look on them as potential allies.[45] Their supposed role in the Haitian Revolution, however, is largely myth.[46]

i) *Emancipationist rumors.* The most striking feature in the history of American slave revolts is the claim made by the majority of rebels and conspirators from 1789 onward that they were fighting to seize a freedom already granted them by a distant central government but which local officials and planters were refusing to implement. Sometimes it was a question of only three free days per week, sometimes of full emancipation. Though a few earlier examples can be found (Virginia in 1730, Venezuela in 1749 and 1770, perhaps Peru in 1779), the phenomenon first fully emerged with the uprisings on Martinique (1789), Tortola (1790), and Dominica and Saint Domingue (1791). Such rumors, which were salient in the major revolts in the British Caribbean in the period 1816–1831, also appeared in Charcas (Bolivia) in 1809, in Brazil in 1822, and in the Indian Ocean, on Bourbon, in 1832.[47] They seem most plausibly related to the libertarian ideology of the Age of Revolution and the rise of the antislavery movement.[48] Perhaps rooted in some innate disposition of the powerless to believe hopefully in the beneficent intentions of the powerful, they are also reminiscent of the "naive monarchism" of Russian peasant revolts. It is extremely difficult to know how far such claims were believed or half-believed or if they were merely ruses used by astute leaders.

Some Typologies of Slave Rebellion

The typical American slave revolt was organized by a charismatic leader who was Creole or African, according to which group predominated in the population; it was preceded by oath-taking, either on the Bible or following African traditions; and it was timed to break out on a Sunday or public holiday. Beyond these facts, generalization becomes difficult. Scholars have developed numerous ways of classifying slave insurrections according to their supposed aims and causes, degree of organization, participants, religious content, and so forth.

In an early attempt at typologizing, Marion Kilson identified three varieties of rebellion in the United States: systematic/rational, unsystematic/vandalistic, and situational/opportunistic (the latter being merely nonviolent cases of mass flight).[49] Eugene Genovese has also compared the major U.S. revolts and conspiracies according to their political maturity, distinguishing the well-organized conspiracies of Gabriel Prosser (1800) and Denmark Vesey (1822) from the "messianic," "apocalyptic," and suicidal revolt of Nat Turner (1831).[50] Gerald Mullin, however, reached different conclusions. While all three leaders used religious meetings and to varying degrees invoked religious sanctions, he thought that Prosser and Vesey were too secular in approach and failed because they couched their message, unlike Turner, in political and not religious terms. Neglecting both African sorcerers and Methodist camp meetings, they were unable to mobilize the support of rural blacks.[51]

With regard to Brazil, it is precisely the meticulous organization of the religiously inspired slave revolts of 1807–1835 that was stressed by Edison Carneiro, who contrasted them with the secular, anarchic, and ineffectual insurrection known as the Balaiada.[52] Michael Craton, however, makes no such distinction when discussing the three most important rebellions in the British Caribbean. He points out that while Christian revivalism played a vital role in two of the great nineteenth-century uprisings, it was totally absent from the Barbados revolt of 1816. He concludes it was not a necessary condition for revolt.[53]

From the Santidade of late-sixteenth-century Brazil to Jamaica's Christmas Rebellion in 1831 and the Malé revolt of 1835, religion often provided slave rebels with leaders, organization, ideologies, and a community of feeling.[54] The religion could be a variety of African animism, Afro-Christianity, or Islam, although it appears likely that the greater the cultural distance between slaveowner and slave the more easily resistance was engendered. Yet a religious orientation probably imposed limits on the success of slave resistance, as Genovese implies. Beyond a certain point, belief in supernatural guidance and personal invulnerability became a handicap and was a poor substitute for training and tactics. The Saint Domingue Revolution, the crucial test case, illustrates the point.[55] The highly syncretic vodou religion may have played an important role in bringing together slaves from different religious traditions and, more specifically, in launching the massive uprising of August 1791. Some rebel leaders were vodou priests. However, the most important, and those who were responsible for the revolution's eventual triumph, displayed a rational, secular style of leadership.[56]

A common element in the analysis of the causes of revolution, at least since the time of Marx and de Tocqueville, has been a sense of relative deprivation, caused either by worsening circumstances or by heightened expectations.[57] Various historians have linked slave resistance to the hardship caused by economic depression, although, as noted above, many revolts occurred in times of economic expansion that brought different types of hardship. Brazil and the United States represent conflicting cases in point, perhaps because of their differing systems of slave subsistence. Yet, even in the United States we find the Prosser conspiracy of 1800 linked by Gerald Mullin not only to economic growth but to actual amelioration of the slave regime.[58] According to the former slave Frederick Douglass, resistance resulted more often from "indulgence" and rising expectations than from severity.[59] Marian Kilson argued that revolts and conspiracies in North America were most common in regions of tobacco cultivation and diversified agriculture, where the slave regime was least severe.[60] However, the statistics he used underrepresent rebellions in South Carolina, inflate those in Virginia, and take no account of the longer history of slavery in the tobacco belt.

In the United States and elsewhere in the Americas, slave resistance was most prominent in areas of sugar and rice production, where conditions were harshest, although harsh conditions were perhaps less significant than organizational factors associated with large slave-holding units. In any event, it was the fact of change rather than any absolute level of misery that probably was the important factor. The largest revolts in the British Caribbean (in 1816, 1823, and 1831) took place in a period of falling sugar prices and declining profits. The Christmas Rebellion on Jamaica coincided with the lowest sugar prices for 100 years. The Saint Domingue insurrection of 1791 followed a year of exceptionally severe drought.

However, one cannot simply assume one knows what sort of impact such trends had on the lives of slaves. The theory that Jamaican slaves were being worked harder in the nineteenth century, to which Michael Craton and Barry Higman give some support, is richly problematized in the work of J. R. Ward. He claims that after 1800, slaves in the British West Indies were generally better fed and less severely worked but that the heartland of the 1831 rising probably participated less than other regions in these developments.[61] Higman also contends that demographic changes resulting from the abolition of the slave trade in 1807 restricted the upward mobility of slaves in Jamaica. "The resulting stress," he writes, "was a basic cause of the rebellion of 1831," in which Creole elite slaves were for the first time prominent. Ward, on the other hand, states that the ratio of skilled to field slaves was increasing.[62] The slave elite in Jamaica was, in any case, already being associated with conspiracies as far back as 1776 and 1791, when the causative factors that Higman adduces were not present.

As for the Saint Domingue uprising of 1791, it has frequently been asserted that working conditions in the colony were worsening on the eve of the French Revolution. Far more basic research needs to be done, however, before such claims can be substantiated. If a rapidly growing slave population put pressure on local food production, a new free-port system facilitated food imports. We do know that for the previous twenty years or so, a more humane attitude had been emerging on the part of certain planters and that the government, too, attempted to institute protective legislation, which was bitterly resisted by most whites.[63] This may mean that even before the effects of the French Revolution were felt in the colony, expectations were rising in the slave quarters faster than they could be satisfied.

In the literature on slave rebellion in the Americas, two overarching typologies are of particular interest. In *From Rebellion to Revolution,* Eugene Genovese contrasted "restorationist" and "bourgeois-democratic" slave revolts in the history of the Americas. He depicted the Saint Domingue insurrection as a turning point between secessionist rebellions and true revolutions that, under the influence of the French Revolution, aimed for the first time to eradicate slavery. Slave resistance was thus incorporated into a programmatic history of world revolution.[64] In contrast, Michael Craton, writing on the British Caribbean, argued that structural change within slave society rather than the transmission of ideas was the chief influence in fashioning new forms of armed resistance. He proposed that the transition from an African to a locally born Creole majority in slave communities entailed significant changes in the aims and tactics of rebels. An initial escapist or maroon phase gave way to violent attempts to overthrow the colonial regime and, in the last years of slavery, to Creole-led rebellions that aimed to achieve freedom within plantation society, mainly through passive resistance and limited use of violence.[65] Where Genovese saw increasing radicalism, Craton saw increasing moderation.

Such divergent views are possible because of the extreme difficulty of deciphering rebels' intentions. Apart from problems of evidence, the large-scale revolts appear to have been multilayered affairs which expressed a diversity of aims. This makes classification especially tricky. Each of the two models is open to certain objections.[66] Craton's characterization of the late rebellions in the British Caribbean as "proto-peasant" draws attention to the slaves' known attachment in the late slavery period to their individual provision grounds, on which they worked on weekends. Freedom to become independent small farmers, Craton concluded, was the aim of these nineteenth-century rebels. However, it is far from sure if such aspirations distinguished these revolts from the earlier "African" ones. Craton's own position is unclear. While he describes the late rebellions in socio-economic terms, he categorizes the "African" rebellions largely in political terms. It is not a comparison of like and like. Since one of the defining characteristics of the late rebellions was the apparent willingness of the rebels to continue working part-time on the plantations as wage-earners, one wonders if the term "proto-peasant" is not more applicable to the insurrections of the eighteenth century than to those of the nineteenth century. After all, it was a predominantly African Saint Domingue that produced the classic "proto-peasant" revolt.

The case of Saint Domingue also gives cause to question the validity of Craton's reified cultural constructs. Although a majority of Saint Domingue's adults were African-born, the 1791 revolt, albeit extremely bloody and destructive, was led largely by Creoles. Moreover, in strict demographic terms, Craton's "Creole" Demerara was more "African" than Saint Domingue's northern plain. Finally, Craton's argument accords too little place to the influence of the antislavery movement, which became an unsettling factor in American slave societies from the 1780s onward. It is difficult to know if this development exacerbated the slaves' sense of injustice, but for the first time it certainly gave evidence of divisions in the ranks of the whites and suggested that concessions could be won.

This is one reason why Genovese's stress on the French Revolution seems misplaced. Although the French revolutionary period did see the appearance of a new type of slave revolt, linked to rumors of emancipation, its ideological significance seems questionable. These revolts apparently owed far more to the Anglo-French antislavery movement and pre-revolutionary reformism than to the French Revolution, which clearly had a greater impact on free coloreds (such as Toussaint Louverture) than on slaves. Contrary to Aimé Césaire's assumption, the Martinique uprising of August 1789 occurred before news arrived of the popular revolution in Paris; it was connected with rumors of royalist reforms. Two years later, the slaves of Saint Domingue rose in the name of king and church rather than the rights of man, although they incorporated both into their rhetoric.[67]

Modern studies of revolution tend to downplay long-term change as a causal factor and stress instead control over the instruments of repression. Discontent and "delegitimization" are not enough, it is claimed, to overturn a social system.[68] Or, as James Scott argues, the pragmatic resignation of the ruled is not evidence of hegemonic control; neither accommodation nor revolutionary change are questions of consciousness.[69] Such an emphasis accords well with the known facts about slave rebellion, with the exception, perhaps, of these "late" revolts influenced by antislavery ideas. The exact nature of that influence constitutes one of the most perplexing problems in the study of resistance to slavery. Genovese acknowledges that "the mechanics of ideological transmission remain obscure."[70]

As for the rebellions that Genovese terms "restorationist," he appears to have subsumed under this heading two aspects of revolts perhaps best kept separate—the rebels' aims with regard to the slave society (in this case, withdrawal from it) and the form of social organization they proposed to adopt after the revolt (maroon societies). This blurs an important distinction that Craton, Synnott, and Monica Schuler have all felt necessary to make between escapist rebellions and those aimed at destroying the colonial system, whether or not the envisaged post-revolutionary society was archaic or in some sense modern. These writers see a shift from rebellion to revolution considerably predating the Age of Revolution. Synnott convincingly relates this shift to the diminishing opportunities to establish new runaway communities as the frontier of settlement advanced or became closed off by existing maroon groups who agreed to police the mountains and forests in return for official recognition of their freedom.[71] Thus, Tacky's Rebellion in Jamaica (1760) and Cuffee's in Berbice (1763) were not aimed at withdrawing from colonial society but at overthrowing it.[72]

It is true that some of these African insurgents spoke of enslaving blacks who would not join them. Their ideas were thus premodern, not "revolutionary" in

Genovese's terms. African slaves came from societies where slavery was an accepted institution; there was perhaps no reason why they should regard the overthrow of slavery per se as a moral imperative. Their indigenous traditions of bondage meant they might reject their own enslavement but not single out slavery as an institution to destroy; similarly, maroon communities in Brazil, Surinam, and Jamaica bought or raided for slaves.[73] The issue here is whether Craton's cultural model provides a better explanation of rebels' diverse behavior than Genovese's emphasis on ideological change. Obviously, creolization did not itself create libertarian ideas.[74] But when slave insurgents did espouse them, under the influence of the French Revolution or antislavery movement, those insurgents were Creoles. In African-led revolts, talk of enslaving enemies continued during the Age of Revolution and well into the nineteenth century.[75] However, before we can say with confidence that not until the French Revolution did slave rebels demand the abolition of slavery, one would like to know a good deal more about the earlier insurrections.

On the later slave revolts Genovese says little, other than to observe that they occurred "within the context of the bourgeois-democratic revolutionary wave." He notes that "restorationist" rebellions did not disappear, but it is not clear how he classifies those in nineteenth-century Brazil. He describes as "bourgeois-democratic" the resistance of Prosser, Vesey, and Turner in the United States but admits that their aims "remain debatable" and that they may have been directed toward establishing maroon enclaves. When dealing with Jamaica's Christmas Rebellion, Genovese de-emphasizes its nonviolent, accommodationist aspects, which are stressed by other writers, and observes somewhat surprisingly that it "represented the culmination of a new stage, in which the slaves could look forward to independence in a world of modern nation states."[76] No evidence is put forward to support this analysis.

Genovese's concern with ideology thus led him to see growing radicalism in slave rebellion, whereas Craton and Synnott, concerned with methods as well as aims, saw moderating tendencies. For the latter writers, the force for change came from within slave society (creolization, the closing frontier). Genovese acknowledged the importance of these factors but argued that ideas external to the slave system comprised the main influence shaping new forms of resistance. It is, of course, not the only occasion that he championed the role of ideas against the skepticism of non-Marxist historians. Whether one approach is more successful than the other it may be too soon to say when so much remains obscure about individual revolts.[77]

At present, we know too little about the structure of slave societies in which revolts took place and about the changes they were undergoing, material or otherwise. In particular, there is a need to investigate the impact on slave communities of the libertarian ideals of the Age of Revolution, but also, as Hilary Beckles argues,[78] to uncover what ideologies the slaves themselves fashioned. The influence of ideas needs to be distinguished from the weakening of the forces of social control that sometimes accompanied them. The aims of rebel leaders further need to be delineated and distinguished, if necessary, from those of their followers. The relation between marronage and revolt and the role of religion in slave resistance are other notably murky areas. The comparative analysis of slave resistance has thrown up a number of useful hypotheses which draw attention to similarities and contrasts in the history of servile rebellion. The time would now seem right for a return to more empirical investigations that will serve to evaluate and ultimately extend those hypotheses.

5 Marronage, Vodou, and the Slave Revolt of 1791

Many slave conspiracies in the Americas were betrayed before reaching fruition, and most rebellions were quashed within a few days. Particular interest, therefore, attaches to the circumstances surrounding the Saint Domingue slave revolt of August 1791, which was by far the largest and longest lived of American slave uprisings and perhaps the only one that can be called successful. This chapter briefly surveys some of the evidence concerning two elements that, for at least the last half-century, have commonly been accorded a key role in the August uprising.

Vodou and marronage, or flight from slavery, are controversial topics. They are central to the argument that stresses indigenous influences on the Haitian Revolution, as opposed to external ones, and their supposed historical role has become for many Haitians an object of national pride. First linked in an article published in 1905 by Haitian novelist Justin Lhérisson, they assumed an increasingly prominent place in revolutionary historiography after Jean Price-Mars's *Ainsi parla l'oncle* appeared in 1928. Much writing about them in what Michel-Rolph Trouillot calls "the epic rhetoric of the Haitian tradition" has consisted of unsupported assertions.[1] Expatriate Haitian social scientists have in varying degrees taken a critical stance toward this position elaborated by their predecessors, yet they end up displaying a good deal of solidarity on the issue.[2] European scholarship on vodou and marronage began in 1897 with Lucien Peytraud's book on French Caribbean slavery and after 1960 developed as an empiricist critique of Haitian work. While recognizing its more professional handling of evidence, Trouillot faults such writing for "trivializing" and lacking "ideological respect" toward its subject matter.[3]

This chapter makes no revelations regarding the August revolt's causation; intended as a point of departure toward an understanding of the past, it seeks to distinguish what in the historical record may be termed certain from what was probable or merely possible.

Marronage and 1791

Throughout the period of slavery in Saint Domingue, some slaves fled their captivity, and a few periodically raided colonial settlements in frontier regions. *Grand marronage,* involving communities of fugitives, was infinitely less common than the *petit marronage* of individuals whose absences were short term. Most plantations lost maroons; very few were attacked by them. These differences between micro- and macro-level manifestations of the phenomenon partly explain the divergent depictions of marronage by Haitian and European historians. The armed bands of fugitives that troubled colonial administrators, and whom novelists and nationalists have found so appealing, were far from being "typical maroons" in a colony where hundreds, and later thousands escaped, if only briefly, each year. Nevertheless, a tradition of sporadic guerrilla resistance was established which in the years 1791–1803 became a key element in the slaves' fight for freedom and independence.

Historians have disagreed about the dimensions, causes, and character of marronage, but the argument linking marronage and the Haitian Revolution consists of two core claims: that the slave rebellion grew out of a rising tide of marronage that built up momentum through the colonial period and that it was organized and led by maroons. This thesis was first associated with champions of black culture (as opposed to the more French-oriented "mulatto" school of thought in Haiti), but it has since gained widespread acceptance, particularly through the work of Jean Fouchard.[4] Implicit in this interpretation is a vision of marronage as an "insurrectionary movement," to use Edner Brutus's phrase.[5] Critics of this argument, who are usually European, have downplayed the disruptive impact of slave fugitives on French colonialism; they stress the variety of behaviors marronage encompassed, linking it with ad hoc material causes rather than with an abstract pursuit of liberty and, while accepting the logic of a link between fugitives and rebels in 1791, they claim there is no hard evidence of such a connection.[6]

Some see hidden agendas underlying these opposing positions, which have an unfortunate resemblance to the struggles of colonial times. Michel-Rolph Trouillot believes that explanations of marronage in terms of biological impulses (hunger, mistreatment) deny the slaves' humanity, although this is surely no more true in Haitian revolutionary scholarship than it is of the scholarly attention paid to food prices in the French and Russian Revolutions.[7] In the 1950s, the *noiriste* Emmanuel Paul attacked Haitian leftist Étienne Charlier for depicting marronage merely as an early stage in the national liberation struggle that was supplanted by the uprising of 1791. Paul saw Charlier as a defender of the "mulatto" school of Haitian history, which presented the Haitian Revolution simply as a by-product of the French Revolution and the free coloreds (who rebelled in 1790) as the true initiators of the fight for freedom.[8] For Paul, 1789 was an accident that occurred in the middle of an ongoing struggle that influenced but did not determine its outcome. Like François Duvalier,[9] whose government erected the Statue of the Unknown Maroon in Port-au-Prince, he thought it important to show that the black struggle preceded that of the Europeanized free coloreds, who later formed the country's elite.

This is not the place to assess the militant and quietist aspects of marronage, to seek out its political meaning.[10] A more simple task, apparently, would be to determine if the historical record indeed reveals a rising tide of black resistance that culminated in the 1791 revolt. Although this is treated as an article of faith by many Haitian historians, only Jean Fouchard has seriously attempted to quantify the phenomenon. Using the lists of runaways published in colonial newspapers, he claimed to show that marronage increased steadily during the last thirty years of slavery and sharply in the period after 1784. There are several problems with this approach. Fouchard did not distinguish between lists of fugitives who were missing, recaptured, or for sale or (for the years 1790–1793, when the number of newspapers multiplied) between duplicate lists in different publications. Many cases were thus counted more than once. For the year 1790, the annual total seems overstated by up to one-third, but the total for 1788 is overstated by only one-tenth.[11] In addition, Gabriel Debien observes that Fouchard may really have measured increasing use of the colonial press or the increased efficiency of the rural police force in capturing fugitives, whose number was not necessarily growing any faster than the slave population.[12]

Such advertisements for runaways bear no certain relation to the number of fugitives at large and still less to the number gathered in bands, who intermittently alarmed colonial administrators. Was their activity increasing in the decade before the revolution? This is difficult to answer with certainty, but the evidence seems to suggest quite the opposite. Fouchard's "Chronology of Marronage" conflates all manner of disparate events but is conspicuously thin on material for the 1780s. Conflict with maroon bands (and poisoning scares, too) appear to have been far more prominent in the 1770s or even earlier.[13] In 1785, moreover, the colony's longest-lived maroon band, the Maniel, which actually lived in Santo Domingo, left its mountain stronghold after concluding a treaty with the French and Spanish administrations that provided for the capture and return of runaway slaves. The Maniel then numbered 133 persons, not the "several thousand" mentioned by Eugene Genovese.[14]

It is true that a colonist wrote from Cap Français in 1785 that the number and boldness of maroons were daily increasing—soon whites would be held up on the highway, he claimed.[15] However, such complaints were as old as the colony and in this instance were directed toward the withdrawal of recent liberal legislation on slavery (including the Maniel treaty). In September 1786, the new governor wrote that marronage had been decreasing for two years and that its incidence had probably never been so low. Despite the activities of a small group of fugitives in the mountains of Port Margot at the end of the year, he repeated this claim in August 1787. The great majority of cases were short term and local, he thought. Some nocturnal banditry in a northeast parish in 1787 was discovered to be the work of plantation slaves, not maroons. Despite systematic searches, few runaways could be found anywhere in Saint Domingue and no permanent bands at all.[16] In 1789, at the start of the revolution, public alarm about maroons led to the revival of a free colored corps led by Milscent de Musset, who had gained a high reputation in the previous decade as a maroon fighter. He claimed that although public opinion credited him with combating between two and ten thousand fugitives, he dispersed all bands (numbering perhaps 300) inside three months after killing or capturing seventy people.[17]

Continuity is difficult to find between maroon activity and the revolution in terms of geography, too. Those areas where Jean Fouchard states maroon bands were present on the eve of the revolution[18] were not those where the slave revolt broke out; they in fact tended to be the districts where the slave regime remained intact longest. On the other hand, the newspaper advertisements do suggest a somewhat higher incidence of marronage in the north province than elsewhere. However, further research is needed to confirm this pattern, and it may result merely from a less regular publishing of jail lists in the south and west.[19]

At the level of individuals, it is certainly difficult to find a direct connection between marronage and the slave uprising. Presumably maroon bands did join in the 1791 insurrection, but none is known to have done so. The Dokos maroons in the southeast, who apparently were a branch of the Maniel, took an ambiguous stance throughout the Haitian Revolution. Though generally remaining aloof, in 1793 they sacked the plantations of free coloreds when invited to do so by their white enemies. Like the resettled Maniel, they then fought on the side of Saint Domingue's Spanish invaders, keeping or selling their black captives as slaves, and in 1802 they briefly joined the Napoleonic invasion forces before turning against them.[20]

Quite misleadingly, Fouchard presented a list of seventeen rebel leaders of the mid-1790s as though they were already active maroon leaders in 1789. Although the unwary reader might think he was stating established fact, he was merely giving vent to poetic fancy. Writing of the revolution, Fouchard designated all rebel slaves as maroons, even including Romaine la Prophétesse and Candi, who were not slaves at all but free coloreds, and Jean Kina, who was a slave but commanded a corps raised by white planters.[21] One may accept that the line between marronage and rebellion is not clear-cut, but to make the words synonyms is blatantly to ignore both the ambiguous position of maroons in slave societies and the necessarily violent and collective nature of rebellion. Furthermore, colonists continued during the revolution to distinguish between *marrons* and *insurgés,* and in the areas where slavery survived, *petit* marronage persisted.[22]

What of the leaders of the slave insurrection? Modern historians sometimes present Boukman and Jean-François, occasionally also Biassou and Jeannot, as commanding bands of maroons in 1791, although they put forward no proof of this.[23] Jean Fouchard cited in support of this point the works of Bryan Edwards, Thomas Madiou, and Céligny and Beaubrun Ardouin, but so far as I am aware, none of these writers referred to the rebel leaders as maroons. Fouchard did find an intriguing advertisement for a "fierce-looking" runaway named Bouquemens dated 1779, but this name was not at all rare.[24] In any case, there does exist an early-nineteenth-century memoir whose writer claimed his father had once owned Boukman and described him as "a very bad slave . . . who continually went on the maroon and used to return at night to steal even from his comrades." Apparently the man was caught and sold several times before being bought by the merchant-planter Clément, who was killed on the first night of the uprising.[25] There also exists a letter of November 1793 by Georges Biassou to his Spanish patrons that describes Jean-François as "a poor fugitive" at the time of the revolt, thus substantiating the statements of several nineteenth-century historians to that effect.[26]

Hence, a connection can be established—although no historian has previously done this—between some of the revolutionary leadership and a prior experience of marronage. However, there is no suggestion in the documents that either Boukman or Jean-François was a member, still less the leader, of a band of maroons, and only Jean-François was a fugitive at the time of the rebellion. There is no evidence that Jeannot was ever a maroon, and it is quite clear that Boukman and Biassou were resident on their plantations when the uprising began.[27] Although some fugitive slaves may have served as intermediaries—I have found one probable case[28]—it seems very likely that the insurrection was organized from within the system more than from outside it. Finally, Fouchard's surmise that only maroons could have supplied the early rebels with the (few) guns and cannons they deployed is entirely without foundation; planters' gunracks and ornamental cannon and coastal batteries were the obvious sources of such weaponry.

As discussed in Chapter 2, Carolyn Fick has put forward a scaled-down version of the Haitian nationalist argument that redirects attention to the short-term cases of absenteeism that Fouchard and Manigat excluded from their definition of maroons. She argues such *petit* marronage played a key role in the organization of the 1791 insurrection in the sense that many conspirators must have gone absent without permission in order to meet. Robin Blackburn similarly suggests *petit marronage* provided slaves with vital contacts and knowledge of the wider world.[29] However, slaves had ample opportunities within the system to meet and organize: on the way to provision grounds and at Sunday markets, at weekend festivities, and at vodou ceremonies, which some whites thought harmless.[30] According to Moreau de Saint-Méry, the Cap Français market attracted 15,000 slaves each week; and dances and stick-fighting took place on the city's outskirts, ignored by the police, on Sunday evenings and holidays.[31] The meeting at which the August uprising was planned was held on a Sunday night on the Lenormand de Mézy plantation, which was on the main road to Le Cap. It was a large-scale feast held with the whites' knowledge.[32] There seems no reason to assume that those who participated were maroons. Moreover, Boukman, Jean-François, and other conspirators were coachmen, who routinely would have traveled widely.[33]

To sum up: the evidence regarding the growth of marronage prior to the revolution is mixed, but it does not indicate a sustained increase in activity, especially in the activity of maroon bands. There is nothing at all to support Gérard Laurent's claim that the organization and solidarity of maroons was steadily increasing.[34] Laënnec Hurbon's depiction of Boukman calling together fellow maroon leaders from their camps before giving the signal for revolt is purely imaginative; three of the four main leaders lived on plantations.[35] During the revolution no connection emerges between the slave revolt and marronage beyond the fact that the rebel leader Jean-François had become a fugitive some time prior to the uprising.

This is not to say that marronage had no bearing at all on the slave revolt. It presumably served through the years to keep alive a spirit of resistance, and it may have provided strategic or tactical lessons for the insurgents of the 1790s. Yet its most important connection with 1791 might have been a negative one. In my view, marronage was primarily an alternative to rebellion, a safety valve that helps explain the remarkable absence of slave revolts in eighteenth-century Saint Domingue. However, it must have been increasingly difficult to become a successful (rural) maroon after the enormous expansion of coffee cultivation in the mountains that began at mid-century, the extradition treaty of 1777 with Santo Domingo, and the Maniel treaty of 1785. It should be no surprise that maroon band activity decreased at this time. Anthony Synnott persuasively argued that such a "closing frontier" in the British Caribbean helped generate revolts aimed at overthrowing colonial regimes.[36] This limiting of options for dissident slaves might be considered one of the causes of the 1791 revolt.

Vodou and 1791

Many of those who claim decisive roles for marronage and vodou in the Haitian Revolution also link the two together. According to Odette Mennesson-Rigaud, marronage provided blacks with the freedom to develop their own religion. Willy Appollon argues that while vodou provided escapism for plantation slaves, for maroons it was a political creed essential for their survival, which by 1791 they transmitted to the masses.[37] These are plausible arguments, though purely speculative. Underlying them, and those of others who simply assume a connection between marronage and vodou, appears to be a belief that maroons represented the least acculturated element in colonial society. As Mintz and Price pointed out, this was improbable in colonies where the slave trade remained open.[38] The case of the Maniel, who were for the most part locally born and who, given the chance, baptized their children in church, strengthens such doubts. So does the practice of Christianized rites in maroon communities in other colonies.[39] In any event, the huge disparity in numbers between the slave and maroon populations makes it unlikely that the latter could have significantly shaped the culture of the former.

Another disputable idea underlying these arguments is that whites never tolerated African religious practices and that therefore vodou could develop only clandestinely. If many whites were hostile, some were complacent.[40] Almost everything that is known about vodou in the pre-revolutionary period concerns slaves or free coloreds, not maroons. Sociologist Michel Laguerre quite wrongly implies that the ceremonies described by Moreau de Saint-Méry and Charles Malenfant were conducted by maroons. Moreau de Saint-Méry's account probably referred to a milieu of freedmen and urban slaves located in the environs of Cap Français. Fugitive slaves no doubt blended into this milieu, in the manner João Reis describes for Bahia, but they were not essential components.[41] Despite the assertions of Laguerre and Fouchard, nothing indicates that the eponymous don Pedro or the sorcerers Jérôme Poteau and Romaine Rivière were fugitives; two of them were not even slaves.[42] The first vodou temples may have appeared in maroon settlements, and "the great majority" of maroon leaders may have been *oungans* (vodou priests), as Laguerre claims, but the truth is, nobody knows.[43] A local tradition recorded by anthropologist Luc de Heusch does state that the modern major sanctuary of Nan Soukri was founded by a slave who fled from the north to the west province, but there are reasons to question its validity.[44] Hence there is very little reason to suppose that marronage had an important influence on the development of vodou.

The case of Makandal, the famous long-term fugitive executed in 1758 for distributing poisons, is a rare example that links pre-1791 marronage with religious or magical practices, but his case raises several problems. Although Makandal was a very successful maroon who evaded capture for at least ten, perhaps eighteen, years, the evidence that he led a band of maroons is actually very slim. The 1750s, when he circulated freely, were if anything a low point in the history of marronage.[45] One can follow in contemporary documents the rapid elaboration of his legend during the pre-revolutionary decades. It is remarkable that of all the historians who have written about this charismatic figure, only Pierre Pluchon decided to exploit the judicial records relating to Makandal's arrest.[46] In 1758, those whites who took his case seriously saw in him at most the mastermind of a network of poisoners in the central north province whose victims were far more often black than white. The first time he was referred to as a maroon leader apparently was twenty years after his death in a fanciful and self-interested memoir. The only source that depicts these maroons as raiders is a novelette-like story published in a Paris newspaper in 1787. These texts form the basis of the interpretation found in Pierre Vaissière's 1909 history, of which extracts were cited by Jean Fouchard as if they were contemporary sources.[47] Pluchon's conclusions echo those of Hilliard d'Auberteuil in 1776 and the colonial intendant in 1758: Makandal's clients were local, and they killed for personal, not political, motives; there was no colony-wide revolutionary conspiracy.[48]

Another problem regarding Makandal concerns the question of what should be labeled "vodou." Makandal seems to have been a sorcerer rather than a priest. We have no evidence of his presiding over communal rituals, acting as intermediary between man and god. He was a *bokor,* not an *oungan.* Though the distinction is not always clear, it is a significant one for those who insist that the vodou religion and magic are separate entities. Another aspect of this problem is that even if Makandal were a priest, we find nothing to connect him to the Dahomean traditions that form the vodou religion's framework. Some contemporaries thought he had an Islamic background but only because certain of his invocations seemed to the investigating judge to include a sound like "Alla." His name, on the other hand, suggests the Kongo word for amulet, *mak(w)onda.*[49] The name of his accomplice, Mayombe, and the type of amulet he sold similarly suggest a Central African identity.

In one sense, this may be of little consequence. Although eighteenth-century commentators did attribute *vaudou* to the Aja-Fon slaves they called Arada, it is of course a highly syncretic religion, at least nowadays. More remarkably, the linguistic evidence relating to it from the slavery period is almost all in Kikongo or a related language. This includes the two chants recorded by Moreau de Saint-Méry and Drouin de Bercy and some of the lexical items revealed in the Jérôme Poteau case of 1787. Vodou's Petro cult, though frequently described as "Creole," also has obvious Kongo affinities.[50]

This apparent contradiction between the West and Central African character of eighteenth-century vodou—descriptions of snake cults accompanied by Kikongo texts—might be taken as a demonstration that vodou easily absorbed the mass of Bantu-speaking peoples who were brought to Saint Domingue in the later eighteenth century. On the other hand, it may show quite the opposite. Even today, some scholars object to the word *vodou* on the grounds that it implies a nonexistent homogeneity in Haitian folk religion, whose adepts rarely employ the term.[51] It is all the more likely, therefore, that what eighteenth-century colonists called *vaudou* may have been in reality a multiplicity of ethnic or locally based cults that expressed divergent rather than common identities and only later became integrated. In the 1790s, some colonists wrote of the slaves, "They do not worship the same god. . . . They hate and spy upon one another."[52] This point is worth stressing, because one of the most important contributions that vodou could have made to the slave revolution was the bringing together, physically and spiritually, of the very heterogeneous black population. That it actually did this in the colonial period remains unclear.

Scholars who argue that vodou had become an integrated and cohesive force by 1791 employ a circular argument based on its supposed role in the revolution.[53] However, the umbrella structure that vodou now displays (with its different "nation" rites) does not prove that slave religion helped forge political unity prior to 1791. The revolution itself must have enormously advanced the assertion of racial identity over narrower ethnic identities. Yet evidence is not lacking that during the conflict Africans organized along ethnically exclusive lines to worship, to dance, and to fight.[54] Notwithstanding the unifying experience of confronting a common enemy, interethnic conflict among slaves did not disappear during the revolution.[55] According to Victor Schoelcher, ethnic consciousness was still strong among the descendants of different African peoples in the 1840s; some even practiced marital endogamy.[56] Moreover, tensions and fighting between locally born Creoles and Africans described as "Congos" persisted down to the eve of independence.[57] The plantation manager Charles Malenfant's comment that Creole and creolized slaves (except the children of *oungans*) mocked and rarely participated in vodou should give one pause before ascribing great importance to such practices in a revolution dominated by Creoles.[58]

It is therefore difficult to accept the statement of Michel Laguerre that slave religions were "a symbol of racial solidarity" and that "no ethnic boundary could prevent anyone from taking part." The characterization of vodou by François Duvalier as the "supreme factor in Haitian unity" similarly merits skepticism.[59] If religious organization strengthened, even created, communities at the grassroots level, it did so at the risk of reinforcing old, or creating new, divisions in the wider society. As for the magico-religious practices ancillary to vodou, their influence appears to have been more antisocial than unifying. As Edouard Glissant observes, "the act of sorcery isolates," because it encourages suspicion of neighbors through a worldview that sees misfortune as never accidental but the product of malice.[60]

Apart from promoting social unity in the black population, vodou (loosely defined as supernatural beliefs of African origin) is generally thought to have contributed organization, leadership, and ideological/emotional inspiration to the slave revolution. With regard to the organizational element, the key factor is the famous Bois Caïman ceremony, where the leader Boukman is believed to have taken a blood oath with his fellow conspirators immediately before the slave uprising. I argue in Chapter 6 that, although the event itself was not mythical, as some have argued, accounts of the ceremony have been successively elaborated over the years, as with the Makandal story, so that few details can be considered authentic. Many historians, like Pluchon, have situated the Bois Caïman ceremony on Makandal's old plantation, hinting thereby at a continuous tradition of resistance that is the central theme of Alejo Carpentier's novel *El reino de este mundo.* These historians, however, confused two different plantations in Limbé and Plaine du Nord that were at least ten miles apart.[61] Above all, the Bois Caïman meeting has generally been mistaken for an earlier, probably larger and more important one, at which the insurrection was planned and that appears to have been a predominantly secular occasion. The ceremony's significance was to sacralize a political development already brought to maturity. Oath-taking and divination forged bonds and gave courage, but the conspirators of 1791 were obeying other imperatives than just the voices of the *mystères.* Or, as Haitian peasants still say, "Konplo pi fo pase wanga" (Conspiracy is stronger than a magic charm).[62]

Whether vodou ceremonies in general provided a mechanism for organizing the conspiracy it seems impossible to say. It sounds likely, but there is no evidence of it. Individual priests apparently wielded formidable influence over their followers, but nothing suggests that there existed a network of vodou priests.[63] Much depends on whether the leaders were themselves *oungans.* Here the evidence is mixed.

Modern historical works usually present Boukman as a vodou priest, but the early sources, French or Haitian, generally do not. Even in Céligny Ardouin's *Essais,* the only primary account of the Bois Caïman ceremony that refers to him, written at least fifty years after the event, he does not direct the ceremony but merely takes an oath from the priestess who presided.[64] Boukman was undoubtedly held in high esteem by the slave rebels, but there is little to positively identify him as a religious leader.[65] As for Jean-François, who rapidly became the most important of the rebel leaders, almost no one has ever described him as *vodouisant.* Toussaint Louverture, thought by some to be the mastermind of the 1791 uprising, is occasionally claimed, unconvincingly, by spokesmen for the vodou tradition as a closet worshipper of the *lwa* but never as a religious leader. Biassou and Jeannot, the other two leaders who came to prominence in 1791, are both described in Madiou's 1847 *Histoire* as being advised by sorcerers and surrounded by fetishes, but they are not depicted as priests themselves. Jeannot's title of Médecin-Général, however, probably indicates that he did perform religious functions.[66] Perhaps significantly, he was soon executed by Jean-François, who also tried to have Boukman killed.

On balance, the principal actors in the 1791 revolt do not seem, therefore, to have been religious leaders. Three of the five were fairly certainly secular leaders, and perhaps two were religious specialists. Probably all of them, moreover, were locally born Creoles, a group that, according to Malenfant, included few vodouists.[67] Where we do find cult leaders involved in the rebellion is in subordinate positions, encouraging fighting men before battle, acting as advisers, or leading smaller bands. This was more true later in the revolution and in the west province, where Hyacinthe, Romaine Rivière, and the Yoruba Halaou gained brief notoriety. It was there, where, in C. L. R. James's words, the slaves were most politically "backward," that an autonomous slave revolution was slowest to develop. Coincidentally or not, this was the part of Saint Domingue where vodou was said to be most widespread.[68]

Vodou's impact on the *mentalité* of the black masses is perhaps the most difficult area to assess. Numerous stories attest to at least some rebels' belief that they were personally invulnerable because of the amulets they wore or the rituals they participated in or the belief that death in battle would return them to Africa. The hairs of the pig sacrificed at Bois Caïman served as amulets, although such behavior may have been more typical of the west province after 1791. These beliefs clearly formed an explosive force, but equally clearly, suicidal fervor could also prove counterproductive in the pursuit of military victory. My impression is that cautious guerrilla tactics were probably more common in the north. Belief in magic could also have strange repercussions. In the west, the planter Hanus de Jumécourt, who co-opted the vodou priest Hyacinthe as a policeman for the plantation regime, was credited by local blacks with clairvoyant abilities, while the French civil commissioners were said to be sorcerers and therefore invulnerable.[69] Finally, beliefs in the protection of talismans or the return of the soul to Africa were vehicles that carried the slave rebellion forward, but they did not cause it. Prior to 1791, Africans seeking to return to their homelands committed suicide or fled; after that date, they took up arms.

Did vodou necessarily imply an anti-white ideology? Presumably it intensified among its participants a sense of cultural alienation from the norms of white society, although to the extent that it incorporated Christian elements it may have also lowered cultural barriers. The interrogators of Makandal convinced themselves that his use of Christian symbols in his sorcery was deliberate mockery. However, it is more likely that such syncretism was designed merely to produce more powerful magic.[70] At the Bois Caïman ceremony, Boukman supposedly gave a speech attacking the white man's religion, but this claim is of questionable authenticity. It derives from a poem published in 1824 by Senator Hérard Dumesle and may reflect the senator's love of classical culture more than his inquiries in northern Haiti. Insofar as the black revolution expressed an attitude toward Christianity and the Catholic church, it was generally favorable.[71]

The religious chant recorded by Moreau de Saint-Méry that begins "Eh eh Bomba! heu heu" has also been the subject of much obfuscation. C. L. R. James attached to it a quite spurious translation: "We swear to destroy the whites." With poetic license, Aimé Césaire imaginatively made it part of the Bois Caïman ceremony. The chant is actually an invocation to a Kongo snake/creator divinity and seeks protection against blacks, whites, and sorcerers; the ethnographic literature on the Kongo contains similar examples.[72] If the deity Mbùmba was sometimes a war god, this was because of its protective powers and was not its most common manifestation; in Saint Domingue we find it in the more usual context of initiation rites.[73] The appearance of the violent, fire-oriented Petro cult around 1770 certainly is suggestive of destabilization. Despite the controversy outlined in Chapter 6, the Bois Caïman gathering generally has been considered a Petro ceremony. Although Jean Kerboull claims that the cult spread only after independence, Haitians such as Hénock Trouillot have made a more plausible case for its florescence during the revolution.[74] Prior to 1791, however, it can only have functioned as a "ritual of rebellion."

The religious leader Jérôme Poteau, condemned to the galleys in 1786, provides a case in point. The nocturnal ceremonies he conducted in the mountain parish of Marmelade, where most slaves were Central Africans, resembled those of Kongo secret societies and the modern Petro cult. They attracted up to 200 slaves. Local whites apparently tolerated the gatherings for some time, intervening only when they found them too noisy. Poteau, a mulatto slave, used a crucifix like Makandal, and he sold protective charms. The amulets warded off punishment by slave-owners and provided protection in stickfights, but they also cured fevers and detected poisoners and chicken thieves.[75] Although a colonist accused Poteau of "preaching independence," this probably meant self-assertion rather than, as Adolphe Cabon suggested, "the independence of the entire black race." The word was used with the sense it had in the Police des Noirs law of August 9, 1777, which accused blacks who returned to the Caribbean from France of bringing "the spirit of independence and indocility" so that "they [became] more harmful than useful."[76] The fact that Jérôme was only sentenced to the galleys, and his accomplice to the pillory, indicates that their judges did not regard them as very dangerous. Marmelade, moreover, became a bastion of white resistance during the northern uprising of 1791–1793.

The "revolutionary" implications of vodou seem to have been exaggerated. One might argue that, by enriching the cultural life of the slaves, the development of vodou helped defuse anomic tensions and thus added to the stability of the colonial regime. Anthropologist Alfred Métraux thought that a major and underrated function of vodou was the dissipation of social bitterness. A magical reading of the universe, moreover, tends to promote magical rather than political remedies to real-world problems. Moreau de Saint-Méry certainly feared black religious specialists, but this was because of the control they exercised over the minds of their followers rather than because of their activities or any revolutionary message they propagated. Drouin de Bercy claimed that the aim of the vodou and Don Pedro cults was to drive the whites out of Saint Domingue, but as his book was published in 1814, this may have been an observation after the fact.[77] Like Pierre Pluchon, therefore, I see the role of vodou in the Haitian Revolution as ancillary rather than central.[78]

From the sixteenth to the nineteenth century, Afro-American religions provided slave rebellions with leaders, organization, and a community of feeling. During the revolutionary crisis in Saint Domingue, too, magico-religious beliefs helped to mobilize resistance and foster a revolutionary mentality. Whether vodou played a critical role, however, either as an institution or source of inspiration, particularly in the northern uprising itself, remains to be proven.

This chapter is intended to supply notes toward an evaluation of the Saint Domingue slave revolt. It has been deliberately negative in tone. Too much in the historiography of the Haitian Revolution has gone without critical appraisal. Other aspects of the slave revolt require similar scrutiny, such as the nature of the plantation regime from which it sprang or the supposed involvement of white counterrevolutionaries or dissident colonists or different sections of the free colored community. Only then can one begin to construct an interpretation of this greatest of all slave revolts and its relationship to both indigenous developments and external forces such as the French Revolution.

6 The Bois Caïman Ceremony

During the night of 14 August 1791 in the midst of a forest called Bois Caïman [Alligator Wood], on the Morne Rouge in the northern plain, the slaves held a large meeting to draw up a final plan for a general revolt. They consisted of about two hundred slave drivers, sent from various plantations in the region. Presiding over the assembly was a black man named Boukman, whose fiery words exalted the conspirators. Before they separated, they held amidst a violent rainstorm an impressive ceremony, so as to solemnize the undertakings they made. While the storm raged and lightning shot across the sky, a tall black woman appeared suddenly in the center of the gathering. Armed with a long, pointed knife that she waved above her head, she performed a sinister dance singing an African song, which the others, face down against the ground, repeated as a chorus. A black pig was then dragged in front of her and she split it open with her knife. The animal's blood was collected in a wooden bowl and served still foaming to each delegate. At a signal from the priestess, they all threw themselves on their knees and swore blindly to obey the orders of Boukman, who had been proclaimed the supreme chief of the rebellion. He announced as his choice of principal lieutenants Jean-François Papillon, Georges Biassou, and Jeannot Bullet.[1]

In the words of Haitian statesman Dantès Bellegarde, such was the meeting that set off the largest slave revolt ever seen in the Americas and which led in the space of a dozen years to the creation of Haiti. Accounts of the ceremony vary subtly between one historian and another, but Bellegarde's version may be taken as representative.

Both the centennial and bicentennial of the Bois Caïman ceremony were publicly celebrated in Haiti amid controversy. The event's symbolic importance in the creation of Haitian identity has always been controversial but difficult to avoid even by those who vehemently reject any association between Haitian nationality and vodou. In a speech made in 1979, Franck Sylvain compared the explosive and creative force of Bois Caïman with the Christian Pentecost, although at the same time he denigrated vodou and sought to argue that the ceremony's influence derived from psychological factors separate from the vodou religion.[2] Nationalist writers, who stress indigenous as opposed to external forces in causing the decisive break with the colonial past, usually have put the ceremony in a more positive light. This is especially true of those who, like Jean Price-Mars, Odette Mennesson-Rigaud, Lorimer Denis, and François Duvalier, have asserted that "1804 [national independence] is the result of vodou."[3]

It was especially controversial, therefore, when in 1991 a prominent scholar of Haitian letters, Léon-François Hoffmann, argued in a conference paper that the ceremony in fact never took place. Hoffmann claims that Bois Caïman was a historical fiction elaborated during the nineteenth century by a mixture of disdainful colonists, romantic abolitionists, and spokesmen of the Haitian elite. The latter wished to legitimate their rule by emphasizing the cultural distance that separated them from the masses.[4]

Although Hoffmann's work is very well documented, writing on the Haitian Revolution has rarely been characterized by careful scholarship or extensive research. In this chapter, I propose to examine the historical record relating to the Bois Caïman ceremony in an attempt to sort out what is most and least trustworthy in surviving accounts and to reassess what its significance may have been in the unfolding of the Haitian Revolution. I will suggest that the Bois Caïman ceremony did indeed take place—it is not a case of *barbarisme imaginaire*[5]—but that much of what has been written about it is unreliable. Probably no single account gives its correct date. Most are confused about its location. Few details of what transpired there can be considered authentic, and the ceremony's role in the 1791 uprising requires some reassessment.

The Bois Caïman ceremony is not mentioned in any surviving contemporary manuscript source.[6] There are, however, three published accounts, one French and two Haitian, that apparently derive from eyewitness testimony. By far the earliest is the *Histoire* of the colonist Dalmas, published in 1814 but said to be written in the winter of 1793–1794.[7] Dalmas lived in the northern plain, and his account derived from three slave conspirators who were interrogated on what was probably the day after the ceremony. The second printed version is found in *Voyage dans le nord d'Haïti*, published in 1824 by Hérard Dumesle, senator from the southern city of Les Cayes.[8] Written partly in poetry and partly in prose, the young politician's account appears to draw on oral traditions he collected when visiting the region of Le Cap thirty years after the events. The third account, by Céligny Ardouin, is best known in versions published in 1853 by his brother Beaubrun and in a posthumous collection of essays in 1865. Ardouin's informant seems to have been the ex-slave-soldier Paul Ali, whom he interviewed in 1841.[9]

Taken together, I think these sources prove that a vodou ceremony involving the sacrifice of a pig did take place shortly before the great insurrection. Even if the three authors wished for their own reasons to denigrate or celebrate the "primitivism" of the rebel slaves, the combination of similarity and dissimilarity in their different versions suggests strongly that they represent three separate accounts derived from different sources. One other account should be noted. It is a family oral tradition recounted in a book by Étienne Charlier. It was passed on to him by the grandson of Cécile Fatiman, long-lived wife of mid-nineteenth-century president Louis Pierrot. Their grandson informed Charlier that Fatiman, a woman of mixed racial descent, was a vodou priestess who had participated in the Bois Caïman ceremony, but he apparently provided no further details.[10]

These, I think, are the only credible sources for a study of the Bois Caïman

Map 2. The Cap Français region

ceremony. By virtue of their date and actual or presumptive claim to record eyewitness testimony, they are preferable to any later published source. They are preferable, too, I believe, to modern oral traditions reported in such esoteric works as Milo Rigaud's *La tradition voudoo,* a work which may have shaped modern vodou as much as reflected it.[11] While interesting material might be extracted from chants sung by modern *vodouisants* and the lore expounded by present-day *oungans,* this is largely of a theological nature, concerning the role of various deities. Where historical figures are mentioned, the context is also mythic and metahistorical.[12] One can only be skeptical, moreover, of detailed modern traditions when Thomas Madiou, a pioneer in using oral sources who enjoyed spicing his narrative with picturesque "primitivism," made no mention at all of Bois Caïman in his 1847 *Histoire.*[13]

Albeit a tediously narrow issue, the dating of the ceremony is a topic of some importance, because it concerns what may one day become in Haiti a national holiday and because the chronology of events has a strong bearing on their significance. The exact location of Bois Caïman, aside from its intrinsic historical interest, may also be of importance to the future development of tourism in Haiti. Most historians have assumed that the ceremony took place on the mountain of Morne Rouge, on or near the Lenormand de Mézy sugar plantation in the parish of Plaine du Nord. Many add that this was the estate where the famous sorcerer and poisoner Makandal had been a slave, thereby hinting at a continuous tradition of local resistance. The great majority give August 14th as its date, though a few, such as C. L. R. James and Aimé Césaire, specify August 22nd.[14]

Even the best historians have tended to give a muddled account of the events surrounding the great insurrection in the northern plain. This is in part because contemporaries themselves did so. For example, even the key event, the outbreak of the uprising itself, is sometimes assigned not to August 22nd, its true date, but to the 20th, 21st, 23rd, or 24th in both printed and manuscript accounts, even by people who had lived through it and claimed it had seared their memories.[15] In fact, as will be seen, no single source accurately records the chronology of what happened. Only by considering a wide range of evidence can the puzzle be solved. In her recent book, Carolyn Fick has gone further than any previous scholar in reconstructing these events, but in her narrative, too, I believe, some errors remain, notably concerning the Bois Caïman ceremony.[16]

This is not the place to give a detailed exposition of the events of August 1791.[17] Suffice it to say that after two years of upheaval brought on by the revolutionary changes in France, Saint Domingue seethed with uncertainty and rumor. Radicals talked of secession, conservatives of counterrevolution. Civil war was brewing between whites and free coloreds. In the north, many of the latter had been disarmed following the Ogé rebellion in October 1790, in spite of their importance as an instrument of social control.[18] Since 1789, false rumors of a slave emancipation decree had circulated in the colony and several other parts of the Caribbean.[19] A new wave of such rumors began early in 1791 and may have become mixed up with news of the May 15th decree granting political rights to free coloreds born of free parents. A forged decree on this issue really did circulate in Saint Domingue early in the year. In June and July, slave revolts occurred on three plantations in the vicinity of Port-au-Prince, where the garrison had mutinied.[20] News of the king's flight to Varennes reached Saint Domingue early in August, as did the Abbé Grégoire's *Lettre aux gens de couleur et nègres libres,* which referred to the eventual emancipation of all slaves. A new Colonial Assembly dominated by radicals met in Léogane and then adjourned on August 9th, planning to reassemble in the northern port of Cap Français on August 25th. Normally overflowing with sailors from Europe, the town was relatively quiet at this time of year.[21] And the north's long rainy season was about to begin.

On Sunday, August 14th, a meeting of slave-drivers, coachmen, and other members of the "slave elite" from about 100 plantations took place in Plaine du Nord parish. They gathered on the Lenormand de Mézy estate, a large sugar plantation with at least 350 slaves that lay at the foot of the Red Mountain.[22] After discussion of political developments in France and the colony, they took the decision to rebel. The meeting itself was not secret. Colonists later wrote of the "pretext of a meal" or "a large dinner" that slaves were allowed to attend.[23] The plans for rebellion became known when on the following Tuesday or Wednesday a premature attempt was made to burn the Chabaud plantation in Limbé parish.[24] One of the arsonists was caught and under interrogation revealed the plot and denounced other conspirators, some of whom were arrested. Not till the weekend (August 20th/21st), however, when other confessions were obtained did alarm begin to spread among the whites (and perhaps among the conspirators, too), although even then it remained confined to Limbé parish.

The August 14th meeting on the Lenormand estate is well documented by contemporary sources. The Bois Caïman ceremony is not, and for this reason the two have usually been confused. Of the three eyewitness accounts of the ceremony, that of Dalmas is easily the most important with regard to questions of time and place. As a resident of the northern plain, he must have lived through this crisis; his information was collected probably hours after the ceremony, and his account was written only two-and-a-half years later, a half-century before that of Céligny Ardouin. It is odd therefore that this crucial source has often been overlooked.

Dalmas shows clearly that two separate meetings were involved. He mentions the Lenormand gathering on August 14th and states that there the plan for rebellion was drawn up. However, "before carrying it out," he adds, "they celebrated a sort of festival or sacrifice in the midst of a wooded and non-cultivated area on the Choiseul estate, called Le Caïman [the alligator], where a large number of blacks gathered."[25] The famous ceremony thus did not take place on the Lenormand plantation on the Morne Rouge (which in any case was not the estate where Makandal had lived),[26] but in the plain about ten kilometers to the east, at a place still called Caïman. The marquis de Choiseul's plantation was a large sugar estate like that of Lenormand de Mézy, but it was situated entirely in the plain, in Petite Anse parish, about halfway between Cap Français and the well-known Galliffet plantations.[27]

French sociologist Gérard Barthélemy argues this would have been an improbable place for a clandestine meeting, and he suggests that Dalmas mistook the Caïman savanna or pond that he knew for a little-known place, also called Caïman, in the hills above Lenormand de Mézy. Local tradition, he states, preserves a memory of this designation and of the meeting. A documentary film by Charles Najman, for which Barthélemy was an advisor, features local people talking about the Bois Caïman ceremony and its exact date.[28] Unfortunately, conflicting oral traditions abound on this controversial and politicized topic. Jean-Baptiste Julien, a local scholar with his own theory on the subject, remarked, "Each small group of vodouists in the north concocts fabrications so that, when the great day comes for commemorating the bicentenary of the famous ceremony . . . , their temple will be adorned at the expense of the state."[29] Only a decade before, in 1980, Haitian anthropologist Gerson Alexis, whose work in the northern plain Barthélemy uses, stated that vodou tradition had preserved no memory regarding Bois Caïman.[30] Another problem with the hilly Lenormand location, as Jacques de Cauna remarks, is that it is an unlikely habitat for alligators.[31] One might also wonder how it has escaped mention in the national gazetteer and on any colonial or modern map. Although governments since the 1960s occasionally have put up commemorative signposts in different locations, it does not seem that a place called Bois Caïman has ever existed.

A third rival as the ceremonial site that emerged at the time of the bicentennial is the major vodou temple of Nan Campeche in Acul parish. It was championed by Haitian professor and *homme du nord* J.-B. Julien, who stated its identification with Bois Caïman was supported by both a widespread oral tradition and detailed testimony collected by one of his relatives fifty years earlier from the sanctuary's founder. According to Julien, the region was then a thick logwood forest, planted by Lenormand de Mézy, and took its name from a large Caïmittier tree, popularly called Caïman, that once stood there. Despite the professor's assertions, however, the area was not part of the Lenormand estate, which was four kilometers away and in a different parish. It is also untrue that Moreau de Saint-Méry's *Description de Saint-Domingue* mentions a logwood forest in this location or the western part of the Lenormand estate.[32] And when film director Charles Najman visited Nan Campeche in 1991, its priestess merely stated that Boukman was rumored to have visited the sanctuary before going to Bois Caïman.[33]

In this light, the colonist Dalmas's testimony about the Choiseul plantation that dates from 1793 looks quite good. As for the unsuitability of the Choiseul site, it is nowadays as bare of tree cover as Lenormand de Mézy, Nan Campeche, and most of the rest of Haiti. On the most detailed late-eighteenth-century map of the northern plain, however, the Lagon à Cayman appears as a swamp surrounded by woods spanning the Choiseul and Dustou plantations. Its dimensions appear to have been about 750 by 500 meters.[34] It thus seems a plausible location for the ceremony that has come to be known as Bois Caïman.

The question remains how much time separated the Lenormand de Mézy and Bois Caïman meetings. The implication in Dalmas's narrative is that the sacrifice occurred several days after the Lenormand gathering of August 14th and shortly before a group of twenty slaves attempted to kill the manager of La Gossette, the second of the three Galliffet estates. Dalmas says this occurred shortly after the manager, Mossut, went to bed on the night of August 20th. It is clear, however, he meant the 21st. (He called August 23rd a Wednesday, when it was in fact a Tuesday. He remembered the days of the week but not the dates.) A letter by the manager himself, moreover, written only weeks later, placed this attack on August 21st, twenty-four hours before Boukman began the insurrection in Acul parish.[35] We know therefore that the ceremony occurred before the 22nd. It was during the course of that day that questioning of several La Gossette slaves revealed the story of the sacrifice and the decision to begin the rebellion. As a plantation physician who worked in the area, Dalmas might have been present during the interrogation, although his account implies he later read the slaves' depositions at the seneschal's office in Cap Français.[36]

In my view, the most likely time the ceremony took place was the evening of August 21st. Like the 14th, it was a Sunday, the easiest day for slaves to hold a social gathering. (Like Lenormand de Mézy, the Choiseul estate was well placed for slaves to visit on their way back from Cap Français market.) Hérard Dumesle, although his dates are wrong, also placed the ceremony on the night before the insurrection. And Céligny Ardouin's account, though even more confused, places the ceremony on the same night as the La Gossette attack.[37] According to Dalmas, the night before Mossut was attacked, a message had been delivered to the La Gossette plantation indicating that the long-contemplated day of vengeance had been fixed for the next day and that Mossut should be among the first victims. With regard to the projected date of the uprising, there apparently was a mistake on somebody's part. As the insurrection actually began on the Monday night, the evidence suggests that the La Gossette slaves jumped the gun by at least one day. Nevertheless, it seems probable that the La Gossette conspirators, responding to the Saturday night message, met on the Sunday evening on the nearby Choiseul plantation to sacralize their conspiracy and invoke supernatural aid in the coming rebellion. Returning from the ceremony, perhaps in a state of exaltation, perhaps because of a misunderstanding, they decided to attack the hated Mossut.[38]

This raises the question of when the insurrection was meant to begin. We have seen that there were at least two false starts: at La Gossette on Sunday, August 21st, and on the Chabaud plantation a few days after the Lenormand meeting, probably on Wednesday the 17th.[39] It is known that at the Lenormand meeting conspirators had disagreed about the appropriate day to begin the rebellion. Some wanted to start immediately; others wanted to wait until the arrival of royalist troops, who were expected to be allies. The latter apparently prevailed.[40] Carolyn Fick states that the date of revolt was fixed for August 22nd, but offers no evidence of this, other than the governor's subsequent report that on August 22nd he was informed of rumors of an uprising that was expected that night.[41] However, in documents where a projected date is given, it is the night of August 24th/25th.[42] Fick indeed cites some of these sources but supposes that they refer only to an urban conspiracy in Cap Français, which nonetheless was coordinated with that of the plantation slaves.[43] It seems unlikely that the two conspiracies were timed to break out two days apart.

The fact is that the August insurrection, for all its impressive dimensions, was anything but coordinated. The false starts mentioned above, the disagreements about timing, the failure of the town slaves to rebel, and above all, the sequential way the rebellion spread during its first week, from plantation to plantation, parish to parish,[44] suggest a revolt that broke out prematurely. Indeed, many contemporaries said so, specifying it was two days premature.[45] Moreover, Monday, August 22nd was a strange choice for the launching of an uprising. First, it was a work day. Slave rebels in the Americas tended to choose Sunday nights or public holidays for staging insurrections; presumably so they did not have to begin fighting after a full day's work. Second, a flag-blessing ceremony in Cap Français had been arranged for the morning of August 23rd, which meant that the town militia was assembled and under arms just when news of the uprising arrived.[46]

Assuming that the story about waiting for royalist troops was a fabrication of some sort, my guess is that the conspirators had intended the revolt to begin the night of Wednesday, August 24th. Several sources say so. And if the Chabaud attack indeed occurred on August 17th, this reinforces the idea that the chosen day was a Wednesday. Most important of all, August 25th was the date the Colonial Assembly was to reopen in Cap Français. This was not only a day when the populace of Le Cap would be distracted by pomp and circumstance but a perfect opportunity to eliminate in one go Saint Domingue's political elite. Moreover, these were the leaders of the colony's radical party, then threatening secession, whom the slaves contemptuously called *les citoyens* (the citizens, the fashionably revolutionary term of address). If one accepts the theory that white counterrevolutionaries helped foment the insurrection—and I do not—then this rationale is all the more compelling.[47] Georges Biassou later told the governor of Santo Domingo that the Colonial Assembly would have declared independence if the slaves had not rebelled.[48]

Boukman began the rebellion on August 22nd doubtless because he feared the conspiracy was being uncovered. In the course of Sunday, August 21st, the investigation in Limbé became suddenly more serious. A new, more detailed confession was obtained; further arrests were attempted; warnings were sent by the municipality to other parishes; and some of the prisoners with their depositions were sent by sea to Le Cap.[49] Perhaps it was these developments that led to the calling of the Bois Caïman meeting and the rescheduling of the uprising. Or perhaps, as Dalmas suggests, the decision had already been taken on the Saturday. Or perhaps it was the La Gossette attack following the ceremony, the resultant investigation the next day by the Cap Français seneschal, and the reports the governor then received that precipitated the insurrection. It is difficult to choose among these possibilities, but the uncoordinated manner of the Monday night uprising points to the latter. In this case, the Bois Caïman ceremony may have actually hindered the conspiracy by encouraging the La Gossette conspirators, confident in their invulnerability, to move too soon.

Dalmas reports that, having sacrificed a pig and drunk its blood, the ceremony's participants eagerly took its hairs as protective amulets. The pig was "surrounded with fetishes" and was sacrificed "to the all-powerful spirit of the black race." The white doctor recognized the occasion to be a religious one, but no other details emerge from his account; there is no mention of an oath, a prayer, a priestess, Boukman, or anybody else. Perhaps this should be expected. However, neither an oath nor Boukman appears in Hérard Dumesle's 1824 version either. It was the French abolitionist Victor Schoelcher, writing in the 1840s, who put Boukman into Hérard Dumesle's scenario.[50] Not until Céligny Ardouin's account, fifty years after the event, do both elements become part of the Bois Caïman story. Even then, it is not evident that Boukman was himself a religious leader; the ceremony was directed by a priestess, according to Ardouin. In fact, it is difficult to find any earlier sources, French or Haitian, that refer to Boukman as a priest.[51] Although he undoubtedly wielded great influence over the insurgents,[52] one needs to be cautious in asserting that he was more than a military and political figure.

The first thing to notice about Dumesle's version is that it describes two different meetings with a pig sacrifice at the second. This, I think, gives it an aura of authenticity. Since the author does not seem to have read Dalmas, he may have heard stories of the Lenormand and Choiseul meetings while in northern Haiti. On the other hand, his account has the appearance of a poetic evocation of these events, not a historical description. It is written for the most part in alexandrines and is a poem where most of the references are to ancient Greece, not Haitian vodou. It mentions Attica and Ausonia, Jason and Spartacus, but neither Boukman nor the Bois Caïman. At the second meeting, according to Dumesle, the pig was sacrificed by "a young virgin" and its entrails were used for divination—not a common practice among African peoples.[53] Note also that the familiar backdrop of a dramatic thunderstorm applied not to this ceremony but to the previous meeting on the Morne Rouge, where a priest sacrificed a bull and made an oration.[54] This is the first appearance of the famous prayer later attributed to Boukman, "Bondie qui fait soleil, qui claire nous en haut" (God who made the sun, which sheds light on us from on high).

Léon-François Hoffmann has demonstrated that Dumesle's account owed much to a *Histoire de la République d'Haïti* published in Paris in 1819 by Civique de Gastine. Gastine, a young French radical who had never visited Haiti, was the first writer to give the pre-revolutionary ceremony a specifically anti-Christian coloring and to associate it with a storm, an oath, and divination from entrails, in his case, a black ram's.[55] Although the two-ceremony structure of Hérard Dumesle's account gives it some claim to credibility as an independent source, much of it seems to be an embroidered synthesis of Gastine's description and Antoine Métral's account of 1818 (the first to include an oration and a young priestess).[56] Dumesle's oration, now known as Boukman's prayer, invites particular skepticism and hardly justifies C. L. R. James's comment that the speech "like so much spoken on such occasions, has remained."[57]

If authentic, the prayer presumably would have been spoken by Boukman, although Dumesle does not say so. However, it would have been at the Lenormand meeting, not in the Bois Caïman. Moreover, Dumesle's Creole oration with its rhyming lines is presented (in a footnote to his main poem) only as "the sense of the oracle in the idiom in which it was spoken." Hence it is pointless to speculate, as some have done, on the theological implications of the use of the term "Bondie" (Good Lord). These are Dumesle's words of 1824, not Boukman's of thirty years before. That the slave leader made a speech hostile to the whites one can hardly doubt. But can one say more? Was the speech really as directed against Christianity as Dumesle's classically inspired poem suggests?

This seems a little odd in view of vodou's tendency to absorb Christian elements and the generally good relations the slave insurgents had with the colonial church.[58]

Carolyn Fick argues that the prayer's authenticity is attested by an 1889 publication based on letters by the nuns of Cap Français convent. Apparently the nuns saw and heard Boukman from their convent window reciting his prayer when he was attacking the town and repeating the last line, "Coute la liberte li pale coeurs nous tous" (Listen to liberty that speaks to all our hearts).[59] This would have required exceptional powers of eyesight and hearing. As the insurgents rarely penetrated close to Le Cap in 1791, especially through the mountains to the upper town where the convent was located, the account must refer to events of late August. Some bold spirits did then approach the north side to make acts of defiance and attack the rear of the city barracks. The nuns, however, would have had to make their observations across the rooftops from a distance of at least 300 yards.[60] Moreover, so much incidental detail from Moreau de Saint-Méry's 1797 description of a vodou ceremony reappears, somewhat comically, in this account that one can only conclude (as did missionary-historian Adolphe Cabon) that its nineteenth-century compiler took a good deal of license with his or her sources. One suspects he or she had read the prayer in Victor Schoelcher's *Vie de Toussaint Louverture,* published that year. The French abolitionist, we have seen, was the first to attribute the oration to Boukman.[61]

Poetic license also explains why in Aimé Césaire's *Toussaint Louverture* we find the Bois Caïman conspirators singing the vodou chant that begins "Eh eh Bomba," also taken from Moreau de Saint-Méry.[62] (Furthermore, this chant was not the revolutionary creed many have imagined.[63]) There is likewise no evidence for Dantès Bellegarde's assertion that the leaders of the uprising were chosen at Bois Caïman and that Toussaint Louverture was present. That is simply unknown.[64] As for the identity of the priestess—if priestess there was—Dalmas and Ardouin give no clues. She might have been tall, as Dantès Bellegarde imagined, but for evidence we have only the Hellenic "young virgin" of Hérard Dumesle (probably borrowed from Métral's theatrical account of 1818) and Cécile Fatiman, the green-eyed *mulâtresse* mentioned by Étienne Charlier.[65] This strongly suggests that the "old African woman" described in twentieth-century accounts is apocryphal. In contrast, the animal of sacrifice has quite consistently been represented as a black pig, although it became a black ram in Gastine's account and is rivaled by an ox in Dumesle's. Julien's recent version, however, claiming the sanction of oral tradition, holds that the pig was red, not black, and was not a sacrifice but an emblem of the white man, as the ceremony was political not religious.[66]

The details of what happened at Bois Caïman thus remain elusive, beyond the fact that a pig was sacrificed in some sort of ceremony in preparation for war. No doubt an oath was administered, as Ardouin reports and as the blood-drinking mentioned by Dalmas would lead one to suppose. It may specifically have been a Dahomean blood pact, as the anthropologist Alfred Métraux suggested, although this has been difficult to reconcile with the Haitian tradition that associates the ceremony, because of its violence and the presence of a pig, with vodou's Kongo-influenced Petro cult. Most writers have claimed the Dahomean Rada gods were not invoked at Bois Caïman and that pig sacrifice has never formed part of their cult.[67] Since more than half of the Africans in the north province were West Central Bantu, whereas Aja-Fon (from the culture area including Dahomey) formed only one-eighth, it would not be surprising if Bois Caïman indeed was a Kongolese counterpart to the Creole-dominated Lenormand meeting of the previous Sunday.[68]

However, historian of West Africa Robin Law recently has shown that pig sacrifice was not alien to Dahomean traditions and that ritual blood-drinking oaths were probably unknown in Kongo. The combination of blood oaths and pig sacrifice, in fact, points specifically to an Aja-Fon provenance. With just the sort of comparative analysis long overdue in diaspora studies, he makes a strong case supporting Métraux's argument.[69] This is not just a question of cultural antiquarianism; there is at issue here the time frame in which the revolution's causes need to be set. If Law is right, there is no need to see the growing Kongolese presence in Saint Domingue in the later eighteenth century, and the Petro cult they brought with them, as destabilizing influences on slave society, since the older Rada tradition met the needs of revolutionary mobilization.

In view of the event's political context, and as "Congos" were still only a minority of the slave population in the plain, one may doubt that the Bois Caïman meeting was narrowly identified with one particular ethnic group. Robin Law comments that, in Africa, blood oaths often functioned to bring together people across ethnic boundaries. As cultural syncretism was not an essential part of such practices, the 1791 ceremony did not necessarily exhibit a blending of religious traditions. Such blending is usually taken for granted because of the religion's overtly syncretic structure with its different "national" rites. Yet it is far from clear that this fusion took place before the revolution.[70] It is thus moot whether religious organization facilitated political cooperation or political cooperation fostered religious syncretism. In the same way, one should be wary of projecting back into the colonial period the idea that vodou necessarily expressed a revolutionary ideology; evidence for this has more often been found in the minds of historians than in the historical record.[71] With only slight exaggeration, one can say that the reputation of vodou as a unifying and revolutionary force begins with the ceremony of Bois Caïman.

What, then, can be said of the ceremony's role in the revolt? Principally, that it served to sacralize a political movement that was then reaching fruition. The decision to launch a rebellion, taken seven days earlier at the elite meeting of slave-drivers and coachmen, was at Bois Caïman directly communicated, to a perhaps predominantly African group of field slaves, in a religious setting calculated to mobilize support. A widespread conspiracy was already in place by the time the ceremony was held and, more than this, was slowly being uncovered by the white colonists. It is possible, therefore, that the ceremony was used to bring forward the date of the uprising from August 24th to August 22nd. Yet it is also possible it was the incident on the La Gossette estate immediately following the ceremony that precipitated the revolt's outbreak two days prematurely. Had Boukman waited longer, the conspiracy, like most slave conspiracies, might have been crushed. On the other hand, by waiting until the agreed-upon date, the slaves of Cap Français and the surrounding countryside might well have brought off a spectacularly coordinated uprising even more devastating than the one that occurred.

The Bois Caïman ceremony surely infused its participants with courage and a heightened sense of solidarity, but the number of slaves who took part cannot have been great. If they were more numerous than the 200 or so at the Lenormand meeting, they probably would have left more trace in the historical record. In any event, they cannot have formed more than a small minority of the slaves who took up arms in August 1791. The significance of the Bois Caïman ceremony has been overstated because it is usually confused with the earlier meeting on the Lenormand de Mézy plantation. All the evidence suggests that with regard to the organization of the 1791 insurrection, the Lenormand meeting was the more important. Even the prayer of Boukman, if authentic, was evidently spoken there and not at Bois Caïman. It is therefore entirely fitting that August 14th should be celebrated as an anniversary of national significance in Haiti, although it is not the anniversary of the Bois Caïman ceremony and may have had nothing to do with vodou.

Part Four.

Slaves and Free Coloreds

It is sometimes said that the people in American slave societies least known to historians are those who were neither white nor enslaved. Such gens de couleur libres (free people of color) tend to be less well documented in archives than both wealthier white property-owners and slaves classed as property. Relations between slaves and free coloreds, in particular, remain poorly understood. In the Haitian Revolution they constitute a central theme and an enigma.

As the majority of free persons of color in Saint Domingue were of mixed racial descent, some had relatives among whites and slaves. Many were slave-owners and many were ex-slaves, but free-born or freed, dark or light in complexion, all were subject to a system of racial discrimination that grew increasingly restrictive after 1750 in France and its colonies. Their situation was thus profoundly ambiguous. Free coloreds were often accused of harboring fugitive slaves, but, as they made up half the militia and almost all the rural police, they were also largely responsible for recapturing fugitives. Although whites liked to say that free coloreds were especially harsh to their slaves, as resident planters on small properties they were perhaps more likely to develop paternalistic relations with them; even critics acknowledged that they did not commit the atrocities some whites did, confident in the complicity of the court system. During the late eighteenth century, colonists and administrators privately discussed whether the policy of racial discrimination strengthened slavery, as intended, by encouraging ideas of racial hierarchy or whether it would one day force the free coloreds to unite with the slaves in revolt. On the eve of the Haitian Revolution, the debate continued in the corridors of power with those favoring the status quo prevailing over the advocates of reform.

The French Revolution of 1789 greatly strengthened the case of the free coloreds by legitimating libertarian ideology and providing a political forum, till then nonexistent, where that case could be heard. But by democratizing power, the revolution also strengthened opposition to change. Before 1789, racial equality meant the right to a fair trial and the right to become a doctor or lawyer. Afterward much more was at stake. Equality would bring voting rights and the potential to control colonial society. And by enfranchising the white population, the question was removed from the realm of elite debate to that of popular prejudice.

Saint Domingue's free colored population of about 30,000 people was unusually large for a non-Iberian colony. In the south and west provinces, they outnumbered whites and, because of the prominence among them of small and middling planters, they were the wealthiest such group in the Americas. They were very diverse in wealth, culture, and color, however, and therefore diverse in their relations with whites (where gender was an especially important variable). Historians have tended to treat them as a bloc, but their behavior during the revolution was similarly diverse, and ambivalent, above all on the question of slavery. The abolition of slavery promised to remove the stigma attached to African descent but also to destroy the status that set even propertyless free blacks above the masses. For slave-owning nonwhites, slave emancipation threatened economic ruin, though a revolution that completely overturned white rule might open up dramatically new prospects. The Haitian Revolution thus offers a laboratory for studying the interplay of class and race. The discovery in 1978 that slave leader Toussaint Louverture was himself a freedman adds extra interest to attempts to unscramble the interconnections of class and color loyalties during the revolution.

In the preamble to his slave emancipation decree of August 29, 1793, French civil commissioner Sonthonax exhorted the slaves to remember that the free coloreds gave them the arms that conquered their freedom. What he meant by this, however, remains obscure. The colored merchant Vincent Ogé, who first raised the standard of revolt, demanded only racial equality among free persons and refused to recruit slaves in his October 1790 rebellion. It is true that the year before Ogé had risked making a speech to the planters' club in Paris that evoked slavery's end. And some evidence suggests that the slaves who later launched the northern plain uprising saw Ogé as a precursor. However, only a few partisan historians have claimed a key role for survivors of Ogé's rebellion in the great slave uprising of August 1791. The remarkable coincidence that month of the slave

uprising in the north and the general rebellion of the free coloreds of the west and south nonetheless convinced many colonists
that free and enslaved nonwhites had colluded. Some free men of
color did join rebel slave armies, and others made tactical alliances with them. Many others, however, fought against the slave
insurgents, joined British and Spanish invaders in 1793, and,
long after the slavery question was settled, fought a bitter civil
war against the former slaves in 1799–1800. Until halfway
through the war of independence in 1802, the intermediary free
coloreds hesitated in their choice of allies between the black
masses and French colonizers.

The Haitian Revolution was never just a slave revolution. Although the destruction of slavery constitutes its core, only the simultaneous struggle of free and enslaved nonwhites explains its
outcome. Despite their antagonism, slaves and free coloreds each
owed much of their success to the other. Free people of color won
the abolition of racial discrimination in April 1792 because the
French knew they could not defeat the slave insurrection without
their help. The inability of the French to suppress the slave insurrection had much to do with their having to fight the free coloreds at the same time. And only when the slaves and free coloreds united in the fall of 1802 could they oust the French and
preserve their respective gains by ending colonial rule.

The following chapter examines the first case of collaboration
between free nonwhites and armed slaves and its tragic outcome.
The case of "the Swiss" illustrates the free coloreds' dilemma in
maintaining slavery while fighting for racial equality. It was the
first of many experiments by free persons in arming slaves that
progressively undermined slavery before final abolition. It also
began a long series of deportations of "dangerous elements" that
would be a feature of the French Revolutionary War in the Caribbean. The next chapter in this section analyzes the turning
point of the black revolution, Toussaint Louverture's reversal of
alliances in 1794 when he switched from the monarchical Spanish to the French Republic. Historians of materialist and idealist
persuasions have produced radically different interpretations of
this volte-face and its connection to the Republic's decision to
abolish slavery. Until recently, few knew that Toussaint, like
some 2 percent of the insurgent slave army, was a freedman with
no personal stake in slave emancipation. This chapter stresses
that, because of a traditional focus on the hero, the actions of

other free people of color and slaves have not been given due weight in explaining this realignment of forces. Free coloreds discovered under the Spanish, as they would later under Napoleon, that their own civil rights could not be guaranteed without slave emancipation. Chapter 9 looks at the life of Jean Kina, a slave who made the transition to freedman during the revolution. As a defender of slavery and white supremacy, his career followed a very different trajectory than Toussaint's, although at the end of their lives they found themselves in the same prison in France.

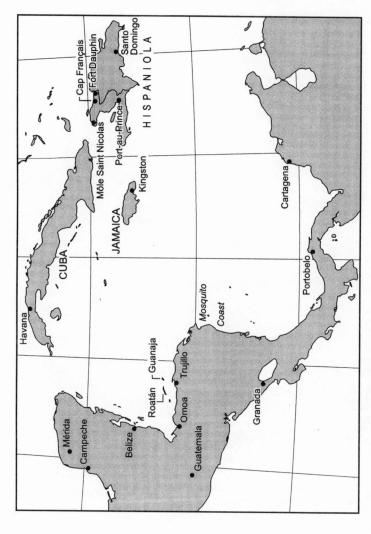

Map 3. The western Caribbean and Central America

7 The "Swiss" and the Problem of Slave/Free Colored Cooperation

In the autumn of 1791, when the slave revolt in Saint Domingue was sending shock waves throughout the Caribbean,[1] British settlers on the Belize River in the Gulf of Honduras were suddenly alarmed to find the slave revolt's threat far closer than they could have expected. On November 14, 1791, a large French ship anchored off Belize carrying more than 200 black rebels, veterans of the recent fighting around Port-au-Prince. Nerves tautened in the logging settlement, whose white inhabitants then numbered scarcely 250. When it was learned that the slaves had been put ashore, the mahogany-cutters "were thrown into great consternation," one of them wrote. "The country in general seems to be panic struck," wrote another, "all is confusion." It was "the most untoward business that has ever attended or threatened this settlement."[2] The blacks concerned, though unknown to the colonists, were a group now famous in the history of Haiti, known as "les Suisses." Their story is one of personal tragedy and of great significance in the development of the Haitian Revolution. To this day, "the Swiss" retain considerable symbolic meaning for students of Haiti's problems.

Origins

The same evening the slave conspirators assembled at Bois Caïman, a group of free men of color met 170 miles away at the widow Rasteau's house just outside Port-au-Prince to launch their own rebellion. They too had been planning for some weeks and needed only to finalize matters. The next night, as Boukman led the Clément and Flaville slaves toward the Noé plantation, Alexandre Pétion, future president of Haiti, slipped into Port-au-Prince to say goodbye to his mother, and around dawn on August 23rd, when the northern plain began to burn, the free coloreds of the west began gathering in arms in the mountains above the capital.[3] The coincidence of the two rebellions is striking, but they were not connected and had quite different goals. The free coloreds wanted legal equality with white colonists; the slaves, an end to slavery. However, just as numerous free coloreds became involved, willingly or not, in the northern uprising, their counterparts in the west soon acquired allies among the enslaved population.

Mounted on ponies and mules and wearing straw hats, the free men of color won two quick victories as they furiously gave vent to long-pent-up frustration. Their white opponents were astonished to find them no longer the humble figures they had known. On August 30th, they fought a brief skirmish against local white militia at Nérette, in the hills near present-day Pétionville. Three days later, at Pernier, at the entrance to the Cul de Sac plain, they routed a column of line troops, National Guards, and waterfront thugs sent out from Port-au-Prince, killing between sixty and eighty of them.[4] They then made their base in the middle of the plain in the village of Croix des Bouquets. At some point around this time, there appeared in the ranks of the free colored army, which numbered some 2,000 to 4,000 men, a body of armed slaves, whom the free coloreds drilled daily and gave the name of "Swiss." The historian Madiou thought the name was meant to honor them as mountain-dwelling and freedom-loving people, but it was more likely used in a then generic sense of "guards," derived from the royal government's Swiss Guards.[5] The origin of these men has long been surrounded by controversy.

Some Haitian historians have stated that the Swiss were mainly domestic slaves armed by their white owners whom they deserted after the skirmish at either Nérette or Pernier. These writers evidently exaggerated. Just as some of them blamed the slave insurrection on white counterrevolutionaries, they wanted to blame the French colonists for being the first slave-owners to arm slaves and thus the authors of their own ruin.[6] Certain colonists had talked of "unleashing the slaves" on the free coloreds even before this civil war broke out, but there is no sign that the whites employed slaves in these two opening encounters, or indeed for several months.[7] If a few domestics accompanied their owners in the militia troop attacked at Nérette, they cannot have been very numerous. Most of the Swiss did have white owners, but it was free coloreds, according to their French enemies, who forcibly recruited them using threats and offers of freedom.[8] The free coloreds themselves claimed that the Swiss were fugitives and rebels who had spontaneously joined them; they prudently strove to keep them under their control.[9] Both versions were self-serving, but each was true to an uncertain extent.[10]

The failure ten months before of the rebellion of Vincent Ogé must have been very much in the minds of the western free coloreds. Against some of his followers' advice, Ogé had turned away slaves who joined them when they launched their revolt for racial equality in the northern mountains in October 1790. Ogé's defeat and grisly death perhaps suggested that a different strategy might be prudent this time. On the other hand, the free coloreds knew that any involvement of slaves in their cause could make their opponents even less likely to yield, and for substantial property-owners, an equality that undermined slavery might prove a Pyrrhic victory. Yet some were willing to take the gamble and to envisage different types of compromise with the slaves. Two who were present at the August 21st meeting left for their home in Petit Trou de Nippes in the south peninsula and encouraged the local slaves to revolt the following week. They then took control of the parish and reestablished slave labor, having freed a few of the slaves' leaders.[11] Free nonwhite insurgents would successfully employ this strategy on several later occasions, as in the Arcahaye, Cul de Sac, and Artibonite plains in March and April 1792. The uprising in the north, however (announced in Port-au-Prince on August 26th), made clear the risks involved.

Numerous plantations in the mountains above Port-au-Prince were pillaged and burned at this time—a fact glossed over in the revolution's "official history" by Garran-Coulon. Free coloreds and slaves, acting independently and in collaboration, killed a score or more of white inhabitants. The few whites who did not flee were disarmed by the men of color.[12] Especially interesting is the accusation that some free coloreds promised the local slaves an extra two free days each week.[13] The rumor of "three free days" conceded by the king had been circulating in the Caribbean since 1789. It reached Saint Domingue in January 1791, when it served to mobilize slaves in a conspiracy at Port Salut on the south coast; it reappeared in June in the Cul de Sac plain and in August among the demands of the slave insurgents in the north. In almost every instance, the rumor seems to have been propagated by free coloreds.[14] It appears to represent a reform of slavery that some free coloreds might have found acceptable as the price for mobilizing slave resistance to pressure whites into agreeing to their demands.

In the Port-au-Prince mountains, a local planter later testified, free colored insurgents told slaves that they would free those who joined their army and that the king had granted them all three free days.[15] In the words of a local slave insurgent, the mulattoes told the slaves they would be free if the mulattoes won and they would have to work only for them; if the whites stayed in power, the mulattoes would not make peace unless the three free days were granted.[16] The slaves armed themselves with machetes and indigo knives tied to sticks, and a few took guns from planters' houses. No doubt many had scores to settle. They killed managers and overseers, a doctor, and a lime-burner, but their vengeance was not random. They did not burn the Montagnac plantation, the slave insurgent said, because the owner had been hospitable to free coloreds and was opposed to the colonial radical party. Both sources mentioned the Robion family's plantation, where pillage was accumulated along with the heads of white victims that were lined up on the platform where coffee was dried.

Unfortunately, it is not clear how much of this rebellion and destruction in the Port-au-Prince mountains had occurred before early September, when the free colored army descended into the Cul de Sac plain and the Swiss were already in existence. Some whites had abandoned the mountains as early as August 10th in fear of the coming conflict, leaving their slaves to their own devices; more fled after the clash at Nérette. Little arson seems to have occurred before September 4th; after that, the slaves in the mountain districts of Charbonnière, Grand Fond, Rivière Froide, and Fond Ferrier remained in revolt, or rebelled spasmodically, until late October.[17] Whether this rebellion was autonomous or was encouraged by free coloreds, it thus remains uncertain if the participants ever formed part of the Swiss. This uncertainty is regrettable, because whether or not the Swiss could be accused of arson and murder is highly relevant to the colonists' reaction to them. It also lends itself to the diversity of images the Swiss have evoked: innocent tools, brave freedom fighters, or sanguinary desperadoes.

A similar and related puzzle is whether the Swiss included in their ranks a group of sugar plantation slaves who had rebelled near Croix des Bouquets in June and who had remained fugitives ever since. Slaves on the Fortin Bellanton estate had killed their driver and decamped to join maroons from other local plantations who were taking advantage of a sudden scarcity of free colored rural police.[18] In two skirmishes with local whites, some seventy or eighty slaves put up bitter resistance; twenty of them were killed or captured. The rest disappeared.[19]

Writing in 1819, Pamphile de Lacroix casually stated that the free colored insurgents later recruited these maroons and they became the Swiss. Most historians apparently ignored this assertion until Carolyn Fick's 1990 history of the revolution, where these events are interpreted as an aborted conspiracy. In fact, Lacroix, Fick, and nineteenth-century historian Céligny Ardouin seem to be the only writers to link the two groups of slaves. No contemporary source did so. Although Lacroix cited two volumes of the *Débats entre les accusateurs et les accusés dans l'affaire des colonies,* they contain nothing that supports this claim. A free colored pamphlet also cited by Lacroix mentions only "several unknown fugitive slaves"; Lacroix himself seems to have presumed who they were.[20] Although it would not be surprising to find these precursors of the August uprising among the ranks of the Swiss, they were not numerous enough, in any event, to have constituted more than a minority of them. Moreover, of the forty-one Swiss whose identity can be established, none came from Fortin Bellanton or any of the estates listed as experiencing heavy marronage in June and July of 1791.[21]

This small sample suggests that the Swiss probably were drawn mainly from coffee plantations in the mountains of Port-au-Prince parish but that at least one-third came from sugar estates in the Cul de Sac plain.[22] During the week following the battle of Pernier, slaves from around Croix des Bouquets flocked to join the victorious free colored army, and their number grew temporarily to about 2,000. With the north province going up in flames, many feared the free coloreds would raise the slaves and march on Port-au-Prince, burning everything in their path.[23] There was no revolt, however, as there was in the nearby mountains, although several whites were killed and seven sugar plantation workforces were described as out of control. According to planter-historian Bryan Edwards, the free men of color found the sugar workers harder to suborn than the highland slaves.[24] But the essential point is that the free coloreds were now in a dominant position. They had won two stunning victories and seemed to hold the future of the west province in their hands. It was a propitious time to negotiate.

Negotiations

Despite the assertions of various historians about the boldness of the Swiss in battle, it is far from certain that many of them ever participated in combat. Their value to the free coloreds was certainly more political than military. They served as an implied threat that if the free coloreds' demands were not met, the *gens de couleur* might raise the slaves en masse. Most sensitive to this threat were the planters and estate managers of the Cul de Sac plain, home to Saint Domingue's largest plantations and about 30,000 slaves. Even before the skirmish at Pernier, they had sent envoys to the men of color, and on September 7th they drew up a concordat or treaty in Croix des Bouquets.[25] By this they finally agreed to accept the May 15th law passed by the National Assembly that, in according equal rights to freeborn people of color, had set off a storm of racist anger in the colony.

Such wealthy rural conservatives who put their property before their prejudices had never been the free coloreds' main opponent. It was the urban working and middle classes—paradoxically, the radicals of colonial politics—that were the most visceral enemies of racial equality. Yet even the Patriots of the capital now realized they had to give ground. Several days in succession, they sent envoys across the plain to conduct preliminary talks. Then, on September 11th, representatives of the town council and National Guard made the 10-mile journey to Croix des Bouquets to agree on terms. The negotiations were long and tense. Most whites now felt compelled to concede political rights to the free coloreds. Yet there remained the problem of what to do with the Swiss.

Slaves who bore arms in rebellion were usually executed. The Port-au-Prince whites wanted the Swiss punished by their owners or by the courts and at least sent back to their plantations; anything less would simply encourage more slaves to rebel. The free coloreds, however, or some of them, had probably already promised the Swiss (or some of them) their freedom. They argued that it would be dangerous to force them, or at least the most assertive among them, back into slavery. According to Thomas Madiou, the whites then suggested deportation as a compromise solution. For the free coloreds, this would be a betrayal of their allies. This recommended the measure to the whites, who were anxious to drive a wedge between the free coloreds and the enslaved masses. When the white delegates became insistent, a moment of crisis arose, and the colored negotiator Daguin shouted the words now famous in Haitian history, "Drummers, sound the alarm!" A treaty eventually was signed in the Croix des Bouquets church, but it said nothing about the Swiss.[26]

It appears that a compromise was reached off the record. A certain number of Swiss would be enrolled in a police force to patrol the plantations, and after eight years' service they were to gain their freedom. This was a device used before the revolution for manumitting certain favored slaves, who were added to the *maréchaussée*, the rural mounted police, which had white officers and free nonwhite troopers. In this case, however, the number and identity of the men involved were radically different. It was not a solution slave-owners wanted to publicize. Yet it was accepted as unavoidable by the Cul de Sac planters and probably by the delegates from Port-au-Prince.[27] By the end of September, a group of 300 Swiss was receiving daily training with weapons. Formerly armed with hoes and lances, some Swiss by now must have had firearms.[28]

Most of the estimated 2,000 slaves who had joined the free coloreds had to be persuaded to return to their plantations and confront angry overseers and owners. As some colonists feared, this was not an easy solution to implement. On September 22nd, the free coloreds' leader, Louis-Jacques Bauvais, reported that angry Swiss being sent back to their owners had rioted in his camp and nearly killed a white colonist. Bauvais opened fire on them, but some fled with their weapons. He urgently asked Port-au-Prince to send field cannon and guns. Probably suspecting a ruse, the authorities in the capital did nothing.[29] Several of the enslaved men who returned to their estates were hanged; the others remained suspects. In a tense atmosphere, which was heightened by news from the north, plantation staff and selected slaves mounted guard every night. Free men of color patrolled the roads through the plain, where many of them had property.[30]

The Swiss posed a dilemma for free colored slave-owners that mirrored perfectly their ambiguous position in colonial society. Class identity clashed with racial sensibilities, self-interest clashed with a sense of justice, and the risks and rewards in challenging the system were finely balanced. Since so little is known about slave–free colored relations at any time, the issue is of special interest for the light it sheds on free colored attitudes toward slavery at a moment when the balance of power between white, black, and brown was about to careen out of control. As the slave revolution raged in the north, a few free coloreds in the west privately argued that a controlled and compensated end to slavery might be a prudent policy.[31] Yet evidence for this argument is very sparse. The enigmatic rumors about "three free days" seem to have originally come from free non-whites, but no one was publicly advocating the idea.[32] The free colored leadership was intent on maintaining slavery. In late September, they sent 400 men to fight alongside the whites in the north. Bauvais refused to meet with slaves who came to see him.[33] A real alliance against the French was still eleven years away. Nevertheless, most men of color wanted to emancipate several hundred of the Swiss.

Ultimately at stake was the free coloreds' moral authority to speak for all the colony's nonwhites and thus their ability to exploit politically their intermediate position in the social hierarchy. The free coloreds, who were a privileged as well as an oppressed sector of society, were not obviously the "natural allies" of the slaves. In the midst of Ogé's rebellion in 1790, a white colonist had written from the north, "Thank goodness the slaves are generally for us and enemies of the mulattoes; but who knows?"[34] As noted above, some whites had been curiously confident that they could always "unleash" the slaves on the free people of color, exploiting an antipathy built on envy and class prejudice. The twin uprisings of August 1791 seriously undermined that confidence. The free coloreds' ability to control the countryside in the south and west provinces (where they were most numerous) was the main reason those regions did not experience an uprising like the one in the north.[35] This enabled the free coloreds to pursue their own ends while claiming to mediate the threat to property symbolized by the Swiss. However, although the threat of slave revolt brought the whites to the negotiating table, it was also an obstacle to reaching an agreement.

Hostility to the two concordats in any case remained strong among the white populace of the capital, and in faraway Cap Français, the governor and Colonial Assembly refused to accept them. Colonists' correspondence of this time frequently describe the treaties as humiliating. The nonwhites' pursuit of equality also ran afoul of some radical leaders' desire for secession. On September 29th, two British warships anchored off Port-au-Prince in response to official requests for aid and to secret feelers from the radicals regarding a protectorate. Their presence excited hopes among disaffected colonists that the British might intervene and take over the colony. Jean-Baptiste de Caradeux, the Patriot leader, now hinted to free colored leaders that recognition of racial equality would be contingent upon their support for independence. They rebuffed and denounced him, and the town council, in return, canceled the concordat. With British support, the Patriots could still hope to return the free coloreds to what some called "their natural place." Only when the warships left on October 7th were the Patriot leaders again forced to cooperate with the free colored insurgents.[36]

In an abrupt about-face, de Caradeux proposed a new concordat that would cover the entire west province. On October 19th, more than sixty white and colored delegates gathered on the Goureau plantation to sign a treaty. Bolstered by new arrivals from surrounding parishes, the men of color were this time more demanding. The whites not only had to accept racial equality and the compensation of recent victims of persecution; they also had to dissolve all political bodies so new elections could be held. It was a resounding victory. Once again, however, the Swiss were not mentioned. The oral agreement presumably still stood.[37] On Sunday, October 23rd, at a ceremony on the Damiens estate midway between Port-au-Prince and Croix des Bouquets, the new treaty was proclaimed. The next morning, a free colored army of 1,500 men and some 300 armed Swiss marched into the capital, drums beating. In an atmosphere of reconciliation, they drew up in formation on one of the main squares, attended a thanksgiving service in the city church, and then attended a banquet with speeches and toasts in the barracks, where they took up residence. Bauvais and Caradeux walked arm in arm. Saint Domingue had never seen anything like it.[38]

The Swiss must have been jubilant. "Impudently," a contemporary wrote, "they walked the streets with the assurance of free men."[39] Their triumph, however, was short lived. White residents denounced as dangerous the excitement the presence of armed slaves caused among the city's enslaved artisans and domestic servants. Daily complaints were made to the town council. Swiss were reportedly overheard saying "If you had done like us, you'd be free, too; the country would be ours!" "The good citizens were all seized with panic," a National Guard spokesman later claimed, "everyone was afraid for his property and his life." Referring to the black soldiers as "monsters" and "tigers," some said they should be sold in South America or thrown in the sea, or the west would go the way of the north province. Others still wished to reclaim them as their property.[40] Caradeux and the mayor, Michel-Joseph Leremboure, called a secret meeting of white and free colored leaders to discuss the fate of the Swiss.

Meanwhile, the men of color, clearly aligning themselves with their new allies, had sent forces to put down the slave revolts in the mountains above the capital and further west at Petit Goâve.[41] It is impossible to know how much the whites had planned in advance, but the free coloreds looked outmaneuvered. At the secret meeting in Port-au-Prince, Mayor Leremboure called for the deportation of the Swiss as necessary to colonial security. Although it meant a brutal separation of families, he argued that it was a humane compromise—"immediate freedom." The men should receive agricultural tools, seeds, and supplies for three months and be left on the coast of Central America. André Rigaud, Pétion, and Daguin were among those who objected, but the main free colored leaders—Bauvais, Pierre Pinchinat, and Jean-Pierre Lambert—accepted.[42] Whether or not they had made any commitment to their enslaved allies, they did not wish to jeopardize their new and hard-won acceptance as full citizens in a slave-owning society.

On Friday, October 28th, the whole National Guard was mobilized, whites and free coloreds. Under the pretext of distributing new weapons, the Swiss were disarmed and then marched at gunpoint on board a ship and put in chains. Not only the slaves but the free colored poor in Port-au-Prince were outraged. In the words of a local Patriot, 2,500 "mulattoes who have nothing to lose" threatened to riot unless the Swiss were disembarked and freed. Daguin called for torrents of blood, and the waterfront toughs led by Pralotto were eager to meet his challenge. The crisis was defused on Saturday afternoon only when Bauvais called a meeting of free coloreds on the main square and threatened that the next person who mentioned the Swiss would also be deported.[43]

"I knew all along the blacks would get screwed," a town slave reportedly said. "I always said the mulattoes and whites would make a deal."[44] Although most Swiss were black and most *gens de couleur* were of part-European descent, the betrayal of the Swiss was not, however, a question of color in any precise sense, as Haitian historians from the light-skinned elite have frequently pointed out. Although Bauvais and Pinchinat were light-complexioned (both had only one black grandparent), so, too, was Pétion, who opposed deportation; but Lambert was black and Daguin and Rigaud were mulattoes. Moreover, although most of the Swiss were black, a minority was of mixed racial descent. Age seems to have been a more significant factor distinguishing the supporters and opponents of deportation; the opponents tended to be younger.[45]

Age, like color, perhaps had implications regarding the wealth of these individuals and their personal stake in the slave regime, but this is not known for certain. It is true that Bauvais and Pinchinat both received privileged educations in France, whereas Pétion was not recognized by his white father and was raised by his mother in Port-au-Prince. Rigaud's father, a minor official, did send him to France, but it was to learn a trade. Nevertheless, Bauvais the schoolteacher, Pinchinat the metropolitan lawyer, and Lambert the illiterate carpenter seem to have been no more invested in slave-holding than Rigaud the goldsmith/professional soldier. The only prominent figure known to be from a planter family was Boisrond junior, and he criticized the deportation as politically unwise.[46] Class does emerge as a factor in the popular resistance to the free colored leadership by the "wretched rabble" of the capital, the "mulattoes who have nothing to lose." However, as they also were described as "free blacks and mulattoes with nothing," the color factor, as usual, reemerges to complicate matters.[47] These class divisions within the free colored sector were presumably important in shaping reactions to the slave uprising in the north, as they would be again in the nonwhite response to the British and Spanish invasions of 1793, but their imbrication with differences of color is far from fully understood.

Contemporary local sources give various figures between 230 and 280 for the total number of Swiss initially embarked, all of them guesses; 217 or 218 were finally deported rather than the 300 supposed by most historians. According to the planter Joseph Sartre, about one-third of the 300 in the corps, "the least guilty," were reclaimed by their owners.[48] Some may have escaped. Another dozen, however, "the most guilty," who had not come to Port-au-Prince, were seized in Croix des Bouquets, brought to the capital on October 31st, and put in the ship's hold with the others. These men may have been the recently arrested leaders of the rebellion in the nearby mountains, which had just been suppressed.[49]

One of them, Charlemagne, a mulatto slave of the Carrère plantation, was described as "Captain-General of the Swiss of Fond-Ferrier." Such slaves of mixed racial descent made up between 17 and 23 of the total deported, a presence four times greater than in the slave population as a whole. They had taken a leading role in the rebellion in the mountains.[50] It appears that free colored insurgents sometimes singled them out as recruits, just as some abolitionists in France began arguing in 1789 that slaves of mixed descent should immediately be emancipated.[51] Since such slaves normally were the most likely to be manumitted, it is easy to imagine that those who were not might be especially driven by unrealized ambitions.

The assertion by several historians that the Swiss were the domestic slaves of free colored owners is highly unlikely; no contemporary suggested this, and only one is known to have had a nonwhite owner. However, they probably were drawn in large measure from the slave elite. Some colonists described them as *chefs d'ateliers* (slave-drivers); others said many were artisans. The seven from the Fleuriau estate included a master sugar-boiler and two craftsmen.[52] Other commentators referred favorably to their intelligence and their physique; Admiral Grimouärd thought them "fine-looking men."[53]

For Joseph Sartre, however, they were "monsters," "almost all arsonists and murderers, or at least guilty of open insurrection," and he felt safer as he saw them go and the propertied classes close ranks. Many colonists also took comfort in the divisions the deportation created between free and enslaved nonwhites; slaves would be less willing to join free coloreds in future, they reckoned.[54] For the free people of color, the sacrifice of the Swiss was certainly in vain. Their acceptance as full citizens lasted less than a month. Their Patriot enemies, encouraged by the weakened position of the *gens de couleur* and by new legislation in France, soon sought to suspend the Damiens treaty.[55] Before the end of November, a new, much bloodier civil war had begun throughout the west and south.

Deportation

The Provincial Assembly of the west province hired a transatlantic cargo vessel, the *Emmanuel* of Nantes, to take the Swiss to a destination that was at first kept secret but was later revealed to be "la Baie des Moustiques." There the captain, François Colmin, was instructed to put his captives ashore with their supplies and equipment on a deserted stretch of coast. Rumors circulated in the city, however, that once out of sight of land, the prisoners were to be thrown into the sea. Perhaps because of this, four free colored commissioners were chosen to accompany the expedition in a separate ship. The two vessels set sail on November 3rd. Chained in the hold of the *Emmanuel* as it beat to westward, many Swiss must have relived their middle passage from Africa.

The strange term "Baie des Moustiques" apparently was meant to encompass both the Bay of Honduras and the adjoining Miskito (formerly Mosquito) Coast of Nicaragua.[56] The region was chosen because most of it was not effectively occupied by any European power. Until 1786, the British had claimed a protectorate over Mosquitia, the homeland of the Afro-Indian Miskito that extended from northeastern Nicaragua into the western reaches of Honduras, but since their withdrawal, the Spanish had made little progress in exerting colonial control over the region.

Historians of the Haitian Revolution have usually thought that the Swiss never reached Central America but were dumped by Captain Colmin on the coast of Jamaica after he had treacherously tried to sell them. At first, the destination of the Swiss had been kept secret. Then, soon after leaving Port-au-Prince, the *Emmanuel* became permanently separated from its escort ship, owing either to a storm or to collusion between the two ships' captains. This has added to the mystery surrounding the affair.[57] Documents in the Public Record Office in London allow us to clear up some of this confusion.[58]

The *Emmanuel* did not sail to Jamaica. The ship made its first landfall on November 11th at Guanaja (Bonacca), an island just east of Roatán off the coast of Honduras. There, Colmin later reported, an English captain advised him against a landing because of Spanish hostility and, because of contrary winds, he did not turn south toward the Miskito Coast.[59] Instead, the *Emmanuel* continued westward into the Bay of Honduras and, with the help of a local pilot, anchored at Goff's Cay, some fourteen miles off the main British settlement on the Belize River. From there he sent one of his crew who spoke English to the river mouth, where on November 15th he announced a cargo of slaves for sale.

The seaman was called Peter McCulloch, an old illiterate Scot who had lived in Saint Domingue for almost fifty years. He was not part of Colmin's regular crew but had been recommended by the Port-au-Prince town council as a good pilot for those waters and a good Patriot. Introducing himself as the *Emmanuel*'s supercargo (i.e., the agent for its cargo), McCulloch told the Belize settlers that the Swiss had had nothing to do with the revolution in Saint Domingue. They had been seized from the estates of indebted planters and were to be sold by him for their creditors' benefit. They had various skills; McCulloch proposed to sell in Belize those accustomed to wielding an axe. He was giving the British first refusal, he claimed, out of gratitude for their assistance in fighting the revolt in northern Saint Domingue, which had now been suppressed.

The tale did not inspire much confidence. Whatever their needs for labor, the settlers chose to look on the Swiss as dangerous men rather than as objects for sale. The night before, on hearing of the *Emmanuel*'s arrival at Goff's Cay, twenty-three anxious inhabitants had drawn up a petition against allowing the ship to land a "sett of villians of so horrid a description." Accusing the Swiss of "being the very worst of those concerned in the late dreadful insurrection," they predicted the direst consequences should they disembark in Belize.

The Europeans of the Honduras settlement, about one-tenth of the total population, were in a particularly vulnerable position. They shared the logging settlement with a sizeable community of free coloreds and more than 2,000 slaves who were to an unusual degree able-bodied males; over half were men.[60] Because the settlement had no regular garrison (until 1797), many of the slaves had been trained as soldiers and had been under arms since the scare about war with Spain the previous year. Some even had had military experience in the war of 1778–1783. The Baymen therefore did not want the message of Saint Domingue spread among them by slaves who had fought for and won their freedom. Only a few weeks before, apparently responding to news of the slave revolt, the settlers had passed a law forbidding on pain of death the practice of witchcraft, the harboring of runaways, and incitement to rebellion.[61] Finally, the inhabitants were temporarily without a leader. The previous superintendent had only recently returned to Europe, leaving the settlers to be governed by their elected magistrates.

A public meeting was called to hear both the petition and McCulloch's statement. It voted unanimously to refuse entry to the Swiss. The magistrates then decreed that any inhabitant tempted to trade illicitly with the *Emmanuel* would have to pay a 100-pound fine for every slave purchased. The pilot (who had already been given two slaves) would be fined 200 pounds if ever again he brought the ship into Honduran waters. Meanwhile, not a half day's sail away, the Swiss were being disembarked on the tiny island of English Cay.[62] Kept mostly in chains, they had now been cooped up on board ship for over two weeks, and sickness was spreading among them. As on a regular slaving vessel, Colmin had allowed half of them up on deck at a time to exercise, but three or four had already died.[63]

The settlers on the Belize River learned of the landing on November 17th. Out on the cay, it was said, a local inhabitant, Noel Vernon, was urging Colmin to leave the slaves and offering to act himself as an agent for their sale. The magistrates immediately held another meeting and decided to sail out to investigate what was going on. When they arrived the next day, they found 213 Swiss crowded together on the cay and the *Emmanuel* disappearing toward the horizon.

The exact responsibility of Colmin, McCulloch, the Provincial Assembly, and the free coloreds in Saint Domingue for what had happened is not easy to apportion. It is certainly suspicious that, on leaving Port-au-Prince, Captain Colmin so swiftly lost his escort ship and the commissioners monitoring the deportation. Suspicion, moreover, attached to both parties. On their return to Saint Domingue, the free colored commissioners were jailed for neglect of duty. This was evidently a propaganda exercise by the colonists; the commissioners were hardly responsible for sailing the vessel (a French navy brig), but some modern historians have regarded them as complicitous in the affair.[64] One of the four commissioners later claimed in his memoirs that, once out to sea, the two ships' captains secretly agreed to split up.[65] Colmin, in any event, admitted he deliberately left behind the slower ship.[66]

Of course, there is no reason to suppose that a seaman like Colmin from the major slaving port of Nantes would have had any scruples about selling blacks as slaves. The surviving evidence, however, falls just a whisker short of proving that this was his intention. As for the Provincial Assembly of the west, its main concerns were presumably that the Swiss should never return to Saint Domingue and that their deportation should not cause friction with the colony's British or Spanish neighbors. To this end, the Miskito Coast had several advantages beyond its hazy political status. It was sparsely populated and extremely unhealthy. Not even the devil could live there, a French colonist commented.[67] Some Saint Domingue free coloreds subsequently argued that the deportation was intended to cause precisely the diplomatic incident it did in order to worsen Anglo-French relations and further the planters' secessionist ambitions, but this seems entirely far-fetched.[68]

One might guess, therefore, that in avoiding the Miskito Coast and approaching a British settlement, Colmin was flouting his instructions and going against the wishes of the Provincial Assembly. This was the assumption of Saint Domingue's governor when he belatedly learned of the incident; it was also the assumption of the governor of Jamaica,[69] who had loose oversight over the logging settlements. However, Colmin's instructions gave him leeway to land the Swiss on a deserted island should the mainland be unapproachable.[70] Moreover, under the Anglo-Spanish Convention of 1786, the British had no claims to English Cay (beyond the right to career ships there). Colmin, therefore, does seem to have stayed within the terms of his instructions.

More than this, the Provincial Assembly itself may well have secretly ordered the Swiss to be sold.[71] Had they been left on the Miskito Coast, it was noted, they could easily have been rescued by the free coloreds and smuggled back into Saint Domingue. This is why the revolutionary politician Garran-Coulon accused the assembly of secretly instructing Colmin to take the Swiss to Jamaica in order to prevent their return.[72] He was wrong about Jamaica, but both Colmin and the Assembly were doubtless aware that strong young men would find a ready market in the logging camps, whence return to Saint Domingue would be almost impossible.

Doubts remain about Colmin's behavior, because, as he was unable to speak English, it is not certain he was responsible for the actions of his crewman, McCulloch. It appears, for example, that when McCulloch returned from Belize

Point he tried to hide from Colmin the fact that he had presented himself as the ship's supercargo. This we know from the testimony of settler Noel Vernon. When Vernon told Colmin that the magistrates were likely to arrest him, McCulloch wanted to reembark the Swiss (presumably for sale elsewhere), but the captain decided simply to cut his cables and flee.

On the other hand, Vernon also testified that Colmin had headed for Belize because he had learned at Guanaja that the Baymen were in great need of slaves. Colmin had told him that his instructions were "to land or otherwise dispose of" the Swiss and that he was willing to leave them in the hands of an agent. Moreover, Colmin had several times showed him his official instructions and clearance papers. If true, this evidence would condemn both Colmin and the Provincial Assembly. However, as Vernon was himself implicated in the affair, he may have been lying.

It is conceivable, therefore, that the captain fell victim first to bad weather and then to the scheming of McCulloch and Vernon and that he was merely seeking permission to land the Swiss at Belize. It is much more likely that he deliberately planned to turn the voyage to his own profit by selling the Swiss back into slavery, and it is possible that he did this with the connivance of the Provincial Assembly, but neither proposition can be proved. The case recalls another deportation from Saint Domingue in 1787, when a ship's captain had been engaged to sell in the French colony of Cayenne thirty-three slaves judged to be excessively unruly because of the bad treatment they had received. The captain sold them in Tobago in contravention of the trade laws, presumably to pocket a higher price, but the administration in Saint Domingue concluded that the captain was "more unlucky than guilty."[73]

By the time the magistrates' expedition reached English Cay, it was too late to catch the *Emmanuel*. The fate of the Swiss was now in the hands of the settlers. They found that most of the 213 men left on the cay apparently "did not understand any European language."[74] This meant they spoke French Creole (which is indeed not a European language) or that the settlers' French was as limited as the slaves' rather than that they were necessarily Africans. One, however, "a sambo man of Charleston," spoke English. Named Paul Williams, he told the magistrates that all but four or five of them had belonged to white masters and that they had been forced by the free coloreds to join them in their rebellion. Those who refused had been killed, he said. The Belize magistrates were skeptical and tended to confuse the castaways with the black rebels in northern Saint Domingue, where the atrocities committed were making slaveowners throughout the Caribbean shudder. They rapidly decided that the Swiss should be sent back where they came from.

Despite their fear of the Swiss, the settlers were not entirely insensitive to their plight. Abandoned on a minuscule, barren island,[75] they had been left with only three days' supply of food and no water—an opportunity the Baymen did not neglect to criticize the "inhumanity and injustice" of the French. While seeking to charter shipping for a second deportation, the magistrates arranged for water to be brought from a nearby cay and for each man to receive two biscuits and a half-pound of salt meat per day. As provisioning a voyage for 200 men would seriously stretch the settlement's resources, an approach was made to the nearest Spanish town on the Yucatán border, Salamanca de Bacalar. Its commandant was asked to contribute 100 bushels of corn to rid the region of a common threat. This he did, despite Anglo-Spanish tensions, free of charge.[76] It is curious to note, however, that some Baymen hoped that the Spanish might be willing to take the Swiss off their hands; whether as slaves or free settlers, it is not clear.[77]

While these arrangements were proceeding, another scare swept the settlement when it was learned that thirty-two of the Swiss had been carried off from English Cay by three settlers named Tillet, Todd, and Kendall. On November 21st, they had sailed out to the cay in Tillet's boat and then rowed ashore in a skiff. Using one of their free black seamen as an interpreter, they told the Swiss that they were to be sent to Jamaica and then back to Saint Domingue. This, it was later reported, "terrified the negroes and much agitated their minds." Many said they would rather suffer any punishment than return to Saint Domingue, where they would be "hanged, shot, or quartered." As most were already sick, their bodies swollen from drinking the brackish water supplied them, Tillet picked out the healthiest and had no trouble persuading them to come with him. In fact, they rushed into the skiff with such haste that it overturned. The thirty-two were then taken to the mainland to a creek at Manatee Lagoon beyond the Sibun River, just outside the settlement's legal limits. There the three whites planned to use them to cut mahogany before selling them in the Bahamas. This is known from evidence subsequently taken from their black seamen.

Quite a few other Baymen would secretly have liked to follow Tillet's example,[78] but the magistrates continued to insist that public safety should not be sacrificed to private gain. Curiously, the settlement had witnessed a similar incident nearly ten years before. A shipload of convicts sent out by the British government had been refused admission by the magistrates, but two settlers managed to smuggle a number ashore with the intention of selling their labor, only to be arrested.[79] Such clashes doubtless reflected class divisions in the settlement between the wealthy magistrates, who were mainly merchants, and poorer Baymen, who had more need of labor and less to lose. A public meeting voted 30 to 1 to declare Tillet, Todd, and Kendall in "a state of open rebellion." They were arrested, and the thirty-two Swiss were eventually brought back to English Cay.

Just how long they had to stay there, exposed to the elements and brooding on their fate, is not apparent from the record. It was probably about six weeks. Reduced to 208 in number, they were carried into Kingston harbor on board a frigate and a schooner on January 16, 1792.[80]

Aftermath

The departure of the Swiss left the settlers at Belize relieved but anxious to be repaid the thousand pounds expended on their maintenance and removal. Their arrival in Jamaica caused alarm and anger. With events in Saint Domingue already uncomfortably close, the episode reminded Jamaica's planters how easily the slave rebellion could spread.[81] The lesson was not lost on the Spanish, either. The governor of Havana promised vigilance should a similar attempt be made on the coasts of Cuba.[82]

The Jamaicans, however, felt particularly indignant that, having themselves sent assistance to Saint Domingue's beleaguered planters, the French should act this way in return. They realized nonetheless that Saint Domingue's governor and Colonial Assembly were not at fault. The Jamaica Council advised that the Swiss be sent back to Saint Domingue as soon as possible, though not to Port-au-Prince and the Assembly of the West, but to Cap Français "to be safely delivered over to the French Government."[83] They were transferred to a transport ship and, after twelve days in Kingston harbor, they set sail for Saint Domingue accompanied by two warships. The day after they left, the escort ship that had been meant to guard them appeared in Kingston, having sailed from the Miskito Coast to Cartagena still looking for the *Emmanuel*.[84]

The flotilla from Kingston anchored at Cap Français on February 9th bearing an aggrieved protest from Jamaica's governor that was soon echoed in Europe by the British foreign secretary and the British ambassador in Paris.[85] Anglo-French relations at this time were good, and in both Saint Domingue and France, the British protests were met with embarrassed apologies. The captain whose squadron accompanied the Swiss to Cap Français received a fulsome welcome from the Colonial Assembly and governor. Suggesting that Captain Colmin must be guilty of at least negligence, the assembly ordered his arrest and agreed to reimburse the British for their costs.[86] When news of the affair reached France some weeks later, the National Assembly in Paris called for an investigation by its colonial and diplomatic committees. They reported on April 5th, deploring that a group of "dangerous negroes" should have so troubled Anglo-French relations. Although the incident appeared to be of little importance, it had called into question revolutionary France's respect for the law of nations and therefore had to be treated seriously. On their recommendation, the National Assembly then voted for reparations to be made and for Colmin to be brought to trial.[87]

By this time, however, the captain had already accounted for his actions to the Colonial Assembly in Saint Domingue and been acquitted. It was decided he was not responsible for McCulloch's words and that therefore there was no case against him. McCulloch was evidently prepared to accept the blame, and for this he received the derisory sentence of having to report to the authorities when requested for a period of twelve months.[88] Seamen of the coastal trade and other poor whites wielded considerable political power in Cap Français during this turbulent period (when they came close to driving out the governor).[89] Preoccupied with the war against the rebel slaves surrounding the town, the Colonial Assembly wanted to bury a potentially divisive issue as swiftly as possible.

Colmin now returned to France armed with the Colonial Assembly's decision, and he himself demanded compensation. The colonial committee of the National Assembly dismissed his claim for damages, but on examining the instructions he had received for his voyage, it also decided he had not committed any transgression.[90] As the Colonial Assembly of Saint Domingue was still willing to compensate the Belize settlers, by July the matter was closed. Colmin and the *Emmanuel* soon returned to their regular routine.[91]

For the Swiss, the consequences were more grave. The governor of Jamaica had hoped when he returned them that they would be shipped off again to a genuinely deserted spot. The Colonial Assembly should have pardoned them; it had just accepted, on February 12th, the royal amnesty that was decreed on November 5th for insurgents not guilty of serious crimes. Instead, the assembly sent the returnees, still in chains, to the isolated port of Môle Saint Nicolas in northwest Saint Domingue. What happened next remains obscure, but it is evident that a large number were murdered and their bodies were thrown in the sea. Spokesmen for the colonial radicals later blamed their royalist enemies for the killing as an attempt to discredit the Patriots. They claimed that the Swiss were disembarked to work on fortifications at the Môle, but on coming ashore many were cut down by Irish soldiers of the Dillon Regiment; the rest were reembarked and sent back to Le Cap. Neither the story nor those who told it merit much confidence.[92]

An alternative version comes from the French civil commissioner Sonthonax, who served in Saint Domingue from September 1792 to July 1794 and abolished slavery there in August 1793. He stated that the Swiss were held on a prison ship at the entrance to the Môle's harbor far distant from the town. About a month after their arrival, a deputation from Port-au-Prince en route to Le Cap boarded the ship at night and, bringing the Swiss up on deck chained in pairs, beheaded sixty of them. Those who did the killings were called the Saliniers (salt-pan workers), a paramilitary group of poor whites from the Artibonite plain. Like the sailors and urban unemployed of Port-au-Prince, they were then fighting a losing battle against local free coloreds and their white conservative allies, and they may have welcomed such an act of vengeance.[93] Sonthonax thought the Colonial Assembly was behind them. This is quite possible, but letters by the town council and mayor of Port-au-Prince strongly suggest their involvement. "It appears," Leremboure wrote a correspondent on March 12th, "that they will be killed."[94]

The survivors of this massacre were kept confined on their floating prison for over a year. How many they were and how long they remained at the Môle is uncertain.[95] Neglected by all government authorities, the majority apparently died of disease. The historian Madiou claimed that twenty were released at some point and sent back to Port-au-Prince to worsen relations between slaves and free coloreds. A Patriot lawyer living in Le Cap recalled that "fortunately" many died of disease but also that local colonists were allowed to hire them out and, finding them "good slaves," kept them, so their numbers dwindled.[96] In mid-May 1793, when Civil Commissioner Sonthonax finally intervened, there were only twenty-nine still alive on the prison ship. The French Republic was now at war, and Sonthonax had begun to form a regiment of armed slaves. He did not enlist the remaining Swiss, however, to avoid exciting the colonists' hostility. Instead, he freed them and placed the nineteen who were not sick as seamen on board the warship *Jupiter* at Cap Français.[97]

This was not a good choice. The week before, the vessel's French crew had refused to accept a detachment of free colored troops as marines on the ship and chanted in provocation, "No, no! No night-faces!" The next month, the admiral whose flagship was the *Jupiter* noted in his journal his seamen's hatred for "the enemy color."[98] The crew participated in the attempted coup against Sonthonax on June 20th, which was also a race riot and ended in burning Cap Français to the ground. A dozen of the Swiss may have escaped or been killed in the battle, for the crew rolls of the *Jupiter* show only seven left on board in August, after the vessel had arrived in the United States along with thousands of refugees from Le Cap. Thereafter they disappear from view.[99] One of those left behind, named Joseph, "former general of the Swiss," turns up in September 1793, after the abolition of slavery, leading a force of pro-republican blacks in the northwest, between Cap Français and Môle Saint Nicolas.[100] Another, less fortunate, accompanied Sonthonax back to Port-au-Prince only to be imprisoned in June 1794, when the British captured the town and reimposed slavery.[101]

Repercussions

A central enigma of Saint Domingue's slave revolution is the failure of the western plains to produce a major autonomous uprising as in the north. This political backwardness, as C. L. R. James called it, does not seem related to the structure of the slave population so much as to the regional strength of the free colored community and to the fact that it was mobilizing at the very moment the northern slaves rebelled.[102] For potential slave rebels in the west, it made most sense to see what they could get within the ranks of the free colored insurrection. The Swiss episode thus might be seen as co-opting and neutralizing slave dissidence in the countryside round the capital. If the west produced a Jean-François or a Boukman, it is likely he enlisted with Bauvais and Rigaud and died at Môle Saint Nicolas in March 1792.

The deportation of the Swiss was welcomed by whites everywhere in Saint Domingue as creating an obstacle to any future alliance between free coloreds and slaves.[103] Some free coloreds had feared this would be the outcome, and their spokesmen later complained that the slaves blamed them for the killing of the Swiss.[104] Hypocritical Patriot politicians publicized nonwhite complicity in the affair and even accused heartless *gens de couleur* of choosing deportation in an attempt to worsen Anglo-French relations.[105] The nineteenth-century historian Ardouin, however, argued that slaves knew most free coloreds had opposed the deportation, and therefore no such rift developed between them.[106] It certainly did not prevent them from cooperating with devastating effect in March 1792 in three nearly simultaneous revolts in the western plains (although they occurred before the Môle massacre probably was known).[107] In any event, those three rebellions mark a new stage in slave–free colored cooperation, a measured move away from the cautious tactics of the Swiss episode, and a shift in the balance of power between the two sectors. After *l'affaire des Suisses,* the free colored leadership remained committed to slavery but more willing to risk slave revolt.

These rebellions of March 1792 resulted in the freeing and arming as rural police of 100 or more of their participants—the outcome the *hommes de couleur* had sought for the Swiss. Although the arming of slaves was far from novel in 1791, the free coloreds' successful use of the Swiss may have increased slave-owners' willingness to risk the deployment of black soldiery. There was no comparable example during the first two years of the revolution, but by the beginning of 1792, whites and free coloreds, radicals and royalists, were all raising units of armed slaves.[108]

The Swiss also proved to be pioneers in the matter of deportation. During the turbulent years of the French Revolutionary War, the three main colonial powers in the Caribbean were to expel or relocate many groups they regarded as threatening. The Bay of Honduras became a favored destination. The British deported and abandoned there black insurgents from Grenada and Martinique and more than 2,000 Black Caribs from St. Vincent. Slaves from Cap Français also show up in Belize in 1794.[109] The Spanish relocated to Honduras more than 300 of the original 1791 insurgents and their families who had served them as auxiliary troops, besides sending 200 more to Panama, Mexico, and Florida. Prisoners of war were usually jailed in the Caribbean or sent to Europe, but in 1797 we find the British dumping on the Cuban coast ninety-one sick prisoners from Saint Domingue.[110] During the Haitian independence war of 1802–1803, massacre tended to supplant deportation, but the French deported at least 640 prisoners to Europe and abandoned many others on the South American coast.[111] At the same time, they deported at least 2,000 blacks from reconquered Guadeloupe. Apart from 200 discovered on the coast of New Granada and perhaps 700 others jailed in Europe, their final destination remains unknown.[112]

Such actions on the part of vengeful colonialists are perhaps not surprising. It is ironic that the complicity of free colored revolutionaries in the deportation of the Swiss has always attracted more comment than that of their white counterparts. Five years after the deportation, Sonthonax, appealing for black support against his free colored rivals, attacked his political adversary Pinchinat as "this Pinchinat who in 1791 sacrificed 300 blacks to the rage of the Port-au-Prince agitators . . . in payment for their loyalty to the men of color and for the blood they shed for their rights."[113] In 1794, the free coloreds were accused of the murder of the Swiss by the French government agent Victor Hugues, who was then the hero of slave emancipation in Guadeloupe, though formerly a baker in Port-au-Prince.[114] Most striking of all, on the eve of the War of the South that ranged former slaves against former free coloreds, Toussaint Louverture harangued the *gens de couleur* of Port-au-Prince as potential traitors and, seeking a symbol of free colored perfidy, evoked the case of the Swiss, "tied up, thrown in a ship . . . and abandoned on a desert isle, where they perished miserably."[115]

In the propaganda war of the revolution, *l'affaire des Suisses* undermined the moral authority the free coloreds hoped to claim as champions of the colony's nonwhites, and it would long remain a sensitive topic with Haiti's historians. Historians from Haiti's light-complexioned elite have been those most concerned to argue the irrelevance of color to this, as to other, episodes in the country's past and to put the free coloreds' actions in the best light. They foregrounded the roles of Rigaud, Daguin, and Pétion and emphasized the machiavellianism of the French. Beaubrun Ardouin, more than his counterparts Saint-Rémy and Madiou, acknowledged free colored guilt and condemned the deportation as a betrayal, but in a typically paternalistic fashion—the free coloreds should have been the "natural protectors" of the slaves. In the twentieth century, black nationalist historians in Haiti such as H. Pauléus Sannon, Gérard Laurent, Lorimer Denis, and François Duvalier dealt with the free coloreds in a less defensive fashion and usually claimed a more important military role for the Swiss. Stressing class interest or color prejudice, these writers condemned the free coloreds without offering their predecessors' justifications. Edner Brutus claimed that the name *Suisses*, far from being a neutral term or one that expressed admiration, indicated the free coloreds' contempt for their auxiliaries. Emmanuel Paul seemed to disown the Swiss as mere tools of the men of color in contrast to his heroes, the maroons. Conversely, other historians who also put slave agency at the center of their narratives have presented the Swiss themselves as maroons. In the case of C. L. R. James and Jean Fouchard, this was done without elaboration. Carolyn Fick, as seen, makes a historically specific argument. Cuban historian José Luciano Franco romantically reinvented the Swiss as hardened mountain guerrillas and, like many of the black nationalists, considered the free coloreds complicitous in their murder.[116]

How far the Swiss controversy genuinely hindered relations between free nonwhites and the black masses is less certain. The lesson the most militant slaves must have drawn from the episode is that they needed to fight their own battles, and there is no doubt that the emergence of autonomous slave leaders in the west marked the following years. If the enigmatic Hyacinthe could be counted sometimes as an ally, even a tool, of the free coloreds, the hostility to them of leaders such as Dieudonné and Pompé in the mountains behind the capital and Mamzelle and Alaou in the plain is striking. The fact Pinchinat and Bauvais had two of these leaders (Alaou and Bébé Coustard) killed whereas Rigaud (the future ally of Lamour Dérance and Lafortune) immediately pursued a policy of arming and freeing slave soldiers makes an interesting parallel with their respective roles in settling the Swiss crisis. Similarly, although all of the leaders accepted slave emancipation in 1793, only Jean-Pierre Lambert, the elderly free black who supported deportation, rallied the following year to the British invaders who came to restore slavery.[117]

Lambert's actions raise the question of whether free blacks tended to display political tendencies different from those of free people of mixed racial descent. Notwithstanding the apparent irrelevance of color to the case of the Swiss, some evidence suggests that during the revolution free blacks exhibited two contrary characteristics; they were more likely to combine with both slaves and whites than were other free coloreds. Further research is needed to substantiate these contrary tendencies and to know if they can be reduced to differences in economic class or whether status divisions related to phenotype were also a factor.[118] The two tendencies are reflected in the subjects of the two following chapters, Toussaint Louverture and Jean Kina.

8   The "Volte-Face" of
Toussaint Louverture

Historians of the Haitian Revolution invariably consider its turning point to have come some time in the spring of 1794, when the black general Toussaint Louverture rounded on his Spanish allies and rallied to the French Republic, whose fortunes were then near their lowest ebb. France looked close to losing its immensely wealthy colony of Saint Domingue to Spanish and British invaders, who were determined to shore up its crumbling slave regime. In a brief campaign, however, Spain's hopes of conquest were smashed and French rule in Saint Domingue was saved. England's chances of seizing the richest prize in the Caribbean practically vanished, and the cause of black emancipation gained a champion whose talents were to ensure its eventual triumph against all attempts to restore slavery in *la perle des Antilles*.

Historiography

For an event of such significance, there is surprising historiographical confusion about not only why but also when and where this volte-face took place. The main point at issue is its connection with the decree of 16 pluviôse an II (February 4, 1794), by which the French Convention abolished slavery but which became known in its colonies at an uncertain date.[1] How far, one wonders, was Toussaint acting idealistically, throwing in his lot with the underdog to fight for a cause he had long supported? Conversely, to what extent did he change sides for reasons unconnected with the liberty of the blacks?

In the best-known work on the revolution, C. L. R. James stated that Toussaint, learning of the emancipation decree "sometime in May," immediately informed the French he would join them but delayed doing so until "one morning in June."[2] The first major Haitian historian, Thomas Madiou, gave a similar version but specified June 25th and situated the event in the small mountain town of Marmelade.[3] Beaubrun Ardouin, on the other hand, who provides the most substantial treatment of the question, claimed Toussaint was indifferent to the cause of black freedom but, resenting his mistreatment by the Spanish and even fearing for his safety, he began negotiations with the French commander, Laveaux, in April and raised the republican flag in the port of Gonaïves on May 4th.[4] Pauléus Sannon, to many the best of Toussaint's biographers, broadly followed Ardouin but insisted that Toussaint always fought for liberty. He implied, moreover, that Toussaint knew of the emancipation decree before he staged his revolt—not at Gonaïves, nor at Marmelade, where "nothing particular happened," but in the mountain canton of Ennery.[5] A more recent historian of the revolution has asserted that Toussaint, "both a power-seeker and sincere abolitionist," was working with Laveaux as early as January 3rd but that not until May 6th did he strike, massacring the Spaniards in the frontier town of San Rafael.[6]

Toussaint's motivation may well remain a mystery. Like his role in the 1791 uprising, similarly shrouded in conflicting rumor, the events of these months are among the most obscure of that strange twilight period when Saint Domingue was transformed into Haiti. Secrecy and duplicity were perhaps too integral a part of Toussaint's character, some might say, for his actions ever to be satisfactorily explained. The evidence, it must be admitted, will support the most diverse interpretations; hence the many guises of the historiographical Toussaint, from the flawed radical hero of James's *Black Jacobins* to the self-aggrandizing and racist "Ancien Regime revolutionary" of Pierre Pluchon; from Ralph Korngold's altruistic Citizen Toussaint to the ruthlessly calculating *Führer* of Erwin Rüsch.[7] Yet, to date, the evidence has never been either accurately or impartially presented. The purpose of this analysis is to provide as clear a picture of the facts as is possible and to suggest the likeliest lines of interpretation, partly by locating some of the errors in the secondary works, partly by presenting some new material from British and Spanish archives. This includes two previously unknown letters by Toussaint that offer a fascinating glimpse of him at a crucial moment in his life. They are printed at the end of this piece. I have also used some little-known Spanish and French sources and critically reexamined the oft-quoted Laveaux Correspondence.

Taking only the most serious of the secondary works, we find that Toussaint's decisive break with Spain has been associated with four different events, given four different locales, and assigned four different dates. Either on June 25th, May 6th, May 4th, or some earlier occasion, he either attacked the camp of his rival Georges Biassou at Ennery or stormed the town of Gonaïves (and was wounded in the assault) or suddenly massacred either a colonists' patrol or the Spanish garrison at or near Marmelade or San Rafael after one or both parties had attended morning mass. To make matters worse, events, locales, and dates have been permutated by historians seemingly at will. Even then, no one account seems to be completely correct.

James and the other historians who placed the volte-face in June took their chronology from the unreliable Pamphile de Lacroix, who himself seems to have copied with variations from two scurrilous works published in 1802, those of Dubroca and Cousin d'Avallon.[8] Toussaint's famous letter to General Laveaux of May 18, 1794, which James cites, clearly states that by this time he was already fighting on the side of the Republic.[9] The two earliest dates mentioned can also be eliminated. Ott's suggestion of collaboration in early January results from misreading the date of a letter in the Laveaux Correspondence.[10] A massacre at San Rafael is also out of the question, since Toussaint did not capture the town until October.[11]

The story of the revolt at Ennery, found in Pauléus Sannon and many other works, derives ultimately from the writings of Toussaint's son, Isaac.[12] His confused and dateless narrative telescopes all manner of events and is thus chronologically misleading; it is also given to some very dubious assertions. Toussaint's attack on Biassou can be shown to have occurred between March 22nd and 26th, over a month before the Gonaïves affair.[13] Though of great significance, it did not represent a rupture of relations with Spain. Fighting between the black commanders had not been uncommon, and by mid-April a rapprochement between the two generals had been arranged.[14] This was due to Colonel Juan Lleonart, the commander at San Rafael, who actually wrote of Toussaint on this occasion, "It is on him that we can count for his judgment, prudence, loyalty, and piety."[15] Hence, one can disregard Isaac Louverture's claim that his father had announced to Lleonart his change of loyalties and was already acting under Laveaux's orders when he fell on Biassou's troops at Ennery.[16] Equally fanciful is Ardouin's suggestion that Toussaint spent April immolating all he could reach.[17]

Ardouin supported his choice of May 4th for Toussaint's rallying to Laveaux with no evidence at all. He probably took the date from the 1850 biography by Saint-Rémy, although they apparently were not even describing the same event.[18] Setting aside Isaac Louverture's account, we find, therefore, that Dubroca and Saint-Rémy are the most basic of the secondary works and the starting points of two rival interpretations. Dubroca's source is unknown. Saint-Rémy cites as his reference Toussaint's May 18th letter. This, however, makes no mention of May 4th. One thus reaches a dead end.

Marmelade and Gonaïves

Toussaint and Laveaux, in their own versions of these events, unfortunately contradict each other. Toussaint, in later years, claimed to have joined the Republic both after emancipation was proclaimed and after the civil commissioners, Sonthonax and Polverel, had returned to France; that is to say, in June 1794.[19] For the reasons already stated, this cannot have been true, though it doubtless helps explain why so many historians have put the volte-face at so late a date.[20] Laveaux, on the other hand, stated at different times that Toussaint "fought against us until April 6th" and "placed himself under the banner of the Republic on May 6th."[21] Although one of the dates could be a confused version of the other, Ardouin argued persuasively that they refer to the beginning and end of a negotiation between the two men. Yet he rejected the latter in favor of May 4th, which he thought was the day Gonaïves was captured.[22] Although Laveaux's *Compte rendu* is not always accurate, it may on this occasion be correct.

Broadly speaking, there are two main versions of the black general's volte-face: an attack on Gonaïves and a sudden massacre, probably at Marmelade. Either or both seem to have taken place on May 4th or 6th. According to Dubroca, the massacre preceded the assault, which is also what one finds in two manuscript accounts that detail an ambush in the mountains behind Gonaïves.[23] Such a blatant example of personal treachery as is described in these works surely would have left little doubt as to Toussaint's loyalty.[24] Indeed, these sources present the massacre as the occasion when the black leader finally threw off the mask, whereas the documents discussed below suggest that he had not openly broken with the Spanish before May 5th, after the attack on Gonaïves. Since these documents also prove Toussaint to have been in Marmelade on May 6th, there is reason to believe that the time and place of his volte-face might be fixed with a degree of confidence.[25]

Unfortunately, other pieces of evidence suggest that such confidence would be premature. In a little-known letter to the navy minister, written in 1796, Toussaint in fact stated that he joined Laveaux on May 10, 1794.[26] A secretary or typesetter could well have mistaken *dix* (ten) for *six*, which would leave the May 6th hypothesis intact. However, it is strange that the Spanish vicar of St. Rafael made no mention of any event in Marmelade, a dozen miles to the northwest, when he wrote on May 10th of a recent attack on Gonaïves and the panic it was causing among local refugees. This suggests two possibilities. Either the route between the frontier town and the mountains was cut; or, if a massacre did take place in the mountain town, it was not before May 10th. Most disconcerting of all, no documentary proof of any massacre at Marmelade has ever been found.[27]

What, then, had happened at Gonaïves? On May 4th, the British commander of the troops occupying the port of Saint Marc wrote to the governor of Jamaica that at Gonaïves, some twenty-five miles up the coast in Spanish-held territory, there had come about "a most strange circumstance . . . so complicated, so extraordinary, so mysterious as to baffle all conjecture." The black commanders, whose forces the invading Spaniards used as auxiliaries, had suddenly attacked the town—on April 29th. On being repulsed, they sent an ultimatum in the name of "the King of the French" demanding the surrender of the Spanish garrison. Two hundred troops managed to withdraw inland to the Pont à l'Ester, while over 500 inhabitants fled on board ship to Saint Marc. Another 150 were said to have been killed.[28] Further inland, at Petite Rivière, the local Spanish commandant was equally perplexed. "Brigands," most of them *gens de couleur* (a term that usually designated free persons of mixed racial descent), had murdered many of the whites guarding his outposts. Patrols he sent into the area failed to return. It seemed that a general conspiracy was afoot.[29]

On May 18th and on other occasions, Toussaint was to claim responsibility for the events at Gonaïves, though regretting he had been unable to prevent the massacre that took place. Hence, it is of great interest to find him on May 5th, almost a week after the rebellion, violently protesting his innocence of what had happened and asking the inhabitants and parish priest to return to their homes.[30] Furthermore, the sincerity of his protestations was apparently accepted by the Spanish commander who had been driven out of Gonaïves. Having intercepted Toussaint's two letters, he wrote immediately to him expressing his pleasure that his hopes had been confirmed that Toussaint had no part in the rebellion. "No, you will not have forgotten you swore before God and man to serve His Majesty faithfully and to die for him." Rather more significantly, he noted that Toussaint's signature had been absent from the rebels' ultimatum.[31]

Thus, the fact emerges that if Toussaint was behind the revolt at Gonaïves, he was, as late as May 5th, still keeping in the background, sitting on the fence, it seems, between Catholic, royalist Spain and the godless, kingless Republic. Was he waiting for something, reluctant to show his hand? Or had he been overtaken by the onrush of events and had not yet caught up with them? Whichever the case,[32] within twenty-four hours of writing these letters, he left the coastal plain for the mountains of Marmelade and, apparently, went into open revolt.

Toussaint and Slave Emancipation

The chronology of Toussaint's public actions can thus only tentatively be established. His motives and private dealings, still more so, remain matters of conjecture. Given his reputation for cunning and double-dealing, one can well see him secretly organizing the mutiny at Gonaïves, waiting to see its outcome, and covering himself until he could strike again at an unsuspecting target. This is clearly the likeliest interpretation. Yet several points in the correspondence just quoted raise doubts that the seizure of Gonaïves was really the *coup de main* planned to open his republican career that Toussaint later claimed.

First, the rebels were said to have acted in the name of "the King of the French." This could have been some sort of smoke screen put up by the insurgents, a deliberate red herring, but the royalist sentiments of many of James's Black Jacobins appear to have been genuine.[33] It is at least conceivable that some obscure mutiny broke out that Toussaint then turned in a republican direction. On the other hand, this report may simply be in error. Another early, though not eyewitness, account stated that after sacking Gonaïves, the rebels left a republican flag flying in the town.[34] Second, the rebels in the surrounding countryside seemed to be mainly free men of color, not blacks. Although Toussaint himself was a freedman and his army included officers of color, this perhaps suggests a volte-face against Spain that came from another quarter. The point will be taken up later. Third, the postscript to Toussaint's letter to the refugees from Gonaïves shows that he was not, in fact, sure of what he was going to do. The proposed visit to Marmelade actually made him change his mind.

Attention is focused, then, on the events of May 5th. Curiously, it was on this day that news of the emancipation decree, passed February 4th, first reached Guadeloupe.[35] It was also, we are told by Garran-Coulon, the "official historian" of the revolution, the date borne by Laveaux's first letter to Toussaint.[36] This letter seems to have been the cause of Toussaint's (possibly momentous) journey into the mountains and the reason Laveaux dated his volte-face from the following day. Did the French general tell him that the National Convention had agreed to abolish slavery? Apparently not. In this first surviving letter of the two men's correspondence, the general merely informed the black leader that "France would be pleased to count [him] among its children."[37] The emancipation decree would not be officially proclaimed in Saint Domingue until the corvette *L'Espérance* sailed into the south coast port of Jacmel with a copy on June 8th.[38]

Yet in May, the decree was already three months old, time enough for news to seep through to Saint Domingue. Furthermore, in a daring bluff, Civil Commissioner Sonthonax, as Yves Bénot recently discovered, had already stated that the Convention had abolished slavery in all French colonies.[39] This claim (correct, of course, but evidently a guess) was made at the end of a proclamation issued in Port-au-Prince on February 27th. The questions are whether Toussaint knew of this proclamation and whether he believed it. As the colony was then a patchwork of French, Spanish, and British zones, communication was difficult. Presumably the proclamation was known to Toussaint but, by May, enough time had elapsed without any decree being circulated for the true nature of Sonthonax's bluff to have become apparent.

Laveaux later claimed in a speech to the Conseil des Cinq Cents that Toussaint had always fought for black freedom, that he thought only a king could grant it, but that when he, Laveaux, convinced him that the Republic had agreed to it, he changed sides. This became republican orthodoxy. Yet, in his *Compte rendu*, Laveaux implied he did not learn of the decree before the arrival of *L'Espérance*, long after Toussaint's volte-face.[40] It is also evident that when the civil commissioners wrote to Toussaint in June welcoming him to the republican camp, they knew nothing of the Convention's decision, even though Sonthonax, too, in later years sometimes repeated the orthodox version.[41] Garran-Coulon specifically stated that Toussaint joined the French before he knew of the emancipation decree.[42] Toussaint himself gave two different versions of his change of allegiance.[43] One links it with the decree of 16 pluviôse, but the other speaks only of a growing respect for Laveaux and makes an order to attack Cap Français the immediate cause of his break with Spain. In Toussaint's correspondence there is no mention of the decree until early July, when he received a copy. He found it "most consoling."[44] The best way one can reconcile these different versions is to assume that Laveaux, at most, can have told Toussaint off the record that he thought the Republic would abolish slavery as Civil Commissioner Sonthonax had requested. There could only have been expectation, not certitude; it was a gamble.

As a first hypothesis, therefore, one may postulate that until Toussaint had received Laveaux's invitation of May 5th, no matter what had happened before, he was still hesitating about which way to turn and that when he finally decided, he was still unaware that France had abolished slavery. This does not necessarily mean that he was indifferent to the emancipation question. Although his rallying to the Republic was not a direct result of the decree of 16 pluviôse, it was still an act of commitment to the cause of black freedom that Sonthonax had openly espoused eight months before. Perhaps one should ask not why Toussaint joined the French when he did but why he had not done so previously. His aspirations might have remained constant, while the circumstances for implementing them had changed. The question then becomes one of establishing Toussaint's libertarian credentials, of demonstrating his support for a complete abolition of slavery rather than for some compromise solution that rewarded the slave insurgents or only their leaders while leaving most slaves enslaved. Such a demonstration is far more difficult than Toussaint's defenders have imagined, but it is not as implausible as his detractors have claimed.

During the negotiations of December 1791 between insurgents and colonists, Toussaint was closely associated with an offer to help restore slavery in return for the freedom of only a handful of leaders.[45] Less well known is his support for a similar measure in the summer of 1792 that also would have forced most insurgents back onto the plantations.[46] Although these were crisis points for the rebels when the arrival of European troops was imminently expected, there is no evidence of Toussaint supporting general emancipation (as it was called) at any time during the first two years of the slave insurrection. For some historians, from Haitian nationalist Thomas Madiou to French conservative Pierre Pluchon, this did not distinguish Toussaint from any other of the main rebel leaders, who in their view were motivated more by self-interest than by libertarian ideology.[47] Outright demands to end slavery were rare, although there was certainly one, a long letter in very stylish French dated July 1792 and signed "Jean-François, Biassou, Belair."[48] Gérard Laurent's suggestion, however, that the real author was Toussaint hiding behind the name of his adolescent nephew, Charles Belair, has little merit.[49]

Toussaint did stand apart from other major leaders in two important respects. He did not round up enslaved women and children for sale to the Spanish, a practice that became a source of great friction among the rebels.[50] And as a freedman, he was obviously not fighting for his own freedom. In early 1792, he could have abandoned the insurgent slaves, as did other free nonwhites, and taken advantage of a government amnesty and the abolition of racial discrimination. In this light, his advocating a compromise solution to the slave insurrection looks less selfish and more pragmatic.

The main rebel leaders, Jean-François and Biassou, allied with the Spanish in May 1793 in response to their offer of freedom, land, and privileges for slave soldiers and their families. Toussaint followed suit a little later, probably in early June.[51] One must remember that when the insurgents joined the Spanish, the republicans had not yet made any offer to the slaves in rebellion, and they continued for several months to offer them less than the Spanish, apart from having abolished racial discrimination among free persons. In mid-May, the civil commissioners began to free slaves who already had been armed by their owners and local governments, and on June 21st they recognized as free those who would fight for the Republic, provided (a restriction introduced July 2nd) they joined French-controlled units. The offer was extended (July 11th) to soldiers' families, if the soldiers were legally married. Not until August 29th did Sonthonax bring into the picture the majority of the slave population by emancipating all enslaved people in the north province. Even then, the freedom he offered was a form of profit-sharing forced labor. Equally as important, throughout the summer the Spanish looked much more like a winning side than the embattled French Republic, which was suddenly at war with all of Europe.

Nevertheless, some time before the middle of June, before the Spanish had spread rumors of the Republic's collapse, Toussaint made overtures to General Laveaux but was rebuffed because his conditions were unacceptable. We know this because he recalled the incident in his May 18, 1794, letter to the French officer. Neither Laveaux nor Sonthonax ever admitted making such a blunder, but the "Mémoire abrégé" claims that Toussaint, unlike Jean-François and Biassou, was willing to join the French at this time and that this was why the Spaniards initially mistrusted him.[52] Spanish sources show the republicans in the spring of 1793 negotiating with a rebel leader at Haut du Cap, and Toussaint is known in these months to have been camped nearby at Port François (the modern Labadie beach).[53] One further notes that in 1794 both Laveaux and Toussaint referred to his volte-face as his "return to the Republic."[54]

Unfortunately, we do not know what Toussaint's conditions of alliance were. If ever there was a letter containing these overtures, it has not survived, contrary to what some have written.[55] According to biographer Pierre Pluchon, Toussaint called for recognition of the French monarchy. This is true of later letters he sent in the period June to August 1793, but in this instance, the claim was pure guesswork.[56] More influential, and dishonest, was the interpretation of an earlier biographer, Gragnon-Lacoste. When he printed the May 18, 1794 letter, he brazenly interpolated into the text concerning these overtures the words "black freedom and a full amnesty."[57] This was sheer fraud, but it has been copied by the most prominent historians of the revolution—Victor Schoelcher, Horace Pauléus Sannon, and C. L. R. James, among others.[58] James further claimed Toussaint put forward the same demands to the Spanish at this time, but his evidence is extremely flimsy and it refers, moreover, to a later period.[59]

There is nonetheless an intriguing letter that the elderly African leader Pierrot sent to Governor Galbaud that deserves attention. With a false air of naïveté, Pierrot stated on June 4, 1793 he had heard that the French, like the Spanish and English, were advocating general emancipation and that he would like written confirmation of this. Because Pierrot was camped, like Toussaint, behind the Morne du Cap at Port François, the two men may well have acted in concert.[60] Even so, this was (ostensibly) an inquiry, not a statement of terms; Galbaud was not Laveaux, and Pierrot was not Toussaint. There is in fact no documentary proof that connects the black general to the idea of ending slavery before Civil Commissioner Sonthonax adopted the policy. This is one reason why Thomas Madiou wrote of the first years of the slave insurrection that the idea of general emancipation "was not completely formulated in the minds of either the blacks or the men of color. It was the civil commissioners, Sonthonax and Polverel who, by the act of August 29, 1793, rallied liberal-minded men, black, brown, and white, around the tree of liberty."[61]

Madiou perhaps conceded more to the French Revolution's influence on the Haitian Revolution than is warranted. Nevertheless, Toussaint's first recorded statements in favor of completely abolishing slavery were clearly a response to Sonthonax's final decision to adopt general emancipation. In a letter to a camp of Cap Français free coloreds dated August 25th, Toussaint declared himself "the first to stand up for" general emancipation, a cause he had "always supported . . . and having begun, I will finish." Four days later, in a similar letter, he dictated the lines almost all his biographers cite that begin: "I am Toussaint Louverture. . . . I want liberty and equality to reign in Saint Domingue."[62] Although the first letter preceded the emancipation proclamation, Toussaint evidently was reacting to the large public demonstration held in Le Cap on August 25th that presented Sonthonax with an antislavery petition and caused him to draw up his emancipation decree.[63]

Most historians treat these two documents as defining the man and his mission; some see in them proof that he was the instigator of the 1791 uprising. It is therefore striking that the conservative historians Rüsch and Pluchon completely ignore these letters. For Pluchon, the "real" Toussaint is revealed in other letters with a very royalist tone that say nothing of emancipation, which Toussaint continued to send his opponents up to this time.[64] The letters of August 25th and 29th are certainly less dramatic than they appear, in edited form, in the pages of historians such as Schoelcher and James. The references to emancipation in fact were made amid a melange of arguments that mix racial solidarity and the restoration of the monarchy, stability for plantation agriculture, divine punishment, and vengeance for Vincent Ogé. Moreover, although these letters represent the first known usage by the leader of the sobriquet *l'ouverture* (the opening), it had been adopted at least several weeks previously and was thus not necessarily connected with the idea of emancipation.[65] However, if the conservatives are justified in a measure of skepticism toward this suddenly declared interest in ending slavery, simply ignoring it does nothing to strengthen their case.

Here we have Toussaint, a commander attached to the Spanish army, exhorting republican blacks to join him in the fight for liberty and equality and claiming to have been the first to fight for both. If he was sincere, he was deliberately interpreting Spain's limited offer of freedom to mean general emancipation. This may well be how he increased his fighting force from a few hundred to 4,000 while serving His Catholic Majesty, committed though he was to maintaining the plantation regime.[66] On the other hand, Spanish records give no hint for at least six months that Toussaint favored a broader scheme of emancipation than the one the Spanish supported. The evidence is thus difficult to interpret. If he favored general emancipation, why did he go on fighting the republicans until the following spring?

The nineteenth-century radical Victor Schoelcher found the question impossible to answer.[67] Yet reasons are not hard to find. As Sonthonax's decree was "unofficial" and the commissioner's position precarious, one can see why blacks might not have taken him too seriously at first. There was still no point in backing the losing side. In his epistolary jousting with the republicans in August, Toussaint at least pretended to believe the Republic had fallen (as it nearly did) and that the monarchy was restored.[68] Moreover, while Toussaint may have been restrained by his royalist inclinations, as he said at the time, or seduced by the attractions of Spanish service, his forces were not yet large enough to challenge the army Spain was expected to assemble or the other black generals. Finally, the choice between the proslavery Spanish and the abolitionist republicans was not quite as Manichean as it might appear. While freedom under Sonthonax meant little more than remunerated serfdom, the Spanish in 1793 were in no position to be able to force blacks back into plantation work in those areas where they had abandoned it. The nervous Governor García, to his critics' dismay, avoided setting a quota on how many slaves Spain would recruit, and as long as most auxiliary troops had no firearms, the line between slaves and soldiers in the Spanish zone probably remained fluid.[69] Blacks in Saint Domingue therefore spent the fall of 1793 waiting to see whether the Convention would ratify Sonthonax's decree and how Spanish policy would develop once planters sought to return to their estates.

Toussaint's credentials as a libertarian amount to little more than the following two points. First, as a freedman who had remained with the slave insurgents through the dark days of 1792, he must have been committed to at least some reform of slavery, since self-interest and ambition cannot satisfactorily explain this behavior. Second, by the end of August 1793, he was quietly giving lip service to the idea of general emancipation and claiming always to have fought for it. Evidently it was not a cause he was prepared to back without prospects for success, but as with his refusal to sell slaves to the Spanish, it set him apart from the other main insurgent leaders. So, too, did Toussaint's willingness, before joining the Spanish, to rally to the egalitarian Republic—albeit on unknown terms—and he again hinted in early August he was willing to do so.[70] Toussaint's alliance with Spain was thus a slightly shaky affair, belated and something of a second-best choice. Viewed in this light, the volte-face might still be interpreted as an idealistic act, part of a long-term commitment to improving the life of the slaves.

Personal Politics

Yet Toussaint also had good personal reasons for leaving the Spanish. Isaac Louverture described his father's about-face entirely as a reaction to the jealous plotting of Jean-François, the slave-trading of Biassou, and the vindictiveness of certain Spanish commanders. He made no mention at all of the emancipation issue.[71] Documentary support for such an interpretation is quite strong. At some time before joining the Spanish, Toussaint had gained the enmity of the vain and all-powerful Jean-François and, apparently, was briefly held captive by him.[72] Although Biassou came to his rescue, Toussaint progressively wearied, as the Spaniards observed, of the anarchic behavior of this gross and overbearing man, whom he eclipsed as a military leader but who claimed to be his chief.[73] Both men, however, had to take refuge on Spanish territory in the autumn of 1793, when they were threatened by Jean-François, who had Biassou's nephew Michaud shot.[74] Caught in the struggle for supremacy between the two main generals, Toussaint was attacked and routed by Petit Thomas, a disgruntled officer who had been jailed by Biassou and then found protection with his rival. In November 1793, the Spanish managed to patch over these differences by administering oaths of obedience and strictly delimiting the territories of Jean-François and Biassou.[75]

Early in 1794, Spanish troops were sent to garrison the town of Gonaïves that Toussaint had taken in December. In his absence, they victimized several of his subordinate officers who had previously served the Republic but who had been maintained by him in their commands. At about the same time, Toussaint's immediate superior, Matías de Armona, who had notably favored him, was replaced by Juan de Lleonart, a man distrusted by the black auxiliaries. Most important, Lleonart failed to support Toussaint in the feud that erupted in March with Biassou, who had been stealing the supplies of Toussaint's troops and selling their wives and children as slaves. Lleonart arrested Toussaint's nephew Moïse and briefly took hostage his wife and children.[76] This feuding proved a serious threat to Toussaint. It cost the life of his brother Pierre and caused a mutiny among his own troops. It also emphasized his inferior position in the trio of black generals. Although the Spaniards privately acknowledged the exceptional nature of Toussaint's abilities,[77] any ambitions he may have had for higher command remained blocked by the prior claims of Biassou and, particularly, Jean-François.[78] Pamphile de Lacroix was wrong to assert that Toussaint changed sides to gain promotion from colonel to general, since the reverse actually took place.[79] Toussaint doubtless knew, however, that under the Republic he would find more recognition and less rivalry.

To counter the idealistic interpretation of Toussaint's actions, Beaubrun Ardouin stressed these factors and printed two letters to Governor García that he found in the Santo Domingo archives.[80] Dated March 20th and 27th, they show an effusively royalist Toussaint acquiescing in plans to force the blacks back to the plantations. Yet, to the detriment of Ardouin's argument, they also suggest that it was precisely this attempt to restore the slave regime that lay behind the breach with Biassou. Toussaint protested to the governor of Santo Domingo that the move was premature. This might mean that the volte-face was precipitated not so much by French offers of freedom as by Spanish moves to restore slavery.

Finally, in a letter to Governor García dated April 4, 1794 by a colonist in the Spanish-occupied zone named Laplace, we find Toussaint out of grace with the Spanish authorities and accused of stirring up the plantation slaves by declaring general emancipation. The charge was repeated by one of Biassou's white secretaries in May.[81] There might be as much truth to this as in the accompanying allegation that he was plotting to massacre all the whites; the letter's tone is very polemical. Alternatively, Toussaint by now may indeed have been proclaiming the liberty of the blacks but using it simply as a vehicle for his personal ambition. This is the interpretation of Rüsch and Pluchon, and it has a certain built-in invulnerability. However, the weak point in their case is that it omits consideration of Toussaint's curious behavior between June and August 1793.

At the very least, therefore, one can conclude that before the emancipation decree could possibly have been known in Saint Domingue, Toussaint was already at loggerheads with the Spanish and associated with the idea of general emancipation. If we also consider Laveaux's statement that Toussaint fought against the French until April 6, 1794 and Ardouin's suggestion that an undated letter from Toussaint to Laveaux mentioned by Garran-Coulon dates from the same day, one arrives at a second hypothesis.[82] That is, that from early April Toussaint was seeking alliance with France, perhaps because friction with the Spanish had led him to pursue general emancipation or because his pursuit of general emancipation had led to friction with the Spanish.

The Balance of Power

A third hypothesis is that Toussaint's volte-face was motivated not only by frustrated ambition and concern for the liberty of the blacks but also by an appreciation that the tide was turning in the struggle for Saint Domingue. This is not necessarily to imply, as several historians have done, that Toussaint foresaw Spain's defeat in Europe and therefore abandoned her before she abandoned him. This story probably originated in an assertion made by Sonthonax in 1798 after Toussaint had deported him[83] (although in late April 1794 rumors had indeed circulated prematurely in parts of the colony that the anti-French coalition had collapsed).[84] In any event, Toussaint doubtless knew that France had improved her position at the end of 1793 and was no longer the lame duck she had seemed six months earlier. Otherwise the volte-face is scarcely conceivable. Similarly, in Saint Domingue, Toussaint did not exactly snatch the Republic from the brink of disaster. The contrast one finds in many works between the overpowering weight of the English and Spanish invaders and the tiny republican forces clinging on hopelessly at Le Cap and Port de Paix is much exaggerated and usually peppered with errors.[85]

In the first place, the allied invasion was by no means imposing. By mid-April, the British had barely 900 effective troops in Saint Domingue, supported by two or three thousand colonists of limited value. Left seven months without once being reinforced from Europe, their morale was extremely low, while what local enthusiasm they had initially aroused was now turning to sour disillusionment.[86] In 1793, many Frenchmen looked on Britain as a maritime colossus whose fleets and armies would storm through the Caribbean occupying enemy colonies. By 1794, the rather less impressive reality had become apparent. The day before the mutiny at Gonaïves, the commander of the British forces in Saint Domingue wrote to the home secretary that lack of men had brought his operation to a standstill and that in the occupied zone there was a danger of the colonists rebelling.[87]

As for the Spanish invasion, it was hardly an invasion at all, so scared was the governor of Santo Domingo of leaving his frontier undefended.[88] Until a naval squadron arrived in January 1794, very few Spaniards had ventured more than a few miles into French territory. Ott's figure of 14,000 troops is quite illusory.[89] Even after substantial reinforcements arrived in March 1794, it is unlikely that there were ever more than 3,500 Spanish troops in the whole island. Dogged by disease, they were always outnumbered by the republicans. Utterly immobile, refusing to cooperate with the British, they reluctantly relied on their black allies (*tropas auxiliares*) to do their fighting for them. The auxiliaries, however, spent much of their time feuding with one another. The French colonists who rallied hopefully to the Spanish standard were also kept in idleness—not out of ma-chiavellianism, as contemporaries tended to think,[90] but because the blacks would not allow their ex-masters to be armed. The extreme precariousness of the Spanish position has not generally been appreciated.

In nine months, the Spanish had achieved almost nothing in the central region of Saint Domingue, while north of the River Artibonite, they owed half of their gains to Toussaint himself. Left to live off the land, some of their forces actually depended on the tiny British contingent for supplies, and when slaves rebelled in the Spanish zone at the end of the year, British troops had to be called in to suppress them.[91] Whites under Spanish protection began to realize that they had been better off under Sonthonax. By March, moreover, Spanish ranks were being ravaged by fever, and, as Toussaint well knew, the rainy season was soon to begin. Not until May 8, 1794, a year after the declaration of war was announced, did García's army attempt a major offensive. Within three days, it was halted—by disturbing news arriving from the districts under General Toussaint's command.[92]

If the Anglo-Spanish threat has been much exaggerated, so too has the weakness of the republicans.[93] Contrary to what is sometimes implied, they held a good deal more territory than just the towns of Le Cap and Port de Paix. James has the British occupying "the whole of the West Province; most of the South."[94] However, while the south had lost to the redcoats only the four parishes of Grande Anse and the village of Tiburon, in the west they held only a part of the coastal region. The area around the capital, Port-au-Prince, remained in republican hands.

On a map, the Spanish-occupied area seems impressive until one realizes that a good half of it was controlled by black auxiliaries, including Toussaint. Outside the towns of Fort Dauphin and Mirebalais, Spanish troops were rare indeed. About 400 garrisoned the lower Artibonite and one or two hundred more the plain of Le Borgne on the northwest coast.[95] In the districts under Biassou and Toussaint, there were either tiny detachments lately arrived or no troops at all. In the wild mountains of Vallière and Grande Rivière, the Spaniards did not even pretend to have any influence, and though Jean-François and Biassou made forays into the area, they could not control the independent bands that lived there.[96] Those in the Grand Cahos mountains had surrendered to Toussaint in 1793 but soon rebelled. The parishes of Gros Morne and Petit Saint Louis formed a sort of buffer zone where neither side predominated.[97]

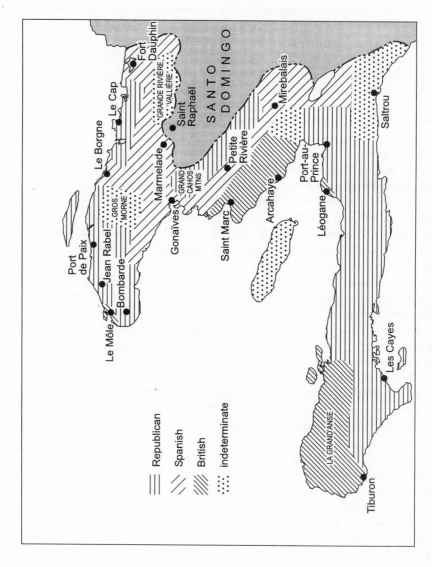

Map 4. Approximate distribution of forces in Saint Domingue, April 28, 1794

Above all, the mulatto commander Villatte, far from being shut up in Le Cap, held almost the entire northern plain for the Republic. Apart from the truly impregnable Camp Martellière, only ten miles from Fort Dauphin, and two forts on the coast at Jacquezy and Caracole, he had no less than 1,200 men in fortified positions guarding the road to Le Cap.[98] Perhaps another 2,000 defended the town, while in the mountains behind he had a long-standing, if independent, ally in the African leader Pierrot. Although one of Jean-François's attacks did apparently penetrate as far as Le Cap, Pauléus Sannon and Gragnon-Lacoste were mistaken to show him occupying the adjacent parishes of Quartier Morin and Limonade.[99] Happy to tell the tale of "Toussaint and Laveaux," and one-sided in their use of source material, historians have invariably failed to appreciate the role of Villatte. Yet one should remember that in early May when Toussaint was raising the tricolor in the parishes under his command with great éclat but probably not too much difficulty, it was Villatte who in the northeastern plain first defeated the massed forces of Governor García and Jean-François.

Another important point is raised by the letter by Laplace to García, dated April 4, 1794.[100] In it we learn not only that the mountain parishes of the interior (Plaisance, Dondon, Marmelade, etc.) were rife with dissent but also that across the northern plain from Limbé to Fort Dauphin, rebel slaves pillaged in the name of the Republic. In stressing the failure of Sonthonax's appeal to the blacks in August 1793, historians have overlooked this collapse of plantation discipline and apparent spread of republicanism in the Spanish zone. Yet in early January, when planters under Spanish protection reinstituted whipping on the plantations, the slaves rebelled at Le Borgne and Petite Rivière, burning numerous plantations and committing "a thousand atrocities."[101] Some sources also show the slaves in Gros Morne parish becoming a significant force from about December 1793 onward.[102] Even if not all these blacks in revolt acknowledged republican control, it would seem that, whatever Toussaint or the Convention was going to do, they intended to be free.

Since early 1794, the Spanish commanders had been subjected to increasing pressure from French planters returning to the Spanish-occupied zone to force those blacks who were not auxiliary troops to resume plantation work. Toussaint, we have seen, protested that such moves were premature and might spread alarm even among the privileged auxiliaries. In fact, the black troops became increasingly agitated, and relations with the Spanish grew extremely tense at this time. In January, some officers feared that the auxiliaries and other blacks would combine and massacre them.[103] In February, Brigadier Petit Thomas and two other leaders revolted at Port Margot. They claimed that the Spaniards had deceived them and that "it was indispensable to follow the maxims of the Republic in order to keep the freedom they wanted so much and for which they had fought."[104] The word "freedom" appeared noticeably more often in auxiliaries' rhetoric after mid-1793. Seeking a Spanish alliance earlier in the year, insurgents had stressed their eagerness to work for, even be slaves of, the Spanish. By the fall, their pronouncements included self-emancipation alongside defense of church and king as the aims of their revolution.[105] Did Toussaint, then, not so much initiate a volte-face as take his cue from the masses and surmise that Spanish policy was doomed?

This appears all the more probable when one realizes that from the end of March, in addition to this agitation on the part of the blacks, a remarkable volte-face in the Republic's favor was already under way. Its protagonists were that most unstable element in Saint Domingue society, the free people of color. Belatedly, they were discovering how little they had to gain from the British and the apparently less-prejudiced Spaniards. As early as December 1793, the Spanish arrested two colored colonels in their auxiliary troops and accused them of stirring up the slaves.[106] By February 1794, wrote Garran-Coulon, Laveaux's firmness had attracted to Port de Paix from the occupied areas black and mulatto leaders as well as many whites.[107] At Gonaïves, the Spanish discovered a conspiracy among local free coloreds. A little later, we find them constantly harried in the Artibonite plain by the mulatto caudillo of the Grand Cahos mountains, Blancazenave, after he renounced his allegiance to the invaders, whom he had joined in summer 1793.[108] Then, at the end of March, the British suffered their first major setback when they lost the valuable parish of Jean Rabel, whose colored commander, Jean Delair, went over to the republicans. On April 16th, the neighboring Bombarde/Plateforme district, where the mayor, Bellisle, was also a mulatto, followed suit, and in the very first days of May the free colored Chevalier raised the tricolor at Terre Neuve and Port à Piment, as did somewhat later the free coloreds of Gros Morne, who had flown the Spanish flag for six months.

One is not surprised, therefore, to find free coloreds so prominent in the uprising around Gonaïves. Free colored commanders of the adjacent parishes, including Chevalier, Gabart, and Vernet, signed the summons to the Spanish to leave the town.[109] The story of the patrol massacred shortly before in the nearby mountains may have been an act of vengeance against local colonists by these men for the mistreatment of their counterparts following Gonaïves's surrender to the Spanish.[110] The rebels then joined with the band of Blancazenave, to whom the Petite Rivière free coloreds deserted in late May. Since we know that Chevalier served as an intermediary between Toussaint and Laveaux, might it not have been his actions that forced Toussaint into the open on May 6th?[111] Even if the black leader controlled the actions of these subordinates from behind the scenes, as is more probable, he could not have achieved his volte-face without their active involvement.

Laveaux, anxious to emphasize the role of Toussaint and in time growing to hate the mulattoes, says as little as possible of this trend in his *Compte rendu.* Indeed, he deliberately passes over what he calls "some events of little importance" just before mentioning Toussaint's defection.[112] Recapping his career to the navy minister in 1799, Toussaint was even more dishonest.[113] Yet if we look forward to the mulatto revolts against the British at Léogane and Saint Marc in the autumn of 1794, the free colored volte-face appears almost as important as that of Toussaint in thwarting foreign attempts to seize Saint Domingue. This is not to deny the paramount significance of Toussaint's volte-face in the history of the revolution. However, only by seeing it in its local (and international) military and political context does it really become explicable.

There is, nonetheless, still more that needs explaining. Astonishingly, Toussaint continued to correspond with the Spanish into the fall, assuring them of his continued loyalty and of his innocence of what his undisciplined subordinates were doing. The Spaniards were not exactly taken in but went along with the deception, hoping for a reconciliation.[114] This was evidently an attempt to keep the Spanish mystified, but perhaps there is a more precise explanation. Although Toussaint's crucial move seems to have come in early May, it transpires that his volte-face was even more of a subtly staggered affair than has already been shown. While he told Laveaux on May 18th that he was besieging the Spanish in Camp Bertin, near Le Borgne, he does not seem to have tried very hard, as it did not fall until July, when Villatte arrived to help.[115] Toussaint's actions were mainly defensive during these months. Far from flying to the Republic's aid, he had to defend himself against his late allies. Then suddenly, during the night of July 3rd, he launched a devastating attack on the army of Jean-François . . . at the very time, one notes, that he received his copy of the emancipation decree.[116] One starts to understand why there are so many versions of Toussaint's volte-face.

The scope for speculation is, of course, still great and will probably remain so. Nevertheless, we have reviewed several hypotheses neither complementary nor contradictory that seem fairly firmly based on the facts. Toussaint's concern for black emancipation would appear genuine and of long standing but not sufficiently important for him to risk making a false move. Toward the spring of 1794, developments in Spanish policy and a deterioration in his personal position made a change of allegiance desirable, while a shift in the balance of power in Europe and in Saint Domingue, partly caused by that policy, made such a move practicable. The timing of his alliance with the French seems determined not by any momentous news arriving from France but by a simple letter arriving from Laveaux, accepting his allegiance. Even then, Toussaint cunningly kept his options open until he was sure slavery was abolished, and he avoided still longer an open breach with Spain.[117]

One can hardly say more; especially after reading these two letters, apparently so sincere, so Christian, yet written perhaps only hours before beginning a sudden and bloody campaign of revenge. The man remains, as ever, an enigma.

Appendix

1. Copy of the letter written by Toussaint Louverture to the Reverend Father, Vicar of Gonaïves.

Gonaïves, May 5, 1794

Most Reverend Father,

I am most sincerely affected by the harsh necessity that compelled you to leave the House of our adorable creator. Having been unable to foresee such a disastrous event fills my soul with despair. You, Minister of Almighty God, instrument of his wishes, come back, I beseech you, come back and reconcile us with Him. Have no doubts as to my sincerity. I dare believe you will give it sufficient credence to return without delay.

I have the honor to be with great respect, most reverend father, your most humble and obedient servant.

Signed Toussaint Louverture,
True Copy, Signed Salazard

2. Copy of the letter written by Toussaint Louverture to Messieurs the refugee inhabitants of Gonaïves.

Gonaïves, May 5, 1794

Gentlemen,

It is without doubt painful for me to have been unable to foresee the unhappy events that have just transpired and have obliged you to leave your properties. Such regret can be felt by me alone. Be assured, Sirs, that I did not at all participate and that everything was done without my knowledge and consequently against my wishes. God who knows our most secret thoughts and who sees all, is witness to the purity of my principles. They are not founded on this barbarous ferocity that takes pleasure in shedding human blood. Come back, Sirs, come back to your homes. I swear before our divine Creator that I will do everything to keep you safe. I have already given my orders on this matter. Nothing will be neglected to ensure they are precisely carried out.

I dare hope that you will have confidence in my sincerity, and believe that I have the honor to be, Sirs, your most humble and obedient servant.

Signed Toussaint Louverture.

P.S. On second thoughts, I request that you do not return until after I have come back from Marmelade, for I am going up there today.

True copy, signed
Salazazy [sic].

Note: These copies, translated by me from the French, were made by the Spanish commander expelled from Gonaïves, Ramón de Salazar, who had intercepted the originals, now apparently lost. They are to be found in Public Record Office, London, CO 137/93, f. 100–102.

9   Slave, Soldier, Rebel: The Strange Career of Jean Kina

At the end of 1791, when Toussaint Bréda began to emerge as a leader among the rebel slaves devastating the north of Saint Domingue, there appeared among the slaves of the south province 150 miles away a leader of a quite different sort. Though a gifted guerrilla fighter, respected by white and black, the equal some would later say (with exaggeration) of Toussaint himself, Jean Kina fought not to overthrow the slave regime but to defend it.

From Carpenter to Colonel

Jean Kina was a little younger than Toussaint; in 1791, he was probably about 40. He may have been born in Africa like the great majority of adult slaves in the district where he lived, but if so, with a son already in his 20s, he must have spent most of his life in Saint Domingue.[1] More probably, he was, like Toussaint, born in the colony to African parents, and, like him, he belonged to the slave "elite." He was apparently a carpenter[2] and lived on a cotton plantation in the tiny bay of Carcasses, near Tiburon at the tip of the southern peninsula. His owner, Guillaume, chevalier de Laroque-Turgeau, had long resided in the colony. Cotton was reputed to be the least demanding of the colony's crops, and one might suppose that the type of slavery Jean Kina experienced was of the small-scale, patriarchal kind, where the workload was relatively light.[3] As a craftsman on a small estate, he probably had a reasonably independent existence, free to "job" in the neighboring village and on the plantations along the coast.

The parish of Tiburon was (and still is) one of the most isolated and sparsely populated districts on the French part of the island. It was an extremely rugged region of small plantations, mainly of coffee, cut out of the forests where the Massif de la Hotte reaches the sea. There were only 4,000 slaves on its ninety or so estates, but the number of whites in the parish exceeded 550. There were also 220 free people of color.[4] Such comparatively high ratios of whites to non-whites and of freemen to slaves undoubtedly facilitated the control of the black population. Apart from simple surveillance and the balance of power, it was in such situations that the cultural hegemony of the master class might be most easily exercised. On small plantations where whites were relatively numerous, African languages and customs probably survived less than well and white values and beliefs were the more effectively imposed.[5] Hence, one can understand how it was customary on this exposed coast for the planters to arm their slaves in wartime. "These brave colonists," an observer wrote in 1788, "are almost all artillerymen and their slaves are soldiers. . . . Experience has shown it has produced nothing but good results so far."[6]

This was the region that would produce, when the French Revolution shook Saint Domingue, the planters' ideal *bon nègre,* a fearless defender of royalty, slavery, and white supremacy. Situated far from any town, the parish of Tiburon survived the early years of the revolution in the colony unscathed. When the great slave revolt broke out in the north in August 1791, Tiburon's slaves continued working, as did most in the south and west. By the end of the year, however, the long-persecuted free colored population had taken up arms throughout these two provinces to demand equality with the whites. In most rural areas, the whites soon had to capitulate to the superior numbers and martial abilities of the free men of color. In Tiburon and the neighboring Grand Anse, however, where free nonwhites were least numerous, white resistance continued, as it did in the cities, which were also dominated by Europeans. Even after April 1792, when the Legislative Assembly in France abolished racial discrimination in the colonies, the region's colonists maintained a white supremacist regime.

As conflict between whites and free coloreds escalated in November and December 1791, both sides in the south province began to arm and recruit slaves. While the slave revolution raged unchecked in the north, both sides took the risk of destroying their own slave-based wealth in the struggle over racial equality. The men of color initially armed their own slaves and then targeted white-owned estates for recruitment with terrorist tactics and promises of freedom. In response, whites armed slaves as plantation guards and for service in military camps. Young African men proved the most likely to abandon the plantations, but slave-drivers and other elite Creole slaves played prominent roles both in protecting estates and in leading insurgents.[7]

Against this background, Jean Kina emerges from anonymity at the beginning of 1792, when we find him commanding a group of sixty armed slaves along the Tiburon River, which formed the front line of the Grand Anse. The local planters first armed their slaves in mid-February, after losing fifty men in an ambush by local free men of color. They apparently placed Kina in command. A letter written in March describes him maneuvering through mountain forests and outwitting a raiding party of "500 blacks and 30 mulattoes." Colonists praised him enthusiastically for his cool head, bravery, and tactical sense and for his devotion to the cause of the white planters. With his master's consent, he was soon given his freedom by Tiburon commune.[8] As early as mid-December, the Colonial Assembly in Cap Français had ordered the manumission of several southern slaves for having defended their owners' plantations; it then sent details of its proceedings to the National Assembly in France.[9] This was good propaganda for proslavery ideologists, and Jean Kina, too, would prove to be a public relations gift for the planter class.

"This Negro," a soldier wrote of Kina at this time, "is absolutely feared by all the brigands and non-brigands, mulattoes and blacks; the sight of him makes them tremble."[10] According to an estate attorney, he mocked free colored prisoners about to be hanged.[11] Although colonists clearly enjoyed exaggerating hostilities among nonwhites, as if it legitimated their own prejudices, Kina appears to have shared in a mentality, common to whites and slaves, which classed the free coloreds as objects of envy but not respect.[12] Certainly it was a paradox, for Kina was now officially a free colored himself. Remarkably, however, he refused to accept his freedom. Even though on May 10th his manumission was ratified by the governor and Colonial Assembly, he seems to have resisted for some time this change of status, to set an example to other slaves, he supposedly said.[13]

The size of Jean Kina's corps soon grew to just under 200 men, who by mid-1793 also had received their freedom. In July 1792, the Colonial Assembly awarded Jean Kina a medal and a pension, which was later fixed at 300 *livres* (about 36 dollars), half the rate paid to free coloreds. It would never be paid, however, as the Grand Anse virtually seceded from the rest of Saint Domingue.[14]

That same month, the hapless Governor Blanchelande visited the region on a tour of the south seeking to reconcile whites and free coloreds in the new spirit of racial equality. When he stated he would like to take Jean Kina along with him, the black soldier replied, "I have been freed, but I have sworn to defend and never leave this region." He also deftly declined as "too great an honor" an invitation to dine with the very unpopular governor, which would have upset his local white patrons.[15] The unfortunate Blanchelande moved on to the Les Cayes region the following month, where he suffered a humiliating defeat leading an expedition against insurgent slaves at Les Platons.

Les Platons was a hilly stronghold overlooking the plain of Les Cayes that lies east of the Grand Anse, a two days' ride on horseback. Several thousand slaves, many of them formerly mobilized by the free coloreds, entrenched themselves there in summer 1792.[16] With the recognition of racial equality, whites and people of color in most of the colony achieved a grudging reconciliation and then had to decide, as with the Swiss nine months earlier, what to do with former slave allies.[17] While supporting the restoration of slave labor to the plantations, the free coloreds, led by André Rigaud, absented themselves from the governor's attack on Les Platons. Acting as intermediaries, they then negotiated an offer to free and enlist 700 insurgents. This failed, however, to disperse the encampment and in January 1793, they joined a second expedition against the stronghold.

Commanding 180 men, Jean Kina took part in this general attack. This time, the insurgent slaves were driven from their mountain fastness, largely thanks to Kina's men. Although the attackers numbered over 1,900, including more than 300 troops of the line, all agreed that it was his ragged and barefoot troop that won the day. Kina himself displayed bravery and intelligence as he led the assault on the camp of the rebel leader Martial. It is not recorded if he participated in the ensuing massacre of noncombatants. Tiburon commune suggested the colony award him a gold medal and a 1,000-*livre* pension, as it would encourage other slaves, they said, to defend their masters. The commune also wanted him back quickly, whereas the regional military commander at Les Cayes wished to retain his services.[18] The parish assembly of Les Cayes proposed to keep "citizen Jean Quina" to finish the defeat of the rebel slaves (and as a counterweight to the free coloreds). As he had lost many men to wounds and disease, the assembly called for reinforcing his corps with 360 Africans. Two months later, on April 13, 1793, the administrative council of the Grand Anse ordered the arming of 600 slaves to be attached to his corps.[19] An estate attorney explained his success:

> Jean Kina . . . came into town because of a ball he got in the left shoulder. He told me that neither the whites nor even the free coloreds were capable of fighting such a war. It was impossible to climb up to the Platons with shoes on your feet, and the tender feet of the whites couldn't stand it. He's dead right.[20]

Whether fighting free coloreds or insurgent slaves, the whites needed men adapted to the climate and terrain who could meet them on an equal footing. The ability to scale precipitous slopes at speed, to march long distances under a vertical sun, and to track and lay ambushes in the highland forests was the basis of Jean Kina's power. But it was not his only use to the planters. He also made the local slaves work, and he had a certain symbolic value, as well, for not only his martial skill but also his example was considered an important prop to the slave regime in the southwest. Besides exemplifying, well beyond the call of duty, how a *bon nègre* should behave, he further demonstrated how well the faithful might be rewarded. Although he never received his pension from the colony, he seems to have lived well. In mid-1793, the food bill for him and his family was running at 100 *pistoles* per month (probably about 108 dollars) and had to be reduced to a monthly payment of 500 *livres* cash instead.[21] At the end of the year, he was able to buy a plot of land in the hamlet of Les Irois, where his corps was then stationed.[22]

During the summer, the free men of color, backed by the new republican government in Paris, had gained control of Tiburon and, temporarily, Les Irois. The republicans ordered Kina's corps dissolved and drafted into the new Legion of Equality under André Rigaud. Kina prevaricated, and when Rigaud marched against the Grand Anse, he avoided contributing soldiers.[23] France and Britain were now at war, and republican officials, fearing an invasion, declared slavery abolished. At the eleventh hour, however, just as a slave revolt was brewing in the southwest, British troops called in by the planters disembarked in the Grand Anse on September 20th. A British enclave was established with its frontier at Les Irois. Kina's men were either already there or deserted from Tiburon a few days later with its white commandant, the chevalier de Sevré. A British captain saw them at the beginning of October. "He is a well looking, middle aged man of great fidelity," he wrote of Kina,

> and has frequently refused the freedom offered him, conceiving his example of more effect on those of his color in arms, while acting apparently from the motives only of duty and attachment to his master. By a superior degree of activity and cunning and more courage than is generally met with in negroes, he has acquired great influence over them and under his orders they have remained uncontami-

nated by the neighbouring disaffected, and in a bush fighting warfare peculiar to themselves have at different times a good deal annoyed them. Their appearance was, as it may be supposed, very grotesque—instead of the drum and fife they used the Banger and Coromantee Flute, the musical instruments of their native country. Some had fire arms, others bill hooks fastened to long poles and plantation watchmen's hangers, and were in general wretchedly attired in their osnaburgh frocks.[24]

They were now, however, promised British pay and clothing and as a first installment were immediately supplied with shoes—a symbolic rather than a practical measure.

The Grand Anse whites stressed to the British the extent of Jean Kina's influence over the blacks, and successive British commanders were careful to award him marks of respect. He was made a colonel and received a sword, sword belt, and high collar as well as gifts of cash. When the British captured Tiburon in February 1794, he was presented with a ceremonial sword, and later gifts included a saber and a portrait of George III.[25]

Before Tiburon was attacked, Kina addressed a number of letters to its black and free colored defenders, hoping to win them over. Though not of his own writing, they provide interesting evidence of his attitudes and of his relations with the free coloreds. To several he wrote as friends. One had already commanded under him. The republicans, he told him, "want only our destruction and your ruin. . . . I have always regarded you as a son." "You never trusted me," he reproached another, "despite my advice. . . . Do you remember how a thousand times happier you were when you had a king?" To the commander, he wrote of "the error which today blinds a great many blacks, who believe in liberty, children of greed and republican fanaticism. . . . Help overcome," he went on, "this class of men without which we can do nothing in this unfortunate isle." Kina did not approve, he said, of the way certain mulatto prisoners had been treated. "I am cruel only with arms in my hand." To the slaves themselves, he wrote, "Unhappy slaves! You have been led along with the fine name of free man, when it is only an illusion. It is in fulfilling your duties to your masters that you will become free."[26]

In their correspondence with London, British commanders wrote of "my friend Jean Kina" or "the gallant Jean Kina," patronizingly no doubt but also with affection and an awareness of the valuable role he played.[27] While British troops were few in number, the unhealthy camp at Les Irois had to fight off many attacks, and no sooner was Tiburon captured and Kina's corps installed than it was subjected to a massive assault by the republicans. When the powder magazine in the fort blew up, killing many of the defenders, all seemed lost. A bold sortie by the remaining colonial troops saved the day, however, Jean Kina's men conspicuously taking most of the risks.[28] He himself was again wounded, and his men were observed to be so angry that before killing their prisoners, they forced them to lick his wounds. "The King had not a better friend," wrote Colonel Whitelocke in July 1794, "than Jean Kina, whose attachment to Royalty is as conspicuous as his Honour and Integrity."[29]

He had only recently accepted his freedom, the colonel added. His "Negro Militia" he described as fluctuating in number between 200 and 500, which suggests there was a core of freed slaves increased on occasion by levies from the plantations. Soon afterward, the British began raising another black corps in the Artibonite valley, promising liberty in return for five years' service, and in September Kina's corps was put on the same footing. Struck down by yellow fever, the British forces were dwindling fast and Jean Kina's importance was now at its greatest. However, in December 1794, his troops, too, were decimated. The republicans returned to besiege Tiburon, this time with artillery and troops of the line. For four days, shells rained down on the hilltop fort with devastating effect. When a bomb exploded in the ditch they were crouching in, Kina's men finally panicked. They lowered the drawbridge and fled, making a desperate retreat through the mountains, and an ambush, to Les Irois.[30]

Thereafter, Jean Kina was to play a less prominent role. He commanded fewer men, and his corps became dwarfed by the regiments of black Chasseurs, 800 strong, which favored colonists were now permitted to recruit. Like his men, the Chasseurs (skirmishers) wore red jackets, coarse trousers, and a round hat with a panache; rank and file carried a musket and a machete. In the period 1795–1798, thousands of Domingan blacks became armed and ostensibly loyal defenders of the slave regime.[31] In colonial societies, the phenomenon is not unfamiliar. Attracted by the opportunities of military life, perhaps by the ideology that went with it, most Chasseurs, like Kina's men, were Africans and were presumably brought up in monarchical societies.

Money, a full stomach, and a prestigious uniform: the attractions were up to a point those that caused young males in any poor and oppressed social group to become soldiers. However, for the slave at the bottom of the plantation hierarchy, the appeal was perhaps unusually great. Ten or twelve ounces of meat every day, sometimes fresh—a soldier's ration represented a substantial improvement in diet, and a daily wage of sixpence (later eightpence) was comparative wealth besides. The uniform, too, for men who normally spent six days a week half naked and, moreover, who prided themselves on their Sunday best, must have seemed singularly attractive, while the transition from bare feet to shoes was itself pregnant with symbolism. For, above all, military service meant freedom—immediate freedom from the plantation and, eventually, the status of a free man.

This was guaranteed, furthermore, not by shadowy authorities born of revolution but by the planters and a king. As the traditional sources of power in the colonial world, they projected a certain security along with a comprehensible ideology of legitimacy and hierarchy that was decked out in the usual trappings of flags, medals, and ceremony. In the distribution of medals to their slaves, the planters had shown since 1792 an uncharacteristic liberality, and the scarlet tunic of course was not just a flamboyant item of clothing but, in the words of the rebel general Jean-François, "the king's uniform."[32] Jean-François and his fellow insurgents in the north had posed as defenders of king and church long before they joined the Spanish. Although left-wing historians have tended to dismiss their royalist rhetoric, Africanist John Thornton argues that it reflects African political ideologies.[33] Under the British occupation, each black corps, Jean Kina's included, had its own chaplain who was instructed not only to inspire his charges with a love of Christianity but also to end each prayer with three shouts of *Vive le Roi!* and each Sunday service with "God save the King," apparently sung in Latin.[34] As for the regimentation, discipline, and flogging, these were nothing new; slaves adapted well to military life.

From then onward, however, Jean Kina's corps was to contain fewer and fewer plantation slaves. Early in 1795, when the remnants of the corps were transferred to the capital, Port-au-Prince, Kina gained leave to go to Jamaica to find recruits on the prison ships of Port Royal. He returned in June with sixty men of all colors, mainly free men of color. They were former deportees from Saint Domingue's British zone, and their reappearance considerably alarmed some white colonists. Kina's activities also aroused the jealousy of the powerful free colored commander, Jean-Baptiste Lapointe, who held the district of Arcahaye for the British. When Kina returned in October from another trip to Jamaica, Lapointe had most of his recruits seized.[35] Many of his men were now evidently property-owners, for a month later we find them naming two representatives to return to the Grand Anse to watch over their affairs.[36] The officers were then living in a derelict house in Port-au-Prince (though they were later evicted to make way for a body of Chasseurs),[37] and the corps performed night patrols in the surrounding countryside. It does not seem to have taken part in any of the major campaigns with which the British consolidated their position in 1795–1796.

Finding new recruits was obviously a problem, as Kina was not allowed to compete with the white colonels of Chasseurs in recruiting on the plantations. However, in the summer of 1796 he began to tap a new source. He was given permission to purchase at his own expense and to enroll newly imported Africans "accustomed to a state of warfare in their own Country." In all, he seems to have bought about forty, probably in Jamaica and at an average price of 2,000 *livres.* Their wages were paid to him, and no provision was made for their eventual emancipation. The ex-slave was now a slave-owner on a large scale, and his "Chasseurs de Georges III" became a curiously hybrid unit. When the colonial corps were reorganized in May 1797, his was formally divided into one company of Chasseurs and one company of free coloreds.[38] Economy was now the order of the day, and he was lucky that such a small unit was allowed to survive. However, as its royal name suggests, it was a much-valued instrument of propaganda, and its disbandment would have posed special problems. Moreover, it was still an effective fighting force. Though during Toussaint's spring offensive it suffered more desertions than most other black regiments, it executed in June a daring attack on the outposts of Léogane, achieving complete surprise.[39] In January, Kina had received his full commission as a colonel and his son, Zamor, was now made a captain.

Although Zamor's mother was still alive,[40] Kina had no wife, and it seems he now wished to marry one Dauphine Guérin, the daughter of a Port-au-Prince free black. Free born and slightly lighter in complexion,[41] she must have represented, whatever her other charms, a degree of social advancement for him. However, Kina had a rival in one of the free coloreds in his corps. On a spurious pretext, Kina had him jailed along with a friend. When the two men were later released, he met them in the street and in a rage beat both of them nearly unconscious with the flat of his saber. Despite the protests of the chief of police, the British commander chose to ignore the incident.[42] It reveals something of Jean Kina's sensibilities, temper, strength, and influence. No marriage took place.

Kina's ability to purchase some forty slaves, if obviously based on credit, shows he was a man of some substance. He received a colonel's pay of about 40 pounds sterling per month, and at the end of 1795 he began to draw his colonial pension from the Administration de la Grand Anse, which in December 1796 was increased to 600 *livres* per year. At the same time, he began drawing the pay of an entire company of Chasseurs. Early in the occupation, it was said that he sent to his master and mistress in Jérémie all he received,[43] but if that was ever true, it was evidently no longer the case. He owned at least one male personal servant and several females.

In October 1797, Kina formally manumitted his son, of whom he had probably been given ownership. He had already informally freed a Grand Anse Creole named Angélique, whom he had purchased and who may have been his son's mistress. These two, Zamor and Angélique, became in 1798 the principal potential beneficiaries of his estate, when, as Toussaint Louverture began his final campaign to expel the British, Jean Kina drew up his will. To Angélique was bequeathed three African slaves and 900 *gourdes* (900 dollars) in cash. Her manumission and that of her daughter were to be paid for by the estate. Florence, a free-born black woman of Port-au-Prince, was to receive 300 *gourdes*, two female Africans, and Kina's plot of land at Les Irois. Dauphine Guérin was also willed a legacy of 300 *gourdes*. To his former *ménagère* (housekeeper), Agnès, now free, Kina willed her daughter (his slave), Marie-Josèphe, and her five children and grandchildren. The remaining property, movables, and cash was left to Zamor.[44] Two weeks later, on February 1, 1798, Kina decided to free Marie-Josèphe and her offspring. Her age was put variously at 35 and 45, and, like her mother, she may have been his mistress at some time.[45] A second will was drawn up in July, after the British had been expelled from Port-au-Prince and had fallen back on the Grand Anse. This time four more slaves were recommended for manumission, bequests were smaller, and Zamor and Angélique were made joint residuary legatees.

A few months before, under rather strange circumstances, Jean Kina had come face to face with one of his earliest opponents. Martial Pemerle, one of the leaders of the rebels of Les Platons, who had been dispersed in January 1793, came into Jérémie with his followers in October 1797 and surrendered. The British commander welcomed him but with suspicion. At the commander's request, Jean Kina and some of his men were sent from Port-au-Prince to join with Martial's group and at the same time spy on them. Kina soon came to the conclusion that Martial was acting for the republicans and denounced him. He was sent before a court-martial.[46]

It does not seem that Kina took much part in the desperate fighting in 1798 that led to the British evacuation. He had been sent to the Grand Anse well before the battle for the west province began. During the spring, he presumably took part in the inglorious defense of Les Irois, but when a daring raid was launched behind the republican lines in the south, it was entrusted to another regiment of Chasseurs. At the beginning of 1797, his corps had contained about 120 men but had been increased by the addition of some Grand Anse free coloreds in May, and in the summer of 1798 it consisted of 148 rank and file with 46 others, including officers, noncommissioned officers, drummers, and ten supernumeraries, who were women or retired officers. Second in command was a Major Schevanard, doubtless a Curaçolien, common on the south coast. All the soldiers in the first company and most in the second and third had surnames. Most of the *bossales* had probably died or deserted.[47]

As the forces of Toussaint and Rigaud pressed forward during these months, liberating the last of Saint Domingue's slaves, Jean Kina must have been anxious about what his future might be. In September, at the Môle Saint Nicolas, he would have seen Toussaint received in state by the defeated British commander. The two may even have met at the banquet given in Toussaint's honor. It must have been a bitter occasion. Most of the Chasseurs wished to leave the colony with the British, much to the latter's embarrassment. Toussaint wanted them to remain. In the event, thousands were left behind or had to return after being refused entry to Jamaica. Naturally suspect to the republicans, they had to return to work on their old plantations. Jean Kina was luckier. On October 1, he and his son sailed from the Môle with the last detachment of British troops. Not seven years out of slavery, he was a colonel in the British Army.

From Hero to Rebel

Kina's movements during the next two years are difficult to pin down. It would seem he spent some time in Jamaica and in April 1799 arrived in England.[48] It is said he received a warm and distinguished welcome.[49] The popular press does not seem to have remarked on his presence, but the French planter community in London, led by Pierre-Victor Malouet, doubtless treated him as a celebrity. He was just the sort of advertisement a hard-pressed, and perhaps guilty-feeling plantocracy then needed. What the British abolitionists made of him, one can only guess. The government awarded him and his son a pension, apparently of 15 pounds per month,[50] but how they lived during the next year in this strange new environment is not known. He spoke only a very broken French and probably no English.[51] It is unlikely that he could read.

We catch a glimpse of him, dejected and anxious to return to active service, in the copy of a letter written by Malouet, dated July 1800 (though the real date may have been 1799). The letter was addressed to a fellow émigré in England but was intercepted by French agents and ended up in Paris.[52] "Keep up the courage of this good negro," the exiled planter wrote from Richmond, "tell him to go and see Mr. King, who has agreed to see him." John King was the principal undersecretary at the Ministry for War. "It is certain they intend to use him and give him a post. New details are expected from General Maitland; in the meantime they will give him something to live on, but they have so much on their minds they can hardly give him a thought. Get him to present himself, to write, or some charitable soul to write for him. I'll help him when I get better." Thomas Maitland had been the last British commander in Saint Domingue and was now negotiating a secret tripartite treaty with Toussaint Louverture and the United States. However, as an adjunct to these negotiations, Malouet had concocted a wild scheme of his own. Toussaint's children were at school in Paris, effectively hostages of the French government. If they could be kidnapped, Malouet reasoned, Toussaint might be willing to sever his links with France. The British government, he admitted, would never approve such a plan, but, he added, if the children could be got to Dover, he was sure their kidnapper would be rewarded and they would be handed over to Jean Kina and sent to Jamaica.

The scheme came to nothing. In June 1800, the government decided to send Jean Kina back to the Caribbean. It was suggested he might command a corps of free coloreds to operate against maroons in the Suriname backcountry, which had been recently seized from the Dutch. Consequently, he and his son, with the pay of captain and lieutenant, were sent out to Martinique to the commander-in-chief, Lieutenant-General Trigge. He arrived in September, but Trigge, for reasons unknown, thought him unsuitable for the job proposed.[53] General Knox in Jamaica heard of the Martinique government's embarrassment and thought that Kina might be of use to him in conducting relations with Toussaint, who had now conquered the whole of Hispaniola and was becoming increasingly independent of France. However, to have him transferred would have required permission from London.[54] Once again, Jean Kina found himself stranded.

Martinique at this time was a politically and socially tense place to be. It had gone through considerable upheaval during the French Revolution and, though the six years it had been under British occupation were a period of stability, there were signs of stress beneath the surface. Its once fractious colonists were in general satisfied with British rule, which had maintained slavery and expelled free coloreds from public office after a brief period of civil equality. It appeared likely, however, that the days of British rule were numbered and that, whenever peace was declared in Europe, Martinique would be restored to France. With slavery abolished and non-whites triumphant in Guadeloupe and Saint Domingue, this was for the (white) planters a grim prospect. The free coloreds of Martinique were less powerful than those of Saint Domingue, but in 1793–1794, they had enjoyed equality and power. The British, therefore, were loath to treat them as harshly as some vengeful whites would have wished.

This was the situation in September 1800, when there disembarked at Fort Royal, the capital, a Domingan black in a colonel's uniform, accompanied by an aide-de-camp and an educated secretary (a "man of quality"). The whites were shocked. Governor Keppel reported a state of "extreme uneasiness."[55] Jean Kina's reaction is interesting.

> He was not long in realizing that such behavior did not fit in with the colonial system and that his presence thus shocked all established opinion. He was soon seen to be behaving in a humble manner, submissive towards the whites, severe with those of his caste who had acted wrongly in the Revolution. He became austere in his habits to the point of excess, rigidly obedient to the precepts of religion, assiduous in his religious observances, at confession and at the altar, with all the appearance of a truly exemplary devotion. . . . Soon people were speaking only of his virtues, when all of a sudden, the alarm rang out.[56]

This hostile portrait makes a fascinating comparison with the traditional, ultra-devious picture of Toussaint Louverture on the eve of his volte-face against the Spaniards in 1794. It may even be the source for that story, which appears only to go back to 1804.[57] In any event, it seems certain that Kina succeeded in allaying the whites' worst fears about him, deviously or not. One might ascribe his (apparently sudden) interest in religion to his courting a young girl who seems to have been of a pious disposition. Rather suddenly, on October 28th, Kina married Félicité-Adelaïde Quimard. She was just 14, the daughter of a free black master mason of Fort Royal.[58] It was in this milieu of free colored master-craftsmen and shopkeepers that Kina seems to have made himself at home.

He also appears to have shared their discontent with a decree that was passed with the approval of the governor on November 3rd by the colony's Superior Council. The decree enacted nothing new but repeated various existing regulations regarding the manumission of slaves that had rarely been enforced. Chief among these was an old law that stipulated that if the regulations were not conformed to, the manumittee could be seized and sold for government profit. Also reiterated was a British decree passed in 1794 which forbade manumission under any pretext without royal assent.[59] The unofficially freed slave, the *affranchi sans l'être,* was then posing a difficult problem for most West Indian administrations. Some were fugitives living by their wits, which often meant crime, in the towns, but others had simply been freed by masters unwilling to pay the cost of an official manumission. Whether they were industrious, destitute, or criminal, their growing numbers were perceived as a threat by declining white populations, particularly after the French Revolution and its repercussions in Saint Domingue. At the same time, to attempt to enslave men who had been free for years was acknowledged to be dangerous, if not unjust. The British military governors in Saint Domingue and Martinique had approached the problem flexibly and resisted pressure on them to round up those without papers. Now, it seems, Governor Keppel wanted to take a hard line.[60]

Jean Kina's wife and mother-in-law were free-born, but his father-in-law was the son of a slave. Had he himself married a week later than he did, he might have faced the humiliation of having to prove to the priest that he was not a slave. During November he was observed to be "attending to some grievances" of the Fort Royal free coloreds. Trigge, the commander-in-chief, considered the new decree both oppressive and dangerous and decided to informally prevent its application.[61] Around the end of the month, however, both he and the governor left Fort Royal to attend to other business.

During the night of December 4th, Jean Kina set out from the town with about twenty blacks and mulattoes armed with muskets, sabers, and pistols, and carrying three small barrels of powder. They had all served in the militia and were apparently wearing their uniforms. At their head they carried a Union Jack with the inscription pinned to it *La Loi Britannique* (British law). They seemed to be making for Morne Lemaître, a natural stronghold, but during the night and early morning they stopped on their way at several plantations and in the hamlet of Case-Navires. No physical violence or pillage took place. Kina merely engaged in a series of extraordinary verbal confrontations.

"Do you like the British laws?" he demanded of bewildered colonists. He asked planters how they treated their slaves. He had heard they were "devourers of human flesh," he said, who whipped their slaves and overworked them so that the women aborted. And, he added, there were three or four Frenchmen who were misleading the British government in trying to sell people who had been free for a long time. This he would never allow. Henceforth, the only punishment he would permit on the plantations was two or three blows with the flat of a saber. Or else! He had also come, he said, to end the practice of shutting up in "dungeons" slaves accused of poisoning. He forcibly freed two, who shouted "Vive Jean Kina!" and joined his band. When asked by whose authority he acted, he gave various answers: that of his own strength, that of Prime Minister Pitt, and that of God, the king, and his British flag.[62]

His manner was hectoring and sometimes disdainful but only obliquely menacing and, in some ways, rather reticent. At one house, he refused the owner's invitation to come in out of the rain, lest he be accused of pillage. By 8 A.M. his band had swelled to no more than seventy; some said forty. The alarm had been raised in Fort Royal, and soon afterward a troop of cavalry arrived accompanied by colonists. Colonel Maitland, the acting commander-in-chief, advanced alone to where Kina's men had taken up position. He promised he would investigate their grievances and offered them all a free pardon. As Kina would capitulate only to the British, the colonists were asked to withdraw. His men then dispersed, retaining their arms, and Kina was taken back to Fort Royal, having been given a horse. Within a few weeks, he and his wife and son were put on a ship for England.

Governor Keppel and the council were furious. The pardon prevented the causes of the uprising being investigated by a judicial inquiry, so the event remains somewhat mysterious and diversely interpreted. Keppel, whose image was that of an authoritarian "strong man," presented it in his dispatches as a slave revolt. Kina, he said, was ambitious and hoped to emulate Toussaint Louverture, to whose example he had been exposed in the Saint Domingue Revolution. Kina had told the slaves, Keppel claimed, that he had been sent from England to instruct them in their rights, saying they were "as free as the air that circulated."[63]

However, there is no record of this, and Keppel seems to have been covering up his own mistakes. To judge from the depositions of eyewitnesses, Kina made no condemnation of slavery itself, nor did he really attempt to raise the slaves.

Apart from the two prisoners he released, he commandeered four slaves to carry his ammunition, but the others he tried to recruit were either free coloreds or light-skinned "privileged" slaves who he said should have been freed by their "scoundrels of fathers." Although not of mixed racial descent himself, Jean Kina appears to have agreed with the proposal voiced early in the revolution by free colored and white activists that slaves of mixed race should be freed.[64] Several of the insurgents were of mixed race, and some must have been slave-owners. Of the ten named by eyewitnesses, four were men in their 40s who came from moderately prosperous families of *petits bourgeois*. One had a shop that sold tobacco, and at least one was a master craftsman. They were friends of the Quimard family, though Kina's father-in-law himself was not mentioned.

Unlike the governor, General Trigge more plausibly blamed the manumission law as the cause of the revolt, and after confirming Colonel Maitland's pardon, he had the law suspended. Agitation among the Fort Royal free coloreds rapidly subsided. There is some irony in Jean Kina's vaunting of British laws. In some ways, notably with regard to rights of inheritance and testimony in the courts, free people of color were treated worse under British law than they were under French law. In the British colonies, however, slaves of very light complexion were automatically freed, and Kina may have known this. He was no doubt also misled by previously lax law enforcement in the British-occupied colonies.

Nevertheless, Kina's concern for the mass of slaves, from which he had risen less than a decade before, is striking. For the first time, Kina appears as a champion of slaves, and he must have known that his claims on their behalf could only have hindered the cause of the free coloreds. Were conditions in Martinique really more shocking than elsewhere? Kina must have seen sugar cultivation in southern Saint Domingue, although perhaps only on isolated estates, and he had visited Jamaica several times in the 1790s. Perhaps this was a belated crisis of conscience.

According to Louis de Curt, however, the Martinique planters' spokesman in London, Kina acted out of "blind vengeance." Having been feted in Saint Domingue and London, he was humiliated at being treated simply as a freed slave in Martinique.[65] De Curt's explanation echoed those of Keppel and the council in rejecting the idea that the November decree was the cause of the revolt. De Curt's address, however, was specifically written to counter yet another explanation. This had appeared in the official French government newspaper *Le Moniteur* and had alleged that Kina was acting for the British government, which wanted to ruin the colony before it handed it back to France. This suggestion seems to have created no impression in Martinique, and de Curt's unnecessary concern to reassure his fellow planters created considerable resentment among them. Loyal addresses were sent to London along with criticisms of the colony's deputy.[66] Others, however, suspected a different sort of government involvement. In Port-au-Prince, it was suggested that certain officials instigated the rebellion as a means of getting rid of Jean Kina.[67] He himself would later claim that he had done nothing without his superiors' advice or consent.[68] Could General Trigge, discreetly or ambiguously, have influenced him, perhaps as a means of reversing the governor's policy? Kina had gotten on well with him and the other officers. Trigge was prompt to affirm Colonel Maitland's pardon and to suspend the offending decree, and when the Home Office, which sided with the governor and council, ordered that all the insurgents be arrested and sent to England, he refused and offered to resign. For many months afterward, relations between the military and civil authorities were considerably strained. In the end, however, Trigge's policy prevailed; the insurgents were left in peace, and the Home Office allowed at least the ban on manumissions to be revoked.[69]

From Newgate to the Côte d'Azur

When Kina was brought to London, he was incarcerated on March 9, 1801 in Newgate Prison. No charges were brought against him, and he was committed under the Aliens Act. It was the government's way of saying it did not know what to do with him. Ironically, a month later the claims board that handled compensation payments arising from the occupation and evacuation of Saint Domingue awarded him in respect of past services the sum of 300 pounds.[70] It was the only good news he would receive for a year. Meanwhile, back in the now peaceful colony, Toussaint Louverture was at his apogee, while in Paris, Napoleon Bonaparte was gathering forces for his overthrow. In August, Kina sent a petition to the commander-in-chief of the army, the Duke of York, declaring he had done nothing wrong and asking to be employed. It was written in badly spelled French by another prisoner (his wife?) and signed with his usual large and clumsy signature. It was passed from one official to another, one of whom wrote on it, "What is to be done with Jean Kina? Wherever he is sent he will do mischief."[71]

The peace signed with France in March 1802 seems to have provided a solution. While French forces were freed for the conquest of Saint Domingue, the Aliens Act ceased to operate in Britain, and Jean Kina and his family were released from Newgate. By the summer, he would have heard that Toussaint had been defeated and that the colonial regime was being restored in all France's colonies, which once again included Martinique. It was thus not such a strange coincidence that a few months after Toussaint had been shipped to France as a prisoner, the Kina family, too, packed its bags and set out for Paris. The contents of those bags revealed that Jean Kina, after a year in prison, was still far from being a poor man.[72] He and his son between them owned about twenty pairs of trousers and knee-breeches, about the same number of waistcoats, and well over twenty shirts. They had also bought two new English razors in a case and possessed three silver medals and a pair of silver spurs. Mme. Kina, now 16, possessed about ten dresses and, more significantly, several music notebooks, a silver crucifix, and numerous works of piety. One of them, curiously, owned a German grammar. Perhaps they were contemplating a European tour.

Their possessions were inventoried because no sooner had they set foot in France than the two men were again arrested. Because they arrived without authorization, they were breaking a new aliens law passed in July. Officials also noted with gravity their connection with Saint Domingue and that they had led an insurrection in Martinique. Any West Indian was a suspect in France at this time, because, shortly before, Toussaint had been sped across the country in a closed carriage and was now being held prisoner under rigid security in its most inaccessible dungeon. The Kinas were initially detained in the Temple Prison in Paris, where the royal family had been held ten years before. It was soon decided that they, too, should be under tighter surveillance. In the depths of winter, father and son were sent south to Besançon and in late January to the fort de Joux in the Jura Mountains. A cell had been specially prepared for them, its windows half walled up and fitted with extra panes of glass. This was to prevent communication with the outside as much as escape, for, unknown to these two exslaves, in the cell beneath their floor, equally unaware of their presence, lay the former coachman of the Bréda plantation, Toussaint Louverture.

The situation was even more bizarre, because the free colored leaders André Rigaud and Martial Besse were soon also sent to the same prison.[73] The prison authorities were under strict instructions not to let the prisoners know of one another's presence. When the Kinas arrived at the fortress, they were so weak that its commandant had to issue them extra food and wine, for fear their health was in danger. Otherwise, the story of their imprisonment, like that of Toussaint, is one of petty bureaucratic meanness. They were all to be fed and housed at the lowest prices possible. It does not seem that the Kinas were any better treated than Toussaint, far from it, but they were able to sell off some of their possessions and doubtless thereby benefited. The family was growing, however. Some time after the two men were incarcerated, Félicité made her way from Besançon and turned up at the prison gate, exhausted, penniless, and heavily pregnant. She could not be admitted and gave birth in the village below the fort. There she was looked after by local people. In April 1803, Toussaint, unaware of all, died of pneumonia.

The Kinas, however, managed to survive the winter, as, far away, did the Haitian people, then driving the last European troops from their soil. In June 1804, the local prefect came to visit the prison, and the Kina men profited from the occasion to request they be let out, offering to work for the government as carpenters. Permission eventually came through from the Ministry of Justice and it was decided they should join the colored battalion of the Army of Italy, then stationed at Menton on the Mediterranean coast.[74] Still weak after their long imprisonment, they were sent to Besançon at the end of August, and the family group disappears from the historical record in a carriage on the Alpine high road, winding its way through the mountains toward the Côte d'Azur.

Part Five.   *The Wider Revolution*

From the slave quarters of the Americas to the council chambers of the European capitals, from the world commodity markets to the imagination of poets, the Haitian Revolution had a multifarious impact. It alarmed and excited public opinion on both sides of the Atlantic, embittering the debates developing about race and abolition. The pro- and antislavery lobbies each found ammunition for their propaganda in the 15-year-long struggle. The revolution inspired a welter of political tracts and poetry, plays, and novels in English, French, and German. These included William Wordsworth's haunting sonnet "To Toussaint L'Ouverture" and Victor Hugo's first novel, Bug Jargal. *In the sphere of great-power politics, the revolution brought humiliating military disasters to the three main imperialist states that cost the lives of about 70,000 soldiers and ended France's standing as a major colonial power.*

In 1791, Saint Domingue went from being the Americas' main destination for migrants from France and Africa to being the source of a multiracial diaspora sending waves of refugees to North America and the Caribbean. The colony lost its entire white population in a dozen years and unknown numbers of slaves and free people of color. As Chapter 12 shows, even the leaders of the slave insurrection died in exile. This diaspora stretched from Trinidad and New Orleans to New York and back to France. It left an enduring cultural imprint in Louisiana and eastern Cuba. Migrants turned Jamaica and Cuba into major coffee producers, and Domingans also helped launch the Louisiana sugar industry. The price rise resulting from the destruction of Saint Domingue's plantations further stimulated the revival of sugar production in Brazil and Jamaica and the opening of new economic frontiers elsewhere. These new expansions of slavery and contacts with Domingan migrants also stimulated slave rebellion, as did news of the unprecedented successes of the black revolutionaries. From the early weeks of the slave uprising to the crowning of Emperor Dessalines in 1804 and of King Christophe in 1811, that news spread rapidly among people of African descent. To the discomfort of white observers, they reacted with subdued pride or open belligerence and celebrated from Brazil to the United States in song, symbol, and ceremony.

Chapter 10 examines the early interaction of the French Revolution and the unfolding crisis in the colonies. The "colonial question" France's new revolutionary politicians were forced to confront consisted of three broad issues: self-government for overseas possessions, racial equality, and the abolition of slavery and the slave trade. Of particular interest is the way the three issues were interconnected and impinged on one another, while metropolitan and colonial developments continually evolved under each others' influence. Despite the ostensibly universal promise of the Declaration of the Rights of Man of August 26, 1789, neither liberals nor radicals in France showed much enthusiasm for changing the colonial status quo. Colonial trade was too valuable and the mercantile lobby too well organized. Colonial whites and free coloreds, nevertheless, seized the opportunity offered by the creation of a metropolitan forum. The Constituent Assembly (1789–1791) rapidly conceded metropolitan representation and a limited local autonomy to the white colonists, but the question of racial equality evoked embarrassed efforts at evasion, timid half-measures, and tergiversation. The slaves were ignored entirely. When the assembly came to an end in September 1791, its members were unaware that slaves and free coloreds were in rebellion in Saint Domingue and its white colonists were making their first attempt at secession.

The following chapter surveys the reactions of the other major powers to the Haitian Revolution from the time of the slave uprising to the winning of independence. As the black revolution simultaneously benefited and threatened Saint Domingue's commercial rivals, their reactions were mixed. Some contemporaries, like later historians, suspected that the British or Spanish governments encouraged the colony's destruction or the subversion of French rule. This was untrue until war broke out in Europe in 1793. Both states then immediately sought to conquer the colony. Military intervention proved a costly failure for all three colonial powers and paradoxically did much to expand the scope of the black revolution. British, Spanish, and U.S. policy toward the revolution fluctuated according to each government's relations with France. Although they sought at certain moments to crush the black insurgents, all three states proved willing to assist them commercially or militarily when they considered France a greater threat. None favored the emergence of an independent black state, although Thomas Jefferson briefly suggested the idea and, with the exception of the Jeffersonian embargo of 1806–1810, none cut off trade relations.

The arming of slaves by slave-owners was an age-old practice that experienced a dramatic expansion during the revolutionary decade of the 1790s. This brought with it a novel problem for the imperial powers: how to demobilize such forces without destabilizing the colonies where the ex-soldiers settled. Chapter 12 surveys Spain's efforts to confront this issue when it evacuated Santo Domingo in 1796. The Auxiliares Negros de Carlos IV constituted a very special case, however, because they were not just slaves who had been armed but the architects of the 1791 uprising who had killed many hundreds of colonists and burned their plantations. Their leaders, moreover, called themselves generals and colonels and had proved extremely self-assertive when in Spanish employ. Spain's efforts to relocate them, first within the West Indies and then in Meso- and Central America, Florida, and Europe, are interesting on two counts. They offer a comparative study of the reactions of different parts of the Spanish empire to this administrative challenge. And they provide a wealth of details about the insurgents as individuals and as members of families.

10 Racial Equality, Slavery, and Colonial Secession during the Constituent Assembly

The colonial question in the French Revolution involved three broad issues: self-government for France's overseas possessions, civil rights for their free colored populations, and the abolition of the slave trade and of slavery itself. This chapter is primarily concerned with the pursuit in France of racial equality and slave emancipation, but it is difficult to understand the progress of these issues without reference to developments in the colonies and to the contemporary debate about the limits of metropolitan control and the threat of white secessionism within the empire. Indeed, one of the chief interests of the colonial question is in studying the interaction between its three component issues and the complex counterpoint that developed between events in Europe and the Caribbean.[1]

Until recently, the colonial question has received remarkably little attention within the context of the French Revolution. As Mitchell Garrett observed in 1916, historians have been less interested in French attitudes toward the colonies during the revolutionary period than "in the colonies as such."[2] The abolition of slavery in 1794, surely one of the most radical acts of the entire revolution, is not even mentioned in the classic studies of Michelet, Jaurès, Mathiez, and Soboul, nor is it mentioned in the recent histories of Rudé, Sutherland, and Schama.[3] Matters of empire, race, and slavery appear nowhere at all in the documentary collections of Roberts and Hardman,[4] or in such different works as those of Kropotkin, Gaxotte, and (barring a misleading half-sentence) de Tocqueville. Even the wide-ranging surveys of Godechot and Palmer accord the briefest of mentions to France's colonies.[5]

This neglect is surprising in view of the importance to ancien régime France of her overseas possessions. The expansion of French foreign trade in the eighteenth century was more rapid than that of Great Britain and was fueled largely by the Caribbean colonies of Martinique, Guadeloupe, and, most important, Saint Domingue (modern Haiti). By the late 1780s, they produced about half of the Western world's sugar and coffee, and three-quarters of this produce was re-exported from France, earning vital foreign exchange. Perhaps more than a million people in France depended on colonial commerce for employment in what was the most dynamic and advanced sector of the French economy. The demise of the Atlantic coast ports during the revolution was in part a product of colonial problems, and Caribbean developments similarly contributed to *la vie chère* on the streets of Paris, where sugar riots broke out in 1792.[6]

The neglect of colonial affairs in French revolutionary historiography is also surprising because of the significance of the issues raised by the colonial question. The world's first examples of colonial representation in a metropolitan assembly, of racial equality in an American colony, of wholesale emancipation in a major slave-holding society, and then the exportation of these policies as weapons of war all date from the years 1789–1794. In the political rhetoric of the mother country, slavery was merely a metaphor,[7] but it was a grim reality in the colonies of the Caribbean and Indian Ocean. The emancipation decree of 16 pluviôse Year II (February 4, 1794) legally freed some 700,000 people without compensating owners for the 1,000 million *livres tournois* in capital investment they represented.[8]

It is of course true that contemporary Frenchmen themselves preferred to avoid the embarrassing problems posed by the colonies. Colonial autonomy, racial equality, abolition of the slave trade, and slave emancipation all were grave threats to French prosperity that the Declaration of the Rights of Man appeared rashly to promote. The colonial question thus tested the universalist claims of the French revolutionaries, and, according to Jean Jaurès, it sapped the self-respect of the revolutionary bourgeoisie, who were forced into a painful confrontation of principle and interest. Foreshadowing the imperial crises of the present century, the colonial question is for Aimé Césaire the crucial question of the revolution.[9] Its neglect by historians of France is therefore all the more surprising.

Yves Bénot suggests that this lack of attention may be attributable partly to the imperialist sensibilities of early writers, who preferred to overlook the struggles of the colonized, and partly to the influence of these writers on later historians, who have absorbed unwittingly their definition of the revolution's agenda.[10] Whether or not this is so, evidently at issue here are perceptions of the meaning and boundaries of the French Revolution.

Dating back to Jean Bodin, antislavery ideas had a long history in France but remained at the end of the ancien régime little more than a superficial embellishment of Enlightenment thought. Slavery's inhumanity had been condemned by Montesquieu, Voltaire, and Rousseau and in the *Encyclopédie*, although with varying degrees of ambiguity, and even those, such as Diderot and Mercier, who wrote of violent self-liberation showed no sustained commitment. The physiocrats had attacked slavery's economic utility incidentally, but their arguments could make little headway, given the institution's role in the dramatic expansion of French commerce.[11] The presence of slaves in France was exploited frivolously in *parlementaire* battles with the Crown, though at the same time explicitly racist attitudes became more prominent in scientific and government circles.[12] Nevertheless, a new practical antislavery concern emerged in the 1780s with the publication of concrete schemes for gradual abolition by Condorcet and in Raynal's best-selling *Histoire des deux Indes*. Necker suggested an Anglo-French initiative to abolish the slave trade. Lafayette sponsored a secret emancipation experiment on a plantation in Guiana. Also in secret, the colonial minister de Castries pondered schemes for reforming and eventually abolishing slavery.[13] In February 1788, Jacques-Pierre Brissot founded the elite Société des Amis des Noirs, which called for the ending of the slave trade and the eventual and gradual, but uncompensated, abolition of slavery.[14] Unlike Britain, however, France never developed a popular abolitionist movement.[15]

Nearly 50 of the 520 surviving general cahiers expressed opinions hostile to slavery or the slave trade, although many of them called cautiously for a compromise between "political interest" and "the sacred rights of humanity [or liberty]."[16] In his long opening speech to the States-General, the king's minister Necker enjoined the deputies to consider the plight of black slaves. And a remarkable pamphlet, perhaps by Brissot, argued that the deputies owed "as much to [their] fellow citizens of the colonies as to those of Europe, as much to black Frenchmen as to white."[17]

The very first question the united three orders had to vote on was the admission of illegally elected white representatives from the West Indies. After some delay, colonial representation was voted by acclamation. The one deputy who argued that colonies were not part of the *patrie* was quickly silenced. However, to the planters' discomfort, these discussions enabled some prominent deputies, notably Mirabeau and La Rochefoucauld, to bring up the issues of slavery and racial equality.[18] During the early summer of 1789, the colonial question certainly seemed to be on the agenda of the revolution.

Yet the Amis des Noirs were to meet with complete failure in the Constituent Assembly. With hindsight this looks like a foregone conclusion, but this was not quite the case for contemporaries. It seemed to the abolitionist Thomas Clarkson, arriving in Paris in early August 1789, that the assembly might abolish the slave trade by acclamation.[19] With Lafayette's prestige and Mirabeau's reputation as an orator at their apogee, he doubtless hoped for another emotional upsurge such as had produced the whirlwind abolition of serfdom and feudal rights on August 4th. Since this was how slavery eventually was abolished in February 1794, one cannot dismiss the prognosis as entirely fanciful. However, it was more significant that during the night of August 4th La Rochefoucauld had brought up the question of slavery without any success.[20] And before then, there were already signs in the Constituent Assembly of the impatience with anticolonial speakers that was soon to become typical.[21] Even so, as the assembly prepared the Declaration of the Rights of Man, planters in Paris were sufficiently alarmed to form a pressure group that became known as the Club Massiac to defend their interests.

On the basis of the fear expressed in colonial correspondence sent from Paris, Yves Bénot suggests that the antislavery cause perhaps missed a promising opportunity in mid-1789.[22] Even seven months later, one might add, when the procolonial lobby had marshaled formidable forces against its opponents, one finds the centrist deputy Régnauld of Saint-Jean-d'Angély fearing that the assembly could still be carried away by emotive eloquence, as the slave trade was an issue on which most deputies, he thought, had feelings rather than an opinion. Others agreed.[23] By the beginning of 1790, when it was clear the antislavery cause had lost much ground, Mirabeau, after personally taking soundings, apparently still reckoned that 300 deputies would support abolition of the slave trade unconditionally and that another 500 would do so if the British agreed to abolish their slave trade.[24]

Thomas Clarkson, who then believed the British trade would soon be ended, in fact considered the French slave trade a more vulnerable target.[25] Smaller and less efficient than its British counterpart, it received annually 2 million *livres* in subsidies from the now bankrupt government. French slave merchants covertly used the services of British ship-owners and brokers, and their export cargoes consisted largely of foreign goods. French planters also purchased many of their slaves from foreign contraband traders. Hence it could be claimed that banning the importation of slaves into France's colonies was not just a moral issue, it was also in the national interest and would hurt foreigners more than Frenchmen. This was the parliamentary tactic that would help terminate the British slave trade in 1806–1807.[26] The Constituent Assembly, however, refused even to hear such arguments. No abolitionists were elected to its Colonial Committee, and on March 8, 1790, it passed a decree which granted the colonies internal legislative autonomy. With a fastidious use of euphemism, it gave assurance that the mother country would respect "local customs," would protect "colonial property," and would not "innovate in any branch of colonial trade." The decree was hurriedly approved without discussion, and the antislavery supporters who endeavored to speak were shouted down. Most newspapers welcomed the outcome.[27]

The colonial deputies boasted to their constituents that almost every clause in the March 8th decree had been suggested by them.[28] This ascendancy of the colonial faction was due to a combination of factors. First, French mercantile interests and the Club Massiac, burying their differences over commercial regulation, proved especially adept at lobbying deputies, publishing propaganda, and piling up petitions and addresses from the port cities that claimed the nation's prosperity was at stake.[29] Suspected of being sold to the British, the Amis were clearly on the defensive by January 1790 in the battle for public opinion. Colonialist pressure forced Olympe de Gouges's play *L'Esclavage des Nègres* from the theatre and then halted publication of Bonnemain's *Régéneration des colonies*.[30] Although the Atlantic ports were not well integrated into the French economy, they (and consequently the slave societies they serviced) represented what was most modern and dynamic in the ancien régime. Serfdom and slavery were therefore not seen in the same light. The support of the wealthy seaports, moreover, appeared to be crucial to the future of the revolution. Its safety, finances, and unity came first, claimed Barnave, the liberal democratic leader and spokesmen of the Colonial Committee.[31]

To criticize the colonial status quo thus came to seem unpatriotic, and the March 8th decree actually made it a crime to incite unrest in the colonies. The stakes were raised this high because the debate was never focused narrowly on the slave trade alone. Though the Amis des Noirs periodically asserted that the slaves were not yet "ready" for freedom, it was clear from their writings that abolition of the slave trade was to be just the first stage in their attack on slavery.[32] The slave regime itself was always in question, and Barnave and the colonial deputies went even further, accusing the antislavery lobby, unfairly, of being opposed to colonization in general.[33]

Finally, the imperial tie also seemed endangered by two elements in the colonies: the slaves and the white settlers themselves. From early in the revolution, Saint Domingue's deputies claimed their colony to be an ally, not a dependent, of France. This outlook had deep roots in Saint Domingue's past, but its articulation became especially strident in response to the revolution's threat to the colonial system.[34] In the winter of 1789, the colonial deputies hinted quite openly that France needed her colonies more than they needed her and that if their wants were not met, secession might follow.[35] Substance was lent to these threats by the overthrow of the old regime administration in the West Indies and the colonists' establishment of their own assemblies, developments that finally forced the Constituent Assembly to pay attention to colonial matters. In addition to influencing the evolution of colonial policy, the autonomist movement in the islands was itself promoted by fears of metropolitan meddling and of slave rebellion.[36] Reports reached Paris in December 1789 of a brief slave revolt in Martinique and of unspecified disorders on plantations in Saint Domingue, supposedly stimulated by news from France.[37] The reports were greatly exaggerated and, coinciding with the Abbé Grégoire's ill-timed call for a "general insurrection" against tyranny,[38] they abetted the merchant-planter campaign to depict abolitionists as short-sighted, possibly criminal, fanatics. The mood of the Constituent Assembly changed considerably.[39] Barnave thus was able to introduce the March 8th decree as a necessary measure for reassuring the colonists and preserving the colonies.

In this manner, the slave trade and slavery became taboo subjects that the Constituent and Legislative Assemblies simply refused to discuss. The demand for reform proved far weaker than even the cahiers had suggested.[40] In May 1791, the assembly passed a constitutional decree that explicitly guaranteed the slave regime against metropolitan interference. Robespierre objected violently, uttering his famous words "Perish the colonies!"[41] However, he also observed, less memorably, in the same speech that "the conservation of your colonies is an important matter." The cause of his outburst was not the institution of slavery itself, which he never displayed any interest in reforming. Rather it was a concern for the impact on domestic politics of a proposal to use the word "slave" in the decree (instead of "unfree person"). But for future dramatic developments in the Caribbean, probably little more would have been heard of these issues. The slave trade, in fact, was never abolished during the revolution and reached an all-time peak during the years 1789–1791.[42]

The Constituent Assembly similarly sought to avoid the question of racial equality, but in a more devious manner and with frank embarrassment. In contrast to the antislavery debate, the cause of the *gens de couleur libres*—the free colored middle class of the colonies—was all but unknown in France. Numbering 40,000 or so in the Caribbean, they were an extremely diverse group. Most were of mixed racial descent, and they included wealthy, well-educated, slave-holding families as well as recently freed slaves. All were subject to humiliating, apartheid-like restrictions. The stability of the slave regime, it was argued, demanded that all descendants of slaves be consigned in perpetuity to a dishonored intermediary class.[43] In 1778, mixed marriages and immigration by non-whites were even banned in France, where there lived several thousand of that group, chiefly in Paris and the Atlantic ports. However, during the twenty years prior to the revolution, government officials began cautiously to discuss ameliorating the position of those in the colonies who were wealthiest and farthest removed from black ancestry. The *Encyclopédie* included a favorable article on *mulâtres*, which was echoed in early pamphlets of Brissot, in the cahier of the Paris Third Estate, and in some early altercations in the National Assembly. Yet in the first years of the revolution, French public opinion still sometimes confused slaves and free coloreds.[44]

Nevertheless, it was the race question that was to prove the most prominent of colonial issues during the Constituent Assembly. Free colored activists in both Paris and Saint Domingue brought their cause to public notice in the fall of 1789, and, taken up by Brissot and Grégoire, it thereafter became the main campaign of the Amis des Noirs. Much remains unclear about the genesis of this alliance and the evolution of free colored demands.[45] Particularly uncertain is the importance attached in the debate to racial intermixture (specifically to white ancestry). Since blacks were only a minority of free nonwhites, in contemporary parlance they were often subsumed within the ambiguous term "people of color." However, phenotypical distinctions were extremely important in the colonies, where they formed the basis of a racial hierarchy and tended to coincide with differences in wealth, literacy, and genealogical distance from slavery.[46] Juxtaposing questions of race and class, the exact importance of these internal divisions within the free colored sector merit much more research.[47]

White colonists doubtless enjoyed exaggerating such divisions, as if they legitimated their own prejudices. Yet one should not be surprised that the first political activities of these nonwhites should reflect a clash between traditional colonial values and the new ideology of equal rights. The first pamphlet written by a free colored appears to be exclusively a plea for fellow "mixed bloods."[48] Its author wanted colonial society to be divided along color lines with the mulattoes and whites grouped together. Mulatto slaves were to be freed at birth. Blacks were referred to as destined for slavery. In late August 1789, we find the wealthy quadroon[49] Julien Raimond seeking political rights only for fellow quadroons, a policy of limited assimilation he had been discreetly urging on the government for some years.[50] Following the Declaration of the Rights of Man, however, some thirty to fifty "citizens of color" in Paris formed the Société des Colons Américains and drew up a much more radical cahier in early September. It called for full equality for all free nonwhites and freedom for mulatto slaves (provisions that respectively negated and subtly affirmed the racist assumptions of colonial society). Raimond and another quadroon, Vincent Ogé,[51] joined the Colons Américains shortly thereafter. French historians Debien and Debbasch treat the Society's cahier with some skepticism, deducing a willingness to compromise on its demands from the fact that Raimond, Ogé, and the society all sought at this period to bypass the Constituent Assembly and negotiate directly with the Club Massiac.[52] When in October and November the society sought representation in the assembly, their addresses spoke only of "citizen landowners of color . . . born free," "mulattoes, quadroons, etc." In the writings of Raimond, too, Debbasch observes, there remained a discordance between an egalitarian program and a discourse impregnated with "sub-racism" that minimized the numbers of free blacks.[53]

Debbasch and Debien do not agree on exactly when free blacks were admitted to the Colons Américains (whose membership grew to eighty), but their numbers were evidently few.[54] In November, an open rift appeared when an anonymous group of free blacks published an address that vaunted their racial purity over the "bastardized" origins of the citizens of color and demanded separate representation for themselves should the mulattoes gain seats in the assembly.[55] Behind this maneuver stood the deputies for Saint Domingue, who claimed fully to represent the colony already and wished to ridicule their rivals' demands. But the document probably was not a forgery, as has been claimed.[56] Its authenticity was not challenged, and Brissot in the *Patriote François* suddenly stopped using "free black" as a synonym for "free colored."[57] The breach was nevertheless of short duration. Though separate identities had suggested separate strategies to these different factions, they were visibly cooperating by early 1790, brought together by the new egalitarian ideology and the increasing intransigence of the colonists.[58]

It is nonetheless striking that the free coloreds' white allies continued to focus on white ancestry as being among the attributes of the free coloreds. Though Abbé Grégoire did support the cause of free blacks, he almost always used the terms "mixed bloods," "mulattoes," and "people of color" in his advocacy, quite unlike Brissot, who frequently referred to "free blacks."[59] The concern with free coloreds as "descendants of Europeans" is quite explicit in the writings of Abbé de Cournand, another Ami des Noirs and early champion of colonial nonwhites. He called for full equality for colored landowners who were two generations removed from slavery and, like Grégoire, for freedom at birth for slaves of mixed racial descent.[60] Even in 1791, the Amis des Noirs' addresses, while asserting the equality of all free nonwhites, describe them as "mulatto Frenchmen." A similar tendency is evident in the addresses of the Jacobin Clubs.[61]

This choice of language was surely not accidental. Though there was probably genuine misunderstanding of the true number of free blacks in the colonies,[62] their activities in Paris meant they cannot have been overlooked. Some reformers perhaps were willing to settle for less than an outright abolition of racial discrimination and merely to shift the line of demarcation. Most likely, it was thought that a discourse that stressed the mixed heritage of the *gens de couleur* would have the best chance of overcoming opposition and persuading Frenchmen to think of colonial nonwhites as their brothers. With the position of Jews and nonwhites in France left in limbo until September 1791, it was the question of free coloreds in the colonies that first tested the racial boundaries of the French Revolution.

Here again, as on the question of the slave trade, the Constituent Assembly came to an end with the status quo intact, and for much the same reasons. The issues were more subtle, however, and there developed a greater diversity of opinion. The campaign began well on October 22, 1789, when at the bar of the assembly the delegates of the Société des Colons Américains received vague but encouraging words from the president of the session. In November, their demand for free colored representation in the assembly was accepted, by a narrow vote, in its Credentials Committee, chaired by Grégoire. Yet because of quite extraordinary obstruction, the committee's report was never presented, and when Grégoire tried to speak, he was shouted down.[63] The proposed deputies could not prove that they had any representative standing, and the Constituent Assembly had already opposed such special-interest representation in the case of the mercantile lobby. However, it was not these arguments but political muscle that denied the free coloreds a voice, first in the National Assembly, and then in the colonial assemblies recognized by the decree of March 8th.

Resting squarely on the Declaration of the Rights of Man, the civil rights of tax-paying, property-owning nonwhites seemed a much safer issue to the Amis des Noirs than did the slave trade. It involved none of the conflict between rights to liberty and property found in the case of human bondage. Yet despite their insistence that the free colored question was quite separate from that of slavery, the Amis never succeeded in divorcing the two issues. Brissot wrote incautiously that free colored citizenship would prepare the way for eventual emancipation of the slaves, and this would remain a constant theme in antislavery literature.[64] It was also thought that free colored deputies would be allies in the fight against the slave trade.[65] Moreover, free colored attitudes toward slavery (an unresearched topic) could be perplexingly ambivalent.

It is broadly true that nonwhite slave-owners generally acted according to their class interests during the struggles of the 1790s. Yet in an early address to the Constituent Assembly, the Colons Américains went out of their way to condemn the institution of slavery. Quite astonishingly, Vincent Ogé made a speech to a stone-silent Club Massiac in September 1789 that alluded to preparing for the end of slavery, which left him a marked man.[66] And as already seen, both free coloreds and white abolitionists linked free colored citizenship with the emancipation of slaves of mixed racial descent. Finally, although antislavery writers were at pains to argue that elevating the status of free nonwhites would strengthen the slave regime (and act as a check on white secessionism), both Grégoire and Brissot also suggested that, if driven to desperation, free coloreds would make common cause with the slaves (or secessionist whites) in open revolt.[67]

The colonists also agreed that the race and slavery questions could not be kept separate. In the Caribbean, colonists and officials had traditionally regarded racial prejudice and discrimination each as necessary bulwarks of slavery that supposedly helped convince blacks of their inherent inferiority and prevented the relatives of slaves gaining access to public office. However, this argument was largely kept in abeyance early in the revolution. Legerdemain was used instead. In February 1790, the Paris Commune warmly received a deputation of nonwhites, but, after hearing arguments from both sides on the colonial question, then passed on to other business.[68] Similarly, Barnave's Colonial Committee wanted the decision on free colored voting rights to be made by the colonial assemblies, but it dared not admit this. Therefore, in defining the franchise in the decree of March 8th and its accompanying instructions it made deliberately ambiguous reference only to "citizens" or "persons" without mention of phenotype.[69] When a debate was finally forced and Grégoire sought clarification, the session was hastily closed, with Barnave and others giving off-the-record assurance that free coloreds' rights were not infringed.[70] In the Caribbean, however, the decree was interpreted according to colonial norms by both white planters and royal administrators. This became the "official" interpretation, and on October 12th Barnave put into another colonial decree, which was forced through without debate, a promise that the National Assembly would not legislate on the "status of persons" in the colonies.[71]

There are a few tantalizing signs that things could have turned out differently. Colonial opinion was by no means monolithic, and the race question exercised merchants notably less than planters. It assumed different proportions in different colonies, and even within the Club Massiac and in different parts of Saint Domingue there was some movement in 1789 toward cooperation between whites and free coloreds.[72] Hence there was some basis for accommodation. The nature and causes of these divergent approaches merit further investigation, but the chances are they were not very substantive.[73] In any event, a polarization rapidly took place as the race and slavery issues became embroiled. While free coloreds were being lynched in Saint Domingue and Martinique, the Constituent Assembly rallied solidly behind Barnave in his desire not to alienate white colonial opinion. This overriding concern for "reassuring" colonists and averting any movement toward secession was particularly explicit in the tormented colonial debate of May 1791, which led to the constitutional guarantee of inviolability for the slave regime but also to a reversal on the race issue.[74]

By May 1791, pro-colonial speakers faced a new degree of opposition on the floor of the assembly, in its public galleries, and in the streets outside. In the previous six months, the political situation had changed noticeably, partly because of a short-lived rebellion in northern Saint Domingue led by an exasperated Vincent Ogé.[75] News of Ogé's torture and being broken on the wheel reached France in early March and helped bring home to the Constituent Assembly the meaning of colonial self-government. Fighting between urban and rural whites in the Caribbean had also caused deputies to want to take a more interventionist line in the colonies. Troops had been dispatched and plans had been drawn up to send out civil commissioners with extensive powers. Concessions to the free coloreds could now seem not only a means of atonement for the dishonest neglect of the past but also a way of strengthening France's loose grip on its colonial populations.[76] The port of Bordeaux announced its support for the *gens de couleur.*[77]

The political climate was also changing in France. Growing antipathy toward aristocracy and dissatisfaction with limitation of the franchise probably put in a more sympathetic light the free coloreds' case against the "aristocracy of the skin." At the very least, free colored rights provided a vehicle for disgruntled Jacobins to attack the political status quo.[78] Michael Kennedy's study of the Jacobin clubs seems to show support for the free coloreds growing in early 1791 more in response to Grégoire's advocacy than to events in Saint Domingue. However, the provincial Jacobins' petitioning campaign was sparked directly by the Ogé affair and was apparently the work of Claude Milscent in Angers, a maverick liberal planter.[79] Some historians see in this period an upswell of popular support for the free coloreds' cause,[80] but the extent of public interest in colonial affairs during the revolution remains problematical. The support of the provincial Jacobin clubs and the Bordeaux merchants appears to have been rather fragile.[81]

After four days of heated debate on the rights of free coloreds and the "necessity" of racial discrimination,[82] a compromise decree was passed on May 15th. It enfranchised only nonwhites born of free parents, not freedmen.[83] It thus kept in existence an intermediary class, as the colonists wished, but one based on legal standing, not phenotype. Furthermore—a point often overlooked —it accorded only voting rights without touching the apparatus of discrimination in any other area. Still, the white colonists regarded it as a dangerous breach in the colonial system. The colonial deputies walked out of the Constituent Assembly. Planters in Saint Domingue spoke ever more loudly of secession, and the colony's governor wrote home that he could not enforce the decree.[84] Meanwhile, in Paris, a climate of political reaction set in following the flight of the king. The interaction between events in the colonies and events in the metropole now grew faster than ever, but colonial policy would remain fatally out of step with developments in the Caribbean. In a remarkable volte-face, Barnave got the decree rescinded in the closing days of the Constituent Assembly (September 24th), just when Jews, actors, and—in a conciliatory gesture—nonwhites in France had their civil rights recognized.[85]

By then, frustrated free coloreds in Saint Domingue had already taken up arms and forced acceptance of their demands from recalcitrant planters. They were able to do this because in August 1791 the largest slave revolt in the history of the Americas simultaneously broke out in the colony's northern plain. Its origins are obscure, but the strengthening of counterrevolutionary currents in Europe and rumors associated with the suppression of the May 15th law seem to have contributed to its outbreak.[86] The prospect of secession also can have aroused no enthusiasm in the slave quarters. The planters, for their part, commonly blamed the insurrection on the interference of abolitionists, free coloreds, or counterrevolutionaries. Whatever its causes, the Saint Domingue slave revolt would decisively change the nature of the colonial question, pushing white planters to their first actual moves toward secession (1791) and then bringing French legislators to concede full racial equality (1792) and eventually slave emancipation (1794).[87]

In a sense, there are good grounds for neglecting colonial affairs in a history of the Constituent Assembly. In October 1791, slavery, the slave trade, and racial discrimination in the colonies all remained juridically unchanged. Although the assembly had admitted seventeen colonial representatives, this fraternity did not extend to the nonwhites who made up more than 90 percent of the colonies' inhabitants. French overseas possessions had been placed outside of the new constitution, and they were self-governing in internal matters, free to choose which aspects of the national regeneration they would adopt. Nonetheless, Caribbean politics could not be kept out of the Constituent Assembly. By early 1791, the creation of civil commissioners and the dispatch of troops were already undermining the colonial autonomy granted a year before. Deputies had to grapple with issues that painfully opposed political principles and national prosperity, and on the racial question they reversed course several times, producing in May one of the great debates of the early revolution. This alone should win a more prominent place in the historiography of revolutionary France for colonial matters.

Also bearing on the question of how integral or peripheral colonial affairs were to the French Revolution is the argument regarding the relative importance of overseas and metropolitan influences both in creating policy and shaping the colonial revolution. To what extent did colonial policy evolve "naturally" out of developments in France, and to what degree was it "imposed" from outside by events in the colonies that may have been only tangentially related to France's revolution? Where in this colonial question should one locate core and periphery?

Perhaps the greatest challenge to the historian of the colonial revolution is in assessing the interaction between metropolitan and colonial developments. The work of the distinguished West Indian Marxists C. L. R. James and, in particular, Aimé Césaire has done much to establish the colonial revolution as an autonomous force that helped radicalize the French Revolution rather than being merely a reflection of it.[88] This view has been especially strongly expressed by writers of the Haitian *noiriste* school and by some right-wing European scholars.[89] Creole autonomism, free colored activism, and slave resistance all certainly had complex prehistories quite independent of the revolution in France, and, as noted above, the Constituent Assembly's colonial legislation came largely as a response to events in the Caribbean.

The recent studies by Bénot and Blackburn develop this viewpoint, achieving a new level in the integration of metropolitan and colonial developments, but they additionally make a strong case, also within the framework of Marxist analysis, for giving renewed emphasis to idealist influences within the French Revolution. Antislavery and antiracism were politically weak forces, they agree, but together with the growth of French radicalism, they helped form the intellectual and emotional climate within which colonial policy was made, and they created political options that could be taken up as the calculations of realpolitik changed.[90]

The evidence that Bénot, Blackburn, and James put forward of a growing popular solidarity in France with colonial nonwhites is suggestive but remains limited, and there seems some contradiction in Bénot's depiction of antislavery as possessing mass support yet remaining the cause of an enlightened handful of individuals.[91] Nevertheless, in exploring the popular press, he convincingly reconstructs the growth of antislavery sentiment beyond the elite Amis des Noirs and highlights the role of several neglected individuals whose interest in the colonies cannot be reduced to a pragmatic reaction to overseas events, though it often did not predate the revolution. Easily the most important of these was Léger-Félicité Sonthonax, the commissioner who unilaterally abolished slavery in Saint Domingue in 1793 and so precipitated the emancipation decree of 16 pluviôse. Although his actions are best understood as a desperate response to a wartime emergency, they take on a new appearance when one realizes that as early as September 1790, Sonthonax was predicting the end of slavery, writing that "the time is not far off when a frizzy-haired African, with no recommendation beyond his good sense and virtue, will come and participate as a legislator in the bosom of our national assemblies."[92]

Perhaps the most important point, however, that one can make regarding the force of antislavery ideas is to note that the moral case against slavery and institutionalized racism was often conceded by their leading defenders. Both were unjust and irrational, they admitted, but unfortunately necessary for French prosperity and the preservation of order in the colonies.[93] It is a measure of antislavery's success that its opponents were often reduced to a defense based on instrumentality that would prove vulnerable to recalculations of self-interest.

Finally, it is impossible to ignore the way the decrees of March 8 and October 12, 1790, and May 15 and September 24, 1791, reflected the changing political climate in Paris—the triumph of bourgeois liberalism, the subsequent radical challenge, and the political reaction of the summer of 1791. Jaurès and James argued that the volte-face on the race question facilitated the post-Varennes reaction,[94] but on chronological grounds alone this would seem unlikely. All in all, while it is clearly fruitless to try to assign primacy to either French or overseas influences in creating colonial policy, there is no doubt it cannot be treated in isolation from the development of the revolution in France.

Defining the French Revolution's impact on the colonies is a rather more difficult task. Despite an abundant historiography, current research does not allow precise formulations, as Yves Bénot observes,[95] and his and Blackburn's excellent studies are notably stronger on metropolitan than colonial events. This is not the place to review the whole colonial revolution, but a few points can be made. Though Césaire's stress on the diversity of the revolutionary experience in the colonies is well founded, it does not entirely undermine the French Revolution's importance in shaping the colonial revolution. One can just as well argue that there was a great deal of similarity between events in the different colonies, that the issues were generally the same, even if differences in demographic balance and geographic size produced different outcomes.

At bottom, the question is one of weighing the ideological influence of the French Revolution against its political influence. Did it create new social and political aspirations in the colonies or merely weaken the institutions that traditionally had held them in check? "Merely" is perhaps an overly dismissive term to describe the disruption of the colonial administration and military that took place in the period 1789–1791. There is certainly, I would argue, a vast difference in scale between pre- and post-1789 developments in white autonomism, free colored activism, and slave resistance.[96] Yet the causation of the colonial revolution and its specificity remain difficult to define, especially insofar as France and its empire were participants in a broader Atlantic Revolution.

French Caribbean whites behaved and spoke much like their compatriots in France, where the great majority had been born. The role of the principal law courts, the hatred of "administrative despotism," the adoption of the tricolor cockade, the creation of municipalities and political clubs, the pursuit of representative government, all were similar in mother country and colonies, even if the seigneurial pretensions of some planter revolutionaries made them look as much like aristocrats in R. R. Palmer's broad definition as the Patriots they usually claimed to be.[97] Anne Pérotin's work on the Jacobins of the Windward Isles brings out their mimesis and fixation on the revolution in France.[98] However, she also underlines the centrality of the race and slavery issues for these "Patriots in the Tropics" and the ways in which colonial values tempered their revolutionary zeal. Eighteenth-century attitudes toward race require much more investigation, but though the difference in social setting was indeed enormous, the gap between France and her colonies was not necessarily so great. Just as metropolitan radicals were slow to take up the race and slavery issues, those in the West Indies generally were obliged to reconcile themselves, at least superficially, to the reforms of 1792 and 1794.[99]

For many others, however, the end of white supremacy and slavery provided grounds for abandoning la France régénérée. The revolution thus reinforced latent desires for independence and freedom from restrictions on foreign trade, the other area where colonial and metropolitan interests clashed head-on. It is remarkable, even so, that if in the Caribbean the trade laws were openly flouted during the revolution, in France the planter lobby scarcely raised the commercial question at all, so anxious was it to secure the port city merchants as allies. As for colonial secessionism, I have argued elsewhere it was a weaker movement than appearances suggested and that, as in France, counterrevolutionary forces played an important role in the rejection of the mother country.[100] The first colonists to break away from France were not the turbulent and ambitious "Americans" of Saint Domingue but the traditionalist planters of the Windward Isles who rejected the Republic in September 1792. While the colonial world had its own social and economic imperatives, historians of France's revolution can find much that is familiar in the revolutionary experience of Frenchmen overseas.

As for the free coloreds, their rapid growth in population suggests that, revolution or not, sooner or later they would have become a political force. The French Revolution, however, gave them a public forum unavailable in the colonies, and the Declaration of Rights seems to have had an immediate impact on their program. When Ogé rebelled, he used as a rallying cry the decree of March 1790.

The element of the colonial revolution whose relationship to the French Revolution is most mysterious is, not surprisingly, the activities of the slave population, which had little opportunity to articulate its views in a durable form. Césaire was wrong to connect the Martinique rising of August 1789 to news of the Bastille's fall, which was then still unknown. Nevertheless, other rumors conflating abolitionism and royalist reforms seem to have been important in mobilizing the rebels.[101] Such rumors also circulated in Saint Domingue late in 1789, along with talk of "the revolt of the white slaves [in France] who had killed their masters and taken possession of the land." Most important, they were instrumental in organizing the great 1791 insurrection.[102] Yet they were not confined to the French islands alone. One of the intriguing features of the period 1789–1791 is the emergence of a new type of slave revolt, soon to become common, in which the rebels claimed to have been officially emancipated by a distant government. The evidence concerning the aims of the Saint Domingue rebels of 1791 is contradictory. However, the commitment of the slaves' leaders to the overthrow of slavery was ambiguous and rarely expressed in idealistic terms. They tended to adopt a conservative church-and-king rhetoric and express contempt for those they called *les citoyens*, which complicates considerably the question of the ideological impact of the French Revolution. Although Eugene Genovese argues that a new "bourgeois-democratic" type of slave revolt developed under the influence of the French Revolution, it seems to me that what is novel about slave resistance in this period is more reliably linked to the international antislavery movement and late ancien régime reformism.[103]

The interaction between events in Paris and the Caribbean during the closing months of the Constituent Assembly was to ensure the colonial question a much greater salience within revolutionary politics in the months to come. Curiously, the first news of the August uprising that reached France was regarded with considerable skepticism, and the concurrent reports of the white secessionist response (this time real) tended to be seen as just as threatening.[104] However, it was the slaves who rebelled in this last month of the Constituent Assembly who were to bring not only racial equality and slave emancipation to the French Empire but also colonial secession and its first independent state.

11 The Great Powers and the Haitian Revolution

This chapter sketches the reactions of the major powers, especially Spain, the least studied case, to this sole successful slave revolt in world history. It distinguishes four phases: initial reactions (1791–1792), military intervention (1793–1798), coming to terms with a black power (1798–1801), and the achievement of independence (1802–1804).

Initial Reactions, 1791–1792

By 1791, French Saint Domingue had developed into the world's major producer of both sugar and coffee. Its half-million slaves and 8,000 plantations made it easily the most important colony in the Caribbean, exporting far more than the British and Spanish islands combined. Supplying some 40 percent of French overseas trade, it was a vital source of profits and foreign exchange for France's otherwise stagnant economy and an object of international envy. Reactions overseas were therefore mixed when there broke out in the colony's densely settled northern plain an enormously destructive slave rebellion, far bigger than any previously seen in the Americas, which, as months went by, proved impossible to suppress.[1]

The great insurrection simultaneously threatened and stimulated the Caribbean economy to an unprecedented degree.[2] Bloodcurdling reports of gruesome massacres and blazing cane fields realized every slave-owner's worst nightmare, not least in neighboring Cuba and Jamaica, which could be reached from Saint Domingue by canoe. Nearly 350,000 slaves lived in Cuba and Jamaica, and within one month of the uprising, Jamaican slaves were singing songs about it.[3] During the previous two years the Caribbean had already witnessed an increase in slave protest. This was associated with the onset of the British antislavery campaign and the French Revolution and with hesitant government reformism by the three major powers—trends which themselves increased planter nervousness.[4] On the other hand, the same period also had brought reviving prosperity to the British islands and rapid development to Cuba, and when the price of sugar and coffee skyrocketed in 1791, opportunities for expansion increased dramatically.

"The era of our happiness has arrived," announced Francisco Arango y Parreño, spokesman of the Cuban planter elite. As Cuban sugar and coffee prices tripled, slave imports multiplied, and through the 1790s, thousands of acres of Cuba's forests and tobacco fields were cleared each year for planting cane.[5] Even so, it was Jamaica which for the next few decades would be the world's major producer of sugar and, more briefly, of coffee as well. Through the 1790s, the much smaller but more developed British island would import nearly twice as many slaves as Cuba.[6]

The first concern of colonial governments was security for their increasingly valuable and vulnerable assets. The Assembly of Jamaica called for more troops and reluctantly agreed to pay for them when London refused to do so. It also established local watch committees, deported some foreigners, and passed a few minor laws to improve the lot of the slaves. In the Spanish colonies, extreme hostility to the French Revolution had already produced measures to restrict the entry of people and publications from French territories. In Santo Domingo, the foreign colony most directly threatened by the slave insurrection, the governor established a military cordon along the long common frontier with Saint Domingue using troops transferred from Puerto Rico.

A more delicate problem was the question of sending assistance to a commercial rival. The desperate appeals for aid sent out by the Colonial Assembly of Saint Domingue met with a limited display of class and racial solidarity from Jamaica and a seemingly callous neutrality on the part of the Spaniards, which helped add an additional chapter to the *leyenda negra* of Spanish cruelty. The governor of Jamaica refused to part with any troops—he dared not—but he did send some arms and ammunition to Cap Français, along with several warships for temporary moral support. The Jamaican assembly approved these actions, but it divided over providing a loan or credit to its insolvent French counterpart. Liberal planters, those who most readily identified with Saint Domingue's revolutionary assembly, were defeated by conservative and populist elements who opposed raising taxes to help foreigners.[7]

The funds needed to fight the rebel slaves were to come instead from the United States. The United States had a large debt to France left over from the American Revolutionary War. Washington now chose to repay it to the colonists of Saint Domingue, advancing some 726,000 dollars in two years, though Paris was reluctant to approve the arrangement, remaining suspicious of an attempt to make Saint Domingue independent.[8] Most of the money went into the pockets of North American merchants, who became increasingly indispensable to Caribbean trade in the 1790s.[9]

As for the Spanish, though the governor of eastern Cuba sent food to south and west Saint Domingue, the governors of Havana and Santo Domingo claimed they were unable to spare any resources and announced their neutrality toward what they called an internal conflict in the French colony.[10] The French felt that the Family Pact of 1764 and extradition and mutual assistance treaties of 1765 and 1777, or at least "the laws of humanity," entitled them to active Spanish cooperation in defeating the rebel slaves. Count Floridablanca, the first secretary of state, specified in November 1791 that white colonists forced to flee from "brigands" should be given protection and arms where possible but that "neutrality" would be official Spanish policy toward the colonists' own internecine conflicts. His successor, the conde de Aranda, reiterated the same policy, simultaneously approving the colonial governors' glib excuses for not parting with any resources.[11]

Hostile to the French Revolution and the social groups it brought to power, Governor García of Santo Domingo argued that white revolutionaries were so thoroughly mixed up with slave and free colored insurgents in Saint Domingue's complicated revolution that he could not pick sides.[12] The archbishop of Santo Domingo proclaimed the revolution divine punishment for the colonists' irreligion and insubordination, and for this he was reprimanded by Madrid.[13] On the Santo Domingo frontier, many male French colonists fleeing the uprising were at first refused asylum, and some were sent back to their deaths.[14] Other refugees were robbed or were treated with hostility by Spanish officers or the local inhabitants. Some may have been sold to the black insurgents. Various factors were at work here: soldierly contempt for terror-stricken civilians, the genuine poverty of the Spanish colony, passionate detestation of godless French radicalism, and perhaps long-standing resentment of French economic success on formerly Spanish soil.[15] French prejudices magnified these complaints, and some blatantly false reports appeared in the colonial and metropolitan press. True or false, they further envenomed Franco-Spanish relations.[16]

Still more controversial were accusations that the Spanish actively assisted the slave insurgents. Of the few historians who have studied this subject, Maria Rosario Sevilla Soler and Carlos Esteban Deive implicate Governor García y Moreno and contrast his behavior with the genuine neutrality of the Spanish government. They depict him as assisting the black rebels from 1791 onward. Alain Yacou, on the other hand, argues that the initial Spanish response was one of solidarity with the French but that hostile intentions emerged in Spain by April 1792.[17] Neither version, I think, is correct, although García y Moreno's intentions remain difficult to decipher. The rebel leaders clearly sought to cultivate good relations with their Spanish neighbors; this was one reason why they adopted an extravagantly royalist rhetoric, posing as defenders of church and king.[18] And there is little doubt that Spanish inhabitants and soldiers in the frontier zone traded ammunition for plantation pillage. French radicals and counterrevolutionaries and black rebels—all said so. But it remains uncertain how much official connivance there was in this conduct and whether it was machiavellian or just opportunistic.[19]

Ordering his officers to neither irritate nor encourage the black insurgents, Governor García forbade such trading, and he strongly denied accusations of duplicity. He claimed the frontier zone contained no significant quantities of gunpowder and that it was foreign vessels off the Saint Domingue coast that supplied the slaves.[20] Moreover, the rebels' frequent written requests to initiate trade perhaps suggest it was a less-than-routine occurrence, notwithstanding pre-revolutionary links between free colored smugglers and Spanish soldiery.

García certainly disliked the French, who he felt should have been able to defend themselves. Despite Madrid's suggestions, he refused to let refugees settle in Santo Domingo. Furthermore, his correspondence reveals a degree of sympathy with the slave insurgents. He contrasted their martial spirit with that of the once arrogant, now barefoot French colonists. He described slavery in Saint Domingue as "horrifying," and apparently found reasonable the rebels' pursuit of freedom, albeit believing they were secretly led by white liberals. His letters, however, also expressed hopes for peace; disappointment when negotiations failed; contempt for the "ferocious brigands," "that barbarous people"; and orders that none be allowed to cross the frontier.[21] Spanish officers on the frontier, unlike García, formally corresponded with, and occasionally met, the rebel leaders, but that they encouraged them remains unproven.[22] The governor of Spanish Louisiana did believe reports of Spanish complicity, but that does not justify the confident assertions of some historians that Spain was seeking to destroy Saint Domingue or even helped cause the slave uprising.[23]

Fear of a massive invasion, rather than machiavellian meddling or graft, was probably the guiding force in Governor García's declared policy of perfect neutrality. It is also the best reason for thinking he did not assist the black rebels. He sought to appease them, not make them stronger. This remained true even after May 1792, when García hinted to his subordinates that war with France was a possibility: "We do not know in the end which side will be our enemy."[24] He refused all French requests to pursue insurgents into Spanish territory, because he feared having to repel a large-scale incursion precipitated by a French attack. He suggested to Madrid that, in such a case, humanity and the law of nations demanded the granting of asylum. Madrid discouraged the idea but left the way open for him, in consultation with the regent of the *audiencia* (supreme court), to react as circumstances dictated. García interpreted this to his subordinates as "almost carte blanche."[25] Nonetheless, they continued, at least selectively, to expel insurgents who crossed the frontier, handing slaves over to the French in accordance with the treaties in force.[26]

Spain's policy toward the slave insurrection was thus one of non-intervention and neutrality, modified to provide humanitarian aid to white refugees and continued enforcement of treaties regarding fugitives. Officials in Santo Domingo interpreted this policy with an anti-French bias and took pains not to alienate the black insurgents. However, even after the overthrow of the French monarchy in August 1792 and the further radicalization of the Saint Domingue Revolution, there is no evidence of official Spanish complicity in the slave uprising. Only in 1793, once war became likely, did García and the new government of Godoy decide to make overtures to the black insurgents. In March 1793, the governor cautiously suggested such an alliance to Madrid,[27] only to find the decision had already been taken.[28]

Like the Spanish, the British also have been frequently accused of seeking to profit from Saint Domingue's revolution to gain revenge or compensation for the loss of their North American colonies. Even before the slave uprising, rumors circulated in Europe and the Caribbean that England sought to encourage the independence of Saint Domingue or would seek to seize it with the help of secession-minded colonists. *The Times* openly recommended this course. Following the slave insurrection, both radical Anglophile and counterrevolutionary colonists secretly sought British assistance against revolutionary France and the slave insurgents. Various British ministers and officials granted them interviews and revealed varying degrees of enthusiasm for the possibility of acquiring Saint Domingue or taking over its trade. Nonetheless, the British government, like the Spanish, dared do nothing that would jeopardize the European peace. Down to the French declaration of war in February 1793, William Pitt's ministry avoided any interference in the colony.[29]

Military Intervention, 1793–1798

The outbreak of war in Europe and the revolutionary turbulence in Saint Domingue gave the British and Spanish the opportunity to seize one of the world's wealthiest colonies. The intentions of both powers were aggressive rather than defensive. The governments did not yet see the slave revolt as a danger to strongly garrisoned colonies. Rather, both hoped to win an enormous prize at relatively little cost. Despite the expectations of counterrevolutionary colonists and royalist émigrés, neither power intended to return the colony in the event of a Bourbon restoration in France.[30] Nor, despite contemporary suspicions, did they coordinate their policies.[31] British and Spanish planters were left to contemplate uneasily the prospect of a revived Saint Domingue incorporated within the British or Spanish empires.

However, as soon as war began, the balance of power in Saint Domingue dramatically shifted. The whites and free coloreds divided for and against foreign intervention, and all sides turned to the blacks to do their fighting for them.[32] The Spanish recruited most of the slave rebels as *tropas auxiliares* with offers of land, honors, and freedom, though only for soldiers and their families. Although it was a daring experiment, the policy grew out of long Spanish American traditions of arming blacks, making treaties with maroon communities, and welcoming foreign slave fugitives.[33] The Spanish decision also reflected the high stakes the colonial powers were playing for and a desire to recover from the French what had been part of Spain's first American colony. Intense conservative antipathy for the French Revolution and for the type of secular, individualist society exemplified by Saint Domingue perhaps also formed part of the equation, along with the low moral profile and financial problems of the Godoy government that had recently come to power. To outbid the Spanish, the French Republic was forced in February 1794 to emancipate all the slaves, thus turning the conflict into a war of liberation for the entire black population.[34]

The British and Spanish had stumbled into far more than they expected. Though many historians have reflected contemporary opinion that the great powers purposefully marshaled massive forces to seize Saint Domingue, it was never a high priority in their overall military strategy. Other theatres of war always took precedence, and Governor García proved a very cautious general.[35] A striking feature of the Spanish strategy was the use of priests as intermediaries, some of whom became enthusiastic advocates for the black generals. Spanish officers complained it was a "war of Pater Noster and Ave Maria." None, however, proved able to control the black soldiers, who tended to avoid combat and live it up in style in the frontier towns.[36] When they massacred in one day in July 1794 more than 700 French colonists who had allied themselves with the Spanish, it became clear that the policy of using ex-slaves to restore slavery was unworkable.[37] Notwithstanding the 4,000 Spanish troops transferred there, the future of Santo Domingo itself became doubtful.

Since Spain already had more land than it could cultivate, it was easy to imagine that Godoy's government, perhaps in league with the British, had concocted a plot to destroy Saint Domingue and end France's control of the international sugar and coffee markets.[38] Santo Domingo was certainly expendable.[39] Governor García regarded most French colonists with contempt.[40] And the predatory but otherwise passive behavior of the two Cuban regiments sent to Santo Domingo certainly invites speculation about their officers' intentions.[41] Nevertheless, this was not a sinister master plan. Fear of invasion by thousands of armed blacks dominated thinking in Santo Domingo.[42] Criminality, cowardice, and perhaps a lack of supplies best explain the behavior of the Cuban troops.[43] Spanish policy was to conquer, not destroy, Saint Domingue.

In 1794, the French won over from the Spanish the leading black general, Toussaint Louverture. This was the turning point of the Haitian Revolution.[44] Thereafter, the forces of black self-liberation were combined with the resources of a modern state that espoused slave emancipation as a weapon of war. The threat to the slave colonies of middle America escalated, and the chances of conquering Saint Domingue rapidly vanished. Spain was forced to cede Santo Domingo to France, leaving its colonial officials to sort out what to do with the black auxiliaries.[45] Refused entry to Trinidad and Cuba, about 800 (including women and children) eventually were distributed between the neglected regions of Florida, Yucatán, Panama, and Honduras, where some provided valuable military service.[46] The British clung on for five years in Saint Domingue, successfully maintaining slavery in several substantial enclaves. Though they sent more than 25,000 European soldiers to the colony, they too came to rely on black troops. The heavy costs of occupation, however, compelled them to withdraw in 1798. Far from suppressing the threat to their slave colonies, Britain and Spain's military intervention had only succeeded in magnifying the scope of the black revolution.[47]

A Black Power in the Caribbean, 1798–1801

In the next three years, the ex-slave Toussaint Louverture built up a black state in the heart of slave-owning America that remained ostensibly a French colony but in effect was autonomous. The colonial powers looked on with alarm. In the Caribbean, waves of refugees from Saint Domingue were feared as agents of revolutionary "contamination" but also were welcomed for the skills, capital, and slaves they brought with them. Jamaica and Cuba both benefited, despite an increase in slave resistance on the latter island.[48] Spain, now an ally of revolutionary France, found its harbors in Cuba and Venezuela visited by multiracial privateers from Saint Domingue who made common cause with disgruntled local radicals, though not with approval from Paris.[49] In an ironic reversal of policy, the British now decided the best way to control the threat to their colonies and, at the same time, weaken France was to help Toussaint Louverture extend his rule throughout Saint Domingue. It is not true, however, despite many assertions, that the British tried to encourage him to declare outright independence.[50] They thought the potential effect on nonwhite opinion would be too dangerous, and the black general shrewdly showed no desire to take this step.

Toussaint signed a nonaggression pact and limited trade treaty with Britain that in 1799 was expanded to include the United States. John Adams's Federalist administration was chiefly concerned with U.S. commercial interests, which were then being threatened by French privateers. The black leader denied them bases in Saint Domingue and in return received U.S. naval support in his conquest of Saint Domingue's southern peninsula (the first armed intervention overseas by the United States). The Federalists' anticolonial, antislavery, and anti-French bias created some sympathy in the administration for an independent black-ruled Saint Domingue. However, like the British, Adams refrained from encouraging such an inflammatory development and, once peace with France was achieved in 1800, his support for the blacks slackened.[51] Meanwhile, in France, Napoleon Bonaparte had come to power and Jacobin idealism retreated before plans to reassert French control in Saint Domingue and perhaps restore slavery.[52]

The War of Independence, 1802–1804

For the British, still more than for the Americans, relations with France determined policy toward Saint Domingue; it was construed as choosing the lesser of two evils. Though as a goodwill gesture Toussaint had secretly betrayed to the British a French attempt to cause a slave rebellion in Jamaica in 1799, his regime was always perceived as a potential threat to other slave colonies.[53] Hence when peace preliminaries were signed with Napoleon in October 1801, the British government made a cynical about-face and discreetly acquiesced in a French expedition of reconquest.[54] Thomas Jefferson, the new U.S. president, more concerned with southern slaveholders than northern commerce, had already done the same, hinting to the French ambassador in July that he would embargo Toussaint while supplying a French invasion force.[55] Napoleon needed these assurances, because the United States supplied Toussaint's munitions and the British controlled the sea lanes. Spain, France's ally, agreed to supply the expedition with ships, cash, and livestock from its colonies. The Batavian Republic (the Netherlands) also contributed ships and supplies.[56] All the major powers with Caribbean interests were implicated in the French attempt to reconquer Saint Domingue.

There ensued an apocalyptic, almost genocidal war against the former slaves. Since 1791, all parties to the conflict had massacred noncombatants, tortured prisoners, and collected severed heads as trophies, but the War of Independence set new standards in barbarity. In addition to the more than 25,000 French, British, and Spanish troops who had already died in Saint Domingue, perhaps another 40,000 French soldiers now perished. No one knows the number of black dead. Europeans who believed in the progressive civilization of mankind found cause for reflection.[57] Yellow fever, fierce black resistance, and a final twist in great power relations together ensured a French defeat. On learning of Napoleon's designs on Louisiana (secretly purchased from Spain), Jefferson decided to disrupt his plans by allowing the continued supply of the black forces in Saint Domingue along with the French forces.[58] Then the resumption of war in Europe in 1803 caused the British to blockade the French and prevent them from being reinforced. The devastated colony declared its independence on January 1, 1804.

Jamaican and Cuban planters no longer needed to fear the specter of a revived Saint Domingue that would undercut their renewed prosperity.[59] Few predicted a vibrant economic future for the new state. However, slave-owners and the colonial powers now faced a new type of challenge. The choice of an Amerindian word to celebrate Haiti's rupture with Europe and the ensuing massacre of perhaps 4,000 surviving white colonists underscores that Haitian independence carried a more radical message than that of the United States two decades earlier or that of Spanish America two decades later.

In England, the victory of the former slaves stimulated the revival of the abolitionist movement, which could now argue more plausibly that future revolts were inevitable as long as the slave trade and slavery continued. This argument probably did not contribute much to the antislavery movement's future successes, as Seymour Drescher demonstrates. However, by ending British legislators' fears of French commercial rivalry, the Haitian Revolution facilitated Britain's disengagement from slave-trading in 1807 and from slavery itself in 1833.[60]

Despite contemporary and modern claims about "Haitian agents," the new Haitian state did not prove a direct threat to neighboring slave regimes, and early heads of state were at pains to allay such fears.[61] Alexandre Pétion provided assistance to the Miranda expedition of 1806, however, and ten years later as president, he re-equipped Simón Bolívar at the nadir of his fortunes and sent him back to South America after he promised to end slavery in his homeland.[62] Beyond this, Haiti was a symbol of black achievement in a world dominated by Europeans, where slavery and racism were gaining strength. For proslavery and antislavery forces it became a crucial test case for the next few decades regarding ideas about race, slavery, and the future of the Caribbean, a debate to which Haitian publicists and statesmen contributed.[63] Though its revolution was never emulated, it was not easily forgotten.

12 The Slave Leaders in Exile: Spain's Resettlement of Its Black Auxiliary Troops

On the eve of declaring war against the French Republic, the Spanish government took an extraordinary decision. With a view to conquering the whole of Hispaniola, it instructed the governor of Santo Domingo in February 1793 to recruit as "auxiliary troops" the men who had devastated Saint Domingue's northern plain eighteen months before. They were to be offered freedom for themselves and their families; "exemptions, favors, and privileges"; and land in the French or Spanish part of the island or elsewhere. The governor, Joaquín García y Moreno, cautiously began suggesting such an alliance to the home government at about the same time.[1]

This decision to restore slavery with an army of revolted slaves grew out of long Hispanic traditions of arming blacks and encouraging the resettlement of fugitive slaves. However, even in the context of international and local trends toward arming slaves, it represented a daring experiment.[2] In their bid for freedom, the recruits in question had killed, burned, raped, and tortured on a scale that terrified American whites, although their present leader, Jean-François, had intervened early in the insurrection to limit atrocities. The alliance also grew out of the adroit diplomacy of the insurgents themselves. From the start of the uprising, they had assiduously cultivated contacts with the Spanish, presenting themselves as defenders of church and king. As soon as they had access to the frontier, insurgents were telling border guards "The Spanish are good, love God and their king," or "Long live God and the king, and death to the nation."[3] In what measure this behavior was cynically instrumental or grounded in African or other monarchical ideologies remains controversial, but major and minor rebel leaders played the role consistently until the alliance with Spain was formalized in May 1793.[4]

By the early months of 1794, insurgent leaders had occupied most of the northern half of Saint Domingue in the name of the king of Spain. The number of black auxiliaries recruited is impossible to ascertain, but in mid-1793 Jean-François claimed to command 6,647 men (6,522 slaves, 67 free mulattoes, 58 free blacks). His rival, Georges Biassou, claimed a slightly smaller number that included forces under Toussaint Louverture. Governor García reckoned in May 1794 there were perhaps 14,000 in all, and in October 1795 he stated that Jean-François commanded more than 7,500.[5] The same month, however, Toussaint Louverture (now an opponent) reckoned that their armies totaled 4,000 soldiers.

All these figures were doubtless exaggerated in the interest of graft and self-promotion. Toussaint's desertion to the French in spring 1794 reduced Biassou's army probably by three or four thousand, and in late 1795 it amounted to just two companies. A French colonist in Fort Liberté estimated Jean-François's army at 3,000 men in late 1794 and 1,000 in February 1795, though there were other insurgents whom the Spanish supplied, such as Charles Lesec, who also claimed 1,000 men in early 1795.[6]

The rank-and-file soldiers officially received no pay and at first were expected to feed themselves. They later qualified for rations, apparently paid in cash at the rate of 7.5 dollars per month. The Spanish were very slow in supplying uniforms and very cautious in supplying weapons. The monthly salary of Jean-François and Biassou was fixed at 250 dollars (though Jean-François later received a 100-dollar supplement). Other officers received the equivalent of skilled artisans' wages. Colonels, who were numerous, were paid 20 to 30 dollars and captains were paid 15 dollars. (A Spanish captain was paid 40 dollars but commanded more men.) The official wage bill in late 1795 was just under 4,000 dollars per month for 191 officers. Jealous French colonists in the Spanish-occupied zone reckoned the army cost anything from 12,000 to 25,000 dollars per month, and some said Spanish officials pocketed half the sum budgeted.[7]

The Spanish found their allies maddeningly independent. Appreciating how much the Spanish depended on them, they insisted on being cajoled, flattered, and bribed. The Spanish had no say in their organization, least of all in the distribution of ranks. Jean-François called himself grand admiral; Biassou adopted various titles. Biassou quickly established himself in the Spanish frontier town of San Miguel and called himself its governor, running up large bills for food and drink. Black officers sometimes refused to recognize local commanders or demanded precedence over Spanish counterparts. The inability of the Spanish to control the situation became spectacularly evident in July 1794, when Jean-François's men massacred in one day some 700 French colonists under the eyes of an immobile Spanish garrison in the occupied town of Fort Liberté.[8]

Spain's intervention in the Haitian Revolution was doomed by the decision of Toussaint Louverture in the spring of 1794 to go over to the French Republic. Although Toussaint was not the only senior officer in the *tropas auxiliares* to rally to the French after they abolished slavery, the two principal generals, Jean-François and Georges Biassou, remained loyal to Spain and fought a holding action against the resurgent republicans until October 1795.[9] This continued loyalty presented Spanish officials with a dilemma when, by the Treaty of Basle of July 1795, a defeated Spain abandoned its oldest colony and surrendered Santo Domingo to France.

Evacuation from Santo Domingo

Santo Domingo was one of the most neglected and least valued parts of Spain's empire.[10] This may explain why government instructions to Governor García regarding the colony's evacuation carelessly made no mention of the black auxiliary troops. Perhaps it was a problem ministers were happy to leave in the hands of someone else. García thus had to decide himself in light of the February 1793 instructions what should be done with the soldiers and their families. Many of the black officers, and the French, seem to have agreed it might be dangerous for them to remain on the island. The governor was no doubt anxious to be rid of them too, as his relations with the auxiliaries had always been difficult. However, as living embodiments of the 1791 uprising, they were unlikely to be welcome in another slave society. The year 1795 had seen widespread rebellion across the Caribbean, not least in Spanish colonies.[11] Since the republicans, who had abolished slavery, proved willing to accept the rank and file as French citizens, García determined to demobilize some and send the remainder to Cuba, the main destination for Santo Domingo evacuees.[12] The details of this demobilization he left to his subordinates.

The black officers' reaction was that the whole army should be embarked; they should retain their ranks and pay and should be given land to farm and form a village. They would become a reserve army of soldier-farmers. To control their fate, they knew they had to stick together. Different officials in Santo Domingo gave them mixed signals about what they could expect.[13] The government in Spain was taken by surprise. Although the Treaty of Basle mandated the removal of Spanish troops, the auxiliaries evidently were not included in this term. Ministers complained that García had foolishly foreclosed their options, especially that of leaving the black army in Santo Domingo on the grounds that it had not demonstrated due obedience to the king. The ministers agreed that the men should be paid a modest pension but not that they should be sent to a Spanish island or, above all, to Spain itself.[14] The ministers remained months behind events, however, and would play no active role in the evacuation.

Matters were complicated temporarily by competition between the British invaders in western Saint Domingue and republican leaders in the north to win over the auxiliaries as allies. Jean-Louis Villatte, the free colored commandant of Cap Français and rival of the French governor Étienne Laveaux, made discreet approaches to Jean-François's advisor, Padre Vásquez, at Fort Liberté.[15] Villatte was perhaps seeking support for a bid for independence and doubtless wanted a counterweight to the growing power of Toussaint Louverture within the republican zone. At the same time, Laveaux and Toussaint similarly hoped to win over Jean-François.[16] From their forward positions at Banica on the central plateau, the British also sent out feelers to the auxiliaries, who were still ensconced in the mountains of the north province. The British would have liked to add them to the growing number of black regiments they were then forming. Biassou tried on the red jacket the British sent, and Benjamin, Jean-François's number two, expressed interest, but they did not want to be incorporated into white-officered corps.[17] The negotiations ultimately led nowhere but served to strengthen the black troops' bargaining position with the Spanish.

On November 5, García informed Las Casas, the governor of Cuba, of his decision to send him the black auxiliaries along with the other refugees from Santo Domingo. He felt justified in doing so, because the Crown had promised the soldiers land on Hispaniola "or elsewhere," and Las Casas supposedly had once offered García Cuba's almost uninhabited Isle of Pines to house prisoners of war.[18] In December, Jean-François's contingent was embarked on four ships at Fort Liberté. According to the local commander, Casa Calvo, who haplessly sought to restrict departures to officers, they numbered 707 persons: 91 officers, 240 soldiers, 284 women, and 92 children. As García claimed that the black army had 191 officers in December, presumably at least half were left behind, unless the numbers had been inflated to hide graft. In a remarkably bitter accompanying letter, marked "secret," Casa Calvo vented to Las Casas the frustrations he had accumulated during his two years in Santo Domingo:

> [Alliance with the blacks] cost us our self-respect and mine in particular. . . .
> [I have been] obliged to alternate with a black who, although called general, remained confined within the limitations created by his birth and the nature of slavery. . . . For the sake of peace, I have suffered there to grow up between them and us a perfect equality and reciprocity . . . which are in some measure shameful and harmful [and, now the war is over, must cease. So must] their jobs, or at least the military ranks they have arbitrarily conferred on themselves, the toleration of which has contributed to that harmful equality and even caused them to think themselves superior to us. . . . Although they paint themselves in different colors, they are the same men who, at the start of the insurrection, killed their masters, raped their mistresses, and destroyed anyone owning property.[19]

Having embarked shortly before Christmas, Jean-François's group left Fort Liberté on January 1 and reached Havana on January 9. Georges Biassou sailed with an entourage of only twenty-four from Ocoa on Santo Domingo's south coast and arrived a few days earlier.[20] They had escaped the land of their enslavement and possible French revenge but faced a very uncertain future. Sometimes abandoning family and property, they trusted in their new identity as soldiers of the king of Spain. Official correspondence reveals little about how these people were selected or the reactions of the thousands who were left behind.

Cuba and Trinidad

The reaction of Governor Las Casas to news of their impending arrival in Havana was anger and panic. He complained to his counterpart in Santo Domingo and to the government in Spain. Cuba contained the largest concentration of slaves in Spain's empire and was in the midst of an economic boom fueled by the slave trade from Africa, the economic collapse of Saint Domingue, and an influx of Domingan refugees. As early as May 1790, Spain had closed its colonies to all slaves from French settlements and to all nonwhites considered dangerous. The governor saw no place for the men who had destroyed Saint Domingue in the new boom society, where slave resistance was starting to show disquieting developments.[21] Tall, stylish, and strikingly handsome, the charismatic ex-coachman, Jean-François, would be especially unwelcome. In a revealing diatribe, Las Casas wrote:

General (as he calls himself) Jean-François has filled the inhabitants of the city and the island with terror. Every colonist imagines his slaves will rebel and the colony will be totally destroyed the moment these individuals arrive. Wretched slaves yesterday, they are today the heroes of a revolution, triumphant, wealthy, and decorated. Such things should not be seen by a population composed primarily of people of color oppressed by a smaller number of whites. Nothing has such a vivid effect on most men as the perceptions they receive via the sense of sight. It is not easy to foresee how the lower orders and people of color would react and how excited they might get in the presence of Jean-François, decked out in the sash of a general officer of the king's army and navy, with a large following of his subordinate generals and brigadiers wearing the insignia of the ranks he awarded them, dazzling with astonishing pomp in a magnificent coach with six horses, an elaborate household, etc., much superior to that ever seen by the public in the head and principal officer of this island. . . . [Jean-François's] name resounds in the ears of the populace like an unconquerable hero, a redeemer of the slaves . . . at a time when the voice of freedom resounds everywhere and the seeds of rebellion are sprouting.[22]

Finding it too late to delay the embarkation from Fort Liberté, Las Casas consulted with top officials and the Havana town council about the best course of action. Already facing a huge influx of refugees from Santo Domingo, including some French colonists and their slaves, they determined that when the black soldiers arrived, they should not be allowed to land in Cuba. Instead they should be given a choice between the following destinations: the isolated Isle of Pines; the sparsely populated frontier colony of Florida; Cádiz, the commercial center of the Spanish empire, conveniently far from the Americas; and perhaps the Canary Islands, a colony without slaves.[23]

Biassou's small group was the first to arrive and the easiest to deal with. Refused permission to land and given a choice between the Isle of Pines and Florida, the caudillo chose the latter and sailed for St. Augustine on January 13, 1796. Jean-François proved more of a problem. In the first place, his party numbered not 707, but 780 people: 70 officers, 282 troops, 334 women, and 94 children.[24] The Havana junta, echoing Casa Calvo's term of "venomous vipers," suggested they be split up; the leaders could go to Spain if they wished, while the remainder would be sent, if its governor agreed, to Trinidad, another underdeveloped colony where the government was distributing land.

On January 10, Jean-François accepted; he wanted to go first to Trinidad and then to Spain to plead his case directly. He resented being confined to ship, however, and his relations with the Cuban administration soon deteriorated. Reminding it of his men's distinguished service, obedience, and personal sacrifice, he demanded to know if his followers were prisoners of war or vassals of the king. Adding a touch of blackmail, he rhetorically asked if the British would have rewarded them with less. Havana, the largest city in the Caribbean, must have looked very tempting from across the harbor. Jean-François declared he would not leave until his advisor, Father Vásquez, arrived and if not allowed to disembark, he would return to Fort Liberté. An irritated Las Casas shot back that he should return to Fort Liberté. So Jean-François shifted his ground; he wished to see Governor García in Santo Domingo. He wanted the genuine orders of the king and no others. This was a device the auxiliaries had previously employed, refusing to recognize Spanish commanders by claiming they owed obedience only to the governor. The Havana junta commented on the "bold character" of the black soldiers and how they hid their plan of remaining together beneath expressions of loyalty. A Cuban officer who had accompanied them from Fort Liberté observed they had always displayed strong esprit de corps and that, therefore, it would be dangerous not to split them up, wherever they were sent.[25]

Informed of the auxiliaries' negotiations with the British and republicans, the junta decided to send the officers to Spain rather than Trinidad and to further divide their forces. By February 19th, Jean-François's group had been scattered as follows: 136 (or 142) sent to Spain, 144 to Trinidad, 115 to Campeche in the Yucatán, and 307 (or 308) to a settlement that was rebuilding on the Honduran coast at Trujillo. After delays caused by lack of shipping and the weather, another 86 (or 87) would leave for Panama on August 23rd.[26] The junta favored places with few slaves and tropical lowland locations needing settlers.

Trinidad fit this description but proved a poor choice. The Spanish government, seeking to create a plantation economy, had developed the island primarily with French settlers. The governor, José María Chacón, thought their loyalty to Spain was "precarious" and that, as all the black population spoke the same language as the auxiliaries, they would regard the soldiers as comrades and brothers. "The blacks who have arrived know how to use weapons and, what is worse, have used them in disobedience to a Spanish governor in committing what can only be called an atrocity," he wrote, alluding to the Fort Liberté massacre. If he had 1,000, instead of 112, regular troops, Chacón concluded, he would try to employ the black soldiers, but as Trinidad had none of Cuba's impressive defenses, he would be "an imbecile" to do so. The 76 men and 68 women and children were therefore sent back to Santo Domingo. They arrived in mid-May after nearly five months on board ship. García went to greet them. Shouting loudly "Long live the king!" they protested they did not want to live under French rule.[27] In the event, they did not have to. Although the capital city was then overflowing with French refugees, the French Republic did not take formal possession of the colony, and the Spanish administration remained in place until Toussaint Louverture's invasion in 1801.

Florida

The smallest group of exiles, led by Georges Biassou, is to date the best known, thanks to the work of Jane Landers.[28] She describes the mixture of consternation and curiosity the 25 newcomers[29] initially aroused in St. Augustine, whose population of 3,000 or so was equally divided between black and white. Expecting to be invited to dinner on his arrival, the irascible Biassou rapidly raised the hackles of the local governor, who found he was paid not a great deal more than the former slave. Biassou's pride, temper, and excessive drinking early attracted comment, as they had in Santo Domingo. Provided with an interpreter, he made frequent demands and sometimes complained over the head of the governor to his superior in Cuba.

Despite these tensions, the migrants proved a welcome addition to the armed forces of the frontier colony. Florida was increasingly vulnerable to foreign incursions in these years, and its small but long-established black militia was a valued institution. Biassou became its head and continued using his title of general. He saw action in 1800–1801 against Creek Indians. The militia also served as a vehicle for integrating the new migrants with local free blacks, many of whom had fled slavery in the United States. Although their young men sometimes fought one another in the street, Landers shows that the two groups soon began to intermarry and establish godparent relationships. Biassou lived with his wife, her mother, and her three siblings. The Domingan group also included two female slaves. Of the seven other males Landers identifies, four were mulattoes, one African, and another apparently French. At least one of the mulattoes had been a freeman before the revolution.[30] Two found work as masons, two as bakers, and one as a shoemaker.

One sergeant and three soldiers received rations and clothes during their first year in Florida, but only Biassou was paid a salary.[31] He went heavily into debt providing patronage for his followers and seeking to maintain his high-profile lifestyle. Although wealthy by St. Augustine's standards, he had to adjust to straitened circumstances. For four years he had been a warlord commanding sometimes thousands of men. He petitioned several times to leave Florida; to find the soldiers, and mother, he had left in Santo Domingo; or to do military service elsewhere, but without success. Until the archbishop of Santo Domingo had persuaded him to marry in 1794, he had lived with a retinue of concubines.[32] In 1800, his wife moved to Havana with her family for reasons of health, leaving the aging leader alone. He died the following year and received a full military funeral that was attended by the governor. His corpse went to the graveside wearing the gold medal awarded him by the king, which then was removed to be sold to pay his debts.[33]

Other Domingan exiles continued service in the black militia until Spain surrendered Florida to the United States in 1821. They were then relocated to Cuba, the island where they had not been permitted to land a quarter-century before.

Honduras

The Honduras coast, destination of the largest group of auxiliaries, was, like Florida, vulnerable to foreign depredation. Like Trinidad, it was a region where the government was seeking to attract settlers. Sandwiched between the British in Belize and their Miskito allies to the east, the coast was wide open to contraband and was frequently raided in wartime. The port of Trujillo, where the Domingans disembarked, had been destroyed several times since the sixteenth century. Since the late 1780s, it had been the site of a floundering colonization scheme that had been launched after the British had abandoned their claims to nearby Roatán Island and the Miskito Coast (see Map 3, p. 98). The region, however, was notoriously unhealthy for Europeans and highland Indians. Its sparse population was mainly poor and of varying degrees of African ancestry, but slaves were few. The Indians of the coastal highlands remained unconquered and hostile to the Spanish.[34] In terms of imperial planning, the location looked ideal for the ex-auxiliaries. A few years before, the inhabitants of Trujillo had in fact asked the government to purchase 200 slaves who would double as soldiers and as canoemen in the port.[35]

The 310 blacks from Saint Domingue who landed there on March 10, 1796, had spent eleven weeks on board ship in cramped conditions under military escort. Their food had rotted. They numbered 41 officers, 74 soldiers, 121 women, and 74 children. Two babies were born on the voyage. Apart from 26 single men in a grenadier company, they were divided into 36 family groups containing from 2 to 27 persons.[36]

Their leader was Marshal Jean-Jacques (alias Juan Santiago), who along with Benjamin had held the second-highest rank in Jean-François's army. He was accompanied by his wife, their two adult sons, and their wives and children. Most officers were accompanied by either a wife (*esposa*) or consort (*muger*) and fragments of extended family. Some had been free and had owned slaves before the revolution. Brigadier Gilles Narcisse (Gilé) brought his wife, son, mother-in-law, sister-in-law and her two daughters, two brothers, five cousins, and two female slaves. Colonel Bivet's family of nine included six slaves; Captain Fantaisie's consisted of seven brothers. Five of the officers had been awarded medals in Santo Domingo. Apart from two men and a child called Sénégal and another soldier named Mamu, very few can be identified as African. As on the slave lists of the period, the great majority were identified by only one name, although family names would soon start appearing in the records. None of the main officers could sign their names, although over the years that, too, would change.

Trujillo was a small garrison town with a few, mainly wooden, public buildings and more shacks than houses. Though its trade had been expanding, it was still a backwater in a wretchedly poor province. Its commandant hastily organized lodgings for the new arrivals by putting the officers' families in the jail and the others in the militia barracks. He found them "very civilized but also very proud because of their distinguished record." Accustomed to "superabundance," they complained at getting the basic soldier's ration of one pound of meat, one pound of bread, and two ounces of vegetables per day. The officers were used to a daily barrel of wine, and they expected to be paid, he reported to the captain-general in Guatemala City. "For this reason, it is essential they receive special treatment that neither exasperates them nor tolerates the continuing lack of distinction between them and white people." It would be a good idea, the commandant thought, to invent a pretext to separate the leaders from the rest, "so their pride might be gradually worn down."[37]

These ideas gained approval as the problem was passed up the administrative hierarchy. In the capital city, a week's journey away, the public prosecutor of the high court was asked to draw up a report. He outlined three aims: 1) assist the black families; 2) make all possible use of them; and 3) avoid the problems their opinions and conduct might cause. Although they had fought on the right side, they needed "to be treated like people coming from a country where there is plague, with whom no precaution is excessive." The bureaucrat then made specific recommendations. The soldiers should be persuaded to deposit their weapons in the local armory. They perhaps might form an all-French colony at the mouth of the Motagua River (which separates Honduras and Guatemala), but it would be safer to disperse the officers and those with a trade among the cities of the interior and the Pacific coast; settling in small groups would encourage intermarriage with locals. Some soldiers could stay in Trujillo as an adjunct to the militia, and those families judged to be good Christians might settle as farmers on the Motagua frontier, which was judged more suitable for white migrants. Those who became sailors or ship's carpenters could continue to receive a soldier's wage and ration. Above all, none should settle at Río Tinto near the Afro-Indian Miskitos, who were traditional enemies of the Spanish, or on Roatán, which had recently been abandoned by the British. Nor should they move to the fortress town of Omoa, where they might "teach the Saint Domingue path to liberty" to the slave soldiers of the garrison.[38] The captain-general and high court concurred.[39]

Back in Trujillo, these proposals were not well received. An extensive fire at the beginning of April made life in the town more difficult, and a recommendation that the Domingans be drafted to build huts probably did nothing to improve relations.[40] Moreover, the black families were angry about numerous thefts from their belongings during the voyage from Havana. Sailors supposedly had stolen 400 dollars from Marshal Jean-Jacques. The group said they were determined not to split up, as Jean-François had told them to stick together. They also proved very reluctant to part with their weapons. It took the local commandant a 4-hour debate to persuade them to deposit a total of fifty-two carbines and muskets in the militia armory; all refused to sell their arms. Contrary to previous expectations, only four men could be identified as carpenters, and none had experience as a sailor. Three of the black officers, who spoke Spanish well, acted as interpreters. Local officials reported that, in view of the soldiers' attitudes, it might be best to settle them as a group, after getting rid of certain "troublemakers" such as the vociferous Adjutant Michel-Claude (also called Caudio or Candio).[41]

The administrators in the capital, however, still favored dispersing the group and were particularly adamant about keeping the black troops away from the slaves at Omoa. It is therefore ironic that the commandant at Omoa was the only official to welcome the auxiliaries' arrival and Governor García's suggestion they be settled as soldier-farmers. If placed under Spanish officers, they would not be dangerous, he thought. Their homes, fields, and families would be a stabilizing factor and an example to local blacks. If the British at Belize managed to control their slave population, so could the Spanish. The commandant offered to provide cash and oxen for house-building, hoping to see Omoa and the Motagua region develop at the expense of Trujillo.[42]

At this point, three months after their arrival, about fifty of the Domingans made the 300-mile journey to the capital in the Guatemalan highlands to settle the question of salaries. It is not clear if they took the initiative or were invited: perhaps both. In Santo Domingo, they favored face-to-face audiences with officialdom, and their representatives tended to impress, even when they had to speak through an interpreter. The result was agreement to continue the main officers' pay at their former rates, while the ordinary soldiers accompanying them received the basic stipend of 2 *reales* (25 cents) per day to cover subsistence; dependents received 1 *real*. Colonel Desombrages made two successful return trips to see treasury officials, first to correct an underpayment and then to claim back pay.[43] Recent migrants or not, they knew how to play the system.

Governor Las Casas had promised 6,000 dollars to help with resettlement costs in Guatemala, but the funds never arrived from Cuba. Captain-General Domas therefore turned to the viceroy of Mexico, as was customary in the poorer Spanish colonies, for funds to meet the additional expense. The viceroy's first response was a refusal, since Guatemala already had large debts. The government in Spain, however, supported the request, and it was folded into increased defense expenditures following the outbreak of war with England in October 1796. Support for the immigrants averaged more than 20,000 dollars per year until the beginning of the new century.[44]

The group in Guatemala City appears to have stayed there until February 1797, lodged at public expense.[45] It was probably during this period that sixteen of them married in the church of the Franciscan monastery, which became their parish church. The priest who examined them found them "to be good Catholics beyond any doubt, well instructed in obligations of the faith."[46] Given the church's neglect of slaves in Saint Domingue, this may indicate that some had been free before the revolution. However, although church marriage was extremely rare among nonwhites, Christianity was not quite as absent from Saint Domingue society as has often been supposed. One colonist claimed that the slaves had been the most Christian part of it.[47] In 1798, one of the ex-auxiliaries, whom the Spanish called Silvestre (probably Captain Sylvain, uncle of Jean-Baptiste Desombrages), entered the monastery as a lay brother.[48]

War with Great Britain focused the attention of the Guatemalan administration on the vulnerable Honduran coast and gave the exiles an opportunity to prove their worth. The captain-general may not have expected much of them, as his correspondence regarding his preparations for war does not mention them, and they were outnumbered by the local militia units transferred to the coast. The leaders and their families, nevertheless, were sent back to Trujillo with substantial pay raises under the command of one of Guatemala's leading citizens, José Rossi y Rubí.[49] They nearly found themselves reunited with Jean-François, who was ordered to leave Cádiz for Guatemala in October. However, the outbreak of war prevented his departure, as it would again in 1803.[50]

British ships threatened Trujillo in March 1797, and a month later forces landed by a British squadron briefly seized the town from its fleeing defenders. Local officials and troops proved negligent, drunken, and incompetent. What was looking like a debacle for the Spanish was suddenly reversed when the Saint Domingue soldiers, together with local black militia, launched a furious attack during the night and drove the British back to their ships with heavy losses. The ships then bombarded the town, but accurate fire from local batteries, notably from a Domingan artilleryman, forced them to exchange prisoners and leave. Several of the soldiers, led by Commandant Suasi (Pierre Dieu-Choisi), received medals from the captain-general and pay raises. Juan Luis Santillan, the artilleryman, was admitted to the (primarily white) royal artillery corps.[51]

The British left behind a major challenge for the local administration. A few weeks before attacking the town, they had disembarked and abandoned more than 2,000 people, who, like the auxiliaries, were condemned to exile, on Roatán, a few miles from the port. These were the Black Carib (Garifuna) of St. Vincent. Deported after a pro-French uprising, they had already lost more than half their number to disease during the previous nine months of detention.[52] Like the local Miskito, the Black Carib were Afro-Indians, determined to resist the encroachment of the white colonial world around them. Unlike the Miskito, they were anything but pro-British, but their alliance with French revolutionaries who had just ravaged the British Windward Isles made them even more threatening to the Spanish. Black rebels from Martinique, and perhaps Grenada, seem to have been included among the deportees. This is probably why the Spanish would refer to them over the next few years as *negros republicanos.*[53]

As all these people spoke similar varieties of French Creole, the Domingans were able to perform valuable service as interpreters when the Black Caribs sent three envoys to Trujillo and later in May when Rossi y Rubí and a dozen Domingan officers landed on the island and negotiated terms with them. Led by Colonel Desombrages, they assisted in the evacuation of the Caribs to the mainland, a process that continued until year's end. On one trip out to the island in July, the Domingans in a canoe attacked a British schooner and captured it.[54] Meanwhile, in Guatemala City, administrators argued whether to deport the Caribs to a French colony or to disperse them locally. Although the colonial and metropolitan government favored deportation, no one cared to implement the policy, so the black population of the coast became much larger and more polyglot than ever.[55]

This must have increased pressures to disperse the Domingans, despite their useful services. In October 1797, Jean-Jacques, Michel-Claude, Choisi, Santillan, and ninety others were relocated to the city of Granada 280 miles to the south on Lake Nicaragua.[56] Most of the rest seem to have remained in the Trujillo area with Desombrages, although his uncle, Sylvain, moved to the capital and, until December 1798, a half-dozen commanded by Colonel Joseph Bivet did military service on Roatán. The original plan to scatter them between the towns of the interior was not carried out. According to the 1801 census, most must have settled among the Garifuna "on the slopes and summits" of the hills behind Trujillo. However, land distributions were not made until the first half of 1803.[57]

Those with salaries continued to receive them. In the summer of 1798, the colonial government announced it would cut off ration payments to those who could work, but it continued to pay half or full rations to the old and sick. To judge from the group living in Trujillo, most seemed to be adapting well, far better than the wretched immigrants from Spain who arrived in the 1780s. Desombrages, a man in his mid-30s, supplemented his 40-dollar salary by growing vegetables for sale, as did several others on plots near the town. As late as mid-1803, their *huertecitas* were described as Trujillo's sole source of vegetables. Desombrages, Major Bruneau de Clerc, and the 70-year-old Pierre Delacour were also charged with policing the local Caribs. De Clerc later secured a contract to supply the town with lime. Delacour's teenaged son was earning 2 *reales* per day in 1798 as an apprentice carpenter on government building sites. So was another adolescent, who worked with his father, Manuel Chatard (later Zatá), whom the government paid 1 dollar per day as a cabinetmaker and 28 dollars per month as a captain. Four other men worked as cabinetmakers or carpenters. Thirty-six of the common soldiers served in the local garrison in the *compañía fija*. Two others acquired a boat. Most of the women did laundry and ironing or sewing. Apart from the ailing and elderly, the only person in difficulties was the 35-year-old bachelor Jean-Louis, who was in jail. Formerly a soldier, he had gone to Roatán and returned and was unemployed.[58]

The 1801 census of Honduras showed some 200 Domingans in the Trujillo area. The decline in numbers since 1796 was due to the division of the group in 1797 rather than deaths from disease, as some have supposed.[59] Although thirty-five were hospitalized in their first year in Trujillo, only one died, and deaths among them in the following years were few.[60] Those who died in the 1790s did not speak enough Spanish to be confessed, but by the time Pierre Delacour (De Cur) died in 1802, most were confessed. Baptismal records begin only in 1814 but they show that by then, godparent relationships involving "French blacks" usually also involved local people.[61] Marriage records have not survived, but they presumably would also reflect a gradual integration with the local communities. By 1803, both Captain Guillaume Agnus and Sublieutenant Hyppolite Payeau (Payo, Pajo) had married Hispanic women, whose relatives then counted among their dependents.[62] While Domingans made up nearly a third of the permanent garrison, it is interesting that the black militia with whom they cooperated in April 1797 came from the settlement outside Trujillo called Campamento. As this was the home of 300 "English blacks," who were no doubt fugitive slaves from Belize, the situation very much recalls the parallel incorporation of Anglophone and Francophone black communities that Jane Landers found in St. Augustine. Intermixture with the Black Caribs also occurred. In 1799, Domingans and Caribs together repulsed a British naval attack with a display of impressive marksmanship, and the same year they jointly raided the

Miskito at Río Tínto. Anthropologist Nancie Gonzalez has found that the genealogies of many Garifuna families include a "Haitian" ancestor.[63]

Early in the new century, conditions worsened for the *morenos franceses* (French blacks). The peace with England of March 1802, which reduced their military value, initiated a period of retrenchment in Spain and Guatemala that threatened their salaries. The arrival of a new captain-general in 1801 accentuated the trend. Antonio González Saravia was a cost-cutting hard-liner who expressed contempt for his predecessor's fiscal laxity. By cutting expenditure on coastal defense and state support for all settlers, he reduced Trujillo's budget by 60 percent in one year. Observing that Spanish policy was to endow the ex-auxiliaries with land, not pensions, he ordered in September 1802 that their salaries and rations be ended and that they become self-supporting by August 1803.[64]

The forced transition to becoming self-supporting farmers went more smoothly in the Trujillo region than among the Granada group, but it caused conflict in both places and proved to be a long, drawn-out process. A few of the black officers in Trujillo responded that the Spanish had deceived them. They said they wanted to be reunited with Jean-François, or they refused to make any choice about their futures. The local military commander exchanged nervous letters with the colonial governor recalling the men's past, characterized as one of bloodshed, pillage, and treachery to their former masters. The two men agreed to proceed carefully and to try to persuade the recalcitrant to accept land, preferably in remote regions far from the Miskito.[65] The affair seems to have blown over, but it helped persuade the governor to limit the new settlements' degree of self-government.

Most of the men at Trujillo appeared pleased with the offer of land grants. Slaves in Saint Domingue usually grew their own food. Those who declined the offer generally did so because they already had alternative employment. Several stated that their wounds prevented them from clearing land in the mountains and that they were content with their market gardens near the town. Most of the woodworkers wanted to stay in Trujillo; so did the barber-musician Joseph Gilles. Commandant Bonhomme requested a permit to trade between coastal ports but perhaps because of official concern with smuggling, he ended up driving a stagecoach.[66] Reserving the land closest to Trujillo for other settlers, the Spanish granted the Domingans land in the hills a dozen or so miles away at Chapagua and Saladillo. The main obstacles encountered concerned land titles and the weather. For a while, it appeared that land where the officers intended to graze livestock near the mouth of the Aguan River had been already conceded to a local planter, who, bizarrely, was a French marquis. The officers protested they did not wish to be "shut up" in the mountains and that the future they envisaged for themselves included raising cattle. Either the planter's claim proved false or he was compensated elsewhere, for the crisis soon subsided. Nothing could be done, however, to shorten the rainy season. This meant land clearance and planting could not begin before April 1803, delaying the first harvest until the fall. State support, made contingent upon progress in land clearance, thus had to be continued until November, by which time two new villages were taking shape.[67]

Ten of the officers, who intended to grow coffee and cotton as well as vegetables, asked the government to provide credit to buy fifteen slaves, whom they would pay for in two years. Local officials explained that several had been free and had owned slaves in Saint Domingue; they were now getting old, and their pride made them look down on agricultural labor, although their children would still work under their direction. As noted above, a few had arrived with slaves attached to their households. The type of slavery implied was familial, clearly closer to African practice than to practice in the Caribbean.[68] Nevertheless, the irony of the leaders of the great slave uprising investing in slavery long after the French had abolished it provides further evidence that the ideological commitment to eradicating slavery entered the Haitian Revolution in 1793 rather than 1791.[69]

By October 1802, the number of ex-auxiliaries who had been transferred from Honduras to Nicaragua had grown to 107. Marshal Jean-Jacques remained in the town of Granada; Pierre Dieu-Choisi led a rival faction in nearby Masaya, and others were stationed at Fort San Carlos on the south shore of Lake Nicaragua. The new captain-general offered them tools, seeds, poultry, and land to clear at Mateare, to the northwest of modern Managua. Most responded either that they preferred to remain in royal service or to rejoin family in Trujillo or that they would defer to their superior officers. The three or four men who had found civilian employment in Granada rejected the farming option but welcomed freedom from military service; these included Augustin Azor, a successful barber with a white clientele who had bought his own house. Although the common soldiers sometimes seemed favorable to the plan, their officers, who had salaries to lose, used their influence to organize a lengthy and generalized resistance. It was painful for them to think of no longer being colonels and commandants, thought the local military commander, Brigadier Ansoategui. In a series of stormy interviews, they sought to argue with him about the justness of the decision. In a stream of complaints to the captain-general, he criticized their "deep-rooted disobedience," "lack of rationality and discipline," "indomitable pride," and "impertinence." He claimed it was the worst task he had ever undertaken.[70]

From Cádiz in April 1802, Jean-François had informed Jean-Jacques he would be arriving in Central America, where the Spanish government was giving him land.[71] Despite his urging on his followers obedience to Spanish officials, the caudillo's seemingly imminent arrival gave them a reason to delay any decision about their future. Jean-François's misleading assurance that officers' salaries would continue to be paid must have also created problems. So too did the rumor, reported by Ansoategui, that some of the soldiers in Granada were saying privately that Trujillo belonged to them, since they had reconquered the town after the whites had lost it. This increased the captain-general's hostility to allowing any migrations back to the coast.[72] Nevertheless, despite official fears of concentrating too many blacks in one location, he eventually allowed the fractious Commandant Choisi to leave Nicaragua and reunite his large entourage in the new settlements near Trujillo. Around the same time, in early June 1803, a group of thirty-three led by Gilles Narcisse finally began staking out farms in Mateare.

Negotiations about relocation dragged on for about eighteen months. Marshal Jean-Jacques and three companions made the long journey to Guatemala City in February 1803, but the alternative offer they extracted from Captain-General González was not much more attractive—garrison duty in the two remote fortresses that guarded the approaches to Lake Nicaragua. Their salary would be reduced to 20 dollars per month; others with less distinguished records would get $10.50. Like all troops under the new regime, they would receive land, tools, and seeds and have to feed themselves.[73] These forts were "hardship locations," among the worst postings in Central America. Fort San Carlos, at the far end of the lake, was garrisoned by criminals and vagrants; Castillo San Juan lay in the jungle to the southeast and had been in ruins for two decades.[74]

Governor González then added insult to injury by forbidding the Domingans further use of their military titles. This led to a sharp exchange between Jean-Jacques and the military commandant of Granada. Disdainfully inviting the "Saint Domingue blacks," in the third person, to show him any "real royal titles" they might have, the brigadier threatened to put in the stocks any who appeared in public wearing their existing emblems of rank.[75] Jean-Jacques went on using the titles in his correspondence and, employing a familiar tactic, said he again wanted to speak face to face with the captain-general. Most of his followers, when interviewed in August, rejected both the options offered them.[76] Although government support was then cut off, many were still holding out the following spring, accumulating debts they could not repay. Juan Luis Santillan, the artilleryman, successfully petitioned for the 20-dollar wage granted to Jean-Jacques. This encouraged the truculent Michel-Claude to buy a mule and go to lobby in the capital, where he appealed on behalf of seven other "true Catholic Christians who had served the king with love and loyalty."[77] Meanwhile, house-building and ground-clearing at Mateare proceeded slowly. The government only belatedly provided tools; draft animals had to be borrowed from local peasants. Planted late, the first harvest was poor. Local officials continued paying cash rations to the settlers until October 1804.[78]

Thereafter most of the Domingans disappear into an anonymous life of farming and garrison duty. In 1812, for the third time, the arrival of former comrades from Cádiz was anticipated, but none came. However, several left Honduras that year for Cuba. The same year, the Wars of Independence began, and it is likely that some of the former auxiliaries participated, like the Garifuna, on the royalist side. In 1818, Jean-Jacques, still "Marshal," reappears in the records leading his own corps. In 1820, we find a unit of thirty-six Domingans attached to Trujillo's part-time artillery corps, apparently led by "Colonel" Desombrages, who won praise for his contributions to agriculture and the army.[79] While the migrants were achieving integration into local society, they thus retained their separate military identity until the end of the colonial period.

The Slave Leaders in Exile 193

Yucatán

The 115 auxiliaries sent to Campeche arrived there on February 10, 1796 and consisted of 4 officers, 59 soldiers, 35 women, and 17 children. They were led by commandant Jean-Pierre Marceau (a.k.a. Marcos). The governor of Yucatán brought him and his officers to the regional capital of Mérida, where they requested tools and good agricultural land and that their salaries be continued. The governor and his advisers decided they should establish a town about fifteen miles east of the city. Although Indians made up half the local population, at least one in eight were people of African descent, as was half of Yucatán's militia. The area had plenty of uncultivated fertile land, was relatively distant from any Indian community, and yet was not too far from urban garrisons. There were, in fact, 1,000 troops in the vicinity. It is clear that the new arrivals were valued not as a potential defense force but as farmers. It was hoped that because of their association with the "Pearl of the Antilles," they might introduce "the true method of cultivating the sugar cane" and other cash crops.[80]

The viceroy of Mexico was less enthusiastic. He remarked that Yucatán was a bad choice of destination, as the Domingans would increase the region's population of "loathsome castes," and their "proud character and dangerous customs" would set a bad example. Officials in Mérida drew up a detailed plan to regulate their conduct. The group would be obliged to live in the same location. They should not be sold alcohol or visit Indian villages without a permit. At first they would be housed in three large buildings and provided with a jail. The group was assigned an interpreter, whose duties included spying on them. "At the slightest sign of insubordination, discontent, or propagation of the pernicious maxims of liberty and equality [he was to report] immediately and with the utmost secrecy."[81]

The black officers' request for salaries was accepted in Campeche but denied in Mérida. Instead, each migrant was allotted a convict's allowance of 1 *real* (12.5 cents) per day that was to cease once the group produced its first harvest. This included a daily ration of 1.5 pounds of meat on the bone. The cost of their food, tools, and seed corn and the wages of their interpreter and a surveyor would be deducted from each family's allowance. Old cannon were melted down to make the machetes and axes required. Whereas the governor of Guatemala requested 100,000 dollars from Mexico's viceroy to cope with the arrivals in Trujillo, the governor of Yucatán asked for no additional funds at all.

In a landscape of pre-Columbian ruins, there slowly took shape the village of San Fernando Aké, named for the patron saint of the Spanish monarchy. Following government instructions, it was laid out on the traditional grid plan around a central plaza. Work on a stone church began in 1798, but it seems that official graft prevented its completion. In 1809, the village had a thatched church but no resident priest; priests were notoriously few in the countryside.[82] By 1806, the population had doubled to 233 people. This was mainly due to migration, as the birth rate was low. Four Indians and forty-four local women of mixed racial descent had married Domingan men, and other blacks from New York, Charleston, and Jamaica had taken up residence. French (presumably Creole) was the common language, but Senegalese, Mandinga, and Kongolese were identified as also speaking their own languages. The town's Spanish commissioner described the population as ethnically divided, licentious, and physically ugly.[83] According to local historian Jorge Victoria Ojeda, the community retained its distinctive identity well into the national period, but during the Caste War that began in 1847 and largely depopulated the region, its members emigrated to Belize.[84]

Panama

The 46 men, 32 women, and 7 children who arrived in Panama may have been the lowest-ranking group among the auxiliaries. They included only one officer, a captain-commandant named Sanson, a 60-year-old Kongolese.[85] Of all the exiles, their social composition is the best documented. They thus provide a rare, though not necessarily representative, sample of the 1791 insurgents. They were relatively young: in 1797, only twelve of the men were thought to be at least 40 years old. Just over half of the adults were single, and most of the nineteen couples were childless. There were none of the extended families common in Guatemala, Florida, and Cádiz. This was because more than two-thirds of the group were African. Two-thirds of the Africans were Kongolese, and a quarter were Mandinga. The great majority of them had been field slaves, whereas most of the Creole men had been household servants or had held some other specialized post. Sanson gave his occupation as surgeon.[86]

For unexplained reasons—though Sanson mentioned a shipwreck—it seems that the group did not reach Panama before late December 1796. They were probably in a very weak state, especially if they had been confined to shipboard all their time in Havana. They spent a month or two on the coast at Chagres and then had to walk about thirty miles to Portobelo, an old fortress town with fewer than 3,000 inhabitants, which was the main Atlantic coast port of Central America. There they were lodged in empty barracks in an isolated fort across the bay from the town. The local officials were adamant they should not mix with local slaves, who, given the newcomers' "pernicious example," might revolt "to see if they can achieve the same liberty [the Domingans] had gained in the same manner."[87] Since it was wartime, the men were put to work on the fortifications to defray the cost of their upkeep while the administration decided what to do with them. Sanson was allowed his captain's salary of 15 dollars monthly, and the others received 25 cents per day. Because of their ragged state, they were given cloth and thread to make new clothes. Sanson received a beaver hat; the others, straw hats. The cost to the colony through March 1797 was 2,400 dollars.

When interviewed, the ex-soldiers asked for land to farm and assistance in building houses. They described themselves as expert agriculturalists and even offered, if the government built a sugar plantation, to make it as good as any in

Saint Domingue. In search of suitable locations, officials from the governor of Portobelo up to the viceroy, who was three weeks away in Bogotá, weighed the attractions and disadvantages of four different options. The first places suggested were two mainly black townships that lay a safe distance to the east and west of Portobelo. If divided between two existing towns, the Domingans would be more likely to adopt local customs and religion, and they could also strengthen the military roles of the towns. Palenque, which had once been a maroon settlement, served as a bulwark against the raids of the Indians of Darién. Santa Rita protected the westward approach to the city. Further east into Darién was another potential site along the Bayano River, a frontier where Indians had destroyed many plantations. The presence of black slaves there, however, was considered a negative factor by some officials, though others reckoned the Domingans would make just as effective police as the treaty maroons of Jamaica or Palenque. A third choice was the decayed mining town of Cana, also in Darién. It had no slaves to worry about, and with Domingan defenders, its militia garrison could be withdrawn. Like all the locations considered, Cana offered abundant land, wood, and water but also the lure of gold. Yet it was Punta Gorda, the closest of the sites to Portobelo, that was selected. Although it was private land that would have to be leased, there were no slaves in the vicinity, it was easier to supervise, and it offered the best prospects for supplying food cheaply to Portobelo. Economic considerations seem to have outweighed strategic ones.[88]

The process was painfully slow. After vice-regal approval arrived in August 1797, twenty of the men set out in October to clear land and erect temporary shelter so that work could begin in earnest in early summer 1798. A military captain was named to supervise the project, and a platoon of soldiers was assigned to keep order. The lure of gold in Darién and the invitation of its governor temporarily sidetracked the project when Sanson and two companions were sent to inspect a site in that province. However, the progress made at Punta Gorda finally settled the issue. Despite a lack of tools, the seventy-two surviving immigrants had all moved there by April 1798 and were staking out houseplots to be cleared when planting was over. Some had already bought small canoes for carrying produce to market. In July, the superintendent announced that there were large fields of rice and corn, 4,600 stands of plantains, and manioc and beans. Unlike some of their counterparts in Honduras, the group apparently enjoyed farming.[89]

This may be because it paid better than being a common soldier and only one of them received an officer's wage. Several of the Africans had claimed to be officers and Sanson said he was really a colonel, but the papers sent from Santo Domingo and further inquiries showed the claims to be false. The Spanish regarded the old man as an intelligent and effective leader who exacted strict obedience from his followers. However, the group was split into two hostile camps, African and Creole. Dominated by the Kongolese, the other Africans sided with them, but the Creoles obeyed only grudgingly, and, despite a limited amount of intermarriage, most Creole women did not want to marry African men. A communal agricultural project, therefore, did not seem a good idea, and land was distributed on an individual basis.[90]

Free from slavery, the migrants do not seem to have been set on abandoning their "slave names." The list of their names drawn up in Portobelo contains perhaps slightly more African names than is usually found on a slave list, but most of the Africans, even those described as heathens, still had European names. Only three of the group, all of them Kongolese, were considered heathens, but as others were reckoned to be merely neophyte Christians, the administrators agreed that a priest should be assigned "to root out the corrupt ways they may have acquired, to teach them at the same time our language, and inspire them with affectionate loyalty to the king." The Franciscan college in Panama City sent a friar to Punta Gorda, but when he died there in 1801, it refused to send another until 1803. The replacement soon retired because of ill health, and his successor also died at Punta Gorda after only a few years.[91]

Whatever "corrupt ways" the Domingans may have brought with them, modern Panama shows no sign of African influence in religion, magic, or medicine, but it does have, curiously enough, well-established "Congo" traditions associated with carnival along the coast east and west of Portobelo. These include a burlesque "Congo dialect" and public rituals that act out, among other things, slave rebellion, cruel slave-owners, and maroon life. Scholars are probably correct to locate the roots of these traditions deep in Panama's history of slavery, but it could be, as with Jamaican Kumina and Trinidad Shango, that they are creations of free migrants who arrived very late in the colonial period. Alfredo Castillero Calvo remarks that the Domingan families "are the obvious answer to one of the great cultural enigmas of the coast around Portobelo, where 'Congos' are very numerous and where, to the confusion of anthropologists, some French words are still preserved."[92]

Cádiz

The transfer to Spain of Jean-François and his retinue of staff officers and family considerably embarrassed the Spanish government. It was a fait accompli by the governor of Cuba, not the planned reward French contemporaries imagined. Caught off guard, the ministry hastily ordered the governor of Cádiz to house the families when they arrived and to watch them closely.[93] In mid-March 1796, 141 blacks from Saint Domingue disembarked in the bustling port, which was a fortified town of about 70,000 people, five times the size of Cap Français. Nineteen of the group were officers; about sixty were women and children related to them, and another sixty or so, equally divided between the sexes, were described as "servants." One officer had died during the voyage. Jean-François's first impulse was to seek an audience with a minister, but the government was adamant that "[the blacks'] remaining in Europe is not desirable, and in no manner is their coming to Madrid."[94]

The officers' monthly wage bill in Saint Domingue had been 955 dollars. By far the best-paid figures after Lieutenant-General Jean-François were Marshal Benjamin (160 dollars per month) and Inspector-General Bernardin (100 dollars per month). Most of the others had received, as colonels or captains, 15 to 30 dollars per month. The governor of Cádiz at first provided them with rations only and then, awaiting royal approval, paid them their salaries reduced by 25 percent (an adjustment from *pesos fuertes* to *pesos sencillos* to reflect living costs). Jean-François complained that they risked falling into poverty. They had no land, did not know the language, and were entirely dependent on the state. They also had large retinues to support: Bernardin had 13 family members and 13 servants; Jean-François, 16 family and 19 servants. Jean-François's dependents included his mother, his wife, two stepdaughters, a sister, four cousins, an aunt, and various of these women's children. The story told by Toussaint Louverture about Jean-François's family refusing to join him in exile is therefore misleading.[95]

Although a wealthy man, the general had lost much of his fortune in the evacuation, and not just the plantations he had occupied. Before his departure, he had sold thousands of head of livestock to the republican government and many slaves to Cuba, but he relied on his enemy Casa Calvo at Fort Liberté to collect payment for him. His baggage was also detained in customs at Havana. He asked for it to be sold but without success.[96] Finding that the ministry ignored his letters, Jean-François tried sarcasm. Seeking to shame the government, he sent a list of his officers to the chief minister, the Príncipe de la Paz, asking if their pay could "maintain, with honor and a decency befitting their rank, officers who have no other resource or means, and who have sacrificed their fortune without hesitation to be able to deserve the honors showered on them by His Catholic Majesty."[97]

Cádiz must have felt unpleasantly cold in March. It was a very cosmopolitan city, and among its many foreign inhabitants were some slaves and even a few French Caribbean blacks. The new arrivals in their elaborate uniforms with extra gold braid, nonetheless, created quite a stir. The governor called it "no more sensation than a normal curiosity about seeing them." Crammed into two large houses, many soon contracted smallpox. They also attracted the disapproving attention of the cathedral authorities, because not all the couples were married. A French friar was later assigned to give them religious instruction.[98]

The government's first priority, however, was to divide the group while it sought a permanent solution. The governor of Cádiz recommended that the men be stripped of their military titles; he particularly wanted to isolate the black army's white secretary, Nicolas Préau (a.k.a. Réaux, Perró, Pertero, etc.), whom he considered "a captious agitator." Jean-François, on the other hand, impressed him as moderate, loyal, and deserving. He expressed much love of the king and reminded the Spanish that he had resisted advantageous offers from the British. He pressed the government to award his men lands in Trinidad or Puerto Rico, where they could grow coffee and cotton, as they had in Saint Domingue. Their large entourage of "servants" was obviously destined for agricultural labor on the officers' farms. As Jean-François did not declare them to be soldiers, they were legally his slaves.

Discussions continued through the summer about how much to pay the ex-auxiliaries and where they should go. Jean-François turned down the warmer climes of Ceuta in Morocco, preferring somewhere in Andalucia. He liked Jerez, but when told that only his family could settle there, he insisted that everyone remain together in Cádiz. Meanwhile, Florida, Venezuela, and Cartagena were suggested as permanent destinations for the group. In October 1796, the ministry finally decided to send them to Honduras, where they would continue receiving their salaries until lands were distributed to them. But just at that time, war broke out with England, Cádiz was blockaded, and the plan had to be shelved.[99]

Information on the migrants thereafter becomes sparse. When the British bombarded the city in 1797, some of the soldiers served behind the fortifications, as they did again in 1800. At some point, their allowances were increased by 25 percent, which left them 6 percent below their 1795 level. By November 1798, the retinues of the leading officers had all shrunk; Jean-François's from 36 to 30. That year, the men were obliged to give up their military ranks, as the war and interior ministers found that they were not conferred by royal command.[100] This must have been a blow to their prestige. Although Governor García had issued orders that the auxiliaries' ranks be recognized and Jean-François had received his general's uniform from the hands of a prominent admiral, who conferred on him the Order of Alcántara, he was now merely "leader of the troops who were auxiliaries in Saint Domingue." Further indignities followed. As they could not produce a document stating that the king would continue their salaries in exile, the men had their pensions reduced in 1803. During the brief peace of 1802–1803, preparations again were made to send the group to Honduras, but the resumption of war once more prevented their departure. In Jean-François's last surviving letter, he recapitulates his complaints and difficulties and somewhat poignantly returns to using what once must have been his nickname when he was a dashing young coachman, "Petecou" (breakneck).[101] Having lost his military title, the former grand admiral decided, like most ex-slaves, to adopt a surname.

It was thus a rather disgruntled Jean-François who heard the news of Haitian independence early in 1804. His scornful comments about Dessalines and Christophe, the new powers in the land, attracted the attention of the French consul in Cádiz, who put him in touch with the Saint Domingue planter lobby. They were thirsting for vengeance and placed their hopes in the resistance to the Haitians of the Spanish in Santo Domingo. If the Spanish government, concerned to protect Cuba, would ship Jean-François to Santo Domingo, the colonialists reasoned, he might become a rallying point for opposition to Dessalines. The merchant Stanislas Foäche thought the idea dangerous in view of Jean-François's ambition. "You remember Mr. King," he wrote dryly, alluding to the title the black leader supposedly adopted at the start of the slave insurrection. The former legislator Charles Tarbé, however, envisaged Jean-François conducting subversive operations against the new state while missionaries preached to peasants in favor of "the justice and humanity" of Bonaparte; a new French invasion would follow. This unlikely scenario failed to appeal to Bonaparte himself, and the project went no further.[102]

Within little more than a year, Jean-François was dead.[103] In 1809, a royal decree ordered for the third time the Domingans' removal from Spain to Honduras. This decree suggests some change in official attitudes, for it referred to the deportees as "honorable relics of a unit that did honor to our armed forces." According to historian Carlos Deive, no departures seem to have taken place before 1813, when several families left for the Caribbean and settled in Cuba and Santo Domingo.[104] This meant the ex-auxiliaries must have lived in Cádiz when it was besieged by French troops in 1810–1811. These were also the years of the Cortes of Cádiz that gave Spain its first liberal constitution. The *cortes* did little to change race relations, still less slavery, but it is interesting that one of the few deputies who called for citizenship for people of African descent chose to invoke the case of the *auxiliares*.

> I beseech you not to commit such an injustice [as to deny citizenship], so we do not repeat those sad examples that, when my memory stirs, awaken in my heart a terrible, still-fresh emotion. After the illustrious blacks of Saint Domingue, those 63,000 men, chose Spain as their fatherland and willingly shed their blood for it, and when their leaders were sent to this city, they were robbed of their freedom, their titles, and their honors. And why was this? . . . The guilt is not yours. These were the despotic deeds of earlier governments, relics of the barbarous past.[105]

Return to Santo Domingo

It is odd that just when Spain was trying regroup the Domingan exiles in Honduras, some of those who had been living there for fifteen years left to return to Santo Domingo. Brigadier Gilles Narcisse, Captain Juan Luis Santillan, and two other officers from the Granada group turned up with their families in Havana in December 1811. They said they were on their way to Santo Domingo, where a royal decree had permitted their return. Fearing their impact on the local black population, as in 1796, Cuba's governor had them lodged in a fort across the harbor. Word spread, nevertheless, about a black brigadier, which led many locals to visit them and sometimes ask to see their uniforms.

Three months later, a revolt on a nearby sugar estate led to investigations that uncovered the extensive, and now famous, conspiracy of the free black carpenter José Antonio Aponte. Its coincidence with the arrival of these veterans of the 1791 uprising caused the administration to question them. Some of the Aponte conspirators admitted visiting the Domingans in their lodgings, but all concerned denied discussing anything incriminating. One of the foreign-born plotters pretended to be Jean-François when he went recruiting and claimed the new arrivals were his officers. The Domingans were thus at least the object of inspirational rumors. But did they provide advice or encouragement, or more? Cuban historian José Luciano Franco, citing oral traditions of the Abakuá secret society, stated that they did participate in the plot and that Gilles Narcisse promised to lead the rebels once they were armed. The Spanish found no proof of this, however, and the men were soon permitted to continue their journey to Santo Domingo.[106]

Santo Domingo at this time was rife with conspiracies against its weak Spanish regime. According to J. L. Franco, Gilles Narcisse became implicated just months after his arrival in an aborted slave revolt, which was linked, like Aponte's, to false rumors concerning the Cortes of Cádiz. The prolific historian of Dominican slavery Carlos Deive apparently does not agree, but he does mention a pro-Haitian plot that was betrayed in 1818 by a black captain named José Fantasín, who evidently was Gilles Narcisse's comrade, Jean Fantaisie Gaston. An earlier pro-Haitian plot in the colony in 1810 involved many people with French names, but Deive does not seem sure that they included former auxiliaries; the best known of them, Paul Ali, kept out of the plot.[107]

Paul Ali's career exemplifies the degree to which some auxiliaries maintained a pro-Spanish and anti-Haitian stance. An early participant in the 1791 uprising, he became a captain in Biassou's army but was left behind in Santo Domingo in 1795. His salary then ceased, and for several years he lived in poverty in Santo Domingo city working for himself. Many ex-auxiliaries went on fighting the French Republic in these years, some of them joining the British forces that remained in Saint Domingue until 1798.[108] Ali turned down financial inducements from the British and was acquitted in 1797 on charges of complicity in a pro-British conspiracy. Several times he asked to join Biassou in Florida. After resisting Toussaint Louverture's occupation of Santo Domingo in 1801, he took refuge in Puerto Rico but returned to fight against Dessalines's invasion of 1805. The Spanish government awarded him a gold medal in 1809 and made him lieutenant-colonel of a black corps. In the crisis of Spanish power in 1820, he ignored Haitian overtures and stuck by the governor, until he learned his request for Spanish citizenship had been rejected. He then switched sides and joined, not the pro-Haitian faction, but the white Creole independence movement that looked to Simón Bolívar. When the Haitians conquered the country in 1822, they nonetheless gave him a military command. In 1843, Paul Ali became commander of the Santo Domingo garrison, where Juan Santillan was head of the arsenal. Until his death in 1844, he remained in the Spanish part of the island, and as a very old man he recounted his memories of the early slave revolution to historian Céligny Ardouin.[109]

The men who launched that revolution and diverted it two years later into the service of Spanish imperialism ended up on the wrong side of history. For that reason, the story of their exile has found little room in the master narrative of the Haitian Revolution. It turns out to be less picturesque than historians have often imagined. Biassou did not die in a brawl or a Mexican mine or vanish without trace. Jean-François did not live in splendor in Cádiz or become a Spanish grandee or the governor of a North African city.[110] If Gilles Narcisse sponsored slave revolts in Cuba and Santo Domingo, no one has been able to prove it. Instead, these men sought to make new lives for themselves and their follow-ers in several different Hispanic societies, usually as soldiers or farmers, while conserving the patronage of the Spanish state.

For the Spanish government, as Joaquín García put it, there were two essen-tial points: keeping the king's pledge to the auxiliaries and taking maximum advantage of them. Advantage proved to be military (guarding the Central American coast and Indian frontiers in Panama and Florida) and economic (provisioning poorly supplied cities such as Portobelo and Trujillo). Much in this story appears to support Frank Tannenbaum's thesis regarding Iberian tol-erance for racial difference and willingness to integrate former slaves into free society.[111] However, the metropolitan government's honoring of its 1793 pledge was not entirely of its own volition, and Governor García, who initiated the process, had his own selfish motives for doing so. Moreover, he drastically lim-ited the number of beneficiaries. It was a pledge somewhat reluctantly and very selectively honored. Besides, in the societies chosen to host the exiles, adminis-trators were inclined to see security as the essential point and the migrants as a threat more than a resource; hence their outright rejection in Cuba and Trinidad and the desire to split them up, even in Honduras, where they performed valu-able military service. The rare administrators who took a more positive view, such as the commandant of Omoa and the governor of Darién, failed to have them settled in their provinces.

The sources reveal little of the reactions of other sectors of society. Bystand-ers gathered to gawk at the newcomers in Cádiz and St. Augustine; black admir-ers in Havana were numerous, some of them with revolutionary ambitions of their own. Contact with the Catholic church was tenuous in the rural settle-ments in Yucatán and Panama but was more evident in other locations. Inter-marriage with local black and Indian women occurred quickly and extensively in Yucatán, where the migrant group had a large excess of males over females. Integration was probably less rapid elsewhere, but intermarriage and godparent relationships with other recent migrants (Anglophone blacks, Garifuna) oc-curred in Florida and Honduras.

The study of their exile shows the insurgents of 1791 in a somewhat new light, notably as members of families and as a diverse range of individuals rather than as one-dimensional "rebels." They were of all ages and persuasions, from the overbearing drunkard Georges Biassou to the Franciscan lay brother Sylvain and the enterprising barber Augustin Azor. The discovery of the large extended families of the Creole leaders makes more vivid the contrast between them and their socially more isolated African followers. Although the data on the group's social composition is very uneven, it invites speculation about the propensity of different parts of the slave population to join the revolution. The prominence of domestic slaves and the apparent underrepresentation of arti-sans is striking. The numerical dominance of Kongolese among the Africans is much what one would expect (especially taking age structure into account), but the salience of Mandinga among both the Panama and Yucatán migrants is par-ticularly noteworthy. Together with the few references to Senegalese in the Honduras group, this may suggest that Muslims or Senegambians were disproportionately present among the insurgents.

Despite their counterrevolutionary rhetoric, the ex-auxiliaries were greeted with unease everywhere they settled. Although they had fought against the French Revolution, they were the visible embodiment of the black revolution that had become its most feared expression. Yet having adopted a conservative posture, they maintained it to the end. Some of those who formed this transatlantic diaspora and their descendants eventually moved to Cuba, where slavery flourished. None is known to have returned to independent Haiti.

Part Six. *Epilogue*

Although the nationalism of the Americas' white revolutionaries expressed little animosity toward the colonial rulers they much resembled, Haitian nationalism, to a large degree defined by race, was understandably born in bitterness. Not only did Haitians pass from slavery to independence in the space of a decade, but that independence was won in an extraordinarily brutal war. The ceremony on January 1, 1804 at which the new state was baptized began with a speech by Jean-Jacques Dessalines reminding his audience of the atrocities they had suffered at French hands. The following speech by Louis Boisrond-Tonnerre, which served as a prologue to the proclamation of independence, emphasized the difference between French and Haitians in terms of cruelty, color, adaptation to local climate, and the distance that separated them. Boisrond vowed "eternal hatred of France" and called for the massacre of the remaining French colonists. More than 3,000 were killed in the following four months.

French, nevertheless, would remain the national language, even though most Haitians did not understand it, and the country, unlike most American states, had its own indigenous language, kreyol, understood by everyone. The Roman Catholic church, too, was to enjoy under most governments a privileged status, although most inhabitants had had little access to it. The retention of the colonizer's language and religion reflected the predilections of the Haitian elite more than strictly rational decision-making in the national interest. Against this background of cultural Francophilia and intense hostility to the French, the name Haïti was chosen for the new state.

Until the 1950s, at least, decolonization was rarely accompanied by a radical change of name. The choice of an Amerindian name for the first modern black state is therefore all the more noteworthy. It raises interesting questions about ethnicity, memory, and identity among the former slaves and free coloreds who created Haiti, whose aboriginal population had died out centuries before. By 1804, a revalorization of Amerindian culture was already beginning in Latin America, but the vogue for nostalgic *or nationalist indigenism still lay well in the future. As interest in the symbolic Indian has tended to be inversely proportional to the presence of real Indians, it may be that the Haitian case makes perfect sense. Surveying sources from the sixteenth to the twentieth century, this final chapter traces use of the word "Haiti," and seeks to understand the meanings attached to it by different sections of Haitian society.*

13 The Naming of Haiti

When the first modern black state declared its independence on January 1, 1804, it adopted an Amerindian name, although its population was overwhelmingly African and Afro-American and it had been ruled by Europeans for three centuries. The renaming of French Saint Domingue as Haïti remains the only case in which a Caribbean colony underwent a radical change of name on achieving independence.[1] In this it resembles Europe's former colonies in Africa rather than those in the Americas. The word Haïti, apparently meaning "rugged, mountainous" in the Taino Arawak language, was assumed to be the aboriginal term for the island Columbus had christened La Española.[2] The choice of name raises interesting questions about ethnicity and identity and historical knowledge in the Caribbean, yet the circumstances surrounding its selection have gone entirely unrecorded. Haiti's earliest historians, Vastey and Madiou, were able to reveal little on the matter.[3] Modern historians have found almost nothing new to add.[4]

Having fought an extremely bitter war to expel French colonists and British and Spanish invaders, Haiti's victorious ex-slaves and mixed-race elite evidently wished to emphasize symbolically their break with Europe. After completing the massacre of the remaining colonists in April 1804, head of state Jean-Jacques Dessalines proclaimed that no European would ever again be a proprietor in Haiti, and he declared enigmatically, "I have avenged America."[5] There are few clues, however, about how the decision was made in Dessalines's entourage of black and colored generals to anchor the new state to an American and noncolonial past. Historian Thomas Madiou merely tells us that, when the last French troops left in December 1803,

> People immediately thought about giving a new name to this land that formed the new state. On everyone's lips was the name of "Haïti," a reminder of the island's native inhabitants, who had been wiped out defending their freedom. It received an enthusiastic welcome, and the local people called themselves "Haïtiens."[6]

One might wonder why a place-name that had scarcely been used for three centuries came so spontaneously and universally to mind in an almost entirely illiterate population that had had little leisure for investigating the past. Those accustomed to thinking of the Taino Arawak as helpless victims of genocide also might be surprised to find them symbolizing violent resistance for the first black Haitians. This chapter seeks to explore what the makers of Haitian independence might have known of those past victims of European imperialism, whose patrimony they came to inherit.

Haiti and Africa

First, it is not entirely surprising the founding fathers did not pick an African name for their state. It is true that *ayi* is the word for "earth" in Fon, a language that has left a marked imprint on the lexicon of Haitian vodou. However, a recent claim that this was the source of Dessalines's inspiration has little linguistic or historical basis.[7] The "y" in the Fon word is usually a consonant; the "y" used interchangeably with "ï" in the state's name is a vowel.[8] The state was not called "Hayiti"; nor "Ayi," of course. And at no time do Haitians ever seem to have believed their state to have an African name. Aja-Fon, furthermore, constituted no more than 15 percent of Saint Domingue's African slaves in the later eighteenth century. Although half or more of Haiti's population had been born in Africa, they spoke dozens of different languages, which rendered difficult the choice of an acceptable term.[9] A decision to name the country something like "Nouveau Kongo," building on nostalgia for a prestigious African state, the homeland of close to half the Africans in Saint Domingue, would have had little appeal for the other half of the African-born population and probably would have been offensive to locally born Haitians.[10]

Most important, few of Haiti's most prominent leaders were African. Though some hostile commentators identified Dessalines and other ex-slave leaders of the Haitian Revolution as African-born, they used the term indiscriminately as a pejorative.[11] African guerrilla leaders in the mountains—often called "Congos" —had played critical roles at different stages of the revolution, but their power had been broken by the Creole (i.e., locally born) generals of the colonial army, who were backed, so Madiou claimed, by the Creole population of the plains. According to him, this had been a precondition for achieving national independence.[12]

Louis Boisrond-Tonnerre, who wrote the declaration of independence, was passionately anti-European but, Paris-educated, of mixed racial descent, and several generations removed from slavery, he had little personal connection to Africa.[13] Dessalines entrusted him with writing the independence proclamation on December 31st after rejecting as too staid an earlier attempt by another French-educated mulatto, Charéron. Boisrond supposedly declared, "To draw up the act of independence we need the skin of a white man for parchment, his skull for an inkwell, his blood for ink, and a bayonet for a pen."[14] He sat up all night to work on the document. On the morning of January 1, 1804, before the proclamation was made public in the seaport of Gonaïves, a group of senior military officers met to swear support for independence and to name Dessalines head of state. "They were agreed," Joseph Saint-Rémy tells us with tantalizing imprecision, "on giving back to the country its aboriginal name of 'Haïti.'"[15] Of the thirty-seven officers who signed the declaration of independence, more than two-thirds were of mixed racial descent, and none was African.[16]

Race and Color

The Haitian Revolution had never been just a revolution of slaves, and with a near monopoly on literacy, the former "free colored" minority of colonial times was disproportionately represented in the new state apparatus.[17] This was the milieu that had to validate, and very probably suggested, the new state's name. Spokesmen of this new ruling class tended to share Europeans' deprecation of African and African-derived culture.[18] Vodou was repressed; Christianity was the only religion recognized by the state.[19] Dessalines's courtiers danced minuets and gavottes, along with the local *carabinier*, but not the *calenda* or *chica*. And no one seems to have suggested that Creole, the language of the masses, replace French, even though Dessalines himself did not speak French.[20]

On the other hand, Haitian spokesmen did assert that the racial identity of all Haitians was African, and this unifying stress on a shared racial heritage served to counteract mutually reinforcing divisions of class and color.[21] Léon-François Hoffmann observes that mixed-race Haitians seem very rarely to have disowned their African ancestry by substituting a supposed Indian ancestry, as their Dominican neighbors generally are supposed to have done.[22] A few sought to do so in court cases of the colonial period in order to be classified "white," just as others falsely claimed pure European descent.[23] Yet after the revolution, the opposite occurred: certain white allies of the black revolutionaries claimed to be of mixed racial descent.[24] The constitution of 1805 defined all Haitian citizens as "black" and banned the use of colonial terms denoting phenotype.[25]

Nevertheless, appeals to "blackness" seem to have been rare during the revolution. In a mixed-race, color-conscious population, they were potentially divisive. In Paris in 1789, a group of free blacks seemingly excluded from the activities of "colored" activists had criticized the latter's "bastardized" origins while vaunting their own racial "purity."[26] Haitian ethnographer and statesman Jean Price-Mars argued that *sentiment de race* (racial awareness) motivated revolutionary leader Toussaint Louverture and that he wanted to make blackness a subject for pride. I would contend that instead of valorizing biological attributes, Toussaint fought to remove the stigma Europeans attached to blackness by pointing out that race does not determine behavior.[27] After Dessalines's assassination in 1806, the article defining Haitians as "black" was dropped from all subsequent constitutions.

Haiti and the Taino

Amerindian symbolism provided a sort of neutral, non-European reference point for a diverse population, some of whose most influential figures had every reason to hate Europeans but who, in ancestry as well as culture, were much more European than African. Though light-skinned Haitians have rarely claimed Amerindian ancestry, it is generally they who have shown the most interest in their country's Native American past. From the beginning of the Haitian Revolution, mixed-race activists, but not their black counterparts, called themselves "Americans."[28] Dessalines adopted the name "Haïti," but it was the 1816 constitution of Alexandre Pétion, leader of the former free coloreds in the War of Independence of 1802–1803, that admitted to Haitian citizenship all African and Amerindian migrants.[29] Whether or not the choice of an Amerindian name had especial appeal for Haitians of mixed racial descent, it surely was valued by a ruling class that rejected both African culture and European rule and which was charting unknown terrain in a difficult search for national identity. There are strong reasons therefore for thinking that the preponderant influence in the naming of Haiti came from members of the mixed-race elite and that part of the name's attraction was that it was neither European nor African.

Even so, if we believe Madiou's account, the name must at least have resonated with a large section of the population. But what can the mainly African ex-slaves have known of a world that had collapsed at the time of Columbus? Some modern Haitian scholars such as Jean Fouchard and Louis Élie have suggested that Taino Arawaks or their descendants survived in numbers into the late colonial period.[30] Along with others, such as Jean Price-Mars, godfather of the indigenist movement, they have argued for a Taino cultural influence in Saint Domingue down to the Haitian Revolution (and beyond), claiming certain vodou chants of the revolutionary period to be Arawak war chants. One chant was supposedly written by the ruler Anacaona, who was executed in 1504.[31]

Price-Mars's source for attributing a late colonial vodou chant to the Taino was apparently the mid-nineteenth-century work *Histoire des caciques d'Haïti* by Émile Nau. Nau, however, stated that this linking of the vodou chant with the Taino was a fiction. It had been invented, he claimed, by courtiers of King Henry Christophe (1811–1820) to flatter the monarch, who liked hearing stories about his namesake, Enrique, a sixteenth-century Taino leader who fought against the Spanish.[32] Unknown to Nau, the chant was genuine but of African origin; the proposed translation, "Death rather than slavery," was false and was taken from an earlier French author.[33] It thus provides further evidence that elite Haitians in the nineteenth and twentieth centuries have sometimes been attracted by Hispaniola's Arawak past, but it is not proof that Taino traditions continued through the time of independence.

In more recent years, Hungarian ethnographer Maya Deren and other scholars have suggested a more encompassing Amerindian influence on Haitian vodou.[34] Part of Deren's case rests on general similarities between African and Native American religions, which she acknowledged to be merely similarities rather than products of diffusion. Her argument is centered, however, on an outmoded understanding of vodou's violent Petro cult as being an American rather than an African creation. An ethnographically and historically more plausible interpretation of Petro sees it as related to the huge influx of Kongo slaves into Saint

Domingue in the late eighteenth century.[35] Many of its deities, its drumming, its dances, and its magical accoutrements seem related to the Congo region. Deren was clearly wrong to derive the Kongo words *zombi* and *Simbi* from the Arawak *zemi*.[36] Even those who regard Petro as a New World creation tend to see its violent features as a reaction to enslavement rather than a product of Amerindian influence. The same can be said of vodou's decentralized nature, which Deren also linked unconvincingly to the Arawak past. Finally, the inclusion of Taino axe-heads and figurines among the sacred objects of some vodou temples does suggest an awareness among Haitians of the vanished Amerindians, but it is not evidence, as Louis Maximilien claimed, of Arawak influence on the formation of vodou.[37] Vodou has no counterpart to the Brazilian candomblé caboclo.[38]

Nothing is known for certain about the ex-slaves' knowledge of Native American culture. The sixteenth century no doubt saw some cultural transmission between the last survivors of the pre-Columbian population and the first generations of African slaves, although the two groups tended to live in separate locations. Suzanne Comhaire-Sylvain stated in the 1930s that 10 percent of Haitian folktales were "clearly of Indian origin." However, she acknowledged the paucity of sources available to her concerning Caribbean Indians, and other folklorists have seemed less convinced.[39] Moreover, while traditional foodways or fishing techniques may have been transmitted, directly or through European intermediaries, there seems little reason to think a redundant place-name would have been preserved among the enslaved blacks. Above all, such Amerindian-African contact as occurred on sixteenth-century Hispaniola was likely to involve Indians other than the aboriginal Taino, who numbered fewer than 1,000 by 1550 and only a few dozen in the 1560s, when the black population was estimated at between 12,000 and 25,000. According to Carlos Deive, by that time, Hispaniola's colonists had imported tens of thousands of Indian slaves from all round the Caribbean and from Mexico and Brazil.[40] By the time the French began large-scale importations of black slaves in the late seventeenth century, the native Arawaks had been almost extinct for about 100 years.[41]

Dominican ideologues obviously exaggerated when they denied any Amerindian input into the creation of the Haitian people.[42] Early French censuses record small numbers of enslaved *sauvages* and *Indiens,* notably on the neglected south coast, though they were probably not descendants of the pre-Columbian Taino.[43] Like the Spanish before them, the French enslaved other Amerindian peoples and brought them to the colony. It is true that in the pre-Columbian Caribbean use of the term "Aytí" was probably not confined to the Taino.[44] However, the few *Indiens* who appear in plantation inventories and colonial newspapers in the eighteenth century were likely to be Natchez and others deported from Louisiana, Canada, and South America or Asian Indians shipped through Isle-de-France (modern Mauritius).[45] By the 1780s, even with their mixed-race descendants (*mulâtres indiens*), they represented a small fraction of 1 percent of the slave population.[46]

Boyá and Enrique

Nevertheless, there were some Indians on Hispaniola in the eighteenth century who apparently did claim descent from the original Taino. They were found not in Saint Domingue but in the neighboring Spanish colony of Santo Domingo. From 1519 to 1533 the *cacique* (chief) Enrique and a small band of followers had waged a successful guerrilla war against the Spanish and forced them to pass the Americas' first maroon treaty.[47] In an embroidered account of these events, written around 1730, French historian Charlevoix claimed that Enrique had subsequently settled with the last of the Tainos in the village of Boyá some forty miles north of Santo Domingo city, where he and his group were granted extensive autonomy. Charlevoix added that down to the beginning of the eighteenth century, the head of the Boyá community had used the title "Cacique of the Island of Haiti."[48]

The modern Dominican historian Utrera has shown that there were in fact no historical links between Enrique and Boyá, which was founded years after the *cacique*'s death. Moreover, the village's original inhabitants seem to have died out in the 1650s and been replaced by a small group of Campeche Maya rescued from the French of Tortuga.[49] By the 1700s, residents of Boyá were mainly mestizos. They numbered fewer than 100 by 1720 and supposedly only 25 or 30 in the 1780s. Their population was probably further thinned by the migration of 1796, following Spain's transfer of Santo Domingo to France. Several eighteenth-century writers recognized that they were not descended from the Taino, among them the French colonial lawyer Moreau de Saint-Méry. He observed, nonetheless, that in 1744 several Indians in the frontier town of Hinche had legally proved their descent from the followers of Enrique and that the inhabitants of Boyá continued to exhibit extreme pride in their supposed heritage.[50]

This community clearly caught the imagination of Philippe-Rose Roume, a prominent official of the French revolutionary government who served in Saint Domingue from 1791 to 1801. After Santo Domingo was made a French colony in 1795, he was posted there for eighteen months. He never visited Boyá or saw any of its residents, whom he thought reclusive. Yet in a report of October 1797, he recounted the story of Enrique and added,

> Thus it might be possible that, despite considerable decline, these men may have passed from father to son some tradition regarding the former state and history of the Haitians (Haytienes). This information would be very important to philosophy, and if the Indians have been able to keep their secrets from the Spanish, they will certainly reveal them to the French.[51]

Inspired by revolutionary egalitarianism, the "noble savage," and the "black legend," Roume called for French officials to carry out the "sweet and sacred duty" of extending the benefits of republican rule to "the wretched remains of a simple and virtuous people" while resisting the temptation to exact on the

Spanish Creoles the vengeance that their conquistador ancestors had merited. This report was intercepted by the local Spanish governor, who remained in office after the French takeover. Forwarding the report to Madrid, Governor García denied that the Boyá mestizos were descendants of Enrique or that they were reclusive: "He who seeks tradition among them will find less than among any other people."[52] Anxious to present the colonial population as loyal Spanish subjects, he claimed the mestizos were better off simple and ignorant without having the French awaken in them ideas of tradition and history.

Whatever the truth about the Boyá community of the late eighteenth century, there is a possibility that it served as a source of inspiration for Haitian revolutionaries. Though situated more than 200 kilometers from the colonial frontier, indirect knowledge of it might have come through the enthusiastic conversations of Agent Roume or through the black rebels earlier recruited as soldiers by the Spanish for their failed invasion of Saint Domingue in 1793–1795.[53] The blacks' invasion and occupation of Santo Domingo under Toussaint Louverture (1801–1802) could conceivably have resulted in some direct contact. Yet surely the likeliest source of knowledge about Boyá and Enrique for residents of Saint Domingue were the same books that no doubt provided Roume himself with much of his information—Charlevoix's 1730s *Histoire*, which was reprinted in the 1780s, and Moreau de Saint-Méry's *Description de la partie espagnole*, published in French and English in 1796.[54]

The reason many Haitians, from Dessalines's secretary Juste Chanlatte to the twentieth-century indigenists, have viewed the Taino as a symbol of resistance has much to do with the personal epic of Enrique and his long campaign in the mountains of Baoruco.[55] More generally, as David Lowenthal remarks, the Caribbean Indians' rapid disappearance has helped foster in the region a romantic stereotype of a population that preferred death to slavery.[56] Enrique's story, however, was particularly apt for Haitians, as he was apparently joined in his mountain retreat by African fugitives from the first generation of plantation slaves.[57] Africans and Indians resisted slavery together, wrote Beaubrun Ardouin in the mid-nineteenth century, seeking to explain the naming of Haiti.[58] "The African and the Indian held hands together in chains," observed his more poetic contemporary Émile Nau.[59] Such knowledge of the Arawak past in Haiti seems to have had little to do with the survival of a Taino population into the eighteenth century or the continuous transmission of ancestral traditions, as Fouchard, Maximilien, and Élie apparently believed. No Haitian scholar of the early nineteenth century adopted such an interpretation, and Madiou and Nau explicitly denied there were any biological or cultural links between the pre-Columbian and modern Haitian populations.[60]

Haiti and the Inca

The name of Haiti was surely transmitted through written sources, to which only a minority of the new elite could have had access. Both the rapid demise of the Taino population and the change in pronunciation between the

Taino and French versions of the word point to this conclusion.[61] Another reason is the curious and temporary adoption of the name "Incas" by the black insurgents at the outset of the final phase of the War of Independence. According to Madiou, when Dessalines went into revolt in the fall of 1802, he "gave to the people that accepted his authority the name of Incas or children of the sun." For some months his soldiers called themselves "Sons of the Sun" until these terms were abandoned in favor of the word *indigène*, which means "native."[62] Madiou provides almost no explanation for the practice, and most other historians have ignored it. Only one surviving letter by the black general Capoix seems to testify to its existence.[63] If Madiou's version is correct, this use of Amerindian symbolism prior to the adoption of the word "Haïti" appears to show Dessalines's desire to identify with an Amerindian past even in the absence of reliable information about that past.

It may be, as Jean Fouchard argued, that the insurgents were remembering news of the 1780–1781 uprising in the Andes of Tupac Amaru and Tupac Katari.[64] Although an attractive hypothesis, this seems unlikely. The uprising received very little mention at the time in the colonial press, and more than twenty years had passed.[65] It is more probable that the Taino were thought to be descendants of the Incas. Evidence for this comes from the novel *Zoflora ou la bonne négresse*, published in Paris in 1799. Its author, who had spent a short time in Saint Domingue, suggested that Hispaniola's aboriginal population had come from Peru.[66] He claimed, moreover, that pre-Columbian underground burial chambers still survived in the Artibonite plain, which is where Dessalines made his headquarters.

Whether or not *Zoflora* reflected ideas already popular in the colony, the book surely must have reached Saint Domingue during the period 1799–1803; it was one of the first novels written about the Haitian Revolution. Alexandre Pétion and other free colored exiles from the War of the South who reached France in 1800 and returned in 1802 in the Napoleonic invasion fleet could well have encountered the book in Paris or in the hands of fellow officers. As Pétion broke with the French at the same time as Dessalines and joined him in the Artibonite in late November 1802, it is tempting to believe that he or someone in his circle played a major role in choosing the term "Government of the Incas." The term probably derived from literary sources, and Dessalines was illiterate. Pétion, his second in command, had received at least a basic education.[67]

The historian Joseph Saint-Rémy's version of events is rather different than Madiou's. He believed the colored officer Étienne Gérin, future signatory of the declaration of independence, invented the designation "Incas" and that its usage was confined to the south during the early months of 1803. Whereas Dessalines adopted the term *indigène* early on, Saint-Rémy claims, the title "Army of the Incas" cannot have been used before January 1803. This was when Gérin joined the insurgent army of fellow southerner Nicolas Geffrard, which Dessalines and Pétion had sent from the Artibonite to raise the southern peninsula against the French. Use of the title was supposedly reproved at the so-called Congress of

Arcahaie in May, when the insurgent officers met to coordinate their actions.[68] Madiou confirms, at least, that Geffrard used the term. What is most interesting about this version is its connection with *hommes de couleur* and the south. Dessalines had ravaged the region only three years before, executing thousands of his light-complexioned opponents during the war of 1799–1800. Now he needed their alliance. Dessalines chose Geffrard, on Pétion's advice, because he himself was so unpopular in the south.[69] Like Geffrard, the designation "army of the Incas" was perhaps chosen with the sensibilities of the southern population in mind.

These officers were all literate, but they were military men, not intellectuals. If we accept the evidence of the letter of Capoix, the insurgents abandoned the term "Incas" not in May but some time after July 1803. This was the month that Dessalines recruited Louis Boisrond-Tonnerre from his home on the south coast to be his secretary.[70] Boisrond-Tonnerre and Juste Chanlatte are generally recognized as the most learned of early Haitian political advisors.[71] They were the most able to point out the awkwardness of the Inca trope. Since Chanlatte did not return from exile until the end of the War of Independence, one suspects here the influence of Boisrond-Tonnerre.

As Boisrond-Tonnerre wrote the declaration of independence, one might assume he also chose the state's name. If that were the case, however, he perhaps would have mentioned it in his *Mémoires*.[72] Madiou seems quite clear the name was chosen before Boisrond was asked to draw up the document on December 31st. Joseph Saint-Rémy, writing slightly later, implied the name was formally approved only after the declaration was written, but no more than Madiou did he attribute the choice to Boisrond. It remains possible that Boisrond's great unpopularity with the mulatto elite caused successors to minimize his role in the founding of the state. But it may well be that the obscure figure Charéron had already used the word in his draft declaration of independence that Dessalines rejected on December 31st. On balance, it would appear that the name "Haïti" enjoyed a certain currency among the men surrounding Dessalines and that no one person was responsible for its selection.

Haiti and Quisqueya

This directs attention to the survival of the word in printed texts since the fifteenth century. Columbus never used it in his writings. Peter Martyr, the court cleric who interviewed returnees from the Americas through the 1490s, recorded three terms he thought the Taino had used over time: "Quizquella," "Haïti," and "Cipango."[73] In a classic study of the early contact period, geographer Carl Sauer implied that "Haiti" referred not to the whole of Hispaniola but to only one part of it.[74] He noted that the pilot-cartographer Andrés Morales, who surveyed the island in 1508, applied the term to a region approximating the modern Montes Haitises in the eastern Dominican Republic. He added that Morales's report, as recounted in Peter Martyr's *Third Decade* (published in

1516), represented "the first appearance of the name 'Haiti.' " This is true, however, only with regard to publication. Dr. Chanca, the official physician on Columbus's second voyage, wrote to the Seville town council in 1494 that "Haití" was the easternmost province of Hispaniola.[75] Ramón Pané, a friar who lived among the island's natives in the mid-1490s, recorded that they called the whole island "Ahití."[76] Since he was one of the first Europeans to learn an Amerindian language and lived among Arawak speakers for several years, his testimony carries weight. Bartolomé de Las Casas, it is true, cast aspersions on his linguistic knowledge, but he, too, believed "Haití" was the aboriginal term for Hispaniola.[77]

Las Casas's firsthand experience of the island dated from nearly a decade later, but his knowledge of the Taino was probably unrivaled among his European contemporaries. Neither he nor the chronicler Oviedo used the term "Quizquella," which some modern scholars consider bogus.[78] Nevertheless, from the sixteenth to the early eighteenth century, European writers tended to record "Quisqueya" and "Haiti" as alternative aboriginal names for Hispaniola.[79] In the course of the eighteenth century, however, "Haiti" began to emerge as the preferred of the two terms. Raynal did not mention "Quisqueya" at all in the three editions of his *Histoire des deux Indes*.[80] Nor did Antonio Alcedo in his *Diccionario* of 1786. Moreau de Saint-Méry and Sánchez Valverde, also writing in the 1780s, mentioned the two alternatives but tended to privilege "Haiti."[81] In his novel *Zoflora*, J.-B. Piquenard referred to "the former island of Ohaïti now called Saint Domingue."[82] Much more striking, in a letter to the archbishop of Santo Domingo of July 1796, the civil commissioner Roume referred to the ex-slaves as "the new French of Haiti," as if the colony had already changed names.[83]

Yet the most remarkable usage of the word came in an obscure anonymous pamphlet published in 1788, supposedly at Les Cayes on Saint Domingue's isolated south coast.[84] It was a plan for colonial reform probably written by a lawyer. This region had a tradition of autonomist, even secessionist, leanings among its planter class.[85] Besides advocating a system of representative government for the colony, this pamphlet suggested the renaming of colonial place-names. "Saint Domingue" was to become "Aïti," which the writer thought to be the aboriginal name for northern Hispaniola, and a new capital city was to be called "Royal-Aïti." As in Spanish America, a degree of indigenism was perhaps emerging among some of the colony's white Creoles who were disgruntled with metropolitan rule.[86] Along with printed works, such colonists might have been another source of influence for south coast free coloreds such as Boisrond-Tonnerre.

Nevertheless, it seems reasonable to suppose that even if literate *anciens libres* suggested the new state's name, its adoption was predicated on some wider, if more vague, awareness of a vanished civilization among the ex-slave population. This is because of the visibility of Taino physical remains in many parts of Saint Domingue. In his 3-volume *Description* of the colony, Moreau de Saint-Méry made frequent references to Arawak rock carvings, tombs, earthen mounds, and artifacts that were strewn on the ground.[87] Slaves who worked the land and hunted in the woods could hardly have ignored them, even if they knew nothing of the colonial scientific society's museum of pre-Columbian artifacts in Cap Français or of the occasional ballet or poetry collection with an Indian character then produced in the colony.[88] Dessalines, born on the border of Dondon parish, must have known of its caverns with their petroglyphs and burials, fetishes and axe-heads. Of Limonade parish, in the plains below, Moreau wrote that "every step you take, there are the remains of Indian utensils."[89] Twenty years later, extensive remains of a large Amerindian settlement still surrounded the town of Gonaïves, where national independence was proclaimed.[90] The baron de Vastey, a leading statesman of the new Haiti, began his *Système colonial dévoilé*, published in 1814, with a long reflection on the fate of the Tainos.

> O soil of my country! . . . Is there another whose unhappy inhabitants have experienced greater misfortune? . . . Everywhere I tread or cast my gaze, I see shards, jars, tools, figurines, whose form bears witness to the infancy of art [and, in mountain caverns, whole whitened skeletons] . . . these remains that attest the existence of a people who are no more.[91]

The few Amerindians that slaves encountered in colonial times may have served a similar function as these archaeological remains. Although not Tainos themselves, such Indians still provided a living reminder of the Caribbean before the Europeans came and enabled Africans and Afro-Americans to visualize their distant predecessors. The new nation's name was thus perhaps more meaningful to its inhabitants than were "Colombia," "Venezuela," or "Ecuador" to the Indians and blacks of northern South America.

The choice of the Taino name "Haiti" for the new state probably derived from literary sources, and the colored elite must have played a preponderant role in its selection. It had little to do with the survival of Arawak culture or of an ancestral Taino population. One may suppose, however, that the widespread physical remains of the vanished civilization and the continued presence of isolated Amerindians and mestizos in Hispaniola's population created among the mass of former slaves a vague awareness of their Taino predecessors, and the choice of name probably was predicated on this awareness.

The Haitians of 1804 were not alone in their symbolic manipulation of the Taino. Even before Dessalines declared "I have avenged America!" and before early nationalist writers presented the slave insurgents as avengers of the Arawak,[92] certain English writers had employed the same conceit, depicting the black revolutionaries as punishing the cruelties of the conquistadors.[93] For the Haitians, it was a rhetorical device that amplified their indictment of imperialism and added legitimacy to their cause. For their English contemporaries, it was a way to criticize Britain's French and Spanish opponents simultaneously, and for proslavery apologists among them, such as Bryan Edwards, it helped obscure, via a flashback to the sixteenth century, the planter-slave conflict at the heart of the Haitian revolution.

For some Haitian intellectuals, the Taino have tended to symbolize resistance, embodied in certain individuals like Enrique and Caonabó.[94] In the Spanish West Indies, their image has been appropriated to sell products associated with strength (e.g., Hatuey beer in Cuba and the Dominican Republic). "Hatuey" was even the choice of the black and mulatto conspirators of the 1843 Escalera for renaming Cuba.[95] North Europeans, on the other hand, in their desire to emphasize the evils of the Spanish conquest, have tended to overlook Enrique and to stress the Tainos' pacific tendencies.[96] A peculiarly idiosyncratic version of this trope appeared in the published reminiscences of a former French colonist, who wrote in the aftermath of the slave revolution,

> The French creole was born in Saint Domingue under the influence of these innocent martyrs [the Taino]. . . . His heart was compassionate and sensitive. . . . The black is lazy and a thief; he used to get beaten sometimes; but in France didn't schoolboys used to get beaten?

After the Haitian occupation of Santo Domingo during 1822–1844, an interesting reaction took place among scholars in the neighboring Hispanic population. Until the Haitian invasion of 1822, Spanish writers had freely accepted "Haití" as an indigenous term for Hispaniola; indeed, the Dominicans who briefly sought independence in 1821 called their state "Haití Español." Thereafter, "Quisqueya" became the preferred term, and some claimed that in pre-Columbian times it had referred specifically to the eastern end of the island.[97] This was despite the absence of any supporting evidence, the presence in the Dominican Republic of several local place-names incorporating the word "Haití," and the letter of Dr. Chanca cited above.[98] This post-facto rationalization was nonetheless subsequently accepted by several Haitian writers.[99] Dominican antipathy for the word "Haiti" became publicized in the early 1930s, when the United States adopted "Hispaniola" as the name for the whole island. Haitians and Dominicans both objected, preferring national alternatives. However, the Academy of History and the National Teaching Council of the Dominican Republic each issued statements to the effect that "Hispaniola" would be preferable to "Haiti," which would be unacceptable to most Dominicans.[100]

The relationship between the color question in Haiti and interest in the country's Amerindian past remains controversial. From the writings of Juste Chanlatte to the government of Jean-Claude Duvalier, which attempted to establish a national Day of the Indian in 1983,[101] concern with Amerindian symbolism has tended to come from the light-skinned elite. Yet it has rarely been attached to claims of biological descent in the manner sometimes attributed to Dominicans and Cubans.[102] Such cases have existed, doubtless reflecting the impact of scientific racism; historian Louis Élie is the notable example, and Emile Roumer devoted a poem to the subject.[103] Nonetheless, according to Suzanne Comhaire-Sylvain, the contrary tendency has been more pronounced, that of individual

Haitians refusing to acknowledge their Indian ancestry for fear public opinion would perceive it as an attempt to minimize their African heritage.[104] Moreover, it would seem that popular (as opposed to elite) attitudes in Haiti link Amerindians with weakness and primitivism.[105]

Henock Trouillot saw the Amerindian vogue in Haitian literature as a way of avoiding the color question. Léon-François Hoffmann disagrees, noting that many of its protagonists did stress blackness as a component of Haitian identity. Indeed, even a prominent *noiriste* like Lorimer Denis claimed an Amerindian heritage for modern Haitians.[106] Haitian "indianism," however, doubtless has reflected national tensions related to color. It is probably not accidental that Émile Nau's *Caciques* and Joseph Saint-Rémy's *Pétion* appeared simultaneously. Both works, published in the mid-1850s, gave non-black national icons to a light-skinned elite suddenly forced to come to terms with the aggressive "black" populism of Emperor Faustin Soulouque, whose rule was widely ridiculed abroad. The indianist writings of Henri Chauvet and Arsène Chevry around 1900 also might be related to the elite's loss of control of the presidency to black military figures in those years. Evocations of the Indian past were an indirect way of insisting that Haiti was not just a black or neo-African state.

One could further read a rejection of the homogenizing claims of *négritude* that were ascendant after the 1930s in the concern with Amerindian heritage expressed by a Louis Élie or a Jean Fouchard or in the claims of others that the Haitian carnival or the Creole language reflect strong Amerindian influence.[107] Writing of "our Indianness," Toussaint Desrosiers recently contended that common French words of African or Asian derivation, such as *igname* or *sucre,* in fact have an Arawak origin.[108] And Michelson Hyppolite pleads that Haiti's Indian heritage is in some way authentic, whereas affiliation with both Africa and Europe evinces "Bovaryism."[109] Such romantic speculations in the more inclusive spirit of *antillanité* seem to reflect a desire to reduce Haiti's exceptionalism, claiming for it a closer affinity with the states of Latin America that traditionally have shunned it. They no doubt have been reinforced by a reluctance to locate the origins of the national culture solely within the dismal boundaries of the slave plantation.

In 1803, the Haitian revolutionaries' revival of the Tainos' name for their most important settlement betokened above all a rejection of Europe and its colonial claims. It was a legitimizing link with the pre-Columbian American past, of which all Haitians could approve and which resonated with people of all social levels. However, for Haitians of partly European ancestry—who played a dominant role in the name's selection—Amerindian symbols had perhaps a special appeal. After the war of 1799–1800, which to a large degree divided the population by phenotype, people of mixed heritage risked a sense of alienation or marginalization in a state where African descent was the basis of national identity, and all citizens (temporarily) were defined as "black." They thus may have welcomed an alternative construct that defined Haitians as successors of the Taino.

Whatever sectional interests have been reflected in Haitians' concern with the Amerindian past, the men of 1804 clearly chose well when naming their new country. Through scission, secession, and the rise and fall of republican and monarchical regimes, the name has survived, suggesting its validity in the eyes of a broad spectrum of the population, even if it has not meant exactly the same thing for all Haitians.

Chronology

1789

January–March	Wealthy colonial activists illegally elect deputies to the States-General in France.
August	White and free colored colonists form separate political clubs in Paris to press their interests.
October	Inspired by the Bastille's fall, democratic protesters force the intendant to flee Saint Domingue. Free coloreds calling for political rights meet with persecution. Slaves voicing protests on some plantations are brutally suppressed.

1790

March	National Assembly allows colonies internal self-government under metropolitan supervision. Is deliberately evasive about the rights of free people of color.
July	Governor Peinier closes the autonomist Colonial Assembly at Saint Marc.
October	Vincent Ogé leads brief free colored rebellion in the north.

1791

February	Grisly execution of Ogé.
March	White radicals drive governor out of Port-au-Prince.
May	National Assembly decrees political rights for freeborn men of color.
July	White colonists discuss secession and organize to resist the May 15th decree.
August	Insurrections of slaves in the north and free coloreds in the west.
September	National Assembly annuls the May 15th decree.
November	Port-au-Prince burned in fighting between white radicals and free coloreds.

1792

January–March	Slave rebellion spasmodically spreads in west and south.
April	Legislative Assembly ends racial discrimination in the colonies.

| September | Arrival of second Civil Commission with 6,000 soldiers. France becomes a republic. |
| October–December | Commissioners form alliance with free coloreds and deport white conservatives and radicals. |

1793

February–March	War begins with Britain and Spain.
May	Spanish conclude alliance with Jean-François and Biassou.
June	Civil commissioners' struggle with Governor Galbaud causes burning of Cap Français and emancipation of slave recruits.
August	Sonthonax abolishes slavery in the north. Abolition extended to the west in September and south in October.
September	British forces begin 5-year occupation in parts of south and west.

1794

January	Fall of Fort Dauphin completes Spanish conquest of most of north.
February	Jacobin government ends slavery in all French colonies.
April–July	Toussaint Louverture turns on his Spanish allies and joins the French.

1795

| July | Spain makes peace and transfers Santo Domingo to France. |
| December | Jean-François and Biassou leave for exile. |

1796

March	Toussaint foils free colored coup against Governor Laveaux and becomes deputy-governor.
May	Sonthonax returns with new civil commission.
October–December	Toussaint and Sonthonax consolidate their control of the north. British switch to a defensive strategy.

1797

| May | Sonthonax names Toussaint commander-in-chief. |
| August | Toussaint forces out Sonthonax. |

1798

| March–October | General Hédouville's mission creates friction with emergent power of ex-slaves under Toussaint. |

May– September	British withdrawal. Toussaint signs trade and nonaggression treaty.
November	Toussaint orders army to impose forced labor on the plantations.

1799

June	War of the South begins.
December	Napoleon becomes head of state. Colonies lose right of metropolitan representation.

1800

August	Completing his defeat of Rigaud, Toussaint controls all Saint Domingue.

1801

January	Toussaint flouts French orders and occupies Santo Domingo.
February	Toussaint announces project for a constitution. Napoleon names him captain-general of Saint Domingue but not commander-in-chief, then retracts his decision.
July	Toussaint's constitution makes him governor for life.
October	Franco-British peace preliminaries permit the Leclerc expedition.
November	Rebellion of Moïse.

1802

February– May	Leclerc conquers Saint Domingue.
June	Toussaint deported to France.
August	News of reestablishment of slavery in Guadeloupe rekindles resistance in Saint Domingue.
October	Dessalines and Pétion unite in rebellion.

1803

May	Franco-British war resumes.
December	Last French troops evacuated.

1804

January	Dessalines declares independence at Gonaïves.

Notes

PRO, CO	PRO, Colonial Office
PRO, FO	PRO, Foreign Office
PRO, T	PRO, Treasury
PRO, WO	PRO, War Office
RSHHG	*Revue de la Société Haïtienne d'Histoire et de Géographie*
SHM	Service Historique de la Marine, Château de Vincennes
UCMM typescripts.	Universidad Católica de Madre y Maestra, Santiago de los Caballeros, Dominican Republic, Colección Incháustegui, Documentos AGI-AGS 1750–1799 II.
UF	University of Florida Libraries, Gainesville, Fla.

1. The Haitian Revolution

1. Although the Code Noir of 1685 did not recognize any distinction between free persons based on phenotype, it was not enforced in the Caribbean and soon was contradicted by local legislation.

2. In practice, the decree could only apply to children of legally married parents, given the difficulty of proving the status of fathers. This greatly limited its application.

3. Meaning "the opening," this is how he spelled his name, not "l'Ouverture." Similarly, "Bauvais" is preferable to the etymologically correct "Beauvais."

4. ANOM, CC9B/23, proclamation of April 28, 1804.

2. New Approaches and Old

1. C. L. R. James, *The Black Jacobins: Toussaint L'Ouverture and the San Domingo Revolution* (London, 1938; 2nd ed., New York, 1963; 3rd ed., London, 1980; 4th ed. [in French], Paris, 1983); P. I. R. [*sic*] James, *Les Jacobins noirs*, trans. Pierre Naville (Paris: Gallimard, 1949). The new French edition, unlike the first, managed to get the author's name and place of origin right. All references are to the second edition.

2. G. Debien, "Les travaux d'histoire sur Saint-Domingue (1938–1946): essai de mise au point," *Revue d'Histoire des Colonies* 34 (1947): 31–86; James, *Black Jacobins*, 140, 159. French readers are also more likely than others to be discouraged by minor errors in the opening chapters, such as the statements that Condorcet sat in the States-General, that Mirabeau was deputy for Marseille, and that that city is in the Dauphiné.

3. See D. Geggus, *Slavery, War and Revolution: The British Occupation of Saint Domingue, 1793–1798* (Oxford: Oxford University Press, 1982), 82, 85, 103, 415, 439; Geggus, "The Volte-Face of Toussaint Louverture," *Revue Française d'Histoire d'Outre-Mer* 65 (1978): 483–484, 488–489.

4. C. Frostin, "Histoire de l'esprit autonomiste colon de Saint-Domingue aux XVIIe et XVIIIe siècles," Thèse de doctorat d'état, Université de Paris I, 1972; Frostin, *Les Révoltes blanches à Saint-Domingue aux XVIIe et XVIIIe siècles* (Paris: L'École, 1975).

5. Publications of useful new source materials on the whites' revolution include F. Thésée, "Les assemblées paroissiales des Cayes à Saint-Domingue (1774–1793)," *RSHHG* 137 (1982): 5–212; J. Cauna, "La Révolution à Port-au-Prince (1791–1792): relation inédite du négociant Lajard," *RSHHG* 152 (1986): 5–28 and 153 (1986): 1–26; R. Beckerich and J. Cauna, "La Révolution de Saint-Domingue vue par un patriote," *RSHHG* 161 (1988): 1–34.

6. J. Garrigus, "Between Servitude and Citizenship: Free Coloreds in Pre-Revolutionary Saint Domingue" (Ph.D. diss., Johns Hopkins University, 1988); Garrigus, "Colour, Class, and Identity on the Eve of the Haitian Revolution: Saint Domingue's Free Coloured Elite as *Colons Américains*," *Slavery and Abolition* 17 (1996): 20–43; Garrigus, "Blue and Brown: Contraband Indigo and the Rise of a Free Colored Planter Class in French Saint-Domingue," *The Americas* 50 (1993): 233–263; Garrigus, "Catalyst or Catastrophe? Saint Domingue's Free Men of Color and the Battle of Savannah," *Revista/Review Interamericana* 22 (1992): 109–125; S. King, "Blue Coat or Lace Collar? Military and Civilian Free Coloreds in the Colonial Society of Saint-Domingue, 1776–1791" (Ph.D. diss., Johns Hopkins University, 1997).

7. J. Garrigus, "The Free Colored Elite of Pre-Revolutionary Saint Domingue: The Case of Julien Raimond," forthcoming in *Brown Power in the Caribbean,* ed. D. Barry Gaspar and G. Heuman; C. B. Auguste, "André Rigaud, leader des anciens libres," *RSHHG* 187 (1996): 15–39; 188 (1996): 30–40; 192 (1997): 1–29; 193 (1997): 1–23.

8. G. Debien, *Les esclaves aux Antilles françaises, XVIIe et XVIIIe siècles* (Basse-Terre: Société d'histoire de la Guadeloupe, 1974).

9. D. Geggus, "The Slaves of British-Occupied Saint Domingue: An Analysis of the Workforces of 197 Absentee Plantations, 1796/97," *Caribbean Studies* 18 (1978): 5–43; Geggus, "Les esclaves de la plaine du Nord à la veille de la Revolution française, partie IV," *RSHHG* 149 (1985): 16–52; Geggus, "Les derniers esclaves de Saint-Domingue," *RSHHG* 161 (1988): 85–111; Geggus, "Sugar and Coffee Cultivation in Saint Domingue and the Shaping of the Slave Labor Force," in *Cultivation and Culture: Labor and the Shaping of Afro-American Culture in the Americas,* ed. I. Berlin and P. Morgan (Charlottesville: University Press of Virginia, 1993), 73–98; Geggus, "The Sugar Plantation Zones of Saint Domingue and the Revolution of 1791–1793," *Slavery and Abolition* 20 (1999): 31–46; Geggus, "Indigo and Slavery in Saint Domingue," *Plantation Society in the Americas* 5 (1998): 189–204.

10. See the publications cited in notes 9 and 12.

11. The contemporary estimate that two-thirds of the colony's slaves were Africans may be broadly correct, but on sugar estates in the northern plain, Creoles constituted more than half the adult slaves and nearly two-thirds overall.

12. Slave trade data compiled in J. Mettas, *Répertoire des expéditions negrières françaises au XVIIIe siècle,* ed. Serge Daget and Michelle Daget, 2 vols. (Paris: Société française d'histoire d'Outre-Mer, 1978, 1984) is analyzed in D. Geggus, "The Demographic Composition of the French Caribbean Slave Trade," *Proceedings of the 13th and 14th Meetings of the FCHS* (Lanham, Md.: University Press of America, 1990), 14–30. French data from D. Eltis, S. Behrendt, D. Richardson, and H. Klein, *The Transatlantic Slave Trade: A Database on*

CD-ROM (Cambridge: Cambridge University Press, 1999) is analyzed in Geggus, "The French Slave Trade: An Overview," *William and Mary Quarterly* 58 (2001): 119–138. In 1790, slave imports increased by 50 percent above the annual average of the previous five years, and more than 19,000 Africans arrived in Cap Français alone, easily a record number for any American port till that date.

13. T. Madiou, *Histoire d'Haïti* (Port-au-Prince: H. Deschamps, 1989), 2:395–396. In Madiou's version, the revolutionary leadership and the Creole workers of the plains combined to overcome the anarchic particularism of the Africans in the mountains. Madiou is usually depicted as favorable to the black masses, and he indeed used oral sources for his *Histoire,* but they seem to have been mulatto generals rather than ordinary folk. This may be why he made no mention of Bois Caïman and almost none of Boukman. His oft-cited references to vodou were sensationalist rather than respectful, and he also thought the Creole language a lamentable barbarism. Jean Fouchard's co-opting of his name to argue the importance of former maroons in the Haitian Revolution is quite fallacious. He did take a more sympathetic view of Toussaint and Dessalines than did his fellow historians, the Ardouin brothers, but he also claimed that, because of the harshness of their rule, most rural and urban blacks welcomed the French as liberators in 1802 and refused initially to take up arms against them. As Madiou has been more venerated than read, the republication of his *Histoire* with an index in 1989–1991 was a great boon for historians.

14. G. Barthélemy, *Le pays en dehors: essai sur l'univers rural haïtien* (Port-au-Prince: Deschamps, 1989); Barthélemy, *Dans la splendeur d'un après-midi d'histoire* (Port-au-Prince: Deschamps, 1996); Barthélemy, *Créoles-Bossales: conflit en Haïti* (Petit-Bourg: Ibis Rouge, 2000).

15. James's choice of title was intended, I think, simply to draw a parallel between French and Haitian revolutionaries. However, identifying Toussaint Louverture with the Jacobins also suggests comparison between the relationship of the slave leadership and masses on the one hand and that of middle-class Jacobins and sansculotte workers on the other. That this was not James's intention is shown by the following extract (*Black Jacobins,* 286): "Robespierre's problem was inevitable; he was bourgeois, the masses were communist. But between Toussaint and his people there was no fundamental difference of outlook or aim."

16. Geggus, "Sugar and Coffee," 79, 90–91.

17. However, see Geggus, "Sugar Plantation Zones," 34–36. Rather unnecessarily, James retracted his argument in the third edition of *Black Jacobins* (xiii).

18. Geggus, "Sugar and Coffee," 73–75; R. Korngold, *Citizen Toussaint* (New York: Gollancz, 1945), 51. Studies of individual plantations before and during the revolution, the sort of monograph Debien pioneered, include two exceptional works: J. Cauna, *Au temps des isles à sucre: histoire d'une plantation de Saint-Domingue au XVIIIe siècle* (Paris: Karthala, 1987); and Bernard Foubert's massive *Les habitations Laborde à Saint-Domingue dans la seconde moitié du XVIIIe siècle: contribution à l'histoire d'Haïti,* 2 vols. (Lille: Université de Lille III, 1990). See also Geggus, "Une famille de La Rochelle et ses plantations de

Saint-Domingue," in *France in the New World: Proceedings of the 22nd Meeting of the French Colonial Historical Society,* ed. D. Buisseret (East Lansing: Michigan State University Press, 1998), 119–136.

19.　Geggus, "Sugar and Coffee," 79. Men were never "more than twice as numerous as the women," as reported in C. Fick, *The Making of Haiti: The Saint Domingue Revolution from Below* (Knoxville: University of Tennessee Press, 1990), 51. Still less did females constitute 5 percent of the slaves, as suggested in Marietta Morrissey, *Slave Women in the New World: Stratification in the Caribbean* (Lawrence: University of Kansas Press, 1989), 35.

20.　Debien, *Les esclaves,* 52–68, summarizes this work.

21.　Geggus, "Sugar and Coffee," 81; D. Richardson, "Slave Exports from West and West-Central Africa, 1700–1809: New Estimates of Volume and Distribution," *Journal of African History* 30 (1989): 14; D. Geggus, "Sex Ratio and Ethnicity: A Reply to Paul E. Lovejoy," *Journal of African History* 30 (1989): 395–397. Debien's samples greatly underrepresented the north province and coffee plantations in general.

22.　Fick, *The Making of Haiti,* 57–59, 241, 264–266; D. Geggus, "Haitian Voodoo in the Eighteenth Century: Language, Culture, Resistance," *Jahrbuch für Geschichte von Staat, Wirtschaft und Gesellschaft Lateinamerikas* 28 (1991): 21–51; S. Mintz and R. Price, *An Anthropological Approach to the Afro-American Past* (New Haven, Conn.: Yale University Press, 1976), 8, 25–26.

23.　J. Thornton, "On the Trail of Voodoo: African Christianity in Africa and the Americas," *The Americas* 44 (1988): 261–278; H. Vanhee, "Central African Popular Christianity and the Making of Haitian Vodou Religion," in *Central Africans and Cultural Transformations in the American Diaspora,* ed. Linda Heywood (New York: Cambridge, 2001).

24.　However, Sylviane Diouf's *Servants of Allah: African Muslims Enslaved in the Americas* (New York: New York University Press, 1998) limits itself, when dealing with Saint Domingue, to repeating the least scholarly work and actually misses the most striking case of Muslim cultural survival in the Americas, the Mandingues of northern Haiti. They are described in G. Alexis, *Lecture en anthropologie haïtienne* (Port-au-Prince: Presses Nationales, 1970), 173–185, and C. Najman, *Haïti, Dieu seul me voit* (Paris: Balland, 1995), 158–160.

25.　J. Thornton, "African Soldiers in the Haitian Revolution," *Journal of Caribbean History* 25 (1993): 58–80; Thornton, " 'I Serve the King of the Kongo': African Political Ideology in the Haitian Revolution," *Journal of World History* 4 (1993): 181–214; Geggus, *Slavery, War and Revolution,* 182, 185, 199, 442; Geggus, "Haitian Voodoo," 37, n. 71.

26.　E. Genovese, *From Rebellion to Revolution: Afro-American Resistance in the Making of the Modern World* (Baton Rouge: Louisiana State University Press, 1979).

27.　General studies include E. Córdova-Bello, *La independencia de Haití y su influencia en Hispanoamérica* (Caracas: Instituto Panamericano, 1967); A. Hunt, *Haiti's Influence on Antebellum America: Slumbering Volcano in the Caribbean* (Baton Rouge: Louisiana University Press, 1988); K. Schüller, *Die deutsche Rezeption haitianischer Geschichte in der ersten Hälfte des 19 Jahr-hunderts* (Cologne: Böhlau, 1992); D. B. Gaspar and D. P. Geggus, eds., *A Tur-bulent Time: The French Revolution and the Greater Caribbean* (Bloomington: Indiana University Press, 1997); D. Geggus, ed., *The Impact of the Haitian Revolution in the Atlantic World* (Columbia: University of South Carolina Press, 2001); D. Geggus, "The Influence of the Haitian Revolution on Blacks in Latin America and the Caribbean," forthcoming in *Blacks and National Identity in Nineteenth-Century Latin America,* ed. N. Naro (London: Univer-sity of London, 2002).

28. D. Geggus, *Slave Resistance Studies and the Saint Domingue Slave Revolt: Some Preliminary Considerations* (Miami: Florida International University, Occa-sional Papers Series, 1983), 20–23; Geggus, "The French and Haitian Revolu-tions and Resistance to Slavery in the New World: An Overview," *Revue Française d'Histoire d'Outre-Mer* 282–283 (1989): 107–124; Geggus, "Slavery, War, and Revolution in the Greater Caribbean, 1789–1815," in Gaspar and Geggus, eds., *A Turbulent Time,* 1–50.

29. R. Blackburn, *The Overthrow of Colonial Slavery, 1776–1848* (London: Verso, 1988). This work and Y. Bénot, *La Révolution française et la fin des colonies* (Paris: La Découverte, 1988) achieve a new level of sophistication in reassess-ing the relation between the French and Haitian Revolutions.

30. G. Debien, J. Fouchard, and M.-A. Menier, "Toussaint Louverture avant 1789: légendes et réalités," *Conjonction: Revue Franco-Haïtienne* 134 (1977): 67–80. The authors state that Toussaint was freed in 1776, but this dating results from a confused reading of one of the documents they reproduce. He was evi-dently freed earlier: D. Geggus, "Toussaint Louverture and the Slaves of the Bréda Plantations," *Journal of Caribbean History* 20 (1985–1986): 33.

31. He learned to sign his name sometime between 1779 and 1791. Notwith-standing the claims in J. Fouchard, *Les marrons du syllabaire* (Port-au-Prince: Deschamps, 1953), the slave leaders usually relied on free colored adjutants or white secretaries to both write and sign their correspondence.

32. Mediathèque, Nantes, MS 1809, f. 205–206; AN, Section Moderne, Dxxv/1/4 and 63/635. P. Pluchon, *Toussaint Louverture: un révolutionnaire noir d'Ancien régime* (Paris: L'École, 1989), 72, commenting on the signatories of a letter of December 1791, misleadingly groups Toussaint with Jean-François and Biassou (as blacks), rather than with the three *gens de couleur* who were their agents. It is true that white contemporaries often thought he was a slave. How-ever, just once we find him signing a letter (or being signed as) "TNL" (i.e., "Toussaint, Nègre Libre"). See AN, Dxxv/5/48 and 12/118, letter of December 18, 1792.

33. See Chapter 8. The statement in Fick, *The Making of Haiti,* 305, that Toussaint "remain[ed] in the background . . . to save himself from . . . opprobrium" dur-ing the December negotiations seems mistaken. He was not an official negotia-tor, but as C. L. R. James observed (*Black Jacobins,* 103–107), he was in it up to the neck; though James's assumption that Toussaint dictated the rebels' December overtures is yet to be proved.

34. If colonial whites exaggerated internal divisions within the free colored sec-

tor, they did not invent them. Differences of phenotype, wealth, culture, and literacy tended to coincide and to dictate marriage patterns.

35. Geggus, "French and Haitian Revolutions," 110–111.

36. P. Pluchon, *Toussaint Louverture: de l'esclavage au pouvoir* (Paris: L'École, 1979); Pluchon, *Toussaint Louverture: un révolutionnaire noir*. The second book retains much of the text of the former but considerably expands the sections on Toussaint's later career and corrects a number of errors. See review by D. Geggus in *Histoire Sociale* 45 (1990): 201–203.

37. The explanatory power of looking at Toussaint from this angle should not be exaggerated. Dessalines and Christophe, both of whom were slaves until the revolution, followed similar policies as head of state, whereas the freeborn Alexandre Pétion was less authoritarian. The decision to revive the slave trade to replenish the working population apparently divided Africans and Creoles more than *nouveaux* and *anciens libres*: UF, Special Collections, Rochambeau Microfilms, lot 132, Roume to Forfait, 3 vendémiaire X.

38. C. B. Auguste and M. B. Auguste, *L'expédition Leclerc, 1801–1803* (Port-au-Prince: Deschamps, 1985); M. B. Auguste, "L'armée française de Saint-Domingue, dernière Armée de la Révolution," *Jahrbuch für Geschichte von Staat, Wirtschaft und Gesellschaft Lateinamerikas* 28 (1991): 99–100. C. L. R. James's interpretation was that the French government already had secretly determined to restore slavery but that only General Leclerc was informed.

39. See Chapter 8.

40. H. Cole, *King Christophe of Haiti* (London: Eyre & Spottiswoode, 1967); R. L. Stein, *Léger Félicité Sonthonax: The Lost Sentinel of the Republic* (Rutherford, N.J.: Fairleigh Dickinson University Press, 1985).

41. M. Dorigny, *Léger-Félicité Sonthonax, la première abolition de l'esclavage: la Révolution française et la Révolution de Saint-Domingue* (Paris: Société française d'Histoire d'Outre-mer, 1997).

42. G. Mentor, *Histoire d'un crime politique: le Général Étienne Victor Mentor* (Port-au-Prince: Telhomme, 1999).

43. See Fick, *The Making of Haiti*.

44. See Chapter 6, which argues that the revolt broke out prematurely and, had things gone to plan, it would have been even more devastating than it was.

45. Fick, *The Making of Haiti*, Chapter 4; T. Ott, *The Haitian Revolution, 1789–1804* (Knoxville: University of Tennessee Press, 1972); G. Laurent, *Quand les chaines volent en éclats* (Port-au-Prince: Deschamps, 1979); T. di Tella, *La rebelión de esclavos de Haití* (Buenos Aires: Ides, 1984).

46. J. Fouchard, *Les marrons de la liberté* (Paris: École, 1972).

47. So it is by James and Fick, whose claims (*Black Jacobins*, 18; *The Making of Haiti*, 42) that the Petro ceremony included a "vow of vengeance" seem unsupported by the evidence.

48. E. Paul, *Questions d'histoire (Études critiques)* (Port-au-Prince: Imprimerie de l'État, 1955); W. Appollon, *Le vaudou: une espace pour les "voix"* (Paris: Éditions Galilée, 1976).

49. She notes (49) that between four conspiracies recorded in the period 1679–1704 and the 1791 revolt there occurred only the Makandal conspiracy of 1757. The later statement (237) that slave revolts were "proportionately far fewer" in the colony than on slave ships is thus slightly misleading. Regarding Makandal and poisoning, Fick cites approvingly Pluchon's excellent study, although it concludes that there was no revolutionary conspiracy. See P. Pluchon, *Vaudou, sorciers, empoisonneurs: de Saint-Domingue à Haïti* (Paris: Karthala, 1987), 167–177.

50. However, in bracketing together the two pre-revolutionary decades (53), Fick obscures a distinct downturn in maroon band activity between the 1770s and the 1780s. She does imply, on uncertain evidence (241), that clandestine assemblies increased in number during the two or three years before 1791.

51. Fick, *The Making of Haiti*, 94–95, 240.

52. Ibid., 49, 227. The statements (49, 51) that by 1791 marronage had "acquired a distinctively collective characteristic" and that African maroons "rarely if ever" lived alone seem both dubious and contradictory.

53. M.-R. Trouillot, *Ti dife boule sou istoua Ayiti* (New York: Lakansiel, 1977), 75–76. The work is a succinct analysis of the revolution's development in a colloquial style.

54. Ibid., 41. "The people forgot the taste for freedom. . . . This was a very sad situation, but we must not think that it did not happen, because it is precisely that which explains a lot of questions in the history of our country."

55. Most of the participants in the 1791 insurrection had probably never been fugitives. Even on estates where young Africans were extremely numerous, only about 1 in 18 adult males fled each year. See the data in Foubert, *Les habitations Laborde*, 1:531–533. The colonial average was almost certainly lower. See D. Geggus, "The Haitian Maroons: Myth and History," in *Marronnage in the Caribbean: Myth and Reality*, ed. B. Delpêche (Montreal: Centre International de Documentation et d'Information Haïtienne Caraïbéenne et Afro-Canadienne, 2002).

56. On the absence of a word for "freedom" in most non-Western languages, see O. Patterson, *Slavery and Social Death: A Comparative Study* (Cambridge, Mass.: Harvard University Press, 1982), 27. See also S. Miers and I. Kopytoff, *Slavery in Africa: Historical and Anthropological Perspectives* (Madison, Wis.: University of Wisconsin Press, 1977), 17, 54.

3. Underexploited Sources

1. This was true in France (Gabriel Debien, Charles Frostin) and in Haiti (Jean Fouchard).

2. T. Madiou, *Histoire d'Haïti*, 3 vols. (Port-au-Prince: H. Deschamps, 1847–1848); B. Ardouin, *Études sur l'histoire d'Haïti*, 11 vols. (Paris, 1853–1860; reprint, Port-au-Prince: Dalencour, 1958). Citations in this book are to the 1989–1991 and 1958 editions of these works.

3. C. Fick, *The Making of Haiti: The Saint Domingue Revolution from Below* (Knoxville: University of Tennessee Press, 1990); P. Pluchon, *Toussaint Louver-*

ture: de l'esclavage au pouvoir (Paris: L'École, 1979); Pluchon, *Toussaint Louverture: un révolutionnaire noir d'Ancien régime* (Paris: Fayard, 1989).

4. In 1994, Fond des Colonies material housed in the Archives Nationales, Paris, was moved to the Centre des Archives d'Outre-mer in Aix-en-Provence. Microfilm copies are available in Paris.

5. D. Geggus, "Pélage-Marie Duboys, The Anonymous Author of the 'Précis Historique,'" *Archives Antillaises* 3 (1975): 5–10, is an attempt to identify the author by using internal evidence. Although it contains some biographical inaccuracies, its identification of Duboys seems to have been confirmed by the subsequent discovery in the Bibliothèque Nationale (Lk12 213) of a Paris publisher's prospectus entitled *Mémoires pour servir à l'histoire de la révolution de Saint-Domingue par feu P. M. Duboys, publiés d'après les manuscrits autographes de l'auteur par M. P. Lacroix. Prospectus* (Paris, 1826). The publisher, Jéhenne, was seeking subscribers for the first of three 500-page octavo volumes. The work apparently never appeared. According to Gabriel Debien (personal communication), a manuscript introduction to it, now lost, was once held by the Institut Saint Louis de Gonzague in Port-au-Prince.

6. BN, Nouvelles acquisitions françaises 14878–14879; UF, Department of Rare Books. A microfiche version has been published in J.-P. Bertaud, G. Miraval, and D. Geggus, eds., *The French Revolution Research Collection and Videodisk: Section 11, War and the Colonies* (Witney: Micrographix, 1993).

7. PRO, WO 1/59, f. 783–785; J.-P. Garran-Coulon, *Rapport sur les troubles de Saint-Domingue* (Paris, 1795–1997), 2:139; PH, 1:13–19, 65; ANOM, CC9A/5, Duboys to ?, November 9, 1791; AGI, SD 955, Joaquín García to marqués de Bajamar, April 25, 1792; Geggus, *Slavery, War and Revolution,* 257; G. Robin, "La lettre de Saint-Domingue," *Genèse* [e-journal] 1 (April 2000) (www.agh.qc.ca/alaune.htm). Duboys owned eight houses in Port-au-Prince, valued at 157,690 *livres tournois.* See *État détaillé des liquidations opérées par la commission . . . de l'indemnité de Saint-Domingue* (Paris, 1828–1833).

8. Robin, "La lettre de Saint-Domingue."

9. Médiathèque, Nantes, MS 1809, "Histoire de la révolution et des événements de Saint-Domingue, depuis 1786 jusqu'en 1812." The manuscript consists of 598 pages of extremely small and densely packed writing. On the eve of the revolution, seeking employment, the author clashed with the Port-au-Prince commandant Loppinot de Beauport. He shows up again in August 1792 interrogating black prisoners. See AD, Versailles, E 1705; AN, Dxxv/63/635, doc. KK42.

10. BM, Auxerre, MS 331, "Histoire des événemens de Saint-Domingue depuis 1786 jusqu'en 1808."

11. BM, Rouen, MS Montbret 574, "Le paysan du Danube ou considérations . . . sur la révolution . . . de Saint Domingue par un colon de cette isle," 360 pages.

12. BM, Rouen, MS Leber 5847, "Récit du massacre arrivé au Fort Dauphin le 7 juillet 1794."

13. AD, Agen, 5 J 34 (Belin de Villeneuve); AD, Marseille, 1 Mi 34, reel 26 (château de Ribaute); AD, Pau, 5 J 21 (Duplaa); BM, La Rochelle, MS 855 (Boutin).

14. AD, Versailles, E 1705.

15. Published between 1947 and 1984, they are listed in B. Foubert, *Les habitations Laborde à Saint-Domingue dans la seconde moitié du XVIIIe siècle: contribution à l'histoire d'Haïti* (Lille: Université de Lille III, 1990), 1:42–44.

16. Commission des Colonies, *Débats entre les accusateurs et les accusés dans l'affaire des colonies* (Paris, 1795). I am aware of only one copy in France, one in Great Britain, and three in the United States. It is now available on microfiche in Bertaud, Miraval, and Geggus, *French Revolution Research Collection*.

17. G. Laurent's *Trois mois aux archives d'Espagne* (Port-au-Prince: Les Presses Libres, 1956) was a pioneering effort but limited itself to printing only two or three items of minor interest from the AGI collection. Spanish material relating to the later stages of the Haitian Revolution, albeit tangentially, has been published in great quantity by E. Rodríguez Demorizi in *Invasiones Haitianas de 1801, 1805, y 1822* (Ciudad Trujillo: Editora del Caribe, 1955); *La era de Francia en Santo Domingo* (Ciudad Trujillo: Editora del Caribe, 1955); and *Cesión de Santo Domingo a Francia* (Ciudad Trujillo: Impresora Dominicana, 1958).

18. Archivo Histórico Nacional, Madrid, Ultramar 6209, exp. 49. The men included several prominent figures such as Candy, Caze jeune, and Savary.

19. Summaries of the Estado material can be found in C. Bermúdez Plata, *Catálogo de documentos de la Sección Novena del Archivo General de Indias*, vol. 1 (Seville, 1949).

20. For family lists, see AGN, Bogotá, Sección Colonia, Fondo Negros y Esclavos, Panama III, f. 953–956; AGCA, A2/120/2265, f. 5–6, 12–21, A2/120/2275, letter of July 7, 1798; AGI, Estado 3, exp. 10.

21. UCMM, Colección Incháustegui, Documentos AGI-AGS 1750–99, vol. 2.

22. AGN, Santo Domingo, Archivo Real de Higüey, legajos 22/48–52; "Fondos del Archivo de la Nación: documentos de la época colonial, 1733–1795," *Boletín del Archivo General de la Nación* 38–39 (1945): 20–22.

23. Ardouin, *Études*, 2:87–89.

24. In 1975, all that could be located in the Archivo were photocopies of documents concerning a slave conspiracy in Hinche in March 1793. The originals were apparently in Cuba, although they do not appear in Franco's published collection, cited below.

25. J. L. Franco, *Documentos para la historia de Haití en el Archivo Nacional* (Havana: Archivo Nacional, 1954).

26. A. del Monte y Tejada, *Historia de Santo Domingo*, 4 vols. (Santo Domingo, 1890–1892). Volume 4 is available on microfiche in Bertaud, Miraval, and Geggus, *French Revolution Research Collection*.

27. This collection's use is cited only in the brief article by H. B. L. Hughes, "British Policy towards Haiti, 1801–1805," *Canadian Historical Review* 25 (1944): 397–408; and in T. Ott, *The Haitian Revolution, 1789–1804* (Knoxville: University of Tennessee Press, 1973).

28. G. Mentor, *Histoire d'un crime politique: le Général Étienne Victor Mentor* (Port-au-Prince: Fondation Sogebank, 1999).

29. Scottish Record Office, Edinburgh, Steel/Maitland Papers GD 193, boxes 2, 3, and 6. The Toussaint material is in box 2, dossier 12.

30. P. Walne, *A Guide to the Manuscript Sources for the History of the Latin America and the Caribbean in the British Isles* (London: Oxford University Press for the Institute of Latin American Studies, University of London, 1973).

31. Devon Record Office, Exeter, O/10–21, Simcoe Papers. Also at Exeter, the well-catalogued Addington Papers contain a few relevant items. The William Clements Library at the University of Michigan possesses five volumes of Simcoe papers covering the years 1770–1824.

32. Phyllis Spencer Bernard Collection, Nether Winchendon, near Aylesbury, Spencer Bernard Papers, OM dossiers 7–11.

33. Scottish Record Office, Edinburgh, James Guthrie collection, GD 188, box 28.

34. For a general study, see D. Geggus, *Slavery, War and Revolution: The British Occupation of Saint Domingue, 1793–1798* (Oxford: Oxford University Press, 1982).

35. PRO, HCA 30/380–401. Ships seized in the eastern Atlantic were sold in London. Because they had been sailing to Europe, they were likely to be carrying more mail than those seized nearer the West Indies, which were bound mostly for the United States and were sold locally.

36. B. Foubert, "Les volontaires nationaux de l'Aube et de la Seine Inférieure à Saint Domingue," *Bulletin de la Société d'Histoire de la Guadeloupe* 51 (1982): 3–56.

37. Rhodes House, Oxford, West Indies MS, S.7.

38. BL, Egerton MS 1794, f. 255–328.

39. D. Geggus, "Haitian History in North American Archives," *Revista/Review Interamericana* 27 (1997): 151–179, contains brief descriptions.

40. NYPL, West Indies Collection, Santo Domingo Papers, 2 boxes.

41. Hagley Museum, Wilmington, De Tousard letterbook, accession no. 892, 139 pages.

42. Hagley Museum, Wilmington, Longwood MS 5/A/II and 7/A/1; Winterthur MS 2/D/1, 3/A/special correspondence/1, 3/C/1, and 4/D; Joseph Donath & Co. letterbook.

43. L. V. Monti, *A Calendar of the Rochambeau Papers at the University of Florida Libraries* (Gainesville: University of Florida Libraries, 1972).

44. C. B. Auguste and M. B. Auguste, *L'expédition Leclerc, 1801–1803* (Port-au-Prince: Deschamps, 1986); Fick, *The Making of Haiti*; Ott, *The Haitian Revolution*.

45. A short summary is included in D. Geggus, *The Caribbean Collection at the University of Florida: A Brief Description* (Gainesville: University of Florida, 1985), 6–7.

46. Geggus, "Haitian History," 152–153, 162–163.

47. A thorough calendar is accessible on the Internet at www.library.georgetown.edu/dept/speccoll/cl158.htm.

4. The Causation of Slave Rebellions

1.   O. Patterson, *Slavery and Social Death: A Comparative Study* (Cambridge, Mass.: Harvard University Press, 1982).

2.   M. I. Finley, "Revolution in Antiquity," in *Revolution in History,* ed. R. Porter and M. Teich (Cambridge: Cambridge University Press, 1986), 54; E. Genovese, *From Rebellion to Revolution: Afro-American Slave Revolts in the Making of the Modern World* (Baton Rouge: Louisiana State University Press, 1979), xxii.

3.   K. R. Bradley, *Slavery and Rebellion in the Roman World, 140 B.C.–70 B.C.* (Bloomington: Indiana University Press, 1989); M. I. Finley, *Ancient Slavery and Modern Ideology* (New York: Viking, 1980). The argument formerly advanced by Soviet historians and defended by P. Dockès in *Medieval Slavery and Liberation* (Chicago: University of Chicago Press, 1979) that slave resistance caused slavery's demise in Europe at the end of the Ancient World was never put forward by Marx or Lenin: E. Hobsbawm, "Revolution," in Porter and Teich, eds., *Revolution in History,* 9.

4.   A. Popovic, *La révolte des esclaves en Iraq au IIIe/IXe siècle* (Paris: Geuthner, 1976); Tabari, *The Revolt of the Zanj* (Albany: State University of New York Press, 1992).

5.   J. W. Blassingame, *The Slave Community: Plantation Life in the Antebellum South* (New York: Oxford University Press, 1979), 216; P. Kolchin, *Unfree Labor: American Slavery and Russian Serfdom* (Cambridge, Mass.: Belknap Press, 1987), Chapter 5. See also the older studies: H. Aptheker, *American Negro Slave Revolts* (New York: International Publishers, 1943); and M. Kilson, "Towards Freedom: An Analysis of Slave Revolts in the United States," *Phylon* 25 (1964): 175–187.

6.   S. Schwartz, *Sugar Plantations in the Formation of Brazilian Society: Bahia, 1550–1835* (Cambridge: Cambridge University Press, 1986), Chapter 17.

7.   See A. Yacou, "Le projet des révoltes serviles de l'île de Cuba dans la première moitié du XIXe siècle," *Revue du CERC* 1 (1984): 46–67; R. Paquette, *Sugar Is Made with Blood: The Conspiracy of La Escalera and the Conflict between Empires over Slavery in Cuba* (Middletown, Conn.: Wesleyan University Press, 1988); D. Geggus, "Slave Resistance in the Spanish Caribbean in the Mid-1790s," in *A Turbulent Time: The French Revolution and the Greater Caribbean,* ed. D. B. Gaspar and D. P. Geggus (Bloomington: Indiana University Press, 1997), 131–155; R. Duharte Jiménez, *Rebeldía esclava en el Caribe* (Jalapa: Gobierno del Estado, 1992). On Puerto Rico, see G. Baralt, *Esclavos rebeldes: conspiraciones y sublevaciones de esclavos en Puerto Rico (1795–1873)* (Rio Piedras: Huracán, 1981).

8.   M. Craton, *Testing the Chains: Resistance to Slavery in the British West Indies* (Ithaca: Cornell University Press, 1982); A. Synnott, "Slave Revolts in the Caribbean" (Ph.D. thesis, University of London, 1976); H. O. Patterson, *The Sociology of Slavery: An Analysis of the Origins, Development and Structure of Negro Slave Society in Jamaica* (London: MacGibbon & Kee, 1969); W. Westergaard, *The Danish West Indies under Company Rule* (New York: Macmillan,

1917); W. Westergaard, "Account of the Negro Rebellion on St. Croix in 1759," *Journal of Negro History* 11 (1926): 50–61; and C. Goslinga, *The Dutch in the Caribbean and Surinam, 1791/95–1942* (Assen: Van Gorcum, 1991).

9. C. L. R. James, *The Black Jacobins: Toussaint L'Ouverture and the San Domingo Revolution* (New York: Vintage, 1963), 21; C. Fick, *The Making of Haiti: The Saint Domingue Revolution from Below* (Knoxville: University of Tennessee Press, 1990), 49.

10. Among the successful were several in late-seventeenth-century Jamaica which led to the formation of the Leeward Maroons and the 1791–1793 uprising that ended slavery in Saint Domingue.

11. On slave soldiers, see P. Voelz, *Slave and Soldier: The Military Impact of Blacks in the Colonial Americas* (New York: Garland, 1993); C. Degler, *Neither Black nor White: Slavery and Race Relations in Brazil and the United States* (London: Macmillan, 1971), 75–82; D. B. Davis, *The Problem of Slavery in the Age of Revolution, 1775–1824* (Ithaca: Cornell University Press, 1975), 72–83; R. Buckley, *Slaves in Red Coats* (New Haven: Yale University Press, 1979); Patterson, *Slavery and Social Death*, 308–314; P. Morgan and C. Brown, eds., *The Arming of Slaves: From Classical Times to the Modern Age* (Yale University Press, forthcoming).

12. D. Geggus, "Haiti and the Abolitionists, 1804–1838," in *Abolition and Its Aftermath: The Historical Context, 1790–1916*, ed. D. Richardson (London: Frank Cass, 1985), 115–116.

13. Bruce Lincoln concludes his investigation of the relation between discourse and society, "the inquiry is not so much inconclusive as it is unconcluded and unconcludable." See *Discourse and the Construction of Society* (New York: Oxford University Press, 1989), 173.

14. M. I. Finley, "A Peculiar Institution?" *Times Literary Supplement*, 2 July 1976.

15. Kolchin, *Unfree Labor*, Chapter 4.

16. Synnott, "Slave Revolts," 356; L. Peytraud, *L'esclavage aux Antilles françaises avant 1789* (Paris, 1897), 371; D. Geggus, "Esclaves et gens de couleur libres de la Martinique pendant l'époque révolutionnaire et napoléonienne: trois instants de résistance," *Revue Historique* 295 (1996), 109, 127; H. Klein, *Slavery in the Americas: A Comparative Study of Virginia and Cuba* (Chicago: University of Chicago Press, 1967), 220; J. J. Reis, *Slave Rebellion in Brazil: The Muslim Uprising of 1835 in Bahia* (Baltimore: Johns Hopkins University Press, 1993), 184. See also E. Viotti da Costa, *Crowns of Glory, Tears of Blood: The Demerara Slave Rebellion of 1823* (New York: Oxford University Press, 1994), 192, 355; E. Brathwaite, *The Development of Creole Society in Jamaica, 1770–1820* (London: Oxford University Press, 1971), 143, 303; G. García Rodríguez, *La esclavitud desde la esclavitud: la visión de los siervos* (Mexico City: Centro Jorge Tamayo, 1996), 195–197.

17. Patterson, *Social Death*, 97, 100.

18. Varying viewpoints are put forward in S. Elkins, *Slavery: A Problem in American Institutional and Intellectual Life* (Chicago: University of Chicago Press, 1976); K. Stampp, "Rebels and Sambos: The Search for the Negro's Personality

in Slavery," *Journal of Southern History* 37 (1971): 367–392; Blassingame, *Slave Community*, Chapters 5 and 8; A.-T. Gilmore, ed., *Revisiting Blassingame's The Slave Community* (Westport, Conn.: Greenwood Press, 1978); B. Wyatt-Brown, "The Mask of Obedience: Male Slave Psychology in the Old South," *The American Historical Review* 93 (1988): 1228–1252.

19.   E. Genovese, *Roll, Jordan, Roll: The World the Slaves Made* (New York: Pantheon Books, 1974), 3–7, 597–598; Genovese, "Towards a Psychology of Slavery," in Gilmore, ed., *Revisiting Blassingame's* The Slave Community, 27–41.

20.   Patterson, *Social Death*, 72–76.

21.   A. Raboteau, *Slave Religion: The "Invisible Institution" in the Antebellum South* (New York: Oxford University Press, 1978); M. Turner, *Slaves and Missionaries: The Disintegration of Jamaican Slave Society, 1787–1834* (Urbana: University of Illinois Press, 1982); Viotti da Costa, *Crowns of Glory.*

22.   B. Higman, *Slave Populations of the British Caribbean, 1807–1834* (Baltimore, Md.: Johns Hopkins University Press, 1984), 280–292; R. W. Fogel, *Without Consent or Contract: The Rise and Fall of American Slavery* (New York: Norton, 1989), 138–143; D. Geggus, "Sugar and Coffee Cultivation in Saint Domingue and the Shaping of the Slave Labor Force," in *Cultivation and Culture: Labor and the Shaping of Afro-American Culture in the Americas,* ed. I. Berlin and P. Morgan (Charlottesville: University Press of Virginia, 1993), 89; J. R. Ward, *British West Indian Slavery, 1750–1834: The Process of Amelioration* (Oxford: Oxford University Press, 1988), 195–198; J. Meredith, *The Plantation Slaves of Trinidad, 1783–1816: A Mathematical and Demographic Enquiry* (Cambridge: Cambridge University Press, 1988), 60–64.

23.   See P. Manning, *Slavery, Colonialism, and Economic Growth in Dahomey* (Cambridge: Cambridge University Press, 1982), Chapter 2; J. C. Miller, *Way of Death: Merchant Capitalism and the Angolan Slave Trade, 1730–1830* (Madison: University of Wisconsin Press, 1988).

24.   Patterson, *Social Death*, 132–135.

25.   J. Vogt, *Ancient Slavery and the Ideal of Man* (Oxford: Oxford University Press, 1974), 39–102.

26.   Patterson, *Social Death*, 354–356, gives estimates of the incidence of slavery in different populations. On African slavery, see S. Miers and I. Kopytoff, eds., *Slavery in Africa: Historical and Anthropological Perspectives* (Madison: University of Wisconsin Press, 1977); J. L. Watson, ed., *Asian and African Systems of Slavery* (Berkeley: University of California Press, 1980); P. Lovejoy, *Transformations in Slavery* (Cambridge: Cambridge University Press, 1983).

27.   "When a master punished a slave, the others would collect a little earth and put it in the [*nganga*] pot. With the help of this earth . . . the master was imprisoned [in the pot]. . . . This is how the Kongolese revenged themselves on their master," recalled Cuban ex-slave Esteban Montejo. See Montejo, *Autobiography of a Runaway Slave* (1968; London: Macmillan, 1993), 46.

28.   For conflicting views, see M. Schuler's comments in *Roots and Branches: Current Directions in Slave Studies,* ed. M. Craton (Toronto: Pergamon, 1979), 131–133; D. Geggus, *Slave Resistance Studies and the Saint Domingue Slave Revolt: Some Preliminary Considerations* (Miami: Florida International Univer-

sity, Occasional Papers Series, 1983), 17; L. Levine, *Black Slavery and Black Consciousness: Afro-American Folk Thought from Slavery to Freedom* (New York: Oxford University Press, 1977), 55–80.

29.   Vogt, *Ancient Slavery*, 39–102; Lovejoy, *Transformations in Slavery*, 114.

30.   B. Moore, *Injustice: The Social Bases of Obedience and Revolt* (New York: M. E. Sharpe, 1978), 359.

31.   D. Geggus, "The Enigma of Jamaica in the 1790s: New Light on the Causes of Slave Rebellions," *William and Mary Quarterly* 44 (1987): 274–299. More supporting data can be found in R. Devas, *The Island of Grenada, 1650–1950* (St. George's: n.p., 1964), 114, 153; J.-C. Nardin, *La mise en valeur de l'île de Tabago (1763–1783)* (Paris: Mouton, 1969), 211; D. Geggus, "Slavery, War, and Revolution in the Greater Caribbean, 1789–1815," in Gaspar and Geggus, eds., *A Turbulent Time*, 35, n. 31.

32.   Patterson, *Sociology of Slavery*, 273–283.

33.   Moore, *Injustice*, 363–364.

34.   Synnott, "Slave Revolts," 234–235.

35.   The clandestine channels through which fugitives were guided to free-soil areas. About 1,000 may have successfully escaped each year in the late antebellum period. See P. Kolchin, *American Slavery, 1619–1877* (New York: Hill and Wang, 1993), 158; J. H. Franklin and L. Schweninger, *Runaway Slaves: Rebels on the Plantations* (New York: Oxford University Press, 1999), 279, 282.

36.   Aptheker, *Slave Revolts*, 117; Genovese, *From Rebellion to Revolution*, 11–13; H. Aimes, *A History of Slavery in Cuba, 1511–1868* (New York: Octagon, 1967), 145; N. Bolland, *Slavery in Belize* (Belize City: Belize Institute for Social Research and Action Occasional Papers no. 7, 1979), 26–27; R. Dirks, *The Black Saturnalia* (Gainesville: University Presses of Florida, 1987), 165–166; Baralt, *Esclavos rebeldes*, 171–172.

37.   J. Pinto Vallejo, "Slave Resistance in Minas Gerais, 1700–1750," *Journal of Latin American Studies* (1985): 1–34.

38.   G. Mullin, *Flight and Rebellion: Slave Resistance in Eighteenth-Century Virginia* (New York: Oxford University Press, 1972), Chapter 3; Reis, *Slave Rebellion in Brazil*, 41, 185–186; Aptheker, *Slave Revolts*, 115–116, 139.

39.   Thomas J. Davis, *A Rumor of Revolt: The "Great Negro Plot" in Colonial New York* (Amherst: University of Massachusetts Press, 1985); D. R. Egerton, *Gabriel's Rebellion: The Virginia Slave Conspiracies of 1800 and 1802* (Chapel Hill: University of North Carolina Press, 1993); E. Pearson, *Designs against Charleston: The Trial Record of the Denmark Vesey Slave Conspiracy of 1822* (Chapel Hill: University of North Carolina Press, 1999).

40.   Geggus, "Slave Resistance in the Spanish Caribbean," 137; Geggus, "Esclaves et gens de couleur libres," 105–132.

41.   J. L. Franco, *Las conspiraciones de 1810 y 1811* (Havana: Editorial de Ciencias Sociales, 1977).

42.   Patterson, *Sociology*, 273–279; Genovese, *From Rebellion to Revolution*, 11.

43.   D. Geggus, "Les esclaves de la plaine du Nord à la veille de la Révolution française, partie 4," *RSHHG* 149 (1985): 16–51.

44. Genovese, *From Rebellion to Revolution*, 12, 33, 86; Geggus, *Slave Resistance Studies*, 4–10; K. Agorsah, ed., *Maroon Heritage: Archaeological, Ethnographic and Historical Perspectives* (Kingston: Canoe Press, 1994), 2, 4.

45. D. Geggus, "Jamaica and the Saint Domingue Slave Revolt, 1791–93," *The Americas* 38 (1981): 224; Ward, *British West Indian Slavery*, 231; G. Heuman, *"The Killing Time": The Morant Bay Rebellion in Jamaica* (London: Macmillan, 1994), 39, 87–88, 131.

46. See Chapter 5; D. Geggus, "The Haitian Maroons: Myth and History," in *Marronnage in the Caribbean: Myth and Reality*, ed. B. Delpêche (Montreal: Centre International de Documentation et d'Information Haïtienne Caraïbéenne et Afro-Canadienne, 2002).

47. See Geggus, "Slavery, War, and Revolution," 7–11, 35; Reis, *Slave Rebellion in Brazil*, 53. The demand for "three free days," although not as a right, also appeared in Brazil around 1790. See S. B. Schwartz, "Resistance and Accommodation in Eighteenth-Century Brazil," *Hispanic American Historical Review* 57 (1977): 69–81. Compare the 1827 conspiracy in Maranhão described in M. Röhrig Assunção, "Elite Politics and Popular Rebellion in the Construction of Post-colonial Order," *Journal of Latin American Studies* 31 (1999): 23.

48. However, according to Ward, *British West Indian Slavery*, 224, the demand for extra free days "suggests a recollection of African slavery."

49. Kilson, "Towards Freedom," 175–187.

50. Genovese, *Roll, Jordan, Roll*, 592–595.

51. Mullin, *Flight and Rebellion*, 159–160.

52. E. Carneiro, *O quilombo dos Palmares* (Rio de Janeiro: Civilizacão Brasileira, 1966), 3.

53. M. Craton, "Slave Culture, Resistance, and the Achievement of Emancipation in the British West Indies, 1783–1838," in *Slavery and British Society, 1776–1848*, ed. J. Walvin (London: Macmillan, 1982), 117.

54. A. C. Metcalf, "Millenarian Slaves? The Santidade de Jaguaripe and Slave Resistance in the Americas," *American Historical Review* 104 (1999): 1531–1559; M. Reckord, "The Jamaican Slave Rebellion of 1831," *Past and Present* 40 (1968): 108–125; Reis, *Slave Rebellion in Brazil*.

55. Genovese, *Roll, Jordan, Roll*, 175; Genovese, *From Rebellion to Revolution*, 123.

56. See Chapters 5 and 6 in this volume.

57. The classic study is T. R. Gurr, *Why Men Rebel* (Princeton: Princeton University Press, 1970).

58. Mullin, *Flight and Rebellion*, 124–142.

59. F. Douglass, *Narrative of the Life of Frederick Douglass* (1845; reprint, New York: Penguin, 1982), 135.

60. Kilson, "Towards Freedom," 179–183.

61. B. Higman, *Slave Population and Economy in Jamaica, 1807–1834* (Cambridge: Cambridge University Press, 1976), 214, 223; M. Craton, *Searching for the Invisible Man* (Cambridge, Mass.: Harvard University Press, 1978), 99, 109,

113, 143; Ward, *British West Indian Slavery*, 88, 94, 184–186, 194–195, 218–232, 263.

62. Higman, *Slave Population and Economy in Jamaica*, 232; Ward, *British West Indian Slavery*, 226.

63. G. Debien, *Les esclaves aux Antilles françaises, XVIIe et XVIIIe siècles* (Basse-Terre: Société d'histoire de la Guadeloupe, 1974), Chapter 20.

64. Genovese, *From Rebellion to Revolution*.

65. M. Craton, "The Passion to Exist: Slave Rebellions in the British West Indies," *Journal of Caribbean History* 13 (1980): 1–20; Craton, "Proto-Peasant Revolts? The Late Slave Rebellions in the British West Indies, 1816–1832," *Past and Present* 85 (1979): 99–125; Craton, *Testing the Chains*.

66. They are examined in more detail in Geggus, *Slave Resistance Studies*, 19–26.

67. Geggus, "The Enigma of Jamaica in the 1790s," 289, 299; Geggus, "Slavery, War, and Revolution," 6–18; A. Césaire, *Toussaint Louverture: La Révolution française et le problème colonial* (Paris: Présence Africaine, 1962), 177.

68. Moore, *Injustice*, 82–83; C. Tilly, *From Mobilization to Revolution* (Reading, Mass.: Addison-Wesley, 1978); Hobsbawm, "Revolution," in Porter and Teich, eds., *Revolution in History*, 7, 15; and, in a qualified sense, T. Skocpol, *States and Social Revolution* (Cambridge: Cambridge University Press, 1979), Chapter 1. Steve Stern, however, in *Resistance, Rebellion, and Consciousness in the Andean Peasant World, 18th to 20th Centuries* (Madison: University of Wisconsin Press, 1987) emphasizes long-term change, while calling for the use of "multiple time frames."

69. J. C. Scott, *Weapons of the Weak: Everyday Forms of Peasant Resistance* (New Haven: Yale University Press, 1985), 316–341. For a contrary view, see B. Lincoln, ed., *Religion, Rebellion, Revolution: An Interdisciplinary and Cross-Cultural Collection of Essays* (New York: St. Martin's, 1985); and Lincoln, *Discourse and the Construction of Society*.

70. Genovese, *From Rebellion to Revolution*, xx.

71. Synnott, "Slave Revolts," 234–235; Craton, "Passion to Exist," 1–20; M. Schuler, "Ethnic Slave Rebellions in the Caribbean," *Journal of Social History* 3 (1970): 374–385.

72. Like Craton, Jamaican historian Richard Hart also depicted the aims of slave rebellions as becoming less ambitious in the nineteenth century, changing from "nationalistic" struggles to purely class struggles, but he attributed the change to the antislavery movement's influence. (*Black Jamaicans' Struggle against Slavery* [London: Community Education Trust, 1979], 21–22.) Michael Mullin (*Africa in America: Slave Acculturation and Resistance in the American South and the British Caribbean, 1736–1831* [Urbana: University of Illinois Press, 1992]) shares Craton's emphasis on the impact of creolization on resistance at the turn of the nineteenth century. This view is rejected by Seymour Drescher (*Capitalism and Antislavery: British Mobilization in Comparative Perspective* [New York: Oxford University Press, 1986], 104–109), who sees phases of rebellion shaped first by the French Revolutionary War and then by abolitionism.

73.   Genovese, *From Rebellion to Revolution*, 53–57; S. B. Schwartz, "Brésil: le royaume noir des 'mocambos,'" *L'Histoire* 41 (1982): 44; Pinto Vallejo, "Slave Resistance in Minas Gerais," 22; M. C. Campbell, *The Maroons of Jamaica, 1655–1796: A History of Resistance, Collaboration and Betrayal* (Granby, Mass.: Bergin & Garvey, 1988), 198–202.

74.   Creole rebels in the 1736 conspiracy on Antigua spoke of keeping the Africans enslaved. See D. B. Gaspar, *Bondmen and Rebels: Master-Slave Relations in Antigua* (Baltimore: Johns Hopkins University Press, 1985), 253; Craton, *Testing the Chains*, 124.

75.   Geggus, "Slave Resistance in the Spanish Caribbean," 147; Reis, *Slave Rebellion in Brazil*, 121.

76.   Genovese, *From Rebellion to Revolution*, 36.

77.   Nevertheless, the last fifteen years have seen published some excellent in-depth studies of individual revolts and conspiracies. These include Gaspar, *Bondmen and Rebels*; C. Fick, *The Making of Haiti: The Haitian Revolution from Below* (Knoxville: University of Tennessee Press, 1990); Reis, *Slave Rebellion in Brazil*; Pearson, *Designs against Charleston*, 1–164; Egerton, *Gabriel's Rebellion*; and Viotti da Costa, *Crowns of Glory*.

78.   H. Beckles, "The Two Hundred Years War," *Jamaica Historical Review* 13 (1982): 1–10.

5. Marronage, Vodou, and the Slave Revolt of 1791

1.   J. Lhérisson, "Le marronnage et le vaudou," cited in L.-F. Hoffmann, *Haïti: lettres et l'être* (Toronto: Éditions du GREF, 1992), 291; J. Price-Mars, *Ainsi Parla l'Oncle: essais d'éthnographie* (Port-au-Prince: Imprimerie de Compiègne, 1928); M.-R. Trouillot, *Silencing the Past: Power and the Production of History* (Boston: Beacon Press, 1995), 175. Works in this tradition, although certainly varied, include S.-V. Jean-Baptiste, *Haïti: sa lutte pour l'indépendance* (Paris: Nef, 1957); E. Brutus, *Révolution dans Saint-Domingue* (Paris: Éditions du Panthéon, 1973); Odette Mennesson-Rigaud, "Le rôle du vaudou dans la guerre d'indépendance," *Présence Africaine* (1958): 43–67; and the works of Fouchard, Laurent, H. Trouillot, Appollon, and Paul cited below.

2.   L. F. Manigat, "The Relationship between Marronage and Slave Revolts and Revolution in St. Domingue-Haiti," *Annals of the New York Academy of Sciences* 292 (1977): 420–438; M. Laguerre, *Voodoo and Politics in Haiti* (New York: St. Martin's Press, 1989); L. Hurbon, *Voodoo: Search for the Spirit* (New York: Harry Abrams, 1995); M.-R. Trouillot, review of *Les marrons de la liberté*, in *New West Indian Guide* 56 (1982): 180–182.

3.   L. Peytraud, *L'esclavage aux Antilles françaises* (Paris: Hachette, 1897); Trouillot, *Silencing the Past*, 74, 83, 96–97, 102–105, 175; L.-F. Hoffmann, "Un mythe national: la cérémonie du Bois-Caïman" and commentary, in *La république haïtienne: état des lieux et perspectives*, ed. G. Barthélemy and C. Girault (Paris: Karthala, 1993), 434–448; P. Pluchon, *Vaudou, sorciers, empoisonneurs* (Paris: Karthala, 1987); and the works cited below, note 6.

4.   J. Fouchard, *Les marrons de la liberté* (Paris: École, 1972).

5. Brutus, *Révolution dans Saint-Domingue*, 1:70.

6. Y. Debbasch, "Le marronnage: essai sur la désertion de l'esclave antillais," *Année Sociologique* (1961): 1–112 and (1962): 117–195; G. Debien, *Les esclaves aux Antilles françaises, XVIIe et XVIIIe siècles* (Basse-Terre: Société d'histoire de la Guadeloupe, 1974); F. Girod, *La vie quotidienne de la société créole* (Paris: Hachette, 1972); D. Geggus, "On the Eve of the Haitian Revolution: Slave Runaways in Saint Domingue in the Year 1790," in *Out of the House of Bondage: Runaways, Resistance and Marronage in Africa and the New World*, ed. G. Heuman (London: Frank Cass, 1986), 112–128; B. Foubert, "Le marronage sur les habitations Laborde à Saint-Domingue dans la seconde moitié du XVIIIe siècle," *Annales de Bretagne* 95 (1988): 277–310. Published in Haiti, Jacques de Cauna's *Haïti: l'éternelle révolution* (Port-au-Prince: Deschamps, 1997), 213–218, exhibits a creolized mélange of arguments: that marronage contributed personnel and tactics to the revolution but that "real maroons" numbered only one or two hundred, that its dimensions did not increase but it became more systematic and aggressive, that the role of marronage is undeniable but many questions remain.

7. Trouillot, *Silencing the Past*, 83, 103.

8. E. Paul, *Questions d'histoire (Études critiques)* (Port-au-Prince: Imprimerie de l'État, 1955). On *mulâtre* and *noiriste* schools of history, see D. Nicholls, *From Dessalines to Duvalier: Race, Colour, and National Independence in Haiti* (Cambridge: Cambridge University Press, 1979), 86–107.

9. According to Manigat, "Relationship between Marronage and Slave Revolts and Revolution," 426. However, there is no mention of maroons in Duvalier's best-known work, co-authored with Lorimer Denis, *Le problème des classes dans l'histoire d'Haïti* (Port-au-Prince: Au service de la Jeunesse, 1958).

10. D. Geggus, *Slave Resistance Studies and the Saint Domingue Slave Revolt* (Miami: Florida International University, Occasional Papers Series, 1983), 4–10, surveys some of the literature. See also Geggus, "The Haitian Maroons: Myth and History," in *Marronnage in the Caribbean: Myth and Reality*, ed. B. Delpêche (Montreal: Centre International de Documentation et d'Information Haïtienne Caraïbéenne et Afro-Canadienne, 2002).

11. That is the difference between Fouchard's totals and the number of missing and recaptured slaves listed in the main newspaper; I ignored the unclaimed runaways listed for sale two months after recapture. See Geggus, "On the Eve of the Haitian Revolution," 112–128; *Les Affiches Américaines*, 1788.

12. Debien, *Les esclaves*, 467–469. The question of numbers is further discussed in Geggus, "The Haitian Maroons" and Chapter 2, n. 55 in this volume.

13. Fouchard, *Les marrons de la liberté*, 474–525. See AN, Fonds Particuliers, 125 AP 6; Debien, *Les esclaves*, 419, 468; below, note 17.

14. AGI, SD 1102; Genovese, *From Rebellion to Revolution*, 51. Perhaps not all were counted, but their number cannot have been very large.

15. M. Begouen-Demeaux, *Stanislas Foäche: négociant de Saint-Domingue, 1737–1806* (Paris: Librairie Larose, 1951), 110–111.

16. ANOM, C9A/157, comte de La Luzerne to maréchal de Castries, September 8, 1786, and C9A/159, f. 142–143, 162–164. Having arrived only in mid-1786,

La Luzerne was not trying to take credit for this. On the Port Margot maroons, see ANOM, C9A/165, case of April 6, 1786.

17. C. Milscent du Musset, *Sur les troubles de Saint-Domingue* (Paris, 1792), 3–12.

18. The northwest and northeast, southwest and southeast, Mirebalais, and Arcahaye.

19. A higher incidence of marronage in the north would be difficult, although not impossible, to reconcile with the idea advanced in M.-R. Trouillot, *Ti dife boule sou istoua Ayiti* (New York: Lakansiel, 1977), 76–77, that greater population density and the lack of high mountains in the north made marronage more difficult there.

20. AGI, SD 1031, and AGS, GM 7157, correspondence 1793–1794; Debien, *Les esclaves,* 468; H. Dumesle, *Voyage dans le Nord d'Haïti* (Cayes, 1824), 164.

21. Fouchard, *Les marrons de la liberté,* 524, 534, 540, 453–454, 462. On Romaine, who was a landowner, see AN, Section Moderne, Dxxv/110, Ouvière dossier; on Kina, see Chapter 9 in this volume.

22. Debien, *Les esclaves,* 469; D. Geggus, *Slavery, War and Revolution: The British Occupation of Saint Domingue, 1793–1798* (Oxford: Oxford University Press, 1982), 308–310.

23. Fouchard, *Les marrons de la liberté,* 453–454, 526; G. Mathelier, *Tousen Louveti* (Port-au-Prince: Deschamps, n.d.), 5; Mennesson-Rigaud, "Le rôle du vaudou dans l'indépendance de Haïti," 57; L. Hurbon, *Voodoo: Search for the Spirit* (New York: Harry Abrams, 1995), 42–43.

24. In documents relating to late-eighteenth-century Saint Domingue, I have come across a dozen slaves and free blacks with this name, both men and women. It is thus difficult to accept the popular thesis that it, any more than "Makandal" (see below), was a corrupted English name, indicating that its owner had escaped or been deported from Jamaica.

25. ANOM, CC9A/5, "Notes de M. Leclerc." If this was the same Boukman, it is unlikely he could have absconded very frequently and still kept the prestigious jobs of coachman and slave-driver. The bizarre claim in P. de Lattre, *Campagne des Français à Saint-Domingue* (Paris, 1805), 47, that Boukman was one of the Maniel freed by the 1785 Bellecombe Treaty is both nonsense and interesting testimony to the colonists' resentment of the treaty and desire to present the rebel leaders in an unfavorable light. In his novel *Bug-Jargal,* Victor Hugo synthesized this story with rumors of Boukman's "English" origins to produce the claim he was a member of the Blue Mountain Maroons. This claim is repeated as fact in modern works such as C. Najman, *Haïti, Dieu seul me voit* (Paris: Balland, 1995), 149.

26. AGI, SD 956, Georges Biassou to Joaquín García y Moreno, July 15/August 24, 1793; J. Saint-Rémy, *Vie de Toussaint L'Ouverture* (Paris, 1850), 22; P. de Lacroix, *Mémoires pour servir à l'histoire de la Révolution de Saint-Domingue* (Paris, 1819), 1:90.

27. Jeannot was still a slave at the time of Ogé's revolt in October 1790: Gatereau, *Histoire des troubles de Saint Domingue* (Paris, 1792), 80; J. Saint-Rémy, *Pétion et Haïti* (Paris, 1853–1857; reprint, Paris: Berger-Levrault, 1956), 1:29. Fouchard (454) argued that, as he had acted as a guide for a colonial expedition

[in 1789], he must have been a maroon. On Boukmān, see ANOM, F3/141, f. 203–206. On Biassou, see Georges Biassou to Joaquín García y Moreno, July 15/August 24, 1793.

28. François à Chapotin, who attended the August 14 Lenormand meeting, was captured in Limbé on the eve of the revolt and revealed the conspiracy under interrogation. Of the several sources that mention him, only one states that he was a maroon, but it is the most reliable: New York Public Library, Kurt Fisher Collection, Government Papers 8:5, Limbé municipality report.

29. Fick, *The Making of Haiti*, 94–95, 240; Blackburn, *The Overthrow of Colonial Slavery*, 208.

30. D. Geggus, "Haitian Voodoo in the Eighteenth Century: Language, Culture, Resistance," *Jahrbuch für Geschichte von Staat, Wirtschaft und Gesellschaft Lateinamerikas* 28 (1991): 33, 47. In the British Caribbean, too, some whites called slaves' magical practices "harmless stratagems." See A. Richardson, "Romantic Voodoo: Obeah and British Culture, 1797–1807," *Studies in Romanticism* 32 (1993): 7, 22, 25.

31. MSM, 1:433; ANOM, F3/126, memoir by Chambre d'Agriculture, June 2, 1785.

32. SHM, MS 113, f. 655; Mediathèque, Nantes, MS 1809; ANOM, F3/197 and 267.

33. Fick's suggestion (240) that many participants would have had to go absent or forge a pass to attend because of the distance involved seems unlikely. The parishes involved in the August uprising were within walking distance, and anyway some slaves had, or had access to, mules or horses. Jeannot is described as a coachman in Saint-Rémy, *Pétion et Haïti*, 1:29, but as a slave-driver in Médiathèque, Nantes, MS 1809, f. 193.

34. G. Laurent, *Quand les chaînes volent en éclats* (Port-au-Prince: Deschamps, 1979), 10.

35. Hurbon, *Voodoo*, 42–43.

36. A. Synnott, "Slave Revolts in the Caribbean" (Ph.D. diss., London University, 1976). Manigat, "Relationship between Marronage and Slave Revolts and Revolution," 435, contains two similar arguments: the coffee boom forced maroons into closer contact with plantations, and an extension of provision grounds dissuaded potential fugitives from escaping, keeping them (albeit discontented) within the system.

37. Mennesson-Rigaud, "Le rôle du vaudou," 43–67; W. Appollon, *Le vaudou: un espace pour les "voix"* (Paris: Éditions Galilée, 1976). See H. Trouillot, *Introduction à une histoire du vaudou* (Port-au-Prince: Fardin, 1970); G. Alexis, *Vaudou et quimbois* (Port-au-Prince: Fardin, 1976); Laguerre, *Voodoo and Politics*.

38. S. Mintz and R. Price, *An Anthropological Approach to the Afro-American Past* (Philadelphia: Institute for the Study of Human Issues, 1977).

39. See C. E. Deive, *Los guerilleros negros: esclavos fugitivos y cimarrones en Santo Domingo* (Santo Domingo: Fundación Cultural Dominicana, 1989), 274–279; S. Mirot, "Un document inédit sur le marronage en la Guyane française," *Re-*

vue d'Histoire des Colonies (1954): 245–256; G. La Rosa Corzo, *Los palenques del Oriente de Cuba: resistencia y acoso* (Havana: Editorial academia, 1991), 184–186.

40. Geggus, "Haitian Voodoo," 33, 47; Hoffmann, *Haïti: lettres et l'être*, 257.

41. Laguerre, *Voodoo and Politics*, 132; Pluchon, *Vaudou*, 65–66; J. J. Reis, *Slave Rebellion in Brazil: The Muslim Uprising of 1835 in Bahia* (Baltimore: Johns Hopkins University Press, 1993), 41–42.

42. Laguerre, *Voodoo and Politics*, 48, 71; Fouchard, *Les marrons de la liberté*, 524, 539; MSM, 1:69; Geggus, "Haitian Voodoo," 33–47; AN, Section Moderne, DXXV/110, Ouvière dossier. Romaine and don Pedro were supposedly from Santo Domingo.

43. Laguerre, *Voodoo and Politics*, 34, 52.

44. L. De Heusch, "Kongo in Haiti: A New Approach to Religious Syncretism," *Man* 24 (1989): 301. Note that the slave's name was that of a local Gonaïves planter. Moreover, in another local tradition, the same founder appears as the manumitted slave of a local planter. See Najman, *Haïti*, 160.

45. AN, Fonds Particuliers, 125 AP 6; Fouchard, *Les marrons de la liberté*, 474–525; Debien, *Les esclaves*, 419, 468; Milscent du Musset, *Sur les troubles*, 3–12.

46. The relevant texts are reproduced in Pluchon, *Vaudou*, 170–182, 208–219, 308–315.

47. Fouchard, *Les marrons de la liberté*, 490–497. Fouchard does not cite Vaissière's opinion that the texts were exaggerated.

48. Pluchon, *Vaudou*, 165, 177–182; M.-R. Hilliard d'Auberteuil, *Considérations sur l'état présent de la colonie française de Saint-Domingue* (Paris, 1776–1977), 1:137–138.

49. See L. Bittremieux, *Mayombsch Idioticon*, 2 vols. (Ghent: Drukkerij Erasmus, 1922–1927); S. Comhaire-Sylvain, "Survivances africaines dans le vocabulaire religieux d'Haïti," *Études dahoméennes* 14 (1955): 13; H. B. Mulinda, "Le nkisi dans la tradition woyo du Bas-Zaïre," *Systèmes de Pensée en Afrique Noire* 8 (1985): 216. It was not Makandal's fame that made his name synonymous with amulets in Haiti: he was named after them, not vice versa.

50. Geggus, "Haitian Voodoo," 21–51.

51. M. Laguerre, "An Ecological Approach to Voodoo," *Freeing the Spirit* 3 (1974): 3–12; G. Smucker, "The Social Character of Religion in Rural Haiti," in *Haiti—Today and Tomorrow*, ed. C. Foster and A. Valdman (Lanham, Md.: University Press of America, 1984), 56; A. Raboteau, *Slave Religion: The "Invisible Institution" in the Antebellum South* (New York: Oxford University Press, 1978), 27.

52. ANOM, F3/129, "Essai sur l'esclavage." Price-Mars in *Ainsi parla l'oncle*, 172, and others state that this document dated from the mid-eighteenth century, implying that the later development of vodou overcame such differences. Yet the document is dated germinal an VII; that is, 1799. It was written by Saint Domingue exiles in Guyane.

53. Price-Mars, *Ainsi parla l'oncle*, 100–101, 173; L. Maximilien, *Le vodou haïtien* (Port-au-Prince: Imprimerie de l'État, 1945), 154; E. Paul, *Panorama du folk-*

lore haïtien: présence africaine en Haïti (Port-au-Prince: Imprimerie de l'État, 1962), 221–247; and in its most extreme form, F. Duvalier (with L. Denis) in *Oeuvres essentielles du Dr. François Duvalier* (Port-au-Prince: Presses nationales d'Haïti, 1968), 1:172–173.

54. M. E. Descourtilz, *Voyages d'un naturaliste et ses observations,* 3:177–178, 180–187, 196; BN, Manuscrits, NAF 14879, f. 127; ANOM, F3/197, letter of 13 juin 1792; Madiou, *Histoire d'Haïti,* 1:96, 235; Fouchard, *Les marrons de la liberté,* 549.

55. L. Dubroca, *La vie de Jean-Jacques Dessalines* (Paris, 1804), 13, 27; L. F. Boisrond-Tonnerre, *Mémoires pour servir à l'histoire d'Haïti* (Port-au-Prince: Fardin, 1981), 83, 89. For interethnic tensions in Trinidad, see M. Warner-Lewis, *Guinea's Other Suns* (Dover, Mass.: Majority Press, 1991), 20–23; and in Cuba, E. Montejo, *Autobiography of a Runaway Slave,* ed. M. Barnet and A. Hennessy (1968; London: Macmillan, 1993), 57–58.

56. V. Schoelcher, *Colonies étrangères et Haïti* (Paris, 1842–1843), 2:300.

57. UF, Special Collections, Rochambeau Microfilms, lot 132, Roume to Forfait, 3 vendémiaire X; Madiou, *Histoire d'Haïti,* 2:395–396, 468–470, 486–487, 496–498.

58. C. Malenfant, *Des colonies et particulièrement de celle de Saint-Domingue* (Paris, 1814), 215–219. See Trouillot, *Introduction,* 59, 61. It is possible that Creole slaves under colonial domination were more influenced by European attitudes than were their descendants after 1804, notwithstanding their greater familiarity with African culture. In the British Caribbean, magical practices and beliefs were similarly associated with Africans rather than Creoles. See B. Edwards, *History Civil and Commercial of the British West Indies* (London, 1793), 2:84; J. Handler, "Slave Medecine and Obeah in Barbados," *New West Indian Guide* 74 (2000): 69; M. Craton et al., *Slavery, Abolition and Emancipation* (London: Longman, 1976), 95–96.

59. Laguerre, *Voodoo and Politics,* 25; Duvalier, *Oeuvres essentielles,* 173. Laguerre, like Hénock Trouillot (*Introduction,* 30–31, 45, 65), emphasizes the fragmentation of the religious landscape into the national period but attributes this to "ecological," not ethnic, factors.

60. E. Glissant, *Le discours antillais* (Paris: Seuil, 1982), 68. When Frederick Douglass visited Haiti a century later, he commented, "The common people there believe much in divinations, charms, witchcraft, putting spells on each other, and in the supernatural and miracle working power of their voodoo priests generally. Owing to this, there is a feeling of superstition and dread of each other, the destructive tendency of which cannot be exaggerated." See *The Life and Writings of Frederick Douglass,* ed. P. Foner (New York: International Publishers, 1955), 4:481.

61. Pluchon, *Vaudou,* 126; R. Korngold, *Citizen Toussaint* (London: Gollancz, 1945), 60–61; R. Heinl and N. Heinl, *Written in Blood: The Story of the Haitian People, 1492–1995* (Lanham, Md.: University Press of America, 1996), 41. The error may go back to the statement in B. Ardouin, *Études sur l'histoire d'Haïti* (Port-au-Prince: Dalencour, 1958), 1:52, that the conspirators probably sought inspiration from Makandal's memory.

62.   Cited by G. Smucker in "The Social Character of Religion in Rural Haiti," 45.

63.   MSM, 1:68–69. A controversy exists whether even nowadays vodou organization is essentially acephalous: Laguerre, *Voodoo and Politics*, 108.

64.   See below, Chapter 6. Hénock Trouillot (*Introduction*, 56) claims Boukman as a high priest but notes that, unlike Makandal, he is scarcely remembered in modern vodou. He appears nowhere in the long lists of *lwa* in M. Rigaud, *La tradition voudoo et le voudoo haïtien* (Paris: Niclaus, 1953), 141–155, which place Makandal in the Petro pantheon.

65.   Following his death in battle, blacks ran through the plain shouting "Boukman is killed, what a blow!" Some rebel leaders went into mourning and ordered a "solemn [Catholic] service." See ANOM, F3/141, f. 296–297. Two years later, two of his former officers told Santo Domingo's governor that "this loss greatly affected me, losing a man who was worthy of command," and "we keep in our hearts the treasured image of he who first dared put himself at our head." See AGI, SD 1031, Gabriel Aimé Bellair to García, undated, and SD 957, Joseph Laffon to García, March 23, 1794.

66.   Many works attribute this title to Toussaint, I think wrongly. See Médiathèque, Nantes, MS 1809, f. 193, "Grand médecin des armées du roi . . . the slaves had a superstitious confidence in him and called him Great Sorcerer. He had a very strong influence over their minds." The colonist Mazères (*De l'utilité des colonies* [Paris, 1814], 65) called him a general, doctor, and sorcerer.

67.   Malenfant, *Des colonies*, 215–219. See Geggus, "The Sugar Plantation Zones of Saint Domingue and the Revolution of 1791–1793," *Slavery and Abolition* 20 (1999): 40–41.

68.   C. L. R. James, *The Black Jacobins: Toussaint L'Ouverture and the San Domingo Revolution* (New York: Vintage, 1963), 102; MSM, 1:64; Malenfant, *Des colonies*, 215–219.

69.   Geggus, *Slave Resistance Studies*, 17. As a gendarme, Hyacinthe personally meted out punishments of 100 lashes to slaves. See University of North Carolina, Chapel Hill, Southern Historical Collection, Caradeuc Papers, letter of November 13, 1792.

70.   It also reinforces the idea that he was Kongolese, not Muslim.

71.   Geggus, *Slave Resistance Studies*, 14–15. The reference to blacks destroying churches in Laguerre, *Voodoo and Politics*, 36, is misleading. The text cited merely notes that most churches were burned during the revolution (the fate of many towns), and it actually describes the ex-slaves as pious.

72.   James, *Black Jacobins*, 18; A. Césaire, *Toussaint Louverture: La Révolution française et le problème colonial* (Paris: Présence Africaine, 1962), 178. The translation James used was an erroneous rendering of a different chant, printed in L. Drouin de Bercy's *De Saint-Domingue* (Paris, 1814). This chant is more violent, but it is directed against sorcerers and is certainly not an oath. Both are analyzed in Geggus, "Haitian Voodoo."

73.   Geggus, "Haitian Voodoo," 48–49. Hein Vanhee informs me (personal communication) that earlier Yombe scholars were probably mistaken in their identification of Mbùmba as a war god. On the other hand, the Bumba family of

deities in vodou are regarded as warriors. See De Heusch, "Kongo in Haiti," 299.

74. J. Kerboull, *Le vaudou: magie ou religion?* (Paris: Laffont, 1973), 199; Trouillot, *Introduction,* 53–63, 77, 84.

75. ANOM, F3/192, letter by Gressier de la Jalousière, May 26, 1786; G. Debien, "Assemblées nocturnes d'esclaves à Saint-Domingue," *Annales Historiques de la Révolution Française* 208 (1972): 273–284; Geggus, "Haitian Voodoo," 33–39.

76. AD, Dammarie-les-Lys, B 545.

77. A. Métraux, *Haiti: Black Peasants and Their Religion* (London: Harrap's, 1960), 89; MSM, 1:68–69; Drouin de Bercy, *De Saint-Domingue,* 176.

78. Pluchon, *Vaudou,* 136–139.

6. The Bois Caïman Ceremony

1. D. Bellegarde, *Histoire du peuple haïtien (1492–1952)* (Port-au-Prince: n.p., 1953), 63 (my translation).

2. F. Sylvain, *Le serment du Bois Caïman et la première Pentecôte* (Port-au-Prince: Deschamps, 1979), 15–21.

3. J. Price-Mars, *Ainsi parla l'oncle: essais d'éthnographie* (Paris: Imprimerie de Compiègne, 1973), 100–101, 171–173; F. Duvalier (with Lorimer Denis), *Oeuvres essentielles du Dr. François Duvalier* (Port-au-Prince: Presses nationales d'Haïti, 1968), 1:178; Odette Mennesson-Rigaud, "Le rôle du Vaudou dans l'indépendance d'Haïti," *Présence Africaine* 17–18 (1958): 43.

4. L.-F. Hoffmann, "Un mythe national: la cérémonie du Bois-Caïman," in *La république haïtienne: état des lieux et perspectives,* ed. G. Barthélemy and C. Girault (Paris: Karthala, 1993), 434–448. A longer version appeared as "Histoire, mythe et idéologie: la cérémonie du Bois-Caïman," *Études Créoles* 13 (1990): 9–34. Hoffmann's essay, "Le vodou sous la colonie et pendant les guerres de l'indépendance," *Conjonction: Revue Franco-Haïtienne* 173 (1987): 122, adopted a somewhat skeptical stance but did not advance this thesis. The latter two pieces are reprinted in Hoffmann, *Haïti: lettres et l'être* (Toronto: Editions du GREF, 1992), 245–301.

5. See L. Hurbon, *Le barbare imaginaire* (Paris: Ed. du Cerf, 1988).

6. It appears, however, that in recent years Bois Caïman has become a prominent motif in the forgery of historical documents in Port-au-Prince: anon., "Echos et Nouvelles," *RSHHG* 167 (1990): 74.

7. A. Dalmas, *Histoire de la révolution de Saint-Domingue* (Paris, 1814), 1:116–121.

8. H. Dumesle, *Voyage dans le Nord d'Haïti* (Les Cayes, 1824), 85–90.

9. B. Ardouin, *Études sur l'histoire d'Haïti* (Port-au-Prince: Dalencour, 1958), 1:50–51; C. Ardouin, *Essais sur l'histoire d'Haïti* (Port-au-Prince, 1865), 16–18. The preface to the *Essais* notes that the Ardouins began collecting oral testimony regarding the revolution in 1837 and that portions of the work had

been published before 1842. Beaubrun, however, stated that this extract formed part of the "unpublished works" of his brother. One of the changes he made deserves to be noted: where Céligny wrote "terrible influence" of fetishism he substituted "magical influence."

10. É. Charlier, *Aperçu sur la formation historique de la nation haïtienne* (Port-au-Prince: Presses Libres, 1954), 49. The account implies but does not specify that she was the *mambo* who conducted the ceremony.

11. M. Rigaud, *La tradition voudoo et le voudoo haïtien* (Paris: Niclaus, 1953), 62–70.

12. For example, Toussaint Louverture and Jean-François are claimed as active *vodouisants* who, along with Makandal (who died in 1758), acted as mouthpieces for the deities in organizing the rebellion. "The esoteric Kabbala of vodou preserves the memory, in an irrefutable manner, that almost all the fortunate decisions of this era were dictated to the leaders of the day by the Invisible Great Ones of the Solar Tradition of Vodou" (Milo Rigaud, cited in Mennesson-Rigaud, "Le Rôle du Vaudou," 58).

13. T. Madiou, *Histoire d'Haïti* (1847–1848; reprint, Port-au-Prince: H. Deschamps, 1989–1991).

14. C. L. R. James, *The Black Jacobins: Toussaint L'Ouverture and the San Domingo Revolution* (New York: Vintage, 1963), 87; A. Césaire, *Toussaint Louverture: La Révolution française et le problème colonial* (Paris: Présence Africaine, 1962), 178; Dumesle, *Voyage*, 90.

15. E.g., ANOM, F3/267, f. 311; AN, Section Moderne, Dxxv/78/772, letter by Acaby, September 15, 1791; Dalmas, *Histoire de la révolution de Saint-Domingue*, 1:117; BM, Rouen, MS Montbret 619, f. 79.

16. C. Fick, *The Making of Haïti: The Saint Domingue Revolution from Below* (Knoxville: University of Tennessee Press, 1990).

17. See D. Geggus, *The Saint Domingue Slave Revolt and the Rise of Toussaint Louverture* (forthcoming).

18. See C.-L.-M. Milscent, *Du régime colonial* (Paris, 1792), 5. However, other evidence of this disarming is hard to find.

19. Such rumors were implicated in some twenty slave revolts and conspiracies in the period 1789–1832, mainly in the Caribbean but also as far away as Upper Peru and Bourbon (Réunion): D. Geggus, "Slavery, War, and Revolution in the Greater Caribbean, 1789–1815," in *A Turbulent Time: The French Revolution and the Greater Caribbean*, ed. D. B. Gaspar and D. P. Geggus (Bloomington: Indiana University Press, 1997), 5–15.

20. On the military factor in New World slave revolts, see D. Geggus, "The Enigma of Jamaica in the 1790s: New Light on the Causation of Slave Rebellions," *William and Mary Quarterly* 44 (1987): 274–299.

21. See the periodical shipping statistics published in the colonial newspaper *Les Affiches Américaines*, 1788–1790.

22. See the data in MSM, 2:610.

23. BM, Auxerre, MS 331, f. 83; Médiathèque, Nantes, MS 1809, f. 185; SHM, MS 113, f. 665.

24. Most contemporary sources place the attack on the night of August 16th/17th. However, the most reliable accounts (by three Limbé residents, including one of the Chabaud family, written six weeks later) gives August 17th/18th: AN, Dxxv/78/772, doc. KK 178; ANOM, F3/197, "Extraits des détails authentiques"; New York Public Library, Kurt Fisher Collection, Government Papers 8:5, Limbé municipality report. Other sources give August 11 (a number much more easily confused with 17 than with 16 when handwritten): SHM, MS 113, f. 664; Médiathèque, Nantes, MS 1809, f. 184; J.-P. Garran-Coulon, *Rapport sur les troubles de Saint-Domingue* (Paris, 1797–1799), 2:211. This error has led many historians to exaggerate the slowness of the colonists' response.

25. Dalmas, *Histoire de la révolution de Saint-Domingue*, 1:117.

26. The estate where he had been a slave was the Lenormand de Mézy plantation in Bas-Limbé.

27. BN, Cartes et Plans, Ge AA 18; U.S. Army, Carte d'Haïti, feuille 5775 11. Neither modern maps and gazetteers nor colonial maps show a Bois Caïman, but a "Savane à Caïman" is indicated in colonial sources. See AN, Fonds de la Marine, 6 JJ 60/61; AN, Fonds Particuliers, 107 AP 127/2, sketch map, Galliffet estates; MSM, 2:580. C. Girault et al., *Atlas d'Haïti* (Talence: Université de Bordeaux, 1985), planche 2, wrongly places the Bois Caïman in the center of Acul parish, where the revolt began.

28. G. Barthélemy, "Propos sur le Caïman: incertitudes et hypothèses nouvelles," *Chemins Critiques* 2 (1992): 36, 54–56. C. Najman, *Le Serment du Bois-Caïman* (Paris, 1992), film. Barthélemy's argument varies in the course of his article, but he was evidently mistaken to insist (36–37, 51) that certain sources such as Dumesle and Gastine mention only one, instead of two, meetings; that Dumesle did not mention a pig; and that Gastine clearly located the ceremony on the Morne Rouge.

29. J.-B. Julien, *La cérémonie du Bois Caïman* (n.p., n.d.), 45. In C. Najman, *Haïti, Dieu seul me voit* (Paris: Balland, 1995), 165, 184–187, those who pose as mouthpieces of oral tradition appear in a rather dubious light.

30. Cited in Hoffmann, *Haïti: lettres et l'être*, 272.

31. Cited in ibid., 275.

32. Julien, *La cérémonie*, 19–21, 28, 41, 56–60; MSM, 2:613. Among the several original assertions in this interesting text is the *noiriste* claim that Boukman imposed the decision to revolt on August 22nd against the wishes of "mixed-race slave drivers" who preferred to await the arrival of royal troops, who they expected to enforce the "three free days" granted by the king.

33. Najman, *Haïti*, 185. For another case of conflicting oral traditions, see Najman, *Haïti*, 160, and Luc de Heusch, "Kongo in Haiti: A New Approach to Religious Syncretism," *Man* 24 (1989): 301.

34. AN, Fonds de la Marine, 6 JJ 60/61, map of the central northern plain.

35. AN, 107 AP 128/3, Mossut to Galliffet, September 19, 1791.

36. Dalmas worked for the Bréda plantations at this time, but such physicians received a retaining fee from several estates: AD, Nantes, MS E 691, Bréda

Plantations Papers. The name of the Galliffet physician is not recorded, but it was said shortly after his appointment that "the slaves scorn him": AN, 107 AP 128/1, notes of January 2, 1790.

37. See Ardouin, *Essais sur l'histoire*, 16–18. The account places the attacks on the La Gossette (rendered "La Doucette") and Chabaud plantations and the Lenormand meeting all on the same day.

38. D. Geggus, "Les esclaves de la plaine du Nord à la veille de la Révolution, partie III," *RSHHG* 144 (1984): 24–36 sheds light on the Galliffet estates' harsh work regimen and shows how conditions deteriorated, particularly on La Gossette, in the previous few years. Though for convenience I refer to the "La Gossette conspirators," it is not clear that most of Mossut's attackers were from this plantation.

39. Perhaps there were more. About a week before the uprising, Bayon de Libertat recalled in 1799, raiders fired the canes on the Bréda plantation at Haut du Cap, but the slaves led by Toussaint Louverture extinguished the flames and processed the cane. See D. Geggus, "Toussaint Louverture and the Slaves of the Bréda Plantations," *Journal of Caribbean History* (1986): 44. For events on the Vaudreuil plantation, see Fick, *The Making of Haiti*, 107; and Geggus, "Les esclaves de la plaine . . . partie II," *RSHHG* 136 (1984): 12.

40. Garran-Coulon, *Rapport sur les troubles de Saint-Domingue*, 2:211–212; ANOM, F3/267, f. 311–323.

41. Fick, *The Making of Haiti*, 96, 102, 263.

42. ANOM, CC9A/5, "Révolte des noirs"; ANOM, F3/141, f. 238, and F3/197, "Notes de quelques événements"; AN, Dxxv/3/31, report by Roume; D. V. A. E. P., *Historia de la isla de Santo Domingo* (Madrid, 1806), 104; Fick, *The Making of Haiti*, 103. SHM, MS 113, f. 655, refers to August [22/]23 as the "selected date," but only in passing.

43. Fick, *The Making of Haiti*, 103, 263.

44. This is why Johannès Tramond described it, albeit wrongly, as "anarchic, spontaneous, acephalous." See G. Hanotaux and A. Martineau, eds., *Histoire des colonies françaises* (Paris: Plon, 1929), 1:514.

45. AN, Dxxv/78/772, letter by Sabatié Barrau, September 11, 1791; Gros, *Isle de St. Domingue* (Paris, 1793), 9; ANOM, F3/141, f. 238, and F3/197, "Notes de quelques événements"; ANOM, CC9A/5, "Révolte des noirs"; AN, Dxxv/3/31, report by Roume; D. V. A. E. P., *Historia de la isla*, 104.

46. SHM, MS 113, f. 655; ANOM, F3/141, f. 223.

47. The theory has long been popular with Haitian historians, from Madiou to Gérard Laurent, and is accepted but not examined in Fick, *The Making of Haiti*, 92. Some contemporary radical commentators also saw the hand of the counterrevolution in the choice of St Bartholomew's Day, the anniversary of the sixteenth-century massacre: letter by Sabatié Barrau, September 11, 1791.

48. AGI, SD 956, Georges Biassou to Joaquín García y Moreno, July 15/August 24, 1793.

49. ANOM, F3/267, 321 ff., and F3/141, f. 203.

50. V. Schoelcher, *Colonies étrangères et Haïti* (Paris, 1842–1843), 2:99.

51.   I am aware of only one—the mention in a contemporary British newspaper that "he passed for a Magician." See *English Chronicle and Universal Evening Post,* January 14, 1792. This could be a confusion with Jeannot, the "Médecin-Général," who died within a few days of Boukman.

52.   See the citations in n. 65 of Chapter 5.

53.   It is mainly confined to pastoralists, who were few in number among Saint Domingue slaves.

54.   The burning of this sacrifice also suggests Ancient Greece rather than Haiti. Nonetheless, in this story of two meetings with their different sacrificial animals one might find support for the vodou tradition (Mennesson-Rigaud, "Le rôle du Vaudou," 59) that the conspirators consulted first the Rada deities, then the Petro. Rada and Petro are the main subcults within modern vodou.

55.   Hoffmann, *Haïti: lettres et l'être,* 277–280; C. de Gastine, *Histoire de la république d'Haïti ou Saint-Domingue, l'esclavage et les colons* (Paris, 1819), 104–106.

56.   A. Métral, *Histoire de l'insurrection des esclaves dans le Nord de Saint-Domingue* (Paris, 1818), 15–20. Métral cited Dalmas but injected into his narrative a quite absurd speech that is evidently apocryphal.

57.   James, *Black Jacobins,* 87. A literary analysis by Carl Middelanis treats the whole of Dumesle's account as a nation-making myth. See Middelanis, *Schwarze Freiheit im Dialog: Saint-Domingue 1791–Haiti 1991* (Bielefeld: Hans Kock, 1991), 29–32.

58.   D. Geggus, "Haitian Voodoo in the Eighteenth Century: Language, Culture, Resistance," *Jahrbuch für Geschichte von Staat, Wirtschaft und Gesellschaft Lateinamerikas* 28 (1991): 21–22, 46; D. Geggus, *Slave Resistance Studies and the Saint Domingue Slave Revolt* (Miami: Florida International University, Occasional Papers Series, 1983), 15–17. The anti-Christian stance is one reason some claim Boukman as a Muslim. See Sylviane Diouf, *Servants of Allah: African Muslims Enslaved in the Americas* (New York: New York University Press, 1998), 152–153, 229; Barthélemy, "Propos sur le Caïman, 49–59.

59.   Fick, *The Making of Haiti,* 104, 264–266.

60.   BN, Cartes et Plans, Imprimés, plan de la ville du Cap François (1789); MSM, 1:424, 532. The nuns had one of the few 3-story buildings in Le Cap.

61.   MSM, 1:64–69; A. Cabon, "Les religieuses du Cap à Saint-Domingue," *Revue d'Histoire de l'Amérique Française* 3 (1949): 417–418; V. Schoelcher, *Vie de Toussaint-Louverture* (Paris, 1889), 30; Schoelcher, *Colonies étrangères et Haïti,* 2:99.

62.   Césaire, *Toussaint Louverture,* 178; MSM, 1:67. Julien, *Cérémonie,* 17, puts the words into Cécile Fatiman's mouth and offers an interesting but rather strained translation. Why a Kongolese should be called Fatiman he does not explain.

63.   Geggus, "Haitian Voodoo," offers a somewhat different translation and exegesis of this chant to those found in Fick, *The Making of Haiti,* 58, 104, where it is claimed, for reasons that are unclear, to date from "at least the mid-eighteenth century."

64.   General Kerverseau, one of the first to claim that Toussaint was behind the

1791 uprising, said he was present at the meeting where the leaders were selected, but he does not state when or where: ANOM, CC9B/23, report by General Kerverseau.

65. Charlier, *Aperçu sur la formation historique,* 49.

66. Julien, *Cérémonie,* 16, 55–56. Julien, who apparently interprets the ceremony as Kongo-Petro, thus unintentionally throws a life raft to those such as Diouf (*Servants of Allah,* 152–153, 229) who have claimed Boukman and Cécile Fatiman as Mandingo Muslims without explaining their use of the pro-scribed animal. Barthélemy, "Propos sur le Caïman," 49–50, favors the Mus-lim hypothesis and therefore favors Gastine's account.

67. A. Métraux, *Le vaudou haïtien* (Paris: Gallimard, 1958), 35; H. Trouillot, *Introduction à une histoire du vaudou* (Port-au-Prince: Fardin, 1970), 54, 63; E. Paul, *Panorama du folklore haïtien: présence africaine en Haïti* (Port-au-Prince: Imprimerie de l'État, 1962), 247; Mennesson-Rigaud, "Le Rôle du vaudou," 59–60; M. Deren, *The Voodoo Gods* (St. Alban's: Paladin, 1975), 66–67. Kongo influence on Petro is discussed in Geggus, "Haitian Voodoo," 19–21.

68. "Creole-dominated" because almost all northern plain slave-drivers and coachmen (those who attended the meeting) in this period were locally born (Creole). On the structure of the slave population, see D. Geggus, "Sugar and Coffee Cultivation and the Shaping of Slavery in Saint Domingue," in *Cultiva-tion and Culture: Labor and the Shaping of Afro-American Culture in the Ameri-cas,* ed. I. Berlin and P. Morgan (Charlottesville: University Press of Virginia, 1993), tables 8 and 11.

69. R. Law, "On the African Background to the Slave Insurrection in Saint-Domingue (Haïti) in 1791: The Bois Caiman Ceremony and the Dahomian 'Blood Pact,'" paper presented to the Harriet Tubman seminar, York Univer-sity, Ontario, November 1999. An earlier version was presented in Port-au-Prince, December 1997.

70. However, the significance of the chant "Eh eh Bomba" in this respect is noted in Fick, *The Making of Haiti,* 58 and discussed further in Geggus, "Haitian Voodoo," 40–43.

71. Dr. Fick is relatively circumspect in this regard, but nonetheless states (*The Making of Haiti,* 42) that slave worshippers called for "vengeance against their oppressors" and that colonial Petro ceremonies included a blood pact and a "vow of vengeance," although contemporary evidence for this is lacking.

7. The "Swiss" and the Problem of Slave/Free Colored Cooperation

1. For early reactions, see D. Geggus, "Jamaica and the Saint Domingue Slave Revolt, 1791–93," *The Americas* 38 (1981): 219–233; M. Zeuske and C. Mun-ford, "Die 'Grosse Furcht' in der Karibik: Saint Domingue und Kuba (1789–1795)," *Zeitschrift für Geschichtswissenschaft* 39 (1991): 41–60.

2. PRO, CO 125/13, letters of Thomas Potts and James Bartlet, November 26 and 27, 1791.

3. See Chapter 6; J. Saint-Rémy, *Pétion et Haïti* (Paris, 1853–1857; reprint, Paris: Berger-Levrault, 1956), 1:39–42; B. Ardouin, *Études sur l'histoire d'Haïti* (Port-

au-Prince: Dalencour, 1958), 1:52. The 20-year-old Pétion was made a captain in the insurgent army. The main gathering on the Diègue plantation was probably not until August 26; Saint-Rémy and Ardouin disagree on the date.

4. T. Madiou, *Histoire d'Haïti* (Port-au-Prince: H. Deschamps, 1989), 1:102–104; J. Cauna, "La Révolution à Port-au-Prince (1791–1792): Relation inédite du Négociant Lajard," *RSHHG* 152 (1986): 16–17; G. Debien, "Nouvelles de Saint-Domingue," *Notes d'Histoire Coloniale* 59 (1960): 28. As later opponents would also find, the free coloreds ably exploited terrain for their defense and proved exceptionally accurate marksmen. They perhaps carried hunting rifles, which were much more accurate than muskets. See D. Geggus, *Slavery, War and Revolution: The British Occupation of Saint Domingue, 1793–1798* (Oxford: Oxford University Press, 1982), 319. The main military commanders Bauvais, Lambert, and Rigaud had fought in 1779–1780 with the Chasseurs Volontaires in Georgia.

5. See Madiou, *Histoire d'Haïti*, 1:106; Saint-Rémy, *Pétion et Haïti*, 1:42; MSM, 2:631. The free coloreds chose the name, which apparently had neutral overtones. Their white radical opponents probably used the term mockingly, with the connotation of "royalist lackeys," since the free coloreds allied with conservative colonists until mid-1792.

6. Madiou, *Histoire d'Haïti*, 1:102; Saint-Rémy, *Pétion et Haïti*, 1:42; Saint-Rémy, *Vie de Toussaint L'Ouverture* (Paris, 1850), 37; H. Pauléus Sannon, *Histoire de Toussaint Louverture* (Port-au-Prince: Héraux, 1920), 1:90. According to Madiou, the whites did not enlist the Swiss until after Nérette, by which time, according to Saint-Rémy, the Swiss had already deserted them.

7. AN, Section Moderne, Dxxv/78/772, Laborie to Chabanon, July 3, 1791; Commission des Colonies, *Débats entre les accusateurs et les accusés dans l'affaire des colonies* (Paris, 1795), 3:183–187.

8. AN, Dxxv/1/12, Blome, *aîné* to Commission civile, n.d. [late 1792]; AN, Dxxv/78/772, Acaby to the National Assembly, October 5, 1791; AN, Dxxv/78/773, anonymous letter, October 27, 1791; Commission des Colonies, *Débats*, 1:153–155; *Histoire des désastres de Saint-Domingue* (Paris, 1795), 202–203.

9. Chanlatte jeune, Dubourg, Viart, and F. Ouvière, *Mémoire historique des dernières revolutions* (Paris, 1792), in ANOM, F3/267, 360; AN, Dxxv/110/870, Gens de couleur de Mirebalais to Philippe-François Rouxel de Blanchelande, September 26, 1791; and Pierre Pinchinat et al. to Blanchelande, November 19, 1791. The free coloreds' supporters among the white planters and high-ranking officers supported this version: AGI, SD 954, Coustard to García, September 8, 1791, enclosed in García to Bajamar, September 16, 1791; C. Tarbé, *Rapport sur les troubles de Saint-Domingue fait à l'Assemblée Nationale* (Paris, 1792), 86–88; H. de Grimouärd, *L'amiral de Grimouärd au Port-au-Prince* (Paris: Larose, 1937), 29–37.

10. This confusion is reflected in their each appearing in separate volumes of the "official history" of the revolution. J.-P. Garran-Coulon, *Rapport sur les troubles de Saint-Domingue* (Paris, 1797–1799), 2:141–158, 3:65–70.

11. Madiou, *Histoire d'Haïti*, 1:105–106.

12. AGI, SD 954, Comandante de Neybe to García, September 7, 1791; BM, La Rochelle, MS 855, letter of October 1, 1791; Mediathèque de Nantes, MS 1811, letters of September 8 and 18, 1791; P. Blanchelande, *Mémoire de Blanchelande sur son administration. Supplément* (n.p., n.d.), 15–16; Garran-Coulon, *Rapport,* 2:141–158, 3:65–70; and the sources cited below, note 17.

13. AN, Dxxv/1/12, Blome, *aîné* to Commission civile, n.d. [late 1792]; AN, Dxxv/58/574, deposition by Pierre-Louis, October 4, 1791. The free colored *Mémoire historique des dernières révolutions* also acknowledged that "the plotting of some bad elements of their class had perhaps contributed to the corruption and leading astray of certain workforces." See ANOM, F3/267, f. 360.

14. D. Geggus, "Slavery, War, and Revolution in the Greater Caribbean, 1789–1815," in *A Turbulent Time: The French Revolution and the Greater Caribbean,* ed. D. B. Gaspar and D. P. Geggus (Bloomington: Indiana University Press, 1997), 10, 37; C. Fick, *The Making of Haiti: The Saint Domingue Revolution from Below* (Knoxville: University of Tennessee Press, 1990), 91, 137–138; BM, La Rochelle, MS 855, f. 369. For this reason, the demand for three days in the northern uprising is perhaps not "unmistakable evidence" of authentically local "slave demands," free of outside influence, as argued in M.-R. Trouillot, *Silencing the Past: Power and the Production of History* (Boston: Beacon Press, 1995), 103–104, although the free coloreds may have shrewdly judged slaves' aspirations.

15. AN, Dxxv/1/12, Blome, *aîné* to Commission civile, n.d. [late 1792].

16. AN, Dxxv/58/574, deposition by Pierre-Louis, October 4, 1791.

17. Blome, *aîné* to Commission civile, n.d. [late 1792]; deposition by Pierre-Louis, October 4, 1791; AN, Dxxv/78/773, anonymous letter, October 31, 1791; J. Marion, "Un Nantais à Saint-Domingue (1756–1792)," *Bulletin de la Société d'Archéologie de Nantes* 78 (1938): 130; G. Debien, "Histoire de deux plantations à Saint-Domingue," *Revue de la Province du Maine* (1968): 315; Debien, "Nouvelles de Saint-Domingue," 28–35.

18. Whites had disarmed free coloreds in some districts during the aftermath of Ogé's October 1790 rebellion. Then, in the furore that followed the May 15th law, some free colored police seem to have withdrawn their services to put pressure on their white opponents. The extent of these actions is unknown.

19. BM, La Rochelle, MS 855, f. 369; AN, Dxxv/78/773, anonymous letter, August 20, 1791, where the estate is called Fortin Bellantien; Garran-Coulon, *Rapport sur les troubles,* 2:207–208. The first source gives lower figures than the second and states that seventy men and women fled, of whom many were arrested. The plantation still had more than 270 slaves in early 1796: ANOM, Administration Anglaise, 4*bis,* inventory. Given the seaside location of the final skirmish, the survivors most likely fled into mountains north of the Cul de Sac plain, not those around Port-au-Prince to the south.

20. Pamphile de Lacroix, *Mémoires pour servir à l'histoire de la Révolution de Saint-Domingue* (Paris, 1819), 1:119; Fick, *The Making of Haiti,* 86–87, 306; C. Ardouin, *Essais sur l'histoire d'Haïti* (Port-au-Prince, 1865), 21; ANOM, F3/267, f. 360.

21. This sample was assembled from information in AN, Dxxv/55/528, "État des

nègres dits Suisses du Port-au-Prince," May 16, 1793; AN, Dxxv/78/773, anonymous letter, October 31, 1791; Jacques Cauna, *Au temps des isles à sucre: histoire d'une plantation de Saint-Domingue au XVIIIe siècle* (Paris: Karthala, 1987), 211; Debien, "Nouvelles de Saint-Domingue," 35; and PRO, CO 245/5, f. 44.

22. Between 15 and 19 came from between 9 and 12 mountain plantations, and between 10 and 14 came from between 4 and 7 sugar estates. The uncertainty arises where the same proprietor had both highland and lowland plantations. Twelve came from plantations whose location could not be identified.

23. Debien, "Nouvelles de Saint-Domingue," 28–29; AN, Dxxv/46/431, Jumécourt to Blanchelande, September 30, 1791.

24. B. Edwards, *An Historical Survey of the French Colony in the Island of St. Domingo* (London, 1797), 104.

25. AD, Vendée, 1Mi/102/2, September 2, 1791, letter by Hamon de Vaujoyeux; Madiou, *Histoire d'Haïti*, 103–107.

26. AN, Dxxv/110/870, concordat, September 11, 1791; Madiou, *Histoire d'Haïti*, 1:103–107; Ardouin, *Études*, 1:47–48, 56–57. The concordat went further than the May 15th law (which was limited to freeborn persons) and enfranchised all nonwhites who met the property and residence requirements. It did this by insisting on a literal interpretation of the National Assembly's March 28, 1790, instructions, a document whose deliberately ambiguous reference to "persons" had till then been interpreted by colonists as meaning whites only.

27. AN, Dxxv/46/431, Jumécourt to Blanchelande, September 30, 1791. Hanus de Jumécourt, the planter leader, stated that this agreement formed part of the concordat. As it is not in the text, it must have been an oral agreement. The governor of Santo Domingo was informed that the slaves who were not included were to receive a free Thursday each week: AGI, SD 954, García to Bajamar, October 25, 1791, enclosure dated October 1. This is unlikely, as no other source reports this, but it presumably was discussed.

28. AN, Dxxv/78/772, Acaby to National Assembly, October 5, 1791; ANOM, F3/267, 360; Debien, "Nouvelles de Saint-Domingue," 30. Several sources put their number at 600 or 700, but their authors were not eyewitnesses.

29. AGI, SD 954, Coustard to García, September 20, 1791; Georgia Historical Society, Savannah, Caradeuc Papers, doc. 3/19, letter of September 22, 1791; "Le concordat de Damiens," *Chemins Critiques* 2 (1992): 263–281.

30. Georgetown University, Michel Marsaudon Papers, letter 28; AD, Marseille, 1Mi/34/26, letters of October 8 and 28, 1791; AD, La Roche-sur-Yon, 1Mi/102/2, letter of September 2, 1791.

31. Micheau and Frères Jumeaux to president of Mirebalais, September 13, 1791. [I have mislaid the source of this citation.]

32. However, see AGI, SD 954, García to Bajamar, October 25, 1791.

33. AN, Dxxv/78/772, Acaby to National Assembly, October 5, 1791; AN, Dxxv/78/773, anonymous letter, October 31, 1791.

34. Médiathèque de Nantes, MS 846, Sigoigne to Desridelières-Leroux, November 6, 1790.

35. C. Malenfant, *Des colonies et particulièrement de celle de Saint-Domingue* (Paris, 1814), 12.

36. Northern colonists made similar overtures at the same time. See D. Geggus, *Slavery, War and Revolution: The British Occupation of Saint Domingue, 1793–1798* (Oxford: Oxford University Press, 1982), 53–54; Geggus, "The Caradeux and Colonial Memory," in *The Impact of the Haitian Revolution in the Atlantic World,* ed. D. Geggus (Columbia, S.C.: University of South Carolina Press, 2001), 238; Grimouärd, *L'Amiral de Grimouärd,* 32–35.

37. Ardouin, *Études,* 1:56–57.

38. AN, Dxxv/61/610, Assembly of the West to the General Assembly, October 27, 1791; AN, Dxxv/78/773, anonymous letter, October 31, 1791.

39. AGI, SD 955, García to Bajamar, February 27, 1792.

40. AN, Dxxv/61/610, Assembly of the West to the General Assembly, October 27, 1791; AN, Dxxv/78/773, anonymous letters, October 27 and 31, 1791; *Production historique des faits qui se sont passés dans la partie de l'Ouest* (Port-au-Prince, 1792), 14–15; Debien, "Nouvelles de Saint-Domingue," 30; García to Bajamar, February 27, 1792.

41. At Petit Goâve, where seven whites had been killed and two women repeatedly raped, whites and *gens de couleur* massacred 200 slaves: ANOM, F3/267, f. 360; AN, Dxxv/78/773, anonymous letter, October 29, 1791; BM, La Rochelle, MS 855, letter of November 1, 1791.

42. Ardouin, *Études,* 1:57–59; Madiou, *Histoire d'Haïti,* 1:109; and the sources cited below, note 43.

43. AN, Dxxv/78/773, anonymous letters, October 29/31 and October 27/November 3, 1791; Commission des Colonies, *Débats,* 1:311–312; Grimouärd, *L'amiral de Grimouärd,* 37. The sources do not make clear if the protesters formed part of the free colored army or were town residents.

44. AN, Dxxv/78/773, anonymous letter, October 29, 1791.

45. Lambert was 63, Pinchinat was 45, and Bauvais was 35. Pétion was 20; Rigaud, 30; and Boisrond jeune (another critic) probably in his 30s. It is not clear if the most fiery defender of the Swiss was Daguin *fils* or his father; it was probably the former—who acted as secretary for drawing up one of the concordats—thus another young man.

46. ANOM, CC9A/5, Boisrond, Maigret, et al. to Pinchinat, November 9, 1791. The letter lamented that such ingratitude for past services would create discontent that their enemies would be sure to exploit.

47. AN, Dxxv/78/773, anonymous letter, October 29, 1791. Free blacks constituted about one-third of Saint Domingue's *gens de couleur libres,* according to Moreau de Saint-Méry (*Description de Saint-Domingue,* 1:102). They were much rarer among the free colored leadership, especially in the west and south.

48. Debien, "Nouvelles de Saint-Domingue," 35; AN, Dxxv/78/773, letters of October 29/31 and October 27/November 3, 1791; PH, 1:56.

49. It is not apparent if the two groups were separate or one and the same. See

AN, Dxxv/78/773, letter of October 29/31, 1791; ANOM, F3/267, f. 360. As noted above, the connections between the rebellion and the Swiss are obscure.

50. AN, Dxxv/58/574, deposition by Pierre-Louis, October 4, 1791. Another observer (cited in Ardouin, *Études,* 1:58) recalled in the 1820s that twenty-three of 220 deportees were mulattoes. Much perhaps depended on the eye of the beholder. A 1784 inventory of the Carrère plantation lists Charlemagne, a valet and cook, as a black Creole 25 years old: J. Houdaille, R. Massio, and G. Debien, "Les origines des esclaves des Antilles," *Bulletin de l'IFAN* 25 (1963): 236.

51. É. Laveaux, *Compte rendu par le Général Laveaux à ses concitoyens* (Paris, 1797), 11; PH, 1:104; see Chapter 10, pp. 162–163. In late 1792, free coloreds of Saint Marc were freeing slaves of mixed racial descent and blacks fathered by *nègres libres.* See ANOM, CC9A/9, Gasnier to Navy Minister, March 18, 1793.

52. AN, Dxxv/46/438, doc. 66; Commission des Colonies, *Débats,* 1:312; AN, Dxxv/46/433, Adam Williamson to Blanchelande, January 26, 1792; Cauna, *Au temps des isles à sucre,* 211; PRO, CO 245/5, f.44.

53. AN, Dxxv/78/773, letter of October 27, 1791; Commission des Colonies, *Débats,* 1:153; Grimouärd, *L'amiral de Grimouärd,* 37.

54. Debien, "Nouvelles de Saint-Domingue," 35; New York Public Library, West Indies Collection, Box 1, Dinety to de Cressac, November 9, 1791; AN, Dxxv/78/773, letter of October 29, 1791.

55. On September 24, the ever-wavering National Assembly effectively canceled the May 15, 1791 law by handing questions of citizenship over to the colonial assemblies.

56. AN, Dxxv/79/779, memoir by François Colmin, February 25, 1792, enclosing instructions dated November 1, 1791. The captain's instructions stated that if a landing was not possible in the Bay of Honduras, he should try "further down" if this could be done "without problems." Should no landing on the mainland be possible, "any island" would do. The Swiss were in no case to be returned to Saint Domingue.

57. Garran-Coulon, *Rapport sur les troubles,* 3:65–70. This passage in the "official history" of the revolution seems to be the source of the confusion about Jamaica and other aspects of the deportation. Colmin later informed the Colonial Assembly that he abandoned his escort ship because it was too slow: memoir by François Colmin, February 25, 1792.

58. PRO, CO 123/13, reports by the Honduras magistrates, November/December 1791. Except where indicated, these papers are the main source for what follows.

59. AN, Dxxv/79/779, memoir by François Colmin, February 25, 1792. Strictly speaking, Colmin claimed he had faced northerly winds only until reaching Guanaja, and the English captain's signed statement advised only against landing on that island. One suspects Colmin wished to avoid his escort ship, which was heading for the Miskito Coast.

60. O. N. Bolland, *Slavery in Belize* (1979), Belize Institute for Social Research and Action Occasional Papers no. 7, 6–7.

61. J. Burdon, *The Archives of British Honduras* (London: Sifton Praed, 1931), 1:195–196.

62. A mere speck of land, situated about 15 miles from the Belize River mouth, 8 miles west of the Turneffe Islands, and 1.5 miles south of Goff's Cay.

63. Colmin's report states that 218 left Saint Domingue and 215 were put ashore on English Cay: Memoir by François Colmin, February 25, 1792. McCulloch told the settlers on November 17th that 3 out of 217 had died. On November 18, the magistrates found on the cay 213 men, 17 of them mulattoes. It is not clear if these figures include the two men given as payment to the pilot who guided them from Guanaja. At 500 tons burden, the *Emmanuel* was far less crowded than a slave ship. A newspaper advertisement described it as copper-bottomed and a fast sailer: *Les Affiches Américaines* (Port-au-Prince), 28 October 1790.

64. J. L. Franco, *Documentos para la historia de Haití en el Archivo Nacional* (Havana: Archivo Nacional, 1954), 18–19; E. Brutus, *Révolution dans Saint-Domingue* (Paris: Éditions du Panthéon, 1973), 1:331–332; J. Fouchard, *Les marrons de la liberté* (Paris: École, 1972), 526. These writers argue that the free coloreds were involved in the later murder of the Swiss.

65. G. Corvington, *Port-au-Prince au cours des ans: sous les assauts de la Révolution* (Port-au-Prince: Deschamps, 1972), 170.

66. AN, Dxxv/79/779, memoir by François Colmin, February 25, 1792.

67. Garran-Coulon, *Rapport sur les troubles de Saint-Domingue,* 3:65–70.

68. ANOM, F3/267, f. 360.

69. AN, Dxxv/46/434, letters of February 10 and 15, 1792.

70. Memoir by François Colmin, February 25, 1792.

71. Collusion is the easier to imagine in that Colmin and the *Emmanuel* were regular visitors to Port-au-Prince. The ship had brought Jean-Baptiste de Caradeux and his new bride back from France in 1785: ANOM, F5B, passenger lists.

72. Garran-Coulon, *Rapport sur les troubles de Saint-Domingue,* 3:65–70.

73. ANOM, C9A/158, f. 123–124.

74. *Gentleman's Magazine* 62 (1792): 375.

75. The magistrates reported that the island was roughly 300 yards in circumference; hence it was about 100 yards across.

76. Franco, *Documentos,* 70–71.

77. PRO, CO 125/13, letters of Thomas Potts and James Bartlet, November 26 and 27, 1791.

78. Ibid.

79. S. Caiger, *British Honduras Past and Present* (London: George, Allen & Unwin, 1951), 91.

80. Franco, *Documentos,* 70–71. The *Gentleman's Magazine* 62 (1792): 375 gives their number as 201, but the former estimate, which comes from an eyewitness (a spy for the Cuban government), seems preferable.

81. *Royal Gazette* [Jamaica] (1792), no. 5; PRO, CO 137/90, Williamson to Dundas, February 12, 1792.

82. Franco, *Documentos,* 70–71.

83. Jamaica Archives, Spanish Town, Council Minutes, January 20, 1792.

84. *Royal Gazette* (1792), no. 5.

85. *Moniteur de la Partie Françoise de Saint-Domingue* 88 (1792): 357; AN, Dxxv/46/433, Williamson to Blanchelande, January 26, 1792; PRO, FO 27/38, Lord Grenville to Lord Gower, April 2, 1792.

86. AN, Dxxv/46/433, Blanchelande to Ministre de la Marine, February 15, 1792; *Royal Gazette* (1792), no. 8.

87. *L'Ancien Moniteur,* no. 97 (6 April 1792); P.-F. Blanchelande, *Discours justificatif* (Paris, 1793), 9–15.

88. PRO, FO 27/39, *arrêté* of the Colonial Assembly, March 16, 1792.

89. Blanchelande, *Discours justificatif,* 9–15.

90. C. Tarbé, *Rapport et projet de decret relatifs au débarquement . . . par le capitaine Colmin* (Paris, 1792).

91. JA, Spanish Town, Vice-Admiralty Court Papers, 1794, *Maréchal de Lévis* case.

92. Commission des Colonies, *Débats,* 1:153–155, 311–315, 3:200–204; Garran-Coulon, *Rapport sur les troubles de Saint-Domingue,* 3:65–70.

93. Commission des Colonies, *Débats,* 1:153–155, 311–315, 3:200–204; Garran-Coulon, *Rapport sur les troubles de Saint-Domingue,* 3:65–70.

94. Cauna, *Au temps des isles à sucre,* 215; Cauna, "La Révolution à Port-au-Prince," 27; Garran-Coulon, *Rapport sur les troubles de Saint-Domingue,* 3:66–67.

95. The governor had reported only "about 160" arrived from Jamaica: ANOM, C9A/167, f. 44. This seems improbable, as it would mean that nearly fifty had died in the crossing from Kingston. More likely the Swiss were divided between two vessels, as they had been on the voyage to Jamaica, and the harassed and distracted governor overlooked the smaller of them. Hence, perhaps 140 survived the massacre.

96. Madiou, *Histoire d'Haïti,* 1:110; Médiathèque, Nantes, MS 1809, f. 205.

97. Commission des Colonies, *Débats,* 3:200–204; AN, Dxxv/51/488, Sonthonax to Cambis, May 10, 1793; AN, Dxxv/55/528, "État des nègres dits Suisses," May 16, 1793.

98. AN, Dxxv/54/521, Admiral Cambis's journal.

99. AN, Dxxv/53/507, crew lists. A crew list of October 1 (in AN, Dxxv/55/533) does not mention them even among the deserters. Perhaps they had been sold as slaves or murdered by the crew or by some of the 180 refugees on the ship.

100. AN, Dxxv/12/116, Sonthonax to Polverel, September 3, 1793. Another "Suisse" is mentioned near the southern city of Jacmel in A. Corre, *Les papiers du Général A.-N. de La Salle (Saint-Domingue, 1792–1793)* (Quimper, 1897), 48–49. However, this probably was an example of the "generic" use of the term, as he seems to have been a locally armed slave.

101. PRO, CO 245/5, f. 44. This was Jean-Louis, an 18-year-old *mulâtre* from the

Fleuriau plantation. He is not mentioned among that estate's six Swiss named in Cauna, *Au temps des isles à sucre,* 211; but he is listed among its slaves in Cauna, "Une habitation coloniale à la fin du XVIIIe siècle: la sucrerie Fleuriau de Bellevue" (Thèse de 3me cycle, Université de Poitiers, 1983), 88, 406.

102. C. L. R. James, *The Black Jacobins: Toussaint L'Ouverture and the San Domingo Revolution* (New York: Vintage, 1963), 102, 108; D. Geggus, "The Sugar Plantation Zones of Saint Domingue and the Revolution of 1791–93," *Slavery and Abolition* 20 (1999): 31–46.

103. See the sources cited above, note 54.

104. Boisrond, Maigret, et al. to Pinchinat, November 9, 1791; ANOM, F3/267, f. 360.

105. Commission des Colonies, *Débats,* 1:311–313; AN, Dxxv/46/438, doc. 66.

106. Ardouin, *Études,* 1:61.

107. These included Hyacinthe's rebellion in the Cul de Sac. See Madiou, *Histoire d'Haïti,* 1:131–133; Ardouin, *Études,* 1:170.

108. D. Geggus, "The Arming of Slaves in the Haitian Revolution," in *The Arming of Slaves from Classical Times to the Modern Era,* ed. P. Morgan and C. Brown (Yale University Press, forthcoming). The claims in this regard in F. W. Knight, "The Haitian Revolution," *American Historical Review* 105 (2000): 111–112 are not well founded.

109. E. Cox, *The Free Coloreds in the Slave Societies of St. Kitts and Grenada, 1763–1833* (Knoxville: University of Tennessee Press, 1984), 80; N. L. Gonzalez, *Sojourners of the Caribbean: Ethnogenesis and Ethnohistory of the Garifuna* (Urbana: University of Illinois Press, 1988), 39–50; Burdon, *Archives of British Honduras,* 1:208–209. This differed from the common British punishment of "transportation," which for slaves meant sale overseas. In 1760, the Jamaicans had "transported" 600 participants in Tacky's Rebellion to the Bay of Honduras. See R. Hart, *Slaves Who Abolished Slavery,* vol. 2, *Blacks in Rebellion* (Kingston: Institute of Social and Economic Research, University of the West Indies, 1985), 150.

110. See Chapter 12 in this volume; AGI, Estado 1/1, Conde de Santa Clara to Príncipe de la Paz, September 2, 1797.

111. C. B. Auguste and M. B. Auguste, *Les déportés de Saint-Domingue: contribution à l'histoire de l'expédition française de Saint-Domingue, 1802–1803* (Sherbrooke, Quebec: Éditions Naaman, 1979), 40, 43.

112. Historians of Guadeloupe commonly suggest that 2,000 were deported. AD, Périgueux, 2E/1586, letter by de Saintrac, September 1, 1802, claims 8,000. The 200 in New Granada were captured by Indians. See A. Helg, "A Fragmented Majority: Free 'of All Colors,' Indians, and Slaves in Caribbean Colombia during the Haitian Revolution," in *The Impact of the Haitian Revolution in the Atlantic World,* 160; Auguste and Auguste, *Les déportés de Saint-Domingue,* 38, 40, 77.

113. Pauléus Sannon, *Histoire de Toussaint Louverture,* 2:15.

114. See Franco, *Documentos,* 70–71.

115. PH, 2:115; Corvington, *Port-au-Prince,* 168–170.

116. Ardouin, *Études,* 1:46–61; Saint-Rémy, *Pétion et Haïti,* 1:41–43, 47–49; Madiou, *Histoire d'Haïti,* 1:102–110; G. Laurent, *Documentation historique pour nos étudiants* (Port-au-Prince: La Phalange, 1960), 75–81; L. Denis and F. Duvalier, *Le problème des classes à travers l'histoire d'Haïti* (Port-au-Prince: Au service de la Jeunesse, 1958), 12–14; Brutus, *Révolution,* 1:314, 321, 331–332; E. Paul, *Questions d'histoire (Études critiques)* (Port-au-Prince: Imprimerie de l'État, 1955), 15, 18; James, *Black Jacobins,* 98; Pauléus Sannon, *Histoire de Toussaint Louverture,* 2:15; Franco, *Documentos,* 18–19; Fouchard, *Les marrons de la liberté,* 526; Fick, *The Making of Haiti,* 86–87, 306. F. Dalencour, *Précis méthodique d'Histoire d'Haïti* (Port-au-Prince: Dalencour, 1935), 18, offers a modern version of the *mulâtre* viewpoint.

117. Madiou, *Histoire d'Haïti,* 1:235–237, 298–299; Ardouin, *Études,* 1:59; C. B. Auguste, "André Rigaud, leader des anciens libres," *RSHHG* 187 (1996): 17–18; R. Dorsainvil, *De Fatras Bâton à Toussaint Louverture* (Alger: Enal, 1983), 93.

118. Geggus, *Slavery, War and Revolution,* 325–326. On free nonwhites in Jean-François's army, see Chapter 12.

8. The "Volte-Face" of Toussaint Louverture

1. Unilaterally and with limited effect, Civil Commissioner Sonthonax declared slavery abolished in northern Saint Domingue on August 29, 1793. The decree was extended to all Saint Domingue by October. In November, Sonthonax sent deputies to France to request that the decree be ratified. Although they were initially imprisoned, they eventually inspired the Convention to pass the decree of 16 pluviôse an II. Wartime conditions delayed its communication to the colonies.

2. C. L. R. James, *The Black Jacobins: Toussaint L'Ouverture and the San Domingo Revolution* (New York: Vintage, 1963), 143–144.

3. T. Madiou, *Histoire d'Haïti* (Port-au-Prince: H. Deschamps, 1989), 1:250. See also Castonnet-Desfosses, *La Révolution de Saint-Domingue* (Paris, 1893), 158–160; A. Césaire, *Toussaint Louverture: La Révolution française et le problème colonial* (Paris: Présence Africaine, 1962), 203; B. Maurel, *Le vent du large* (Paris: La Nef, 1952), 332.

4. B. Ardouin, *Études sur l'Histoire d'Haïti* (Port-au-Prince: Dalencour, 1958), 2:86–93. See also E. Cordero Michel, *La Revolución haitiana y Santo Domingo* (Santo Domingo: Editora nacional, 1968), 43; L. Nemours, "Pour quelles raisons Toussaint Louverture est-il passé des Espagnols aux Français?" *Annales Historiques de la Révolution Française* (1948): 166–171.

5. H. Pauléus Sannon, *Histoire de Toussaint Louverture* (Port-au-Prince: Héraux, 1920), 1:162–168.

6. T. Ott, *The Haitian Revolution, 1789–1804* (Knoxville: University of Tennessee Press, 1973), 82–83.

7. P. Pluchon, *Toussaint Louverture: un révolutionnaire noir d'Ancien régime* (Paris: Fayard, 1989); R. Korngold, *Citizen Toussaint* (London: Gollancz,

1945); E. Rüsch, *Die Revolution von Saint Domingue* (Hamburg: Friedrichsen, De Gruyter, 1930).

8.   P. de Lacroix, *Mémoires pour servir à l'histoire de la révolution de Saint-Domingue* (Paris, 1819), 1:299–302; L. Dubroca, *The Life of Toussaint Louverture* (London, 1802), 13–14, 72; C. Cousin d'Avallon, *Histoire de Toussaint Louverture* (Paris, 1802), 30–31, which appeared slightly later than Dubroca's book.

9.   BN, Manuscrits, Fonds français 12102, Correspondance du général Laveaux (hereafter cited as "Laveaux Corresp., 1,"), f. 73–75; James, *Black Jacobins,* 124–125.

10.   Laveaux Corresp., 1, f. 41. An unknown hand has added to this and other letters in the collection an incorrect Gregorian equivalent of the "revolutionary" date, which is "le 14 nivose 94: L. 3 d. L. R. F.," that is, January 3, 1795. The "94" is a secretarial error; the contents of the letter clearly refer to a later period of Toussaint's career.

11.   Laveaux Corresp., 1, Toussaint Louverture to Étienne Laveaux, 30 vendémiaire an II; AGI, SD 1089, Joaquín García y Moreno to marqués de Campo de Alange, October 25, 1794.

12.   BN, NAF 6864, f. 37–48, published as I. Louverture, *Notes diverses d'Isaac sur la vie de Toussaint Louverture,* in A. Métral, *Histoire de l'expédition des Français à Saint-Domingue* (Paris, 1825), 333.

13.   See the letters printed in Ardouin, *Études,* 2:87–89 and A. del Monte y Tejada, *Historia de Santo Domingo* (Santo Domingo, 1890), 4:200–201. The latter volume is an invaluable and totally neglected collection of contemporary documents now unavailable in Spanish, Dominican, or Cuban archives.

14.   AGI, SD 957, García to Eugenio Llaguno, April 13, 1794; AGS, GM 7157, Juan Francisco to Fernando Portillo y Torres, September 23, 1793; Monte y Tejada, *Historia de Santo Domingo,* 3:xii–xiii, 161; 4:11–12, 96–98, 115; Louverture, *Notes,* 326. In 1793, Jean-François imprisoned Toussaint, and Biassou imprisoned Petit Thomas. Jean-François had Biassou's nephew, Michaud, shot in September of that year, and Toussaint's brother Pierre was killed in fighting with Thomas early in 1794. At the very beginning of the slave insurrection, Jean-François unsuccessfully ordered the execution of his rival, Boukman, and carried out that of Jeannot.

15.   Monte y Tejada, *Historia de Santo Domingo,* 4:205–207.

16.   Louverture, *Notes,* 333.

17.   Ardouin, *Études,* 2:433.

18.   Ardouin has Toussaint raising the tricolor at Gonaïves. Saint-Rémy, in *Vie de Toussaint Louverture* (Paris, 1850), 119–121, has him raising it simultaneously in seven parishes, while three years later, in *Mémoires du Général Toussaint Louverture* (Paris, 1853), 89n, he wrote that Toussaint "submitted to Général Laveaux on May 4 at Marmelade."

19.   PRO, CO 245/2, Toussaint to Rallier, 26 germinal an VII; Toussaint to Navy Minister, 24 germinal an VII, cited in G. M. Laurent, *Toussaint Louverture à*

travers sa correspondance (Madrid: G. Laurent, 1953), 96–99; *Le Moniteur Universel,* 1 July 1799, 585–586.

20.   Another reason, perhaps, is that if one places the volte-face before the fall of Port-au-Prince (June 4, 1794), the high point of British success in Saint Domingue, a rather pleasing dialectic is spoiled. See James, *Black Jacobins,* 137. Toussaint apparently appreciated this and rewrote his own history in the two "political testaments" just cited.

21.   Speech of September 19, 1797, cited in Ardouin, *Études,* 2:86; E. Laveaux, *Compte rendu par le Général Laveaux à ses concitoyens* (Paris, 1797), 34.

22.   Ardouin, *Études,* 2:86.

23.   One, entitled "Mémoire abrégé des événements de l'île de Saint Domingue de l'année 1789 à celle de 1807," is printed in *Revue Française d'Histoire d'Outre-Mer* 62 (1975): 470–471. The other, probably written by a colonist from the northeast, is in BM, Rouen, MS Monbret 574, f. 311–314.

24.   Both accounts seem to be confused and probably refer to the fighting that took place in March. The author of the "Mémoire abrégé" dictated his story on a prison ship about fifteen years after these events.

25.   Interestingly, in both Rüsch, *Die Revolution von Saint Domingue,* 89, and T. L. Stoddard, *The French Revolution in San Domingo* (New York: Houghton Mifflin, 1914), 248, the massacre is linked with this date but given no location. Since these accounts are based respectively on Castonnet-Desfosses and Lacroix, who placed it June, it is unclear how Rüsch and Stoddard hit upon this date. Neither of them cites Laveaux's *Compte rendu.* They may have taken it from V. Schoelcher, *Vie de Toussaint Louverture* (Paris, 1889), 97. Schoelcher probably combined Lacroix's version with that of Laveaux. He had also read Laveaux's letter to Toussaint of May 5, 1794: ANOM, CC9A/5, Laveaux to Toussaint, May 5, 1794. (The letter is published in Pauléus Sannon, *Histoire de Toussaint-Louverture,* 1:165.) Toussaint may have borne a grudge against the whites of Ennery and Marmelade. In 1793, they had rebelled against him after being granted very favorable terms of surrender. See Monte y Tejada, *Historia de Santo Domingo,* 4:141.

26.   Kindly brought to my attention by Joseph Boromé, it is printed in *Le Moniteur* 265 (1796).

27.   AGI, SD 1031, Pedro Cabello to Portillo, May 10, 1794. The massacre is not mentioned in any Spanish official correspondence. If it was small-scale, it conceivably could have been passed over at a moment of multiple disasters, when the governor, moreover, was incapacitated by fever. Haitian oral traditions of the late 1830s or 1840s ostensibly preserved memory of it, according to Madiou, *Histoire d'Haïti,* 1:251, although his text at this point lumps together various events and cites Dubroca.

28.   PRO, CO 137/93, Brisbane to Williamson, May 4, 1794. A memoir written four months later put the death toll at 120. Archives de la Guerre, Vincennes, MS 590, memoir by Charles Dernanancourt.

29.   PRO, CO 137/93, Antonio Santa Cilia to Brisbane, May 1, 1794.

30.   See the letters printed in appendix.

31.   PRO, CO 137/93, Ramón de Salazar to Toussaint, May 5, 1794.

32.   One is very much reminded of the controversy surrounding Toussaint's role in the 1791 revolt; on which, see D. Geggus, "Toussaint Louverture et l'abolition de l'esclavage à Saint-Domingue," in *Les abolitions dans les Amériques: actes du colloque organisé par les Archives départementales de la Martinique, 8–9 décembre 1998,* ed. L. Chauleau (Fort de France: Société des Amis des Archives, 2001), 110–111.

33.   D. P. Geggus, *Slavery, War and Revolution: The British Occupation of Saint Domingue, 1793–1798* (Oxford: Oxford University Press, 1982), 182, 199, 414, 442; J. Thornton, "'I am the subject of the King of Congo': African Political Ideology and the Haitian Revolution," *Journal of World History* 4 (1993): 181–214. This remains a difficult question, but some rare pieces of evidence suggest that, even among themselves, when not courting royalist allies, rebel leaders could maintain their monarchical rhetoric. A remarkable exchange between the radical but pro-Spanish Petit Thomas and the pro-republican Barthélemy shows both men accepting the legitimist argument: AGS, GM 7157, Citizens Barthélemi and Blondeau to Citizen Thomas, October 24, 1793. Part of Barthélemy's notably unrepublican justification for his allegiance ran as follows: "We are ready [to] fight for a king but only if France (whose sons we are) recognizes Louis XVII. . . . Therefore we stay under the protection of the French Republic, as the representative of the king. . . . We always have been aware of the respect, submission, and obedience we owe to a sovereign, when one exists, but he doesn't exist and his rights are now transferred to the Republic."

34.   AGI, SD 1031, Pedro Cabello to Portillo, May 10, 1794. The vicar provided no date for the attack, which he attributed to "enemigos negros," who forced the Spanish garrison to withdraw, killed the French inhabitants, sacked the town, then withdrew leaving behind "una Vandera de la nación."

35.   The war had brought French shipping to a standstill, and though American ships trading to Saint Domingue could not have failed to pass on such electrifying news, they vanished from French waters following the embargo declared by the United States in April. In fact, from early March the volume of American shipping in the Caribbean seems to have fallen off sharply. See JA, Vice-Admiralty Court Papers, 1794.

36.   J.-P. Garran-Coulon, *Rapport sur les troubles de Saint-Domingue* (Paris, 1797–1799), 4:300n; ANOM, CC9A/8, Laveaux to Commissaires Civils, May 24, 1794.

37.   ANOM, CC9A/5, Laveaux to Toussaint, May 5, 1794.

38.   ANOM, CC9A/8, Léger-Félicité Sonthonax to Laveaux, June 8, 1794; Garran-Coulon, *Rapport sur les troubles de Saint-Domingue,* 4:243

39.   Y. Bénot, "Le procès de Sonthonax," in *Léger-Félicité Sonthonax, la première abolition de l'esclavage: la Révolution française et la Révolution de Saint-Domingue,* ed. M. Dorigny (Paris: Société française d'Histoire d'Outre-mer, 1997), 62.

40.   Ardouin, *Études,* 2:86; Laveaux, *Compte rendu,* 34–35. In his September 1794

report to the Convention, he stated that Toussaint finally saw through the Spanish and Jean-François's slave trading and, "reflecting on France's grant of liberty," attacked Gonaïves: ANOM, CC9A/9, Laveaux to Convention Nationale, 1 vendémiaire an III.

41. AN, Section Moderne, Dxxv/23/232, Commissaires Civils to Toussaint Louverture, "juin 94"; BN, NAF 6846, f. 148–151, Sonthonax to García, 7 fructidor an V.

42. Garran-Coulon, *Rapport sur les troubles de Saint-Domingue*, 4:299.

43. PRO, CO 245/2, Toussaint to Rallier, 26 germinal an VII; Laurent, *Toussaint Louverture*, 96–99; *Le Moniteur Universel*, 1 July 1799, 585–586.

44. Laveaux Corresp., 1, Toussaint to Laveaux, July 7, 1794.

45. AN, Dxxv/63/635, deposition by Guillaume Moulinet; AN, Dxxv/60/600, deposition by Laroque; Gros, *Isle de St. Domingue. Province du Nord* (Paris, 1793), 23, 26, 27.

46. AGI, SD 955, García to Bajamar, September 25, 1792.

47. Pluchon, *Toussaint Louverture: un révolutionnaire noir*, 70–108; Madiou, *Histoire d'Haïti*, 1:431–432.

48. See P. R. Roume, *Rapport de P. R. Roume sur sa mission à Saint-Domingue* (Paris, 1793), 47–48; *Le Créole Patriote*, 9 February 1793 and 19 October 1793. Rebels in Camp Galliffet had drawn up a note before September 26, 1791 demanding that the whites leave the colony, but it was never sent; PRO, WO 1/58, f. 9. The description in S.-V. Jean-Baptiste, *Haïti: sa lutte pour l'émancipation* (Paris: Nef, 1958), 152, of Jean-François and Biassou's overtures of December 4, 1791, is quite incorrect. See Garran-Coulon, *Rapport sur les troubles de Saint-Domingue*, 2:307–312.

49. Laurent, *Toussaint Louverture à travers sa correspondance*, 68–72. The signatory was evidently Gabriel Bellair, one of Biassou's ablest subordinates. The author was probably the Dondon parish priest, Abbé Delahaye.

50. Jean-François and, especially, Biassou sold women, children, and "some adult blacks described as troublemakers." See ANOM, CC9A/9, Laveaux to Convention Nationale, 1 vendémiaire an III (quote); Ardouin, *Études*, 2:87–88; Monte y Tejada, *Historia de Santo Domingo*, 4:141.

51. AGS, GM 7157, Cabello to Portillo, June 12, 1793, shows Toussaint visiting the Spanish frontier town of San Rafael and making a good impression.

52. Clavier, "Mémoire abrégé," 67. However, Spanish documents of June/July show no sign of mistrust and in fact sing his praises. Toussaint did have negotiations with a representative of the civil commissioners in late June at La Tannerie, but he rejected their propositions. See Garran-Coulon, *Rapport sur les troubles de Saint-Domingue*, 3:48–49.

53. Monte y Tejada, *Historia de Santo Domingo*, 4:18–22, 43–44; Ardouin, *Études*, 2:87.

54. Laveaux, *Compte rendu*, 35; Laveaux Corresp., 1, f. 73–75.

55. For example, C. Fick, *The Making of Haiti: The Saint Domingue Revolution from Below* (Knoxville: University of Tennessee Press, 1990), 160.

56. Pluchon, *Toussaint Louverture: un révolutionnaire noir,* 108.

57. T. Gragnon-Lacoste, *Toussaint-Louverture* (Paris, 1877), 78.

58. Schoelcher, *Vie de Toussaint-Louverture,* 98; Pauléus Sannon, *Histoire de Toussaint-Louverture,* 1:165–166; James, *Black Jacobins,* 125; Fick, *The Making of Haiti,* 160; Nemours, "Pour quelles raisons," 166–171; A. Michel, *La Mission du Général Hédouville* (Port-au-Prince, n.d.), 27; M. Laurent, *Erreurs et vérités dans l'histoire d'Haïti* (Port-au-Prince: Telhomme, 1945), 1:26.

59. James, *Black Jacobins,* 124; also Césaire, *Toussaint Louverture,* 176. In 1801, Toussaint told Santo Domingo's governor that he, the governor, could have conquered the French colony if he had accepted the plan of Toussaint's superior, Brigadier Armona, which the black leader had supported. That the plan involved general emancipation is merely guesswork. Armona, a Cuban planter, did not reach Santo Domingo before the end of June and could not have met Toussaint before the second week of August.

60. AN, Section Moderne, AA 54/1510, Pierrot to Thomas Galbaud, June 4, 1793.

61. Madiou, *Histoire d'Haïti,* 1:431–432.

62. AN, Section Moderne, AE II/1375, letter by Toussaint Louverture, August 25, 1793; AN, AA 53/1490, letter by Toussaint Louverture, August 29, 1793. The printed versions of Pauléus Sannon, *Histoire de Toussaint-Louverture,* 1:138–139, and Schoelcher, *Vie de Toussaint-Louverture,* 94, are neither complete nor accurate. In James, *Black Jacobins,* 125, the August 29th letter's location is wrongly given as the BN.

63. AN, Dxxv/5/53, Sonthonax to Étienne Polverel, September 10, 1793. Note that Biassou, too, reacted with a declaration on August 25th, but his stated that only a king could free slaves. See AGI, SD 956, García to Pedro de Acuña, November 25, 1793, enclosures 7–9.

64. Rüsch, *Die Revolution von Saint Domingue,* 86–93; Pluchon, *Toussaint Louverture,* 92–104. See also, AN, AA 55/1511, "Réponse sentimentale," August 27, 1793; Garran-Coulon, *Rapport sur les troubles de Saint-Domingue,* 4:47.

65. See AN, Dxxv12/118, proclamation by Biassou, August 14, 1793.

66. After the Gonaïves mutiny, he himself put down the plantation slaves who had joined in. See Laveaux Corresp., 1, f. 73–75. The letter of August 29th, moreover, stresses how whites and free coloreds were able to continue plantation production untroubled under his command.

67. Schoelcher, *Vie de Toussaint-Louverture,* 101.

68. AN, Section Moderne, AE II/1375, letter by Toussaint Louverture, August 25, 1793; AN, AA 55/1511, "Réponse sentimentale," August 27, 1793.

69. AGS, GM 7157, Portillo to Acuña, May 25, 1793.

70. Laveaux Corresp., 1, f. 27–28. However, Laurent's assertion (in *Trois mois aux Archives d'Espagne* [Port-au-Prince: Les Presses Libres, 1956], 50) that his letter shows Toussaint arranging a secret interview with Laveaux is incorrect. The person in question was another rebel leader, Toussaint d'Aux, who was either the Plaine du Nord blacksmith of that name, a free mulatto, or the future black general, Daux Brave. A vigorous "Capitán Tusen" was also fighting for the Spanish in these months in the Cul de Sac region.

71. Louverture, *Notes,* 332–334.

72. Ibid.; Monte y Tejada, *Historia de Santo Domingo,* 3:xii–xiii.

73. Monte y Tejada, *Historia de Santo Domingo,* 4:88, 106–107.

74. Ibid., 4:137–140; AGS, GM 7157, Juan Francisco to Portillo, September 23, 1793.

75. AGS, GM 7157, Juan Sánchez to Portillo, October 25, 1793; AGI, Estado 11, exp. 98, enclosure 11.

76. Ardouin, *Études,* 2:87–90; Louverture, *Notes,* 331–333.

77. Monte y Tejada, *Historia de Santo Domingo,* 4:107–108, 138–140, 204–205; UCMM typescripts, García to Acuña, August 23 and September 4, 1793; García to Alcudia, January 5, 1794.

78. However, García had been willing for Toussaint to replace Biassou if most of the black commanders agreed: Monte y Tejada, *Historia de Santo Domingo,* 4:88, 106–107.

79. Lacroix, *Mémoires,* 1:229–302.

80. Ardouin, *Études,* 2:87–89. The letters are no longer to be found, but their former existence seems to be corroborated by Monte y Tejada, *Historia de Santo Domingo,* 4:205–207.

81. Laveaux Corresp., 1, Laplace to García, April 4, 1794, not April 14, as given by Pauléus Sannon and others; AGS, GM 7161, May 31, 1794, letter by Casaux de Franqueville. The latter also was describing the situation in early April, when the Spanish deported him to Puerto Rico.

82. Ardouin, *Études,* 2:86; Garran-Coulon, *Rapport sur les troubles de Saint-Domingue,* 4:287, n. 3.

83. See Cousin d'Avallon, *Histoire de Toussaint Louverture,* 56–57.

84. Maurel, *Vent du large,* 300–301.

85. For example, Schoelcher, *Vie de Toussaint-Louverture,* 78, 98, 105; Ott, *The Haitian Revolution,* 78–79; Stoddard, *The French Revolution in San Domingo,* 247; Madiou, *Haïti,* 1:251; Laurent, *Toussaint Louverture à travers sa correspondance,* 108.

86. B. Edwards, *Historical Survey of the Island of St. Domingo* (London, 1801), 186; P.-F. Venault de Charmilly, *Lettre à M. Bryan Edwards* (London, 1797), 147–148.

87. PRO, CO 137/93, Adam Williamson to Henry Dundas, April 28, 1794.

88. The following four paragraphs are based mainly on the UCMM typescripts and Monte y Tejada, *Historia de Santo Domingo,* 4.

89. Ott, *The Haitian Revolution,* 79.

90. See PRO, WO 1/58, f. 170–175; WO 1/59, f. 257–299.

91. PRO, CO 137/92, f. 321.

92. UCMM typescripts, García to duque de la Alcudia, May 16, 1794.

93. For example, in Lacroix, *Mémoires,* 1:296–299; Schoelcher, *Vie de Toussaint-Louverture,* 296–298; Toussaint to Rallier, 26 germinal an VII; Toussaint to Navy Minister, 24 germinal an VII.

94. James, *Black Jacobins*, 135. See the discussion of the fall of Les Cayes (which never took place) in Ott, *The Haitian Revolution*, 78.

95. PRO, CO 137/92, f. 321.

96. Monte y Tejada, *Historia de Santo Domingo*, 4:127, 137–140; Ardouin, *Études*, 2:88, 90.

97. Gros Morne sent envoys to the Spanish in December 1793 and to the British in February 1794, but it seems to have remained unoccupied, maintaining a quasi-independent stance until May or June. See Archives de la Guerre, Vincennes, MS 590; Monte y Tejada, *Historia de Santo Domingo*, 4:164; ANOM, CC9A/8, Laveaux to Sonthonax, February 6, 1794; Laveaux to Commissaires Civils, May 24, 1794; ANOM, CC9A/9, Laveaux to Convention Nationale, 1 vendémiaire an III; Pedro Cabello to Portillo, May 10, 1794.

98. Monte y Tejada, *Historia de Santo Domingo*, 4:201–204.

99. Pauléus Sannon, *Histoire de Toussaint-Louverture*, 1:164–168; Gragnon-Lacoste, *Toussaint*, 76. The former, citing Toussaint's letter of May 18, wrongly has Jean-François's men "poursuivis au Trou et Caracole" instead of "repoussés au Trou et Caracole."

100. Monte y Tejada, *Historia de Santo Domingo*, 4:137–140.

101. ANOM, CC9A/8, Laveaux to Sonthonax, February 6, 1794; Monte y Tejada, *Historia de Santo Domingo*, 4:160–161, 186; PRO, CO 137/92, f. 305, 321.

102. Garran-Coulon, *Rapport sur les troubles de Saint-Domingue*, 4:274–275; Laveaux, *Compte rendu*, 36.

103. Monte y Tejada, *Historia de Santo Domingo*, 4:172–177, 185–186.

104. AGI, SD 1031, García to Alcudia, February 16, 1794.

105. AGS, GM 7157, Jean-François to García, February 13, 1793; AGS, GM 7157, Cabello to Portillo, May 20, 1793; AGS, GM 7157, Citizens Barthélemi and Blondeau to Citizen Thomas, October 24, 1793; AGS, GM 7159, Joseph Laffon to García, March 23, 1794.

106. AGI, Estado 11, José Vasquez to Portillo, December 3, 1793, enclosed in expediente 98.

107. Garran-Coulon, *Rapport sur les troubles de Saint-Domingue*, 4:280–281.

108. PRO, WO 1/59, f. 372; Monte y Tejada, *Historia de Santo Domingo*, 4:204–205.

109. Archives de la Guerre, Vincennes, MS 590, memoir by Charles Dernanancourt.

110. "Mémoire abrégé," *Revue Française d'Histoire d'Outre-Mer* 62 (1975): 470–471; BM, Rouen, MS Montbret 574, f. 311–314. The Spanish deported numerous free men of color to Cuba and Puerto Rico. See Archivo Histórico Nacional, Madrid, Ultramar 6209, exp. 49.

111. PRO, WO 1/59, f. 372; Monte y Tejada, *Historia de Santo Domingo*, 4:204–205.

112. Laveaux, *Compte rendu*, 33–34.

113. PRO, CO 245/2, Toussaint to Rallier, 26 germinal an VII; Toussaint to Navy Minister, 24 germinal an VII, cited in Laurent, *Toussaint*, 96–99. He claimed Jean Rabel was captured by Laveaux after his volte-face.

114. García's sudden abandonment of his offensive on May 11th and his decision a week later to allow Jean-François to free whatever slaves he liked suggest that he knew a watershed had been crossed. Yet he remained unsure and wanted to interview Toussaint personally before deciding. See PRO, WO 1/59, f. 321; AGS, GM 7159, García to Campo de Alange, May 17, 1794. Colonel Lleonart certainly knew what was afoot by May 31st. See Monte y Tejada, *Historia de Santo Domingo*, 4:212–215.

115. Laveaux, *Compte rendu*, 38.

116. AGS, GM 7161, García to Campo de Alange, August 6, 1794. García called Toussaint "a creole black full of maxims, who knows how to keep his hand hidden." The archbishop called him "infamous": AGI, SD 1031, Portillo to Llaguno, August 16, 1794.

117. Toussaint continued to extract supplies from the Spanish frontier towns weekly until he conquered them in mid-October. See AGI, SD 1089, Cabello to García, October 7, 1794.

9. Slave, Soldier, Rebel

1. His age was put at "about 40" in his will dated November 8, 1797 (ANOM, Notariat de Saint-Domingue, maître Cottin), and at "about 42" in his two wills, dated January and July 1798 (collection of Dr. Marcel Châtillon, Paris). These probably understate his age, as his son was then thought to be about 30: ANOM, État Civil, Saint Domingue, 190, f. 133; Notariat de Saint-Domingue, Cottin, October 21, 1797. Kina is twice referred to as an African in contemporary documents by British officers in 1793–1794 and never specifically as a Creole; Lord Colville of Culross private collection, Fife, Scotland, Captain Colville's notebook (unpaginated); PRO, WO 1/59, f. 219. However, in his November 1797 will, he was identified as a native of Tiburon and the natural son of Louison, and at his marriage in 1800 as the son of Louise-Anne. Although his surname is suggestive of African origins, possession of any surname by a slave tended to indicate Creole birth.

2. AD, Besançon, M 696. He was also described as a slave-driver in Jean-Louis Clavier collection, Bordeaux, "Mémoire abrégé des événements de l'île de Saint-Domingue depuis l'année 1789 jusqu'à celle de 1807," f. 50–51. However, the source is not very reliable for events in the south province.

3. F. Carteaux, *Soirées bermudiennes, ou entretiens sur . . . la ruine . . . de Saint Domingue* (Bordeaux, 1802), 297; J.-P. Garran-Coulon, *Rapport sur les troubles de Saint-Domingue* (Paris, 1797–1799), 3:110.

4. MSM, 3:1358. The hamlet of Tiburon contained only thirty-three houses. S. Ducoeurjoly, *Manuel des habitants de Saint-Domingue* (Paris, 1802), part 2, introduction, mentions only 352 whites, but this is clearly a misprint.

5. It is true that the small plantations contained fewer Creoles and in a sense were more homogeneous than the sugar estates in that they contained a much larger bloc of "Congo" slaves, but the probability of two individuals of *any* ethnic group being found on the same plantation was much greater on the large units. See D. Geggus, "Sugar and Coffee Cultivation in Saint Domingue

and the Shaping of the Slave Labor Force," in *Cultivation and Culture: Labor and the Shaping of Slave Life in the Americas,* ed. I. Berlin and P. Morgan (Charlottesville: University Press of Virginia, 1993), 73–98, 318–324.

6. MSM, 3:1355.

7. Commission des Colonies, *Débats entre les accusateurs et les accusés dans l'affaire des colonies* (Paris, 1795), 3:182–187; B. Foubert, *Les habitations Laborde à Saint-Domingue dans la seconde moitié du XVIIIe siècle: contribution à l'histoire d'Haïti* (Lille: Université de Lille III, 1990), 783–823; D. Geggus, "The Arming of Slaves in the Haitian Revolution," in *The Arming of Slaves: From Classical Times to the Modern Age,* ed. P. Morgan and C. Brown (Yale University Press, forthcoming).

8. Letter of March 24, 1792, in *Moniteur Général de la Partie Françoise de Saint-Domingue* 155 (1793); Commission des Colonies, *Débats,* 3:186; PRO, T 81/27, document 26.

9. *Moniteur Général de la Partie Françoise de Saint-Domingue* 40 (1791).

10. Cited in B. Foubert, "Les volontaires nationaux de l'Aube et de la Seine Inférieure à Saint Domingue," *Bulletin de la Société d'Histoire de la Guadeloupe* 51 (1982): 37.

11. ANOM, F3/141, f. 370.

12. See PH, 1:204, 270; P.-F. Venault de Charmilly, *Lettre á M. Bryan Edwards* (London, 1797), 112.

13. See Colville of Culross collection, Capt. Colville's notebook; PRO, WO 1/59, f. 219.

14. PRO, T 81/27, document 26. The Spanish silver dollar, called *gourde* in Saint Domingue, was worth 8.25 *livres coloniales,* or 5.5 *livres tournois.* The corps may on occasion have reached 400 men. See C. Fick, *The Making of Haiti: The Saint Domingue Revolution from Below* (Knoxville: University of Tennessee Press, 1990), 314.

15. ANOM, F3/141, f. 400–401.

16. Fick, *The Making of Haiti,* 142–144. Les Platons is a fairly low, but steep-sided, plateau adjoining the plain, not the high, inaccessible mountain of legend.

17. See above, Chapter 7.

18. Foubert, "Les volontaires nationaux," 37; AN, Section Moderne, Dxxv/20/206, f. 1–3.

19. Françoise Thésée, "Les assemblées paroissiales des Cayes à Saint-Domingue (1774–1793)," *RSHHG* no. 137 (1982): 174–176; PH, 1:105. Neither measure was carried out, apparently because of planter parsimony.

20. Cited in Foubert, "Les volontaires nationaux," 37.

21. PRO, T 81/27, doc. 26. Equivalent to 10 *livres tournois,* the French *pistole* coin was worth 15 *livres coloniales* but probably was used here as a unit of 10 *livres.*

22. See Jean Kina's will, dated January 13, 1798, Marcel Châtillon collection. Les Irois is about four or five hours' walk from Tiburon on the other side of Carcasses Bay.

23. A. Cabon, *Histoire d'Haïti* (Port-au-Prince: Ed. La Petite Revue, n.d.), 3:164; Fick, *The Making of Haiti,* 210.

24. Colville of Culross collection, Capt. Colville's notebook. "Coromantee" flutes cannot be taken as evidence of likely ethnicity. The captain was thinking of Jamaica. "Caramenty" (Akan-Ga-speakers) were rare in Saint Domingue. See Geggus, "Sugar and Coffee Cultivation," 81.

25. PRO, WO 1/59, f. 219; WO 1/623, f. 429–432.

26. AN, Dxxv/20, letters of Jean Kina, "Colonnel des Affricains sous les ordres du Roy."

27. Devon Record Office, Exeter, Simcoe Papers, 0/17/1, June 20, 1797; PRO, CO 137/93, Williamson to Dundas, April 28, 1794.

28. See Venault de Charmilly, *Lettre à M. Bryan Edwards,* 145–147.

29. PRO, WO 1/59, f. 219.

30. PRO, WO 1/62, f. 5–10.

31. Desertions from the Chasseurs were fewer than from other British regiments until the last campaign.

32. BN, Manuscrits, F.fr. 12103, Laveaux Correspondence, letter by Jean-François, June 11, 1795.

33. See David Geggus, *Slavery, War and Revolution: The British Occupation of Saint Domingue, 1793–1798* (Oxford: Oxford University Press, 1982), 182, 199, 414, 447; C. L. R. James, *The Black Jacobins: Toussaint L'Ouverture and the San Domingo Revolution* (New York: Vintage, 1963), 124–126; A. Césaire, *Toussaint Louverture: La Révolution française et le problème colonial* (Paris: Présence Africaine, 1962), 182–184; J. Thornton, "'I am the subject of the King of Congo': African Political Ideology and the Haitian Revolution," *Journal of World History* 4 (1993): 181–214.

34. PRO, T 81/14, decree of December 28, 1795.

35. PH, 1:108 and 204; PRO, CO 245/5, October 30, 1795.

36. PRO, CO 245/5, report, November 28, 1795.

37. PRO, T 64/226B, document 10c.

38. PRO T 81/27, doc. 26; PRO, WO 1/66, f. 529–530. In the latter piece, a letter to the king, Kina referred to himself (in French) as "the no. 1 negro . . . devoted to your government in this island," and signed himself "Colonel Commandant of the Chasseurs of George III, Mountain Warrior of Saint Domingue."

39. Littlehales Papers, collection of Mrs. P. Spencer Bernard, Nether Winchendon, England.

40. Kina's July 1798 will refers to her as "Minerve Nsse L. appartenante [autrefois?] à la dame veuve Dubuq"—hence a freed slave, probably not baptized. She was probably African-born, as in the same sentence another *négresse libre* is referred to as *créole.* Zamor's name would seem further evidence that Christian influences were not strong in the family, although in one document he is referred to as Jacques Zamor.

41. The January 1798 will describes her as *marabout,* that is, "five-eighths black." Her father was a *pêcheur propriétaire* (fisherman with his own boat).

42. PH, 1:270.

43. Venault de Charmilly, *Lettre,* 112.

44. ANOM, État Civil, Saint Domingue, 190, f. 133; Marcel Châtillon collection, testament of January 1798; ANOM, Notariat, Saint Domingue, *maître* Cottin, October 21, 1797.

45. ANOM, État Civil, Saint Domingue, 190, f. 135.

46. PH, 1:298.

47. PRO, T 81/27, doc. 26. Of the thirty-seven purchased in October 1796, eight died in nine months.

48. PRO, WO 1/623, f. 525–535.

49. Address by Louis de Curt in PRO, WO 1/36, f. 195, and in *Paris pendant l'année* 31 (1801): 405–409. This appears to be the source for the extracts in H. Grégoire, *De la littérature des nègres* (Paris, 1808), 101; and S. Daney, *Histoire de la Martinique* (Fort Royal, 1846), 5:404–406.

50. This is the sum Kina mentions in his 1801 petition; PRO, WO 1/623, f. 525–535. However, the Saint Domingo Claims Board Papers mention pensions of only 5 pounds and 2 pounds 10 shillings, based on a ministerial recommendation of April 1799: PRO, T 81/1 (unpaginated).

51. He was described in 1804 as "scarcely knowing the French language": Alfred Nemours, *Histoire de la captivité et de la mort de Toussaint-Louverture* (Paris: Berger-Levrault, 1929), 265. Of course he knew Creole and perhaps African languages as well, but they could have done little to reduce his linguistic isolation, even though London then had a large black population.

52. It is printed in Nemours, *Histoire de la captivité,* 91–92.

53. PRO, WO 1/623, f. 525–535; PRO, WO 1/36, f. 195.

54. PH, 1:184.

55. PRO, WO 1/36, f. 9–18, 503; PRO, WO 1/36. f. 195.

56. PRO, WO 1/36. f. 195; see also PRO, WO 1/36, f. 503.

57. See Chapter 8 in this volume.

58. E. Hayot, *Les gens de couleur libres du Fort-Royal, 1679–1823* (Paris: Société française d'histoire d'Outre-Mer, 1971), is the source of all genealogical details. I have assumed that witnesses at family weddings and baptisms were friends. Fort Royal is present-day Fort de France.

59. PRO, CO 319/6, Trigge to Portland, December 17, 1800.

60. For a fuller account of Kina's stay in Martinique, see D. Geggus, "Esclaves et gens de couleur libres de la Martinique pendant l'époque révolutionnaire et napoléonienne: trois moments de résistance," *Revue Historique* 295 (1996): 121–127, or its abridged version, "The Slaves and Free Coloreds of Martinique during the Age of the French and Haitian Revolutions: Three Moments of Resistance," in *Parts beyond the Seas: The Lesser Antilles in the Age of European Expansion,* ed. S. Engerman and R. Paquette (Gainesville: University of Florida Press, 1996), 291–294.

61. PRO, CO 319/6, Trigge to Portland, December 17, 1800.

62. PRO, WO 1/36, f. 515–520, legal depositions by eyewitnesses.

63. PRO, WO 1/36, f. 9–18.

64. See Chapter 10 in this volume.

65. PRO, WO 1/36, f. 195.

66. PRO, CO 166/5, f. 136–137; PRO, WO 1/36, f. 187–190. For evidence that the insurrection was attributed in Martinique to British machiavellianism, see above, note 54; and Hayot, *Les gens de couleur libres du Fort-Royal,* 134.

67. PH, 1:184.

68. PRO, WO 1/623, f. 525–535.

69. PRO, HO 50/390, f. 189–191; PRO, CO 166/4 and 5, various letters.

70. PRO, T 29/77.

71. PRO, WO 1/623, f. 525–535.

72. The following is based on AD, Besançon, M 696, papers relating to the imprisonment of Jean and Zamor Kina, of which copies were kindly sent me by the late Gabriel Debien. This source was also used in Nemours, *Histoire de la captivité.*

73. C. Auguste and M. Auguste, *Les déportés de Saint-Domingue: contribution à l'histoire de l'expédition française de Saint-Domingue, 1802–1803* (Sherbrooke, Quebec: Éditions Naaman, 1979), 111, 119.

74. The Pioneer (later, Royal African) Battalion was created in May 1803 from metropolitan black companies and deportees from Guadeloupe. Decimated in combat in 1806, it was transferred to Naples in 1807. The Kinas do not appear among its officers. See Auguste, *Les déportés de Saint-Domingue,* 76–80. Hayot (*Les gens de couleur libres du Fort-Royal,* 135) suggested Kina may have died in the United States, but this seems to be a confused rumor.

10. Racial Equality, Slavery, and Colonial Secession during the Constituent Assembly

1. The distant Indian Ocean colonies of Île de France and Île Bourbon were less affected by the French Revolution than were the West Indian islands, and they had little impact on revolutionary politics. Of the Caribbean colonies, Saint Domingue was by far the most important economically and as a foyer of revolution.

2. M. B. Garrett, *The French Colonial Question, 1789–1791* (New York: Negro University Press, 1916), iii.

3. G. Rudé, *The French Revolution after 200 Years* (New York: Weidenfeld and Nicholson, 1988); D. G. M. Sutherland, *France, 1789–1815: Revolution and Counterrevolution* (New York: Oxford University Press, 1987); S. Schama, *Citizens: A Chronicle of the French Revolution* (New York: Knopf, 1989).

4. J. Roberts, *French Revolution Documents* (New York: Blackwell, 1966); J. Hardman, *French Revolution Documents,* vol. 2 (Oxford: Blackwell, 1973); P. Kropotkine, *La Grande Révolution, 1789–1793* (Paris: Stock, 1909); P. Gaxotte, *La Révolution Française* (1928; reprint, Paris: Fayard, 1975); A. de Tocqueville, *L'Ancien Régime,* ed. G. W. Headlam (Oxford: Oxford University Press, 1904), 269. Tocqueville gave the impression that the aristocracy's cahiers called for ending slavery and the slave trade, which was true of only a tiny number.

5. J. Godechot, *La Grande Nation* (Paris: Aubier, 1956); R. R. Palmer, *The Age of the Democratic Revolution*, 2 vols. (Princeton: Princeton University Press, 1959, 1964).

6. R. Stein, *The French Sugar Business* (Baton Rouge: Louisiana State University Press, 1988); N. Deerr, *History of Sugar*, 2 vols. (London: Chapman and Hall, 1949–1950); J. Tarrade, *Le commerce colonial à la fin de l'Ancien Régime: l'évolution du régime de l'Exclusif de 1763 à 1789* (Paris: Presses universitaires de France, 1972).

7. In W. Doyle, *Oxford History of the French Revolution* (Oxford: Oxford University Press, 1989), four of the ten indexed entries under "slavery" refer to metaphorical usage.

8. Published population statistics are very unreliable; they are investigated in D. Geggus, "The Major Port Towns of Saint Domingue in the Late Eighteenth Century," in *Atlantic Port Cities: Economy, Culture, and Society*, ed. F. Knight and P. Liss (Knoxville: University of Tennessee Press, 1991), 87–116. Newly arrived African adults sold in Saint Domingue for close to 2,000 *livres tournois* in 1789. Locally born and skilled slaves could be worth considerably more, but children and the aged were less valued, and prices were somewhat lower in the other colonies.

9. J. Jaurès, *Histoire socialiste, 1789–1900* (Paris: Librairie de l'Humanité, 1924), 1:574; A. Césaire, *Toussaint Louverture: La Révolution française et le problème colonial* (Paris: Présence Africaine, 1962), 21–22.

10. Y. Bénot, *La Révolution française et la fin des colonies* (Paris: La Découverte, 1988), 205–217.

11. D. B. Davis, *The Problem of Slavery in Western Culture* (Ithaca: Cornell University Press, 1966), Chapters 13–15; W. B. Cohen, *The French Encounter with Africans* (Bloomington: Indiana University Press, 1980), 130–154; R. Toumson, ed., *La période Révolutionnaire aux Antilles* (Schoelcher: Groupe de Recherche et d'Étude des Littératures et Civilisations de la Caraïbe et des Amériques Noires, 1989).

12. P. Pluchon, *Nègres et Juifs au XVIIIe siècle* (Paris: Tallandier, 1984), 148–157, 246–247, 263–283; P. Boulle, "In Defense of Slavery: Eighteenth Century Opposition to Abolition and the Origins of a Racist Ideology in France," in *History from Below*, ed. F. Krantz (Oxford: Blackwell, 1988), 219–246; Cohen, *French Encounter with Africans*, 60–99.

13. Bénot, *La Révolution française*, 21–41; G. Debien, *Les esclaves aux Antilles françaises, XVIIe et XVIIIe siècles* (Basse-Terre: Société d'histoire de la Guadeloupe, 1974), 488–490.

14. *Discours sur la nécessité d'établir à Paris une société pour concourir ... à l'abolition de la traite et de l'esclavage des Nègres* (Paris, 1788). For lack of documentation, the society has been the subject of only sporadic, article-length studies; most recently F. Thésée, "Autour de la Société des Amis des Noirs," *Présence Africaine*, 125 (1983): 3–82. However, the appearance of the society's *procès-verbaux* in the 1982 sale of the Brissot de Warville Papers promises to yield more extensive research. For an incisive sketch of the

group's deficiencies, see D. B. Davis, *The Problem of Slavery in the Age of Revolution* (Ithaca: Cornell University Press, 1975), 95–100.

15. Seymour Drescher argues that a mass base was vital to the British antislavery movement, although in France, abolitionism eventually triumphed in the nineteenth century without gaining much mass support: S. Drescher, *Capitalism and Antislavery: British Mobilization in Comparative Perspective* (New York: Oxford University Press, 1986); "Two Variants of Anti-Slavery," in *Anti-slavery, Religion, and Reform: Essays in Memory of Roger Anstey,* ed. C. Bolt and S. Drescher (Folkestone: Dawson Archon, 1980), 43–63. This argument is somewhat modified in Drescher, "British Way, French Way: Opinion Building and Revolution in the Second French Slave Emancipation," *American Historical Review* 96 (1991): 709–734. Moreover, the French Revolution also accomplished many reforms, from civil rights for Jews to the abolition of the nobility, for which popular support was not evident in 1789.

16. B. F. Hyslop, *French Nationalism in 1789 According to the General Cahiers* (New York: Columbia University Press, 1934), 142, 276–277; AP, 7:296–297.

17. *Journal de l'Assemblée Nationale,* 1 (1789): 8; Anon., *Lettre à MM. les députés des trois ordres* (Paris, 1789), 30.

18. *Journal des États-Généraux,* 1 (1789): 260; *Journal de l'Assemblée Nationale,* 1 (1789): 244–248, 255–257; AP, 8:165, 186–187.

19. R. I. Wilberforce and S. Wilberforce, *Life of William Wilberforce* (London, 1838), 1:229–230.

20. J. Thibau, *Le temps de Saint-Domingue: l'esclavage et la Révolution Française* (Paris: J. C. Lattès, 1989), 147.

21. *Journal de l'Assemblée Nationale,* 1 (1789): 249, 257.

22. Bénot, *La Révolution française,* 107–108.

23. *Journal de Versailles* 125 (March 4, 1790); H. Gough, *The Newspaper Press in the French Revolution* (Chicago: Dorsey, 1988), 55; Thésée, "Autour de la Société des Amis des Noirs," 63.

24. Thésée, "Autour de la Société des Amis des Noirs," 59.

25. Ibid., 35–36, 79–82. Abolition had been under consideration by the British Parliament since 1788, and a bill would eventually pass the House of Commons, though not the House of Lords, in 1792.

26. R. Anstey, "A Reinterpretation of the Abolition of the British Slave Trade, 1806–1807," *English Historical Review* 87 (1972): 304–332; S. Drescher, *Econocide: British Slavery in the Era of Abolition* (Pittsburgh: Pittsburgh University Press, 1977), 214–223.

27. AP, 12:68–73; Thésée, "Autour de la Société des Amis des Noirs," 71.

28. *Les Affiches Américaines* (Feuille du Cap-François), 14 July 1790, 1.

29. The classic study is G. Debien, *Les colons de Saint-Domingue et la Révolution française: essai sur le Club Massiac* (Paris: A. Colin, 1953). The statement in R. Blackburn, *The Overthrow of Colonial Slavery* (London: Verso, 1988), 178–179 that articles in the press warned that emancipation would lead to the dis-

tribution of property in France seems to be based on a misreading of Debien, *Les colons de Saint-Domingue*, 185.

30. O. de Gouges, *Réponse au champion Américain* (Paris, 1790); Thésée, "Autour de la Société des Amis des Noirs," 63; A. Bonnemain, *Régénération des colonies* (Paris, 1792), 3.

31. AP, 12:68–69.

32. Marquis de Condorcet, *Au corps électoral contre l'esclavage des noirs* (Paris, 1789), in *Oeuvres complètes de Condorcet* (Brunswick, 1804), 16:147–157; *Lettre à MM. les députés des trois ordres* (Paris, 1789); H. Grégoire, *Mémoire en faveur des gens de couleur libres ou sang-mêlés de St.-Domingue* (Paris, 1789); *Patriote François* 119 (December 5, 1789) and 121 (December 7, 1789).

33. AP, 11:38; 12:68–69.

34. For differing assessments of "Creole autonomism" see G. Debien, *Esprit colon et esprit d'autonomie* (Paris: Larose, 1954); C. Frostin, "L'Histoire de l'esprit autonomiste colon à Saint-Domingue aux XVIIe et XVIIIe siècles" (Thèse de doctorat d'état, Paris I, 1972); D. Geggus, *Slavery, War and Revolution: The British Occupation of Saint Domingue, 1793–1798* (Oxford: Oxford University Press, 1982), 16–18, 31–32, 35–37, 46–78.

35. AP, 8:138, 10:266–267; 11:38; 12:381–387; P. Laborie, *Réflexions sommaires adressées à la France et à la colonie de Saint-Domingue* (Paris, 1789), 13–14; Garrett, *The French Colonial Question*, 12. The deputy de Cocherel's claim to "envision with equanimity the end of the slave trade," mentioned in Boulle, "In Defense of Slavery," 232, was really an artful reminder that planters could buy more cheaply from British than French traders.

36. From August onward, colonists in Paris were writing home that the Amis des Noirs might try to foment a slave revolt. Colonial radicals in Saint Domingue used such fears to mobilize support and undermine the administration. See ANOM, C9/162, Peinier to La Luzerne, October 24, 1790; ANOM, C9/163, Peinier to La Luzerne, November 12, 1789; L. Gatereau, *Histoire des troubles de Saint-Domingue* (Paris, 1792), 12–14.

37. *Patriote François* 117 (December 3, 1789); 133 (December 24, 1789); 144 (December 30, 1789); AP, 11:38, 710.

38. "Yes, the cry of liberty rings out in two Worlds; it needs only an Othello, a Padrejean, to awaken in the soul of the Negroes a sense of their inalienable rights": Grégoire, *Mémoire en faveur des gens de couleur*, 35–36. Padrejean had led a slave revolt in seventeenth-century Saint Domingue.

39. J.-P. Garran-Coulon, *Rapport sur les troubles de Saint-Domingue* (Paris, 1797–1799), 1:127.

40. Only seven deputies had opposed the March 8th decree. Two plans for slave emancipation were put to the assemblies: one by Viefville des Essarts in May 1791, the other by Blanc-Gilli in December 1791. Neither was discussed.

41. AP, 26:60.

42. Brissot's sense of urgency regarding the trade was not misplaced. In 1789, 83 slave ships sailed from Nantes and Bordeaux alone, and in 1790, more than 40,000 Africans were sold just in Saint Domingue. J. Mettas, *Répertoire des*

expéditions négrières au XVIIIe siècle, ed. S. Daget and M. Daget. 2 vols. (Paris: Société française d'histoire d'Outre-Mer, 1978, 1984); *Les Affiches Améri-caines*, 1790, port statistics.

43. A. Lebeau, *De la condition des gens de couleur libres sous l'Ancien Régime* (Poitiers: A. Masson, 1903); Geggus, *Slavery, War and Revolution*, 18–23; J. Garrigus, "Between Servitude and Citizenship: Free Coloreds in Pre-Revolutionary Saint Domingue" (Ph.D. diss., Johns Hopkins University, 1988).

44. Y. Debbasch, *Couleur et liberté: le jeu du critère ethnique dans un ordre juridique esclavagiste* (Paris: Dalloz, 1967), 141–142, 157–159, and passim.

45. Debbasch, *Couleur et liberté*, 144–166, is the most detailed study. The account in Debien, *Les colons de Saint-Domingue*, 153–165, probably overrates the influence of the Amis des Noirs and Julien Raimond but seems the more accu-rate with regard to chronology. Each relied on different copies of the Club Massiac's papers.

46. MSM, 1:83–111. On literacy, see D. Geggus, "Slave and Free Colored Women in Saint Domingue," in *More Than Chattel: Black Women in Slavery*, ed. D. B. Gaspar and D. C. Hine (Bloomington: Indiana University Press, 1996), 271.

47. Highlighted by some right-wing historians, they are generally ignored by those on the left. During the revolutionary era in the Caribbean, free blacks often aligned themselves either with whites or with slaves rather than with other free coloreds: AN, Section Moderne, Dxxv/78/771, Marcat to Brissot, April 30, 1791; Geggus, *Slavery, War and Revolution*, 325–326, 330; D. Geggus, "The French and Haitian Revolutions, and Resistance to Slavery in the Ameri-cas," *Revue Française d'Histoire d'Outre-Mer* 232–233 (1989): 109–111.

48. *Précis des gémissements des sang-mêlés dans les colonies françoises, par J. M. C. Américain, Sang-mêlé* (Paris, 1789), 7, 9, 10, 13. It does call in passing for the implementation of the defunct Code Noir of 1685, which had accorded equal status to all freemen, irrespective of color, but the author's other comments belie this suggestion.

49. Mulattoes were persons of black and white parentage; quadroons, of white and mulatto parentage.

50. Césaire, *Toussaint Louverture*, 86, and Debbasch, *Couleur et liberté*, 151, show a radical change in Raimond's proposals between August 26 and 28, but their accounts are clearly confused. To judge from Debien's earlier study (*Les colons de Saint-Domingue*, 158) they seem to have been misled by a false rumor spread by a colonist. On Raimond's background, see J. Garrigus, "The Free Colored Elite of Pre-Revolutionary Saint Domingue: The Case of Julien Rai-mond," in *Brown Power in the Caribbean*, ed. D. B. Gaspar and G. Heuman (forthcoming).

51. Not the brilliant lawyer of legend, Ogé was an unsuccessful merchant from Saint Domingue who was then pursuing a lawsuit in Paris. When later interro-gated in the colony, he commented that "he had never been friendly with any free blacks and . . . he scarcely knew any." See AN, Dxxv/58/574, interroga-tion of Ogé.

52. Debbasch, *Couleur et liberté*, 146–154; Debien, *Les colons de Saint-Domingue*, 164.

53. AP, 9:476–478; 10:329–333; Debbasch, *Couleur et liberté*, 153–154.

54. Debien, *Les colons de Saint-Domingue,* 164; Debbasch, *Couleur et liberté,* 149, 151.

55. AP, 10:329–334, annex to session of November 28. Apparently not presented to the Constituent Assembly, the address was published in the next day's *Moniteur.* Two weeks before, the society had denied any prejudice toward free blacks and proposed to defend itself in the press against the charge: AN, Dxxv/111, *procès-verbal,* November 14, 1789.

56. In A. Brette, "Les gens de couleur libres et leurs députés en 1789," *La Révolution Française* 29 (1895): 399; and Garrett, *The French Colonial Question,* 4.

57. The change occurred between numbers 110 (November 26, 1789) and 117 (December 3, 1789). See Grégoire, *Mémoire en faveur,* 25; AP, 10:333.

58. In the summer of 1789, a minority of colonists in Saint Domingue and Paris had shown themselves favorable in some degree to the free coloreds' aspirations, and this doubtless had encouraged hopes for an accommodation: C.-L.-M. Milscent, *Du régime colonial* (Paris, 1792), 5; Garran-Coulon, *Rapport sur les troubles de Saint-Domingue,* 1:106, 2:3–8; Debien, *Les colons de Saint-Domingue,* 156–169.

59. See Brissot's *Lettre à MM. les députés; Patriote François* 65 (October 9, 1789) onward; and Grégoire's *Mémoire en faveur* and *Lettre aux philanthropes sur . . . les réclamations des gens de couleur* (Paris, 1790). Only after some free blacks were enfranchised by the decree of May 15, 1789, did Grégoire really begin using the term: *Lettre aux citoyens de couleur, et nègres libres* (Paris, 1791), particularly p. 2, where he switches from the vocative case to refer to his past efforts on behalf of "mixed-bloods." The contrast is all the more striking with his posthumous memoirs, in which he uses the phrases "free blacks and mulattoes" and "free blacks and mixed bloods": *Mémoires de Grégoire,* ed. H. Carnot (Paris, 1837), 1:391–392.

60. A. de Cournand, *Requête présentée à Nosseigneurs de l'Assemblée Nationale en faveur des gens de couleur de l'île de Saint Domingue* [Paris, 1789?], 2, 10, 11.

61. É. Clavière, *Adresse de la Société des Amis des Noirs à l'Assemblée Nationale* (Paris, 1791), xii, 48, 56, 69–70, 111; *Lettres des diverses Sociétés des Amis de la Constitution qui réclament les droits de Citoyen actif en faveur des hommes de couleur des Colonies* (Paris, 1791), 8, 9, 16, 18.

62. In Saint Domingue, they constituted about one-third of free coloreds.

63. AP, 9:476–478; Grégoire, *Lettre aux philanthropes,* 5–6; *Patriote François* 119 (December 5, 1789).

64. *Patriote François* 65 (October 9, 1789); 77 (October 23, 1789); 121 (December 7, 1789); Grégoire, *Lettre aux citoyens,* 13; Julien Raymond, *Réflexions sur les véritables causes des troubles* (Paris, 1793), 21–29; Bénot, *La Révolution française,* 79–80, 128.

65. Thésée, "Autour la Société des Amis des Noirs," 17.

66. AP, 10:330; V. Ogé, *Motion faite par M. Vincent Ogé, jeune à l'Assemblée des Colons* (Paris, 1789), 5; Debien, *Les colons de Saint-Domingue,* 160. Ogé is usually remembered for rigidly excluding slaves from the rebellion he led in Saint Domingue a year later.

67. *Patriote François* 117 (December 3, 1789); Grégoire, *Mémoire en faveur,* 33, 51; Grégoire, *Lettre aux philanthropes,* 14; *Moniteur Universel* (February 16, 1790).

68. *Moniteur Universel* (February 16, 1790).

69. Debien, *Les colons de Saint-Domingue,* 190–196.

70. AP, 12:381–387, 25:738.

71. Grégoire, *Lettre aux philanthropes,* 1–2.

72. Milscent, *Du régime colonial,* 5; Garran-Coulon, *Rapport sur les troubles de Saint-Domingue,* 1:106, 2:3–8; Debien, *Les colons de Saint-Domingue,* 156–169.

73. Gatereau, *Histoire des troubles de Saint Domingue,* 19–21; Debbasch, *Couleur et liberté,* 169–172.

74. AP, 25:636–640, 743, 755.

75. The rebellion remained a local affair, true to Debbasch's characterization of free colored politics as fractured and isolated. The parish where it occurred, however, appears to have been in early contact with the movement in Paris. See Marcel Châtillon collection, Paris, Brissot Papers, petition of Grande Rivière free coloreds, November 11, 1789. Early in 1790, moreover, Ogé's elder brother had been killed leading free colored petitioners in the neighboring west province: AN, Dxxv/72/718, Verrier to Legrand, February 25, 1790; Dxxv/58/574, interrogation of Ogé.

76. Blackburn, *The Overthrow of Colonial Slavery,* 187, 210.

77. AP, 25:737, 26:357–360; *Lettres importantes relatives à la question des citoyens de couleur* (Paris, 1791), 1–3; *Lettres des diverses sociétés,* 6–7.

78. Blackburn, *The Overthrow of Colonial Slavery,* 185–188.

79. See M. Kennedy, *The Jacobin Clubs in the French Revolution* (Princeton: Princeton University Press, 1982), 204–209; C.-L.-M. Milscent, *Sur les troubles de Saint-Domingue* (Paris, 1792), and *Lettres des diverses sociétés.* Like Ogé, Milscent was from the central mountains of the north province.

80. C. L. R. James, *The Black Jacobins: Toussaint L'Ouverture and the San Domingo Revolution* (New York: Vintage, 1963), 67–68, 75–76; Bénot, *La Révolution française,* 86–87, 200–201.

81. Kennedy, *The Jacobin Clubs,* 209; AP, 30:123.

82. Opponents of the free coloreds did not attack them in racist terms in the formal debate; instead, they argued for the utility of prejudice as a stabilizing force in slave society. The role of racist ideas is difficult to pin down; historians disagree about the prevalence of "biological racism" in this period. This is partly because the then influential theories of Buffon can be interpreted as both biological and environmental.

83. The number of beneficiaries would have been further limited by the probable need for the parents to have been legally married in order to prove the father's status. Even so, the oft-repeated statement that in Saint Domingue the decree affected only 400 persons seems scarcely credible.

84. AP, 30:118–119; Geggus, *Slavery, War and Revolution,* 51–52.

85. Slave-holding within France was also abolished at this time, but, like the

status of non-whites in France, this had never been an issue. Even the colonial deputy Cocherel had suggested in November 1789 that all blacks should be free so long as they stayed in France: AP, 10:266.

86. The insurgents claimed to be defenders of the king, who was said to have passed an emancipation decree. This was to be a common feature of American slave rebellions for forty years. See Geggus, "French and Haitian Revolutions," 119–121.

87. Geggus, *Slavery, War and Revolution*, 52–54.

88. James, *Black Jacobins*, passim; Césaire, *Toussaint Louverture*, 21–22, 159, 308–309.

89. See, for example, E. C. Paul, *Questions d'histoire (Études critiques)* (Port-au-Prince: Imprimerie de l'État, 1956); S.-V. Jean-Baptiste, *Haïti: sa lutte pour l'émancipation* (Paris: Nef, 1957); E. Rüsch, *Die Revolution von Saint Domingue* (Hamburg: Friedrichsen, De Gruyter, 1930); J. Saintoyant, *La colonisation française pendant la Révolution*, 2 vols. (Paris: Renaissance du Livre, 1930).

90. Bénot, *La Révolution française*, 7–9, 18–20; Blackburn, *The Overthrow of Colonial Slavery*, 185–190, 195, 222–225, 230.

91. Bénot, *La Révolution française*, 75, 86–87, 200–204, 217; Blackburn, *The Overthrow of Colonial Slavery*, 223; James, *Black Jacobins*, 75–77, 120, 139.

92. Bénot, *La Révolution française*, 130; R. L. Stein, *Léger-Félicité Sonthonax: The Lost Sentinel of the Republic* (Rutherford, N.J.: Fairleigh Dickinson University Press, 1985), 21. Exactly three years later in Saint Domingue, Sonthonax had African-born Jean-Baptiste Mars Belley elected deputy and sent to Paris to plead for general emancipation. Ironically, he was one of the very few former slave-owners to sit in the French Convention: ANOM, Notariat, Saint-Domingue, reg. 1012, contract dated June 19, 1787.

93. AP, 12:68–73; AP 25:749, 755; AP 31:281–282, 294; Thibau, *Le temps de Saint-Domingue*, 252; Bénot, *La Révolution française*, 37–39; Boulle, "Défense," 232, 240.

94. Jaurès, *Histoire socialiste*, 1:574; James, *Black Jacobins*, 80–81.

95. Bénot, *La Révolution française*, 138.

96. On these see Frostin, "Histoire de l'esprit autonomiste"; Debbasch, *Couleur et liberté*; D. Geggus, *Slave Resistance Studies and the Saint Domingue Slave Revolt* (Miami: Florida International University, Occasional Papers Series, 1983); and Chapter 5 in this volume.

97. Geggus, *Slavery, War and Revolution*, 33–37; Palmer, *The Age of the Democratic Revolution*.

98. A. Pérotin-Dumon, "Les Jacobins des Antilles ou l'esprit de liberté dans les Îles-du-Vent," *Revue d'Histoire Moderne et Contemporaine* 35 (1988): 275, 302–304.

99. Pérotin-Dumon, "Jacobins," 284–290, 303; Geggus, *Slavery, War and Revolution*, 43–44.

100. Geggus, *Slavery, War and Revolution*, 46–78.

101. P. Dessalles, *Historique des troubles survenus à la Martinique*, ed. Leo Elisabeth

(Fort de France, n.d.), 17–30; H. Lémery, *La Révolution française à la Martinique* (Paris: Larose, 1936), 22–26.

102. Exactly how such rumors functioned, and their relative importance for leaders and masses, raise the intractable problem of the psychology of subordination, which is likely to remain insoluble: see Chapter 4.

103. E. Genovese, *From Rebellion to Revolution: Afro-American Slave Revolts in the Making of the Modern World* (Baton Rouge: Louisiana State University Press, 1979); Geggus, "French and Haitian Revolutions," 119–123.

104. *Moniteur Universel* 305 (November 1, 1791); J.-P. Brissot, *Discours de J.-P. Brissot . . . sur les causes des troubles de Saint-Domingue* (Paris, 1791), 4; Milscent, *Sur les troubles,* 3, 11–14.

11. The Great Powers and the Haitian Revolution

1. A good recent account is C. Fick, *The Making of Haiti: The Saint Domingue Revolution from Below* (Knoxville: University of Tennessee Press, 1990), Chapter 4. A simultaneous civil war between the white and free colored populations in other parts of the colony does much to explain why the revolt was not suppressed.

2. Both the threat and the stimulus have been generally exaggerated, however. Through the 1790s, the Caribbean witnessed about four slave revolts or conspiracies per year, but the example of Saint Domingue was far from being the only cause: D. Geggus, "The French and Haitian Revolutions and Resistance to Slavery in the Americas," *Revue Française d'Histoire d'Outre-Mer* 282–283 (1989): 107–124. Similarly, even without the slave revolution, the continuing expansion of the Atlantic market would have increased Caribbean production: D. Eltis, *Economic Growth and the Ending of the Atlantic Slave Trade* (New York: Oxford University Press, 1987), 37–38.

3. D. Geggus, "Jamaica and the Saint Domingue Slave Revolt, 1791–1793," *The Americas* 38 (1981): 223.

4. J. Scott, "The Common Wind: Currents of Afro-American Communication in the Era of the Haitian Revolution" (Ph.D. diss., Duke University, 1986); D. Geggus, "Slavery, War, and Revolution in the Greater Caribbean, 1789–1815," in *A Turbulent Time: The French Revolution and the Greater Caribbean,* ed. D. B. Gaspar and D. P. Geggus (Bloomington: Indiana University Press, 1997).

5. F. de Arango y Parreño, *Obras de D. Francisco de Arango y Parreño* (Havana: Ministerio de Educación, 1952), 1:134; M. Moreno Fraginals, *The Sugarmill: The Socioeconomic Complex of Sugar in Cuba* (New York: Monthly Review Press, 1976), 28; M. Zeuske and C. Munford, "Die 'Grosse Furcht' in der Karibik: Saint Domingue und Kuba (1789–1795)," *Zeitschrift für Geschichtswissenschaft* 39 (1991): 51–59.

6. Geggus, "Jamaica and the Saint Domingue Slave Revolt," 222; Eltis, *Economic Growth,* 42, 245; M. Moreno Fraginals, *El ingenio: Complejo económico social cubano del azúcar* (Havana: Editorial de Ciencias Sociales, 1978), 1:40–42; Francisco Pérez de la Riva, *El Café: Historia de su cultivo y explotación en Cuba*

(Havana: J. Montero, 1944), 51; S. Drescher, *Econocide: British Slavery in the Era of Abolition* (Pittsburgh: Pittsburgh University Press, 1977), 79.

7.   Geggus, "Jamaica and the Saint Domingue Slave Revolt, 1791–93," 220–221, 227–228; *Moniteur Général de la Partie Françoise de Saint Domingue* (1792), no. 55.

8.   T. Matthewson, "George Washington's Policy towards the Haitian Revolution," *Diplomatic History* 3 (1979): 321–336; R. Logan, *The Diplomatic Relations of the United States with Haiti, 1776–1891* (Chapel Hill: University of North Carolina Press, 1941), 33–39.

9.   J. Coatsworth, "American Trade with European Colonies in the Caribbean and South America, 1790–1812," *William and Mary Quarterly* 24 (1967): 243–266. However, the claim in Moreno Fraginals, *The Sugarmill*, 27, 158, that in Cuba "the late 18th century sugar boom was largely financed by U.S. firms" remains unproven.

10.   AGI, SD 954–955; J. L. Franco, *Documentos para la historia de Haití en el Archivo Nacional* (Havana: Archivo Nacional, 1954), 81.

11.   AGI, SD 955, Joaquín García y Moreno to conde de Lerena, February 25, 1792; García to marqués de Bajamar, March 25, 1792; and Real Orden, June 25, 1792.

12.   AGI, SD 954, García to Philippe-François Rouxel de Blanchelande, August 31, 1791; AGI, SD 954, García to Bajamar, November 25, 1791; AGI, SD 955, García to Bajamar, March 25, 1792.

13.   AGI, SD 1110, Fernando Portillo y Torres to Bajamar, March 14 and September 25, 1792.

14.   Médiathèque, Nantes, MS 1811, letter of September 28, 1791, attributed 180 deaths to this cause.

15.   The French no longer displayed "the arrogance that they enjoyed in former times," the governor gloated: AGI, SD 954, García to Bajamar, November 25, 1791.

16.   AN, Section Moderne, Dxxv/65/659; AGI, SD 954–955; Commission des Colonies, *Débats entre les accusateurs et les accusés dans l'affaire des colonies* (Paris, 1795–1797), 1:266; *Moniteur Général de la Partie Françoise de Saint Domingue* (1792), no. 47, 67, 68; *Mercure de France,* November 19 and 26, 1791.

17.   M. R. Sevilla Soler, *Santo Domingo, Tierra de Frontera (1750–1800)* (Seville: Escuela de Estudios Hispano-Americanos, 1980), 384–388; C. E. Deive, *Los guerrilleros negros: esclavos fugitivos y cimarrones en Santo Domingo* (Santo Domingo: Fundación Cultural Dominicana, 1989), 197–201; A. Yacou, "L'administration coloniale espagnole à Cuba et les débuts des révolutions française et haïtienne," *Bulletin de la Société d'Histoire de la Guadeloupe* 39 (1979): 47–52.

18.   AN, Dxxv/12/118–119, and Dxxv/20/198; AGI, SD 955–956; D. Geggus, *Slavery, War and Revolution: The British Occupation of Saint Domingue, 1793–1798* (Oxford: Oxford University Press, 1982), 414, 442.

19.   A. del Monte y Tejada, *Historia de Santo Domingo* (Santo Domingo, 1890), 3:160, and appendix; Gros, *Isle Saint-Domingue, Province du Nord* (n.p.,

1793), 13, 27; AN, Dxxv/46/439; AGI, SD 955, García to Bajamar, February 27 and June 25 1792, and enclosures.

20. BM, Rouen, MS Monbret 574, f. 301–302; del Monte y Tejada, *Historia de Santo Domingo*, 3:iii, vii; AGI, SD 955, García to Bajamar, June 25, 1792. Foreign shipping doubtless was the main source of powder, but one suspects that much of it passed via Spanish territory.

21. While one may suspect the testimony of the governor's reports to Madrid, his internal correspondence with the frontier commanders found in del Monte y Tejada's *Historia de Santo Domingo* merits less skepticism.

22. AGI, SD 954–956, 1029–1030; correspondence in del Monte y Tejada, *Historia de Santo Domingo*, 3:appendix, and 4:7–26.

23. J. Saintoyant, *La colonisation française pendant la Révolution*, 2 vols. (Paris: Renaissance du Livre, 1930), 2:77–84; J. L. Franco, *Revolución y conflictos en el Caribe, 1789–1854* (Havana: Instituto de Historia, 1965), 29, 31; T. Lepkowski, *Haití* (Havana: Casa, 1968–1969), 1:62, 69; A. Sanz Tapia, *Los militares emigrados y prisioneros franceses en Venezuela durante la guerra contra la revolución* (Caracas: Instituto Panamericano, 1977), 48.

24. Del Monte y Tejada, *Historia de Santo Domingo*, 3:x. In response to the insurgents' requests for help, García replied through a frontier commander that if they surrendered to the French, he would intercede on their behalf: AGI, SD 955, García to Bajamar, February 27, 1792.

25. AGI, SD 955, García to Lerena, February 25, 1792; García to Bajamar, March 25, 1792; AGI, SD 1110, Portillo to Pedro de Acuña y Malbar, September 25, 1792; del Monte y Tejada, *Historia de Santo Domingo*, 3:xiii–xiv.

26. ANOM, CC9A/6, Rochambeau to Ministre de la Marine, December 27, 1792; AGI, SD 955, Gaspar de Cassasola to García, November 25, 1792; del Monte y Tejada, *Historia de Santo Domingo*, 3:xiv–xv; AGS, GM 7157, José Vásquez to Portillo, April 30, 1793.

27. AGI, SD 956, García to marqués de Campo Alange, March 25, 1793, states that the blacks had been offering allegiance on the "impossible" terms of being fully equipped by the Spanish and that he had made no reply, but that given his lack of troops, "it is a point worth considering," especially as the French were certain to try to turn them against the Spanish.

28. AGS, GM 7161, Acuña to García, February 22, 1793. This was two weeks before war was declared. The letter, when drafted, stated that war was "certain," but this was amended to "probable." Part of the letter is printed in B. Ardouin, *Études sur l'histoire d'Haïti* (Port-au-Prince: Dalencour, 1958), 2:22–23. Several historians have misdated these instructions as 1792, which radically misrepresents Spanish policy. The error of a copyist in Santo Domingo in 1795 probably caused the mistake, which by 1799 was being copied by the king's ministers themselves, as in AGN, Bogotá, Sección Colonia, Fondo Negros y Esclavos, Panama III, f. 991.

29. D. Geggus, "The British Government and the Saint Domingue Slave Revolt, 1791–1793," *English Historical Review* 96 (1981): 285–305; Geggus, "British Opinion and the Haitian Revolution, 1791–1805," in *Slavery and British Society, 1774–1848*, ed. J. Walvin (London: Macmillan, 1982), 124.

30. Geggus, *Slavery, War and Revolution*, 63, 66.

31. Belated British attempts in 1794 and 1795 to coordinate Anglo-Spanish policy were politely rejected: PRO, WO 1/60, 261–267.

32. Geggus, *Slavery, War and Revolution*, 100–105.

33. See P. Voelz, *Slave and Soldier: The Military Impact of Blacks in the Colonial Americas* (New York: Garland, 1993); D. Geggus, "The Arming of Slaves in the Haitian Revolution," in *The Arming of Slaves: From Classical Times to the Modern Era*, ed. P. Morgan and C. Brown (Yale University Press, forthcoming). The century-old fugitive slave sanctuary law was withdrawn in May 1790 in reaction to the French Revolution, but it had not applied to Saint Domingue since the passage of an extradition treaty in 1777.

34. Though primarily an act of realpolitik, revolutionary and antislavery idealism certainly also played a key role in this development of French policy: Y. Bénot, *La Révolution française et la fin des colonies* (Paris: La Découverte, 1987); R. L. Stein, *Léger-Félicité Sonthonax: The Lost Sentinel of the Republic* (Rutherford, N.J.: Fairleigh Dickinson University Press, 1985). See also Chapter 8 in this volume.

35. Geggus, *Slavery, War and Revolution*, Chapter 4.

36. C. Ardouin, *Essais sur l'histoire d'Haïti* (Port-au-Prince, 1865), 55 (quotation); AGS, GM 7157–7159; AGI, SD 1031.

37. The massacre occurred July 7th in Fort Dauphin (Bayajá, modern Fort Liberté) under the eyes of a Spanish garrison weakened by disease and apparently paralyzed by fear and indecision: PRO, WO 1/59, f. 229–299, 611–615; BM, Rouen, MS Leber 5847; AGS, Estado 8150.

38. Moreno Fraginals, *The Sugarmill*, 28; PRO, WO 1/60, f. 199–202; J.-P. Garran-Coulon, *Rapport sur les troubles de Saint-Domingue* (Paris, 1797–1799), 4:72; Page, *Essais sur les causes et les effets de la Révolution* (Paris, 1795), 71–72.

39. The Spanish government valued even undeveloped Trinidad, Puerto Rico, and Florida more than Santo Domingo, and in the peace negotiations ending the American Revolutionary War had been willing to cede it to either England or France, though neither power displayed interest in the colony: *Documentos relativos a la independencia de Norteamérica existentes en archivos españoles* (Madrid: Ministerio de Asuntos Exteriores, 1981), 6:415–418, 438–443, 447; Franco, *Revoluciones y conflictos*, 5–6. In 1795, it transferred Santo Domingo to France rather than Louisiana, which the French preferred.

40. Despite directions from Madrid, he did his best to avoid arming royalist planters who eagerly joined the Spanish. He threatened those who resisted with "[el] mas vil tormento." In addition to selling black prisoners of war, he planned to keep all French slaves who fled across the frontier. See PRO, WO 1/61, f. 181–184; WO 1/63, f. 47–50; AGN, Santo Domingo, Archivo Real de Higüey, 22.

41. At least by late 1794, Spanish officers were pillaging capital equipment and slaves from sugar plantations and shipping them to Cuba: AGS, GM 8150, letter of September 22, 1794; Overbrook Seminary, Philadelphia, Rodrigue Papers, Box 1, letter of June 2, 1794; PRO, WO 1/59, f. 313–320; WO 1/61,

f. 157–167. Brigadier Matías de Armona, who advocated burning plantations and who was chiefly responsible in October 1794 for abandoning the Spanish frontier towns to Toussaint Louverture, came from an elite planter family.

42. As Archbishop Portillo observed of the insurgents, "If they are our friends, as they are, they can cheat us fourfold, but if ill-intentioned, they can hurt us a hundredfold": AGS, GM 7157, letter of June 24, 1793.

43. AGI, SD 1089, García to Alange, November 20, 1794. The principal officers were court-martialed: AGI, Papeles de Cuba 1774B.

44. See Chapter 8 in this volume.

45. E. Rodríguez Demorizi, ed., *Cesión de Santo Domingo a Francia* (Ciudad Trujillo: Impresora Dominicana, 1958), 10–14.

46. See Chapter 12 in this volume. The principal black general, Jean-François, went into pensioned retirement in Cádiz, where he died in 1805.

47. Geggus, *Slavery, War and Revolution,* 388–391.

48. Moreno Fraginals, *The Sugarmill,* 158–159; A. Yacou, "La présence française dans la partie occidentale de l'île de Cuba au lendemain de la Révolution de Saint-Domingue," *Revue Française d'Histoire d'Outre-Mer* 84 (1987): 149–188; Geggus, "Slave Resistance in the Spanish Caribbean in the 1790s," in Gaspar and Geggus, eds., *A Turbulent Time,* 131–155.

49. F. Brito Figueroa, *Las insurecciones de esclavos en Venezuela* (Caracas: Cantaclaro, 1961), 64–81.

50. The often-quoted claim in P. de Lacroix, *Mémoires pour servir à l'histoire de la révolution de Saint-Domingue* (Paris, 1819), 1:346, that General Maitland suggested that Toussaint make himself king seems without foundation.

51. Logan, *The Diplomatic Relations of the United States with Haiti,* 68–113; A. DeConde, *The Quasi-War: The Politics and Diplomacy of the Undeclared War with France 1797–1801* (New York: Scribner, 1966); T. Matthewson, "Jefferson and the New Order of Things: The United States and the Haitian Slave Revolution," unpublished ms.

52. P. Pluchon, *Toussaint Louverture: de l'esclavage au pouvoir* (Paris: L'École, 1979), argues that Napoleon long hesitated to restore slavery. This view is criticized in C. B. Auguste and M. B. Auguste, *L'expédition Leclerc, 1801–1803* (Port-au-Prince: Deschamps, 1986), 16–19, and Y. Bénot, *La démence coloniale sous Napoléon* (Paris: La Découverte, 1992).

53. G. Debien and P. Pluchon, "Un plan d'invasion de la Jamaïque," *RSHHG* 36 (1978): 3–72; "Letters of Toussaint Louverture and of Edward Stevens, 1798–1800," *American Historical Review* 16 (1910): 83.

54. H. Hughes, "British Policy towards Haiti, 1801–1805," *Canadian Historical Review* 25 (1944): 397–408; Geggus, "British Opinion and the Haitian Revolution," 133–136. Colonel Vincent claimed that Bonaparte told him he had threatened to make Toussaint independent if the British did not acquiesce: BM, Rouen, MS Monbret 619, f. 89.

55. T. Matthewson, "Jefferson and Haiti," *Journal of Southern History* 61 (1995): 209–248; Logan, *The Diplomatic Relations of the United States with Haiti,* 120–

121. Jefferson did not long maintain this stance, and, veering to the opposite extreme, in the autumn briefly proposed that the major powers guarantee Saint Domingue's independence.

56.   M. B. Auguste and C. B. Auguste, *La participation étrangère à l'expédition française de Saint-Domingue* (Quebec: Auguste, 1980), 75–126.

57.   M. Rainsford, *An Historical Account of the Black Empire of Hayti* (London, 1805), introduction. Losses of seamen were also very great. On British losses, see M. Duffy, *Soldiers, Sugar and Seapower: The British Expeditions to the West Indies and the War against Revolutionary France* (Oxford: Oxford University Press, 1987), 328–334. French and Spanish losses remain uncertain and controversial.

58.   Logan, *The Diplomatic Relations of the United States with Haiti*, Chapter 4.

59.   The Cuban spokesman Arango y Parreño had supported the Napoleonic expedition to the end, reasoning that, even if they were militarily successful, the French could never effectively restore Saint Domingue's economy: Arango y Parreño, *Obras de D. Francisco de Arango y Parreño*, 1:338–383.

60.   D. Geggus, "Haiti and the Abolitionists: Opinion, Propaganda and International Politics, 1804–1838," in *Abolition and Its Aftermath: The Historical Context, 1790–1916,* ed. D. Richardson (London: Frank Cass, 1985), 114–117; Drescher, *Econocide,* 119, 168–169, 214–223, and *Capitalism and Antislavery: British Mobilization in Comparative Perspective* (New York: Oxford University Press, 1986), 98–99; M. Duffy, "The Impact of the French Revolution on British Attitudes to the West Indian Colonies," in Gaspar and Geggus, eds., *A Turbulent Time,* 78–101.

61.   T. Madiou, *Histoire d'Haïti* (Port-au-Prince: H. Deschamps, 1989), 3:148, 183; D. Geggus, "The Enigma of Jamaica in the 1790s: New Light on the Causation of Slave Rebellions," *William and Mary Quarterly* 44 (1987): 287–288.

62.   P. Verna, *Petión y Bolívar: Cuarenta años de relaciones haitiano-venezolanas* (Caracas: n.p., 1969), 87–298.

63.   D. Nicholls, *From Dessalines to Duvalier: Race, Colour, and National Independence in Haiti* (Cambridge: Cambridge University Press, 1979), Chapter 2; A. Hunt, *Haiti's Influence on Antebellum America: Slumbering Volcano in the Caribbean* (Baton Rouge: Louisiana University Press, 1988), Chapters 3–5; K. Schüller, *Die deutsche Rezeption haitianischer Geschichte in der ersten Hälfte des 19. Jahrhunderts* (Köln: Böhlau, 1992).

12. The Slave Leaders in Exile

1.   AGS, GM 7161, Pedro de Acuña to Joaquín García y Moreno, February 22 and March 26, 1793; Chapter 11 in this volume.

2.   See chapters by Geggus and by Morgan and O'Shaughnessy in *The Arming of Slaves in World History,* ed. P. Morgan and C. Brown (Yale University Press, forthcoming).

3.   AGI, SD 954, reports to García, September 17 and 22, 1791.

4.   See Chapter 8 in this volume.

5. AGI, SD 1031, García to Eugenio Llaguno, June 11, 1793; AGI, SD 956, Gabriel Bellair to García, September 16, 1793; AGS, GM 7159, García to marqués de Campo de Alange, May 17, 1794; E. Rodríguez Demorizi, ed., *Cesión de Santo Domingo a Francia* (Ciudad Trujillo: Impresora Dominicana, 1958), 13.

6. V. Schoelcher, *Vie de Toussaint Louverture* (Paris, 1889), 150; BM, Rouen, MS Leber 5847, f. 60.

7. AGI, Estado, 3, expediente 10, enclosure 8; BM, Rouen, MS Leber 5847, f. 7, 60; BM, Rouen, MS Monbret 574, f. 311. Biassou may have received a 70-dollar supplement, but this is uncertain: AGI, Papeles de Cuba 1439, letter of February 28, 1796.

8. PRO, WO 1/59, f. 229–299; AGS, Estado 8150. Fort Liberté was the former Fort Dauphin, called Fuerte Delfín or Bayajá by the Spanish.

9. See Chapter 8 in this volume.

10. Spain had been remarkably willing to abandon it during the peace negotiations of 1782–1783. See *Documentos relativos a la independencia de Norteamérica existentes en archivos españoles* (Madrid: Ministerio de Asuntos Exteriores, 1981), 6:415–418, 438–443, 447.

11. D. B. Gaspar and D. P. Geggus, eds., *A Turbulent Time: The French Revolution and the Greater Caribbean* (Bloomington: Indiana University Press, 1997), 11, 16, 47, 136.

12. Rodríguez Demorizi, *Cesión de Santo Domingo,* 10–14, 42; AGI, Estado 5, exp. 23, letters by García and marqués de Casa Calvo.

13. AGI, Estado 5, exp. 23, letter by Casa Calvo; and AGI, Estado 5, exp. 36.

14. Margin note dated February 8/12, 1796, in AGI, Estado 5, exp. 176.

15. Rodríguez Demorizi, *Cesión de Santo Domingo,* 52.

16. BN, Manuscrits, Fonds français 12103, Toussaint to Laveaux, 4, 10, and 16 frimaire an IV.

17. D. P. Geggus, *Slavery, War and Revolution: The British Occupation of Saint Domingue, 1793–1798* (Oxford: Oxford University Press, 1982), 181–182.

18. AGI, Estado 5, exp. 23, 36 and 40, letters by García.

19. AGS, GM 7161, exp. 24; AGI, Estado 5, exp. 23.

20. AGI, Estado 5, exp. 23 and 24; BN, Manuscrits, Fonds français 12103, Grandet to Laveaux, 12 nivôse IV. The date of embarkation was deduced from AGCA, A2/120/2265, Salvador Javalois to José Domas y Valle, March 17, 1796.

21. D. Geggus, "Slave Resistance in the Spanish Caribbean in the mid-1790s," in Gaspar and Geggus, eds., *A Turbulent Time,* 132–139.

22. AGI, Estado 5, Luis de Las Casas to Príncipe de la Paz, December 16, 1795.

23. Ibid.

24. AGI, Estado 5, exp. 28, enclosure 4. The "730" reported in C. E. Deive, *Las emigraciones dominicanas a Cuba (1795–1808)* (Santo Domingo: Fundación Cultural Dominicana, 1989), 36, and many other details in this work are inac-

curate. The most surprising discrepancy between the January and December lists is the twenty fewer officers.

25.   AGI, Estado 5, exp. 28.

26.   AGI, Estado 5, exp. 92 and 184. The governor of Portobelo had been passing through Havana and was persuaded to take a contingent. Three sick people remained in Havana; one later went to Honduras, another to Panama. The sources contain frequent minor discrepancies regarding numbers.

27.   AGI, Estado 5, exp. 126 and 132.

28.   J. Landers, "Rebellion and Royalism in Spanish Florida: The French Revolution on Spain's Northern Colonial Frontier," in Gaspar and Geggus, eds., *A Turbulent Time,* 156–177; J. G. Landers, *Black Society in Spanish Florida* (Urbana: University of Illinois Press, 1999), 81, 132–133, 94, 209–218; Landers, "Jorge Biassou: Black Chieftain," *El Escribano* 25 (1988): 87–100.

29.   Although Governor García had announced that two companies of soldiers would sail with Biassou's predominantly family group, it appears they did not. See AGI, Estado 24, exp. 53; AGI, Papeles de Cuba 1439, letter of January 8, 1796.

30.   This was the literate Léon Duvigneau, who as commandant of Ennery had surrendered the district to the Spanish to prevent its slaves from being freed. See PH 1:116; AN, Dxxv/43/415, Sonthonax to Duvigneau, July 18, 1793. Strangely, his wife remained a slave. He became a prosperous shopkeeper in Florida, though in the militia he was still a lowly corporal in 1813.

31.   AGI, Estado 1, exp. 72, Enrique White to conde de Santa Clara, April 6, 1798.

32.   AGI, SD 1031, Fernando Portillo y Torres to Llaguno, September 14, 1794.

33.   UF, East Florida Papers, microfilm 138, death certificate, July 15, 1801.

34.   M. Rubio Sánchez, *Historia del puerto de Trujillo* (Tegucigalpa, 1975), 2:292–316; AGCA, A1/2335/17514, report dated July 1, 1798; AGI, Guatemala 501, 1801 census and report by Ramón de Anguiano, May 10, 1804; A. R. Vallejo, *Primer anuario estadístico* (Tegucigalpa: Tipografía nacional, 1893), 119–135. Microfilm copies of the AGCA materials are available in very poor condition at McMaster University, Hamilton, Ontario; they are best consulted in Guatemala City.

35.   R. Leiva Vivas, *Tráfico de esclavos negros a Honduras* (Tegucigalpa: Guaymuras, 1982), 144–145.

36.   AGCA, A2/120/2265, f. 5–6, 12–21.

37.   AGCA, A2/120/2265, Salvador Javalois to José Domas y Valle, March 17, 1796.

38.   Omoa's "royal slaves," who included a partly African artillery company headed by an Igbo sergeant, would revolt in 1803. See AGCA, A2/121/2283, and A2/33/445. When Omoa was briefly captured by the British in 1779, most local blacks remained loyal to the Spanish, but black deserters and slaves assisted the invaders. See P. Voelz, *Slave and Soldier: The Military Impact of Blacks in the Colonial Americas* (New York: Garland, 1993), 86–87, 92.

39.   AGCA, A2/120/2265, f. 22–30.

40.   Leiva Vivas, *Tráfico,* 145; Rubio Sánchez, *Historia del puerto,* 2:323.

41. AGCA, A2/120/2265, f. 32–36. In Saint Domingue, *candio* had the meaning of "extroverted fancy-dresser, ladies' man."

42. AGCA, A2/120/2265, f. 36–38.

43. Ibid., f. 41–42; and AGCA, A3/1331/22446, f. 57.

44. AGCA, A2/120/2265, f. 32, A3/21/5301 and A3/14/290; AGI, Estado 25, exp. 74, and Guatemala 453, report dated July 14, 1810, item 19. Las Casas cavalierly hijacked 100,000 dollars destined for Santo Domingo, claiming it to cover costs occasioned by the auxiliaries. As the total costs of the Havana-Trujillo voyage were 715 dollars, he clearly gave himself a lot of margin. See AGI, Estado 5, exp. 61; AGCA, A3/1331/22446, f. 77. This was his revenge on García.

45. AGCA, A3/1331/22446, f. 59–76.

46. Enclosures in AGI, Estado 49, exp. 89, Domas to Urquijo, July 16, 1801.

47. F. Carteaux, *Soirées bermudiennes, ou entretiens sur les événemens qui ont opéré la ruine de la partie française de l'isle Saint-Domingue* (Bordeaux, 1802), 81.

48. Enclosures in AGI, Estado 49, exp. 89. Three years later, he petitioned to be naturalized. He claimed to be baptized and of legitimate birth but did not say if he was freeborn. Desombrages was probably a free mulatto. See AN, Dxxv/2/14, deposition by Ambroise, March 27, 1792.

49. AGI, Estado 50, exp. 9, 11, 12; AGCA, A3/2602/38449, entry for February 18, 1797. An Italian-born rancher, Rossi was mayor of Suchitepéquez and lieutenant of the captain-general in Zapotitlán province. His recent imprisonment in Cap Français may have helped him find common ground with his troops.

50. AGCA, A2/130/2344, letter of December 22, 1802, and A2/133/2423, no. 19 and 36. Jacques Houdaille was thus mistaken to depict Jean-François (and Biassou) as leading the Domingans in Guatemala in his exploratory articles, "Negros franceses en América central fines del siglo XVIII," *El Imparcial* (Guatemala), 13 March 1954, 11; "Negros franceses en América central fines del siglo XVIII," *Antropología e historia de Guatemala* 6 (1954): 65–67; "Les Français et les afrancesados en Amérique centrale, 1700–1810," *Revista de Historia de América* 44 (1957): 305–330.

51. *Gaceta de Guatemala,* 17 May 1797; AGCA, A2/120/2268; Rubio Sánchez, *Historia,* 2:339–350. Santillan, Jean-François's captain of artillery, was a free black from Santo Domingo.

52. N. L. Gonzalez, "New Evidence on the Origin of the Black Carib," *New West Indian Guide* 57 (1983): 143–172; and *Sojourners of the Caribbean: Ethnogenesis and Ethnohistory of the Garifuna* (Urbana: University of Illinois Press, 1988), 39–50.

53. Jacques Houdaille ("Negros Franceses," 11; "Les Français et les afrancesados," 319–322) wrongly stated this term was applied to the Domingans. However, the Spanish generally called them "black French royalists," "so-called royalists from Saint Domingue," or "blacks from Saint Domingue"; later just "French blacks," and by 1830, just "French." See particularly Church of Latter Day Saints Microfilms, reels 0637018 and 0637008, Trujillo parish registers.

54. *Gaceta de Guatemala,* 26 June 1797; AGCA, A2/120/2267. Treasury officials recorded that they assisted Rossi on Roatán "with their opinions and their color": AGI, Guatemala 805, entry for May 22, 1797.

55. AGCA, A2/120/2269 and 2274; A2/301/6867 and 6868. In 1804, the governor of Honduras called for "cleansing" the coast of blacks; the proposition was discussed periodically down to 1820. See AGI, Guatemala 501, various reports.

56. AGCA, A2/300/6775. Rivalry between Choisi and Desombrages doubtless facilitated the split, which nonetheless divided several families.

57. AGCA, A2/100/1981 (Bivet); A1(4)/51/520, (land distributions); AGI, Guatemala 501, Census and report by Ramón de Anguiano, May 10, 1804.

58. AGCA, A2/120/2275, and A1(4)/51/520, letters of October 5 and December 15, 1802, and August 8, 1803; Rubio Sánchez, *Historia,* 2:396.

59. Vallejo, *Primer anuario,* 121, 133; Leiva Vivas, *Tráfico,* 148. A1(4)/51/520, "Lista general," December 15, 1802, put the number at 170, including thirty-seven married couples.

60. Rubio Sánchez, *Historia,* 2:327; Trujillo parish registers.

61. Trujillo parish registers. Delacour's wife, Marie, appears in 1825 as godmother to a child born to *padres infieles,* presumably Caribs.

62. AGCA, A1(4)/51/520, "Lista general," December 15, 1802.

63. Rubio Sánchez, *Historia,* 2:355–60; Gonzalez, "New Evidence," 152; Gonzalez, *Sojourners,* 54, 62–63.

64. AGI, Guatemala, 453, report of July 14, 1810; AGCA, A1(4)/51/520, "Plan de reforma," September 30, 1802; AGCA, A1(4)/51/519, proclamation, January 20, 1803.

65. AGCA, A1(4)/51/520, letters of October 20 and November 7, 1802. The proposed destinations included two in El Salvador and the Polochic River valley.

66. AGCA, A1(4)/51/520, letters of October 5, 1802, and August 8, 1803.

67. Ibid., correspondence, February–September 1803.

68. Ibid., letters of October 20 and December 5, 1802. Colonel Joseph Bivet apparently freed four of his six slaves between 1796 and 1802. These included his son, his son's mother, and his two slave-soldiers, who were reclassified as "nephews." See AGCA, A2/120/2275; A2/120/2265, f. 5–6, 12–21; A1(4)/51/520, "Lista general."

69. See Chapter 8 in this volume.

70. AGCA, A1(4)/51/519, correspondence September 1802–June 1803, and (Azor) A2/301/6884.

71. AGCA, A1(4)/51/519, letter of April 21, 1802. The letter shows Jean-François keeping actively involved with his exiled army, responding to their problems, passing on requests to the ministry, and informing them of marriages and deaths among the group in Spain.

72. AGCA, A1(4)/51/519, letters of January–February 1803.

73. AGCA, A2/130/2344, letter of February 7, 1803; AGCA, A2/121/2279, report of August 7, 1803.

74. LC, Manuscripts, Central America, S III, 48A, 1, 6672, "Reglamento de las companías fijas"; *Cartografía de Ultramar* (Madrid: Servicio Geográfica e Histórica del Ejército, 1949–1957), 4:269–271; (atlas) plates 58, 59.

75. AGCA, A2/121/2280, letters of July 26 and August 7, 1803.

76. AGCA, A2/121/2279, report of August 7, 1803.

77. AGCA, A2/301/6867, 6882, 6887, 6890–6892.

78. AGCA, A2/301/6878–6879, 6882.

79. AGCA, A2/133/2423, no. 77–78; and A2/ 301/6893–6897.

80. AGI, Estado 24, exp. 53, Arturo O'Neill to marqués de Branciforte, March 20, 1796, enclosing a "provisional plan" of 26 clauses; F. Fernández Repetto and G. Negroe Sierra, *Una población perdida en la memoria: los negros de Yucatán* (Mérida: Universidad Autónoma, 1995), 19.

81. AGI, Estado 24, exp. 53, marqués de Branciforte to Príncipe de la Paz; and O'Neill to Branciforte, March 20, 1796.

82. J. Victoria Ojeda and J. Canto Alcocer, "Impulso y dispersión de los negros auxiliadores: el caso de San Fernando Aké, Yucatán," *Por Eso! Suplemento Cultural,* 26 July 1998, 3–9; G. J. Méndez, "Mérida, Yucatán, and its Hinterland, 1780–1860" (Ph.D. diss., Washington State University, 1994), 115.

83. Fernández Repetto and Negroe Sierra, *Una población perdida,* 54–57.

84. Jorge Victoria, personal communication; Méndez, "Mérida," 182.

85. AGN, Bogotá, Sección Colonia, Fondo Negros y Esclavos, Panama III, f. 902–995. I am indebted to Marixa Lasso of the University of Florida for locating and sending me copies of these documents. Of the eighty-seven who left Cuba in August 1796, two died in transit and one disembarked in Campeche. One man who was left in Havana reached Panama later in the year. The 6,000 dollars meant to accompany them did not arrive.

86. AGN, Bogotá, Sección Colonia, Fondo Negros y Esclavos, Panama III, f. 953–956, "Lista de los individuos," February 18, 1797.

87. Ibid., f. 916.

88. Ibid. f. 916–17, 945–953, 984.

89. Ibid., f. 976–985.

90. Ibid., f. 951–953.

91. Ibid., f. 953–956; AGI, Panama 294, exp. 26, letter of March 20, 1808 with enclosures.

92. J. Lipski, *The Speech of the Negros Congos of Panama* (Amsterdam: Benjamins, 1989), 2–5, 68–70; A. Castillero Calvo, *Conquista, evangelización y resistencia: triunfo o fracaso de la política indigenista?* (Panama: Mariano Arosemena, 1995), 420. However, on much of the coast, "Congo" traditions make no reference to slavery. See P. Drolet, "The Congo Ritual of Northeastern Panama: An Afro-American Expressive Structure of Cultural Adaptation" (Ph.D. diss., University of Illinois, 1980), 160. Neither Drolet nor Lipski mentions French words.

93. AGI, Estado 3, exp. 10, enclosure 1.

94. AGI, Estado 3, exp. 10, enclosures 2–4 and 11. To be precise, 139 were black, as two adjutant/secretaries were whites married to black women.

95. BN, Manuscrits, Fonds français 12103, f. 273. Still less plausible is the account of Jean-François panicking and swimming out to his ship when Villatte visited Fort Liberté, although the source was an eyewitness (ibid., Grandet to Laveaux, 12 nivôse IV).

96. J. Saint-Rémy, *Pétion et Haïti* (Paris, 1853–1857; reprint, Paris: Berger-Levrault, 1956), 4:103–104; AGI, Estado 3, exp. 10, enclosure 79, letter of May 10, 1803.

97. AGI, Estado 3, exp. 10, letter of April 25, 1796.

98. AGI, Estado 3, exp. 10, enclosure 13; AGS, GM 7161, exp. 32. Archivo Provincial de Cádiz, Gobierno Civil, leg. 1, contains a reference to an African-born master caulker from Martinique who had lived twenty-four years in the city.

99. Correspondence, July–October, in AGI, Estado 3, exp. 10; and AGS, GM 7161, exp. 24.

100. Deive, *Las emigraciones dominicanas,* 126; AGS, GM 7161, exp. 33, doc. 279; AGI, Estado 3, exp. 10, enclosure 77.

101. AGI, Estado 3, exp. 10, enclosure 79, letter of May 10, 1803. "Petecou" is a familiar form of *casse-cou.* Besides meanings of headlong, bold, and so forth, the phrase formerly also signified a groom who broke strong-willed horses. Jean-François also used the name in his letter to Jean-Jacques cited above, Letter of April 21, 1802.

102. AN, 505 Mi 42, part 11.

103. Historians have given several dates from 1806 to 1822 for his death, but Agnès Crouzet (personal communication, citing Cádiz Armada) has discovered that he died September 16, 1805. None of the auxiliaries appears in the municipal cemetery records, although the black general Laplume, another insurgent who turned against the revolution, does.

104. Deive, *Emigraciones,* 126–127.

105. *Diario de las sesiones de las Cortes Generales y Extraordinarias* (Madrid, 1870–1874), 3:1778, session of September 5, 1811. My thanks to Marixa Lasso for this citation.

106. J. L. Franco, *Las conspiraciones de 1810 y 1812* (Havana: Editorial de Ciencias Sociales, 1977), 16, 88–108, 180–183; Matt D. Childs, "'A Black French General Arrived to Conquer the Island': Images of the Haitian Revolution in Cuba's 1812 Aponte Rebellion," in *The Impact of the Haitian Revolution in the Atlantic World,* ed. D. Geggus (Columbia, S.C.: University of South Carolina Press, 2001), 144–147.

107. Franco, *Conspiraciones,* 30–31; AGI, SD 1000, report of March 14, 1811; C. E. Deive, *La esclavitud del negro en Santo Domingo (1492–1844)* (Santo Domingo: Museo del Hombre, 1980), 2:476–481.

108. Geggus, *Slavery, War and Revolution,* 182, 199–202; BN, NAF 6846, f. 151–152, 164–165.

109. AGI, Estado 1, exp. 27, f. 57; Deive, *La esclavitud del negro,* 2:424–427;

Rodríguez Demorizi, *Cesión de Santo Domingo*, 95, 128, 254–256; B. Ardouin, *Études sur l'histoire d'Haïti* (Port-au-Prince: Dalencour, 1958), 1:51; T. Madiou, *Histoire d'Haïti* (Port-au-Prince: H. Deschamps, 1991), 8:92, 95, 102. He was African and presumably Muslim, although he could have been owned by the Cap Français bailiff named Augustin Aly (who evidently was neither).

110. R. D. Heinl and N. Heinl, *Written in Blood: The Story of the Haitian People, 1492–1995* (Lanham, Md.: University Press of America, 1996), 68; C. L. R. James, *The Black Jacobins: Toussaint L'Ouverture and the San Domingo Revolution* (New York: Vintage, 1963), 254; P. V. Vastey, *Essay on the Causes of the Revolution and Civil Wars of Hayti* (1823; reprint, New York: Negro Universities Press, 1969), 20; Saint-Rémy, *Pétion et Haïti*, 4:104; H. P. Sannon, *Vie de Toussaint-Louverture* (Port-au-Prince: L Héraux, 1920-1933), 1:201; L. Dubroca, *Vie de Toussaint-Louverture* (Paris, 1802), 65; P. de Lacroix, *Mémoires pour servir à l'histoire de la Révolution de Saint-Domingue*, (Paris, 1819), 1:300; C. Malenfant, *Des colonies et particulièrement de celle de Saint-Domingue* (Paris, 1814), 64.

111. F. Tannenbaum, *Slave and Citizen: The Negro in the Americas* (New York: Vintage Books, 1946).

13. The Naming of Haiti

1. The name first officially appears, without explanation, in the text and at the head of the proclamation of independence made January 1, 1804, at Gonaïves. An earlier declaration of November 29, 1803, stated only that "L'indépendance de Saint-Domingue est proclamée" and it is probably apocryphal. See T. Madiou, *Histoire d'Haïti* (Port-au-Prince: H. Deschamps, 1989), 3:125 n. 1, 150. Belize exchanged its colonial designation for the name of a local river; most other states have kept their colonial name, whether or not it corresponded to an aboriginal term.

2. Its etymology is discussed in E. Tejera, *Indigenismos* (Santo Domingo: Editora de Santo Domingo, 1977), 2:754–758. Whereas the Spanish rendering of the word "Haití" preserved the Taino stress on the third syllable, the French and Creole versions stress the second syllable, which was to entirely vanish in the American English version.

3. V. P. de Vastey, *Essay on the Causes of the Revolution and Civil Wars of Hayti* (1823; reprint, New York: Negro Universities Press, 1969), 44; Madiou, *Histoire d'Haïti*, 3:140–152.

4. J. Fouchard, "Pourquoi Haïti? Où, quand et par qui fut choisi de redonner à notre patrie le nom indien d'Haïti," *RSHHG* 145 (1984): 13–17.

5. Archives de la Guerre, Vincennes, MS 597; ANOM, CC9B/23, proclamation of April 28, 1804. Exceptions were made for certain whites who had allied themselves with the blacks. In the constitutions of 1805, 1806, and 1816, the ban on Europeans was rephrased to exclude "whites of whatever nation," but it was omitted in the 1807 and 1811 constitutions of Henry Christophe, ruler of northern Haiti between 1807 and 1820. See L.-J. Janvier, *Les constitutions d'Haïti* (Paris, 1886), 30–144.

6.   Madiou, *Histoire d'Haïti*, 3:131. This and other translations from French and Spanish are mine. Baron de Vastey (*Essay on the Causes of the Revolution*, 44) was even more laconic: "The name of the island was altered, and the St. Domingo of the French was superseded by the original name of Hayti."

7.   D. M. Yonker, "From the Belly of Dan: Dahomey in Haiti," Paper presented at the Cultural Vibrations conference, University of Florida, Gainesville, April 1989.

8.   The supposed addendum "ti" also lacks a plausible explanation. If it was the Creole word for "little," it would have preceded the noun.

9.   On the ethnic composition of slave population, see D. Geggus, "Sugar and Coffee Cultivation in Saint Domingue and the Shaping of the Slave Labor Force," in *Cultivation and Culture: Labor and the Shaping of Slave Life in the Americas*, ed. I. Berlin and P. Morgan (Charlottesville: University Press of Virginia, 1993), 79, 81.

10.   "Congo" has acquired the meaning "traitor" in Haitian Creole, either because of the ethnic politics of the revolution or a supposed propensity for acculturation to European norms under slavery. See G. Montilus, "Guinea Versus Congo Lands: Aspects of Collective Memory in Haiti," in *Global Dimensions of the African Diaspora*, ed. J. Harris (Washington, D.C.: Howard University Press, 1982), 164–165; C. B. Auguste, "Les Congos dans la Révolution Haïtienne," *RSHHG* 168 (1990): 11–42. For different reasons, it is also an insult in Jamaican Creole: F. Cassidy and R. Lepage, *Dictionary of Jamaican English* (1967; reprint, Cambridge: Cambridge University Press, 1980), 118.

11.   Dessalines was born at Cormier in Saint Domingue's northern mountains in 1758. See "Documents inédits: Thomas Madiou rend hommage à l'empereur," *RSHHG* 145 (1984): 7. Evidence suggests that other similarly identified leaders, such as Biassou, Moïse, and perhaps even Boukman, were also locally born. See D. Geggus, "The Sugar Plantation Zones of Saint Domingue and the Revolution of 1791–1793," *Slavery and Abolition* 20 (1999): 40–41.

12.   Madiou, *Histoire d'Haïti*, 2:395–396; Auguste, "Les Congos." Tensions between African and Creole insurgents went back to the beginning of the revolution. They were aggravated by Toussaint Louverture's reopening the slave trade and continued after independence: UF, Special Collections, Rochambeau Microfilms, lot 132, Roume to Forfait, 3 vendémiaire an X; Archives de la Guerre, Vincennes, MS 601 (unpaginated).

13.   L. F. Boisrond-Tonnerre, *Mémoires pour servir à l'histoire d'Haïti* (Port-au-Prince: Fardin, 1981), viii–x.

14.   Madiou, *Histoire d'Haïti*, 3:145.

15.   J. Saint-Rémy, *Pétion et Haïti* (Paris, 1853–1857; reprint, Paris: Berger-Levrault, 1956), 4:5. A younger, more partisan but more meticulous contemporary of Madiou, Saint-Rémy similarly collected the reminiscences of participants in the revolution.

16.   See Madiou, *Histoire d'Haïti*, 3:150. The 1847–1848, 1904, and 1922 editions of this work contain an appendix identifying the phenotype of prominent individuals. Even General Yayou was born in the colony: Auguste, "Congos," 29.

17.   Archives de la Guerre, Vincennes, MS 601. See also the essays on leading

administrators in R. Léon, *Propos d'histoire* (Port-au-Prince: Imprimerie de l'État, 1945), 1–115.

18. D. Nicholls, *From Dessalines to Duvalier: Race, Colour, and National Independence in Haiti* (Cambridge: Cambridge University Press, 1979), 11–12; L. Hurbon, *Comprendre Haïti: essai sur l'état, la nation, la culture* (Paris: Karthala, 1987), 128–129.

19. Though Dessalines's constitution of 1805 admitted no dominant religion, he sent Haitians to Rome to be ordained as priests. The constitutions of 1806, 1807, and 1816 gave Roman Catholicism a privileged position (Janvier, *Les constitutions*, 30–144). All heads of state repressed vodou. See J. G. Leyburn, *The Haitian People* (New Haven: Yale University Press, 1966), 139–140; H. Trouillot, *Les Origines sociales de la littérature haïtienne* (1962; reprint, Port-au-Prince: Fardin, 1986), 50; Madiou, *Histoire d'Haïti*, 2:112.

20. However, some historians have suggested that certain leaders' unorthodox French was a means of expressing contempt for the language: Léon, *Propos,* 129. Dessalines spoke no French and liked Boisrond-Tonnerre partly because of his ability to speak a vulgar Creole: Trouillot, *Les Origines sociales*, 90.

21. Trouillot, *Les Origines sociales,* 98–99; Nicholls, *From Dessalines to Duvalier,* passim.

22. L.-F. Hoffmann, "L'Elément indien dans la conscience collective des Haïtiens," *Études Créoles* 17 (1994): 30–33. He characterizes the position of the Indian in Haitian literature as shifting in this century from an object of parallelism to one of identification, with biological descent only rarely being claimed. In the Dominican Republic, mulattoes have, at least in the twentieth century, generally been called "mestizos" or "indios." Some say this is merely an evocation of the aboriginal past, not a sign of false consciousness, but others decode it as deliberate obfuscation, an attempt to lay claim to a bogus ancestry and to reclassify African cultural retentions as Amerindian. See M. Fennema and T. Loewenthal, *Construcción de raza y nación en la República Dominicana* (Santo Domingo: Editora Universitaria, 1987), 25–30, 61–64; E. Sagás, "A Case of Mistaken Identity: *Antihaitianismo* in Dominican Culture," *Latinamericanist* 29 (1993): 1–5; A. Benítez Rojo, *The Repeating Island: The Caribbean and the Postmodern Perspective* (Durham: Duke University Press, 1992), 50; F. J. Franco, "Antihaitianismo e ideología del Trujillato," in *Problemas dominico-haitianas y del Caribe,* ed. G. Pierre-Charles, et al. (Mexico City: Universidad Nacional Autónoma de México, 1973), 83–109; S. Torres Saillant, "The Tribulations of Blackness: Stages in Dominican Racial Identity," *Latin American Perspectives* 25 (1998): 126–146.

23. Y. Debbasch, *Couleur et liberté: le jeu du critère ethnique dans l'ordre juridique esclavagiste* (Paris: Dalloz, 1967), 58–69; J.-L. Bonniol, *La Couleur comme maléfice: une illustration créole de la généalogie des "Blancs" et des "Noirs"* (Paris: Albin Michel, 1992), 101.

24. BM, Rouen, MS Leber 5847, f. 62.

25. Janvier, *Les constitutions,* 32.

26. AP, 10:329–334. The slave-general Georges Biassou was perhaps expressing similar feelings when he informed the governor of Santo Domingo, "I like

only solid and natural colors that nothing can change." See AGI, SD 956, Joaquín García y Moreno to Pedro de Acuña y Malbar, November 25, 1793, enclosure no. 6.

27.	J. Price-Mars, "Toussaint Louverture," *RSHHG* 57 (1945): 7–17. After the revolution, however, King Christophe's spokesman, Baron de Vastey, did note that in keeping with universal prejudices, blacks considered themselves more beautiful than others and that Haitian artists depicted God and the angels as black and devils as white. See D. Nicholls, "Pompée Valentin de Vastey," *Jahrbuch für Geschichte von Staat, Wirtschaft und Gesellschaft Lateinamerikas* 28 (1991): 116.

28.	The free colored political club formed in Paris in September 1789 by Julien Raimond and Vincent Ogé (both "quadroons," as was Boisrond-Tonnerre, according to some) took the name "Société des Colons Américains." It appears initially to have had no black members (Debbasch, *Couleur et liberté*, 144–166). The term Américain was used freely by Jean-Baptiste Chavanne, who rebelled with Vincent Ogé in October 1790 (AN, Section Moderne, Dxxv/58/574, "Interrogation de Vincent Ogé"). In the autumn of 1791, free colored insurgents in northeastern Saint Domingue called themselves "L'Armée américaine" (AGI, SD 954, García to marqués de Bajamar, November 25, 1791, enclosures Y and Z).

29.	Janvier, *Les constitutions*, 117. Son of a white man and mulatto woman, Pétion "with his smooth hair could have been mistaken for an Indian" (Saint-Rémy, *Pétion et Haïti*, 1:11).

30.	J. Fouchard, *Langue et littérature des aborigènes d'Ayti* (Paris: École, 1972), 157–165; L. Élie, *Histoire d'Haïti* (Port-au-Prince: n.p., 1944–1945), 1:201–208, 2:258–259; C. P. Charles, *Christophe Colomb, les Indiens et leurs survivances en Haïti* (Port-au-Prince: Editions Christophe, 1992), 115–223.

31.	J. Price-Mars, *Ainsi Parla l'Oncle: essais d'éthnographie* (Port-au-Prince: Imprimerie de Compiègne, 1928), 113–114; Élie, *Histoire d'Haïti*, 1:197; *Aia bombé: Revue Mensuelle* (Port-au-Prince) 1 (1946): 1, 32; T. Desrosiers, *Civilisation indienne et culture haïtienne* (Port-au-Prince, n.d.), 7, 28–29.

32.	É. Nau, *Histoire des caciques d'Haïti* (1854; reprint, Port-au-Prince: Panorama, 1963), 2:67–68.

33.	On the chants, see D. Geggus, "Haitian Voodoo in the Eighteenth Century: Language, Culture, Resistance," *Jahrbuch für Geschichte von Staat, Wirtschaft und Gesellschaft Lateinamerikas* 28 (1991): 24–31.

34.	M. Deren, *The Voodoo Gods* (St. Alban's: Paladin, 1975), 68–74. In L. Hurbon, *Voodoo: Search for the Spirit* (New York: Harry Abrams, 1995), 31, one reads that "the surviving Carib Indians" contributed to vodou's formation.

35.	J. Janzen, *Lemba, 1650–1930: A Drum of Affliction* (New York: Garland, 1982), 273–292; L. de Heusch, "Kongo in Haiti," *Man* 24 (1989): 290–303; Geggus, "Haitian Voodoo," 21–51.

36.	Also, the problematic name of the agricultural deity Azaka can be traced to an African rather than a Taino source. See G. C. Montilus, "Africa in Diaspora: The Myth of Dahomey in Haiti," *Journal of Caribbean History* 2 (1981): 73–84.

37.   L. Maximilien, "Quelques apports indiens dans la vie haïtienne," in Charles, *Christophe Colomb*, 171–184. M. P. Hyppolite, *Héritage culturel et linguistique des Aytiens de la première civilisation de l'île d'Ayti* (Port-au-Prince: Imprimerie Nouvelle, 1989), 103, aptly calls vodou priests "Haiti's first archaeologists." Certain African peoples such as the Kissi and Mende endow local archaeological finds with "rediscovered power."

38.   See W. Valente, *Sincretismo religioso afro-brasileiro* (São Paulo: Companhia Editora Nacional, 1977), 60–67; R. Bastide, *The African Religions of Brazil* (Baltimore: Johns Hopkins University Press, 1978), Chapter 9. Candomblé caboclo and catimbó are predominantly Amerindian religions reshaped to differing degrees by blacks in Brazil.

39.   Charles, *Christophe Colomb*, 155–157; S. Comhaire-Sylvain, "Les contes haïtiens" (Thèse, Université de Paris, 1937), 1:xxiii–xxiv, 2:275; H. Courlander, *The Piece of Fire and Other Haitian Tales* (New York: Harcourt Brace, 1964), 113.

40.   K. Andrews, *The Spanish Caribbean: Trade and Plunder* (New Haven: Yale University Press, 1978), 15; C. E. Deive, *La Española y la esclavitud del Indio* (Santo Domingo: Fundación García Arévalo, 1995), 11, 359, 367–368.

41.   Official head counts indicated a decline in the Amerindian population from 60,000 in 1509 to about 11,000 in 1518, when imports from Africa were authorized. Modern estimates of the pre-conquest population have ranged from 60,000 to 8 million: D. Henige, "On the Contact Population of Hispaniola: History as Higher Mathematics," *Hispanic American Historical Review* 58 (1978): 217–237.

42.   E. Rodríguez Demorizi, *Invasiones haitianas de 1801, 1805 y 1822* (Ciudad Trujillo: Editora del Caribe, 1955), 50–52, 62.

43.   The 1681 census recorded 480 mulattoes and Indians, all slaves. The south had 128 Indians in 1631 and 83 in 1713. See MSM, 1:84, 3:1164–1165.

44.   Its usage by Amerindians near Cumaná was recorded in the 1540s: S. Loven, *Origins of the Tainan Culture of the West Indies* (Göteborg: Elanders Boktryckeri Aktiebolag, 1935), 68. Seventeenth-century Dominican Caribs also used the word: Tejera, *Indigenismos*, 2:754.

45.   L. Peytraud, *L'esclavage aux Antilles françaises avant 1789* (Paris, 1897), 27–29; MSM, 1:83, 89, 94–95. In 1731, 500 Natchez were deported to Saint Domingue. Moreau also mentions deportations of Fox (Renards), though this is not confirmed by J. Peyser, "The Fate of the Fox Survivors," *Wisconsin Magazine of History* 73 (1989–1990): 83–110.

46.   See the samples of more than 30,000 plantation slaves cited in Geggus, "Sugar and Coffee Cultivation," and more than 5,000 slave fugitives listed in the colonial newspaper *Les Affiches Américaines*, 1788 and 1790.

47.   G. Fernández de Oviedo y Valdés, *Historia general y natural de las Indias* (Madrid: Ediciones Atlas, 1959), 1:124–139; B. de Las Casas, *Historia general de las Indias* (Caracas: Fundación Biblioteca Ayacucho, 1986), 3:Chapters 125–127; A. de Herrera, *Historia general de los hechos de los Castellanos en las islas y Tierrafirme del Mar Océano* (Madrid: Tipografía de Archivos, 1934), 4:357–362, 10:113–122, 355–366.

48. P. F. Xavier de Charlevoix, *Histoire de l'isle espagnole ou de Saint Domingue* (Amsterdam, 1733), 2:219–322. The book is based on the notes of fellow missionary Father Le Pers, who later criticized the use Charlevoix made of them.

49. C. de Utrera, *Polémica de Enriquillo* (Santo Domingo: Editora del Caribe, 1973), 24, 457–461. This indispensable work makes extensive use of archival sources but errs in making Sánchez Valverde the first to link Enrique with Boyá.

50. Charlevoix, *Histoire de l'isle espagnole*, 2:322; A. Sánchez Valverde, *Idea del valor de la isla Española* (Santo Domingo: Editora Nacional, 1971), 150; M. L. E. Moreau de Saint-Méry, *Topographical and Political Description of the Spanish Part of Saint-Domingo* (Philadelphia, 1796), 1:59, 162–163. Among those who abandoned Santo Domingo for Cuba in 1796 were thirteen "Indios blancos." See AGI, Estado 5, exp. 99, Luis de Las Casas to Príncipe de la Paz, April 7, 1796.

51. Cited in E. Rodríguez Demorizi, ed., *Cesión de Santo Domingo a Francia* (Ciudad Trujillo: Impresora Dominicana, 1958), 282–283.

52. Ibid.

53. However, they remained in the frontier region, and many emigrated in 1796. See Chapters 11 and 12 in this volume.

54. The basic printed source on Enrique is Oviedo's *Historia*, which was published in French as early as 1555. Charlevoix' *Histoire de l'isle Espagnole*, reprinted many times in the 1730s and 1740s and again in 1780–1781, was the first work to link Enrique with Boyá. Sánchez Valverde's *Idea del valor* was also published in French in Saint Domingue itself sometime before 1802. Moreau de Saint-Méry mentioned Enrique only briefly, as if he was well known to his readers. Las Casas's account was not published until the nineteenth century.

55. Juste Chanlatte (wrongly) depicted Enrique dying in battle against the Spanish in a poem that is cited in Hoffmann, "L'Elément indien," 26. He was the author of the April 28, 1804 proclamation (ANOM, CC9B/23) that spoke of avenging "America" and of the free coloreds' bloodthirsty call to arms of November 1791 (Madiou, *Histoire d'Haïti*, 3:183, 1:114).

56. D. Lowenthal, *Caribbean Societies* (London: Oxford University Press, 1972), 108.

57. Although not recorded by Las Casas or Herrera, such cooperation is briefly mentioned in Oviedo and Charlevoix, who nonetheless give as much attention to Enrique's subsequent agreement to hand over black fugitives to the Spanish and have them hunted for bounty along with (non-Taino) Indian slaves. In this way, the agreement of 1533 prefigured many later maroon treaties. According to Utrera, *Polémica*, 27, 39, Enrique's Baoruco settlement was destroyed by African slave rebels in 1547.

58. B. Ardouin, *Études sur l'histoire d'Haïti* (Port-au-Prince: Dalencour, 1958), 6:7.

59. Nau, *Histoire des caciques d'Haïti*, 1:12.

60. Madiou, *Histoire d'Haïti*, 2:451; Nau, *Histoire des caciques d'Haïti*, 1:12. Élie,

Histoire d'Haïti, 2:259, argued that in the 1520s the two groups intermingled, apparently leaving numerous mixed descendants.

61. See above, note 2.

62. Madiou, *Histoire d'Haïti*, 2:451, 472. In reply to "Who goes there?" soldiers would answer, "Sons of the sun; they still exist." Madiou explained this meant there were still defenders of liberty.

63. M. Camus, "Une lettre du général Capoix," *RSHHG* 141 (1983): 71, contains a letter of July 3, 1803 apparently headed "Armée des Incas." However, the writing in the original is unclear, and the term was interpolated into the printed version by the journal editor, Jean Fouchard (personal communication from Michel Camus).

64. Fouchard, "Pourquoi Haïti?," 13–17.

65. *Les Affiches Américaines*, 1780, 1781.

66. J.-B. Picquenard, *Zoflora ou la bonne négresse: Anecdote coloniale* (Paris, 1799), 2:209. Various errors suggest that the author did not reside long in the colony. He was a secretary to the second civil commission.

67. Saint-Rémy, *Pétion et Haïti*, 1:11–12. Dessalines supposedly offered the supreme command to Pétion at this time (Boisrond-Tonnerre, *Mémoires*, xviii–xix).

68. Saint-Rémy, *Pétion et Haïti*, 3:75. According to C. B. Auguste and M. B. Auguste (*L'expédition Leclerc, 1801–1803* [Port-au-Prince: Deschamps, 1986], 277), Saint-Rémy overrated the importance of the Arcahaie meeting.

69. Madiou, *Histoire d'Haïti*, 2:79–85, 518.

70. For the date, see Boisrond-Tonnerre, *Mémoires*, ix.

71. Madiou, *Histoire d'Haïti*, 3:183; Trouillot, *Les Origines sociales*, 90. Chanlatte was raised in Paris and spent the period 1798–1803 in the United States. Boisrond was educated in Paris and lived there approximately 1792–1800, when he was aged 16–24. See Saint-Rémy, *Pétion et Haïti*, 4:11, 19; Boisrond-Tonnerre, *Mémoires*, introduction.

72. He mentions the extermination of the Tainos on the first page, but no more than that.

73. C. Columbus, *The Diario of Christopher Columbus's First Voyages to America, 1492–1493* (Norman: University of Oklahoma Press, 1989), 132; C. Columbus, *The Four Voyages* (Harmondsworth: Penguin Books, 1969), 71, 80, 85, 116, 142; P. Martir de Angleria, *Décadas del Nuevo Mundo* (Santo Domingo: Sociedad Dominicana de Bibliófilos, 1989), 1:351, 354.

74. C. O. Sauer, *The Early Spanish Main* (Berkeley: University of California Press, 1966), 45.

75. Columbus, *Four Voyages*, 142. This lends some support to the idea of a regional rather than island-wide application, but the region in question is flat, not mountainous; Chanca did not record a native name for the whole island.

76. R. Pané, *Relación acerca de las antigüedades de los indios* (Santo Domingo,

1988), 26. Long unpublished, Pané's memoir apparently was completed in 1495.

77. B. de Las Casas, *Short Account of the Destruction of the Indies* (London: Penguin Books, 1992), 27; Columbus, *Diario*, 132.

78. Fernández de Oviedo, *Historia*, 1:27, 32, 143; Las Casas, *Historia*, 1:Chapters 45–48; A. Tejera, "Quid de Quisqueya?" *Boletín del Archivo General de la Nación* (Santo Domingo) 8 (1945): 216–221; Tejera, *Indigenismos*, 2:1148–1149.

79. Herrera, *Historia general*, 1:23; J. de Laet, *Novus orbis, seu, descriptionis Indiae occidentalis* (Leyden, 1633), 5; Charlevoix, *Histoire de l'isle espagnole*, 1:4–5.

80. Abbé Raynal, *Histoire philosophique et politique des établissemens et de commerce des Européens dans les Deux Indes*, 1st ed. (La Haye, 1774), 3:13; and *Histoire philosophique et politique des établissemens et de commerce des Européens dans les Deux Indes*, 3rd ed. (Geneva, 1780), 3:346.

81. A. de Alcedo, *Diccionario geográfico-histórico de las Indias Occidentales o América* (Madrid, 1786), cited in Tejera, "Quid," 220; MSM, 1:266; Moreau de Saint-Méry, *Topographical and Political Description of the Spanish Part of Saint-Domingo*, 1:1; Sánchez Valverde, *Idea del valor*, 7, 27. Moreau's books were published in the 1790s but written the previous decade.

82. Piquenard, *Zoflora ou la bonne négresse*, 1:v, 48. The curious form "Ohaïti" suggests some confusion with Tahiti, then called "Otaïti."

83. J. M. Incháustegui, *Documentos para estudio: marco de la época y problemas del tratado de Basilea de 1795* (Buenos Aires: Academia Dominicana de la Historia, 1957), 1:275.

84. *Essai sur l'administration des colonies françoises* (Antonina [Les Cayes], 1788), 9, 12. However, the *National Union Catalog* and M. Bissainthe (*Dictionnaire de Bibliographie Haïtienne* [Washington, D.C.: Scarecrow Press, 1951], 397) attribute this work to one Charles-Jacob de Bleschamp. Bleschamp was a lawyer and French naval bureaucrat who was at that time Intendant de la Marine at Le Havre. He had earlier worked on a geography of France using new provincial boundaries and names. See P. Fleuriot de Langle, *Alexandrine Lucien-Bonaparte* (Paris: Plon, 1939), 12–14.

85. C. Frostin, "L'Histoire de l'esprit autonomiste colon à Saint-Domingue" (Thèse de doctorat d'état, Université de Paris I, 1972).

86. See G. Marchetti, *Cultura indígena e integración nacional: la "Historia antigua de México" de F. J. Clavijero* (Xalapa: Universidad Veracruzana, 1986).

87. MSM, 1:163, 265, 285; MSM, 2:617, 625, 635, 656, 786, 807, 814, 898; MSM, 3:1212, etc. See Dr. Arthaud's account of stone phalluses found in northern caves in ANOM, F3/267, f. 208–211.

88. On these, see J. Fouchard, *Plaisirs de Saint-Domingue* (Port-au-Prince: Deschamps, 1988), 41, 51, 95.

89. MSM, 1:212.

90. L.-F. Hoffmann, "Un Négociant américain aux Gonaïves en 1806 et 1807," *RSHHG* 155 (1987): 9.

91. P. V. de Vastey, *Le système colonial dévoilé* (Cap Henry, 1814), 2–3.

92. Madiou, *Histoire d'Haïti*, 1:viii–ix; Juste Chanlatte cited in Hoffmann, "L'Elément indien," 26; Nau, *Histoire des caciques d'Haïti*, 1:12–13.

93. D. Geggus, "British Opinion and the Haitian Revolution, 1791–1805," in *Slavery and British Society, 1774–1848*, ed. J. Walvin (London: Macmillan, 1982), 129, 146, 242.

94. A parallel tendency, long established in Haitian letters, has been to claim Caonabó as a Carib (a people far more bellicose in reputation) or to describe the pre-Columbian population as a mixture of Taino and Carib or simply to call them "Carib." Edmond Mangonès argued that "Haïti" was a Carib word and "Quisqueya" a Taino word: E. Mangonès, "L'Île d'Haïti: une regrettable initiative de la U.S. Geographic Board," *RSHHG* 15 (1934): 58–59.

95. R. Paquette, *Sugar Is Made with Blood: The Conspiracy of La Escalera and the Conflict between Empires over Slavery in Cuba* (Middletown, Conn.: Wesleyan University Press, 1988), 256, 258. Paquette attributes the choice to the influence of Siboney literature then in vogue among Cuban whites (as it was among Haitians).

96. He is not mentioned in any edition of Raynal's *Histoire philosophique*, nor in Sauer, *Early Spanish Main*, which also presents Caonabó and Hatuey in a rather pacific light.

97. J. Ángulo y Guridi, *Elementos de geografía físico-histórica . . . de la isla de Santo Domingo* (Santo Domingo, 1866), cited in Tejera, "Quid," 220; J. G. García, *Compendio de la historia de Santo Domingo* (Santo Domingo, 1867), 1:12.

98. A map dated 1630 showing Quisqueya in the south and Haiti in the north is reproduced in Hurbon, *Voodoo*, 18–19. A. Mejía Ricart, in *Historia de Santo Domingo* (Ciudad Trujillo: Editores Pol Hermanos, 1948), 1:35–38, commented that the association with the east was erroneous, but he (wrongly) thought it due to an error by Ramón Pané.

99. See the introduction to the 1893 Port-au-Prince edition of Nau's *Histoire des caciques d'Haïti*; J.-B. Dehoux, *Études sur les aborigènes d'Haïti*, cited in Tejera, "Quid," 220; Élie, *Histoire d'Haïti*, 1:86.

100. Mangonès, "L'Île d'Haïti."

101. See Hoffmann, "L'Elément indien," 32; Fouchard, "Pourquoi Haïti?" 221.

102. Note, however, that A. Záiter Mejía, in *La identidad social y nacional en Dominicana: un análisis psico-social* (Santo Domingo: Taller, 1996), does not mention Amerindians, although she does observe (92) that many Dominicans have difficulty accepting the nation's multiethnic, "fundamentally mulatto" identity. Silvio Torres Saillant, in "The Tribulations of Blackness," 126–146, observes that "in the minds of most Dominicans who use it," the term *indio* "merely describes a color gradation." On Cuba, see R. Duharte Jiménez, "Cuba: identidad cultural, mestizaje y racismo," *América Indígena* 52 (1992): 159–167.

103. "The historian Thomas Madiou states in his autobiography he was descended from an Indian woman. The same applies to thousands and thousands of Haitians." "During the [slave] trade, numerous half-caste descendants of Moors and Negresses with fine European features attracted attention. Their language, scarcely corrupted, gave solid evidence of their semitic ancestry. . . .

The country was not populated solely by uneducated primitives" (Élie, *Histoire d'Haïti*, 2:140, 259). See Lowenthal, *Caribbean Societies*, 185; Comhaire-Sylvain in Charles, *Christophe Colomb*, 156. In a highly polemical exchange with Haitian scholars, Dominican historian Rodríguez Demorizi (*Las invasiones*, 51) mocked certain Haitian intellectuals' attempts to "trace back their history to the days of the Discovery rather than to the African jungle."

104. Cited in Charles, *Christophe Colomb*, 156.

105. In the 1940s, Kléber Georges-Jacob wrote that most Haitians believed that Dominicans were inferior because of their Indian ancestry. See Rodríguez Demorizi, *Invasiones*, 55; also, Hyppolite, *Héritage culturel*, 107, 112.

106. Trouillot, *Les origines sociales*, 113; Hoffmann, "L'Elément indien," 23, 31.

107. J. Faine, *Philologie créole: Études historiques et étymologiques* (Port-au-Prince: Imprimerie de l'État, 1936), 2; Charles, *Christophe Colomb*, 115–223; Fouchard, "Pourquoi Haïti?"; and the discussion above, note 28.

108. Desrosiers, *Civilisation indienne*, iii, 7, 28–29, 34.

109. Hyppolite, *Héritage culturel*, 106.

Works Cited

Agorsah, Kofi, ed. *Maroon Heritage: Archaeological, Ethnographic and Historical Perspectives*. Kingston: Canoe Press, 1994.

Aimes, Hubert. *A History of Slavery in Cuba, 1511–1868*. New York: Octagon, 1967.

Alcedo, Antonio de. *Diccionario geográfico-histórico de las Indias Occidentales o América*. Madrid, 1786–1789.

Alexis, Gerson. *Lecture en anthropologie haïtienne*. Port-au-Prince: Presses Nationales, 1970.

———. *Vaudou et quimbois*. Port-au-Prince: Fardin, 1976.

Andrews, Kenneth. *The Spanish Caribbean: Trade and Plunder*. New Haven: Yale University Press, 1978.

Ángulo y Guridi, Javier. *Elementos de geografía físico-histórica . . . de la isla de Santo Domingo*. Santo Domingo, 1866.

Anstey, Roger. "A Reinterpretation of the Abolition of the British Slave Trade, 1806–1807." *English Historical Review* 87 (1972): 304–332.

Appollon, Willy. *Le vaudou: une espace pour les "voix."* Paris: Éditions Galilée, 1976.

Aptheker, Herbert. *American Negro Slave Revolts*. 1943. Reprint, New York: International Publishers, 1969.

Arango y Parreño, Francisco de. *Obras de D. Francisco de Arango y Parreño*. 2 vols. Havana: Ministerio de Educación, 1952.

Archives Nationales. *Guide des sources de l'histoire de l'Amérique Latine et des Antilles dans les archives françaises*. Paris: Archives Nationales, 1984.

Ardouin, Beaubrun. *Études sur l'histoire d'Haïti*. Paris: Dezobry et Magdeleine, 1853–1860. Reprint, Ed. François Dalencour. 11 vols. in 1. Port-au-Prince: Dalencour, 1958.

Ardouin, Céligny. *Essais sur l'histoire d'Haïti*. Port-au-Prince, 1865.

Auguste, Claude B. "Les Congos dans la Révolution haïtienne." *Revue de la Société Haïtienne d'Histoire et de Géographie* 168 (1990): 11–42.

Auguste, Claude B., and Marcel B. Auguste. *Les déportés de Saint-Domingue: contribution à l'histoire de l'expédition française de Saint-Domingue, 1802–1803*. Sherbrooke, Quebec: Éditions Naaman, 1979.

———. *L'expédition Leclerc, 1801–1803*. Port-au-Prince: Deschamps, 1986.

———. *La participation étrangère à l'expédition française de Saint-Domingue*. Quebec: Auguste, 1980.

Auguste, Marcel B. "L'armée française de Saint-Domingue, dernière Armée de la Révolution." *Jahrbuch für Geschichte von Staat, Wirtschaft und Gesellschaft Lateinamerikas* 28 (1991): 99–100.

Baralt, Guillermo. *Esclavos rebeldes: conspiraciones y sublevaciones de esclavos en Puerto Rico (1795–1873)*. Rio Piedras: Huracán, 1981.

Barré de Saint-Venant, Jean. *Des colonies modernes sous la zone torride*. Paris, 1802.

Barros, Jacques. *Haïti de 1804 à nos jours*. 2 vols. Paris: Harmattan, 1984.

Barthélemy, Gérard. *Créoles-Bossales: conflit en Haïti*. Petit-Bourg: Ibis Rouge, 2000.

------. *Dans la splendeur d'un après-midi d'histoire*. Port-au-Prince: Deschamps, 1996.

------. *Le pays en dehors: essai sur l'univers rural haïtien*. Port-au-Prince: Deschamps, 1989.

------. "Propos sur le Caïman: incertitudes et hypothèses nouvelles." *Chemins Critiques* 2 (1992): 33–58.

Barthélemy, Gérard, and Christian Girault, eds. *La république haïtienne: état des lieux et perspectives*. Paris: Karthala, 1993.

Bastide, Roger. *The African Religions of Brazil*. Baltimore: Johns Hopkins University Press, 1978.

Beckerich, Richard, and Jacques Cauna. "La Révolution de Saint-Domingue vue par un patriote." *RSHHG* 161 (1988): 1–34.

Beckles, Hilary. "The Two Hundred Years War." *Jamaica Historical Review* 13 (1982): 1–10.

Begouen-Demeaux, Maurice. *Stanislas Foäche: négociant de Saint-Domingue, 1737–1806*. Paris: Librairie Larose, 1951.

Bellegarde, Dantès. *Histoire du peuple haïtien (1492–1952)*. Port-au-Prince: n.p., 1953.

Benítez-Rojo, Antonio. *The Repeating Island: The Caribbean and the Postmodern Perspective*. 1989. Reprint, Durham: Duke University Press, 1992.

Bénot, Yves. *La démence coloniale sous Napoléon*. Paris: La Découverte, 1992.

------. "Le procès Sonthonax, ou les *débats entre les accusateurs et les accusés dans l'affaire des colonies* (an III)." In *Léger-Félicité Sonthonax, la première abolition de l'esclavage: la Révolution française et la Révolution de Saint-Domingue*, ed. Marcel Dorigny, 55–63. Paris: Société française d'Histoire d'Outre-mer, 1997.

------. *La Révolution française et la fin des colonies*. Paris: La Découverte, 1987.

Berlin, Ira, and Philip Morgan, eds. *Cultivation and Culture: Labor and the Shaping of Slave Life in the Americas*. Charlottesville: University Press of Virginia, 1993.

Bermúdez Plata, Cristóbal. *Catálogo de documentos de la Sección Novena del Archivo General de Indias*. Seville: Escuela de Estudios Hispano-Americanos, 1949.

Bertaud, Jean-Paul, Georges Miraval, and David Geggus, eds. *The French Revolution Research Collection and Videodisk: Section 11, War and the Colonies*. Witney: Micrographix, 1993.

Bigarré. *Mémoires du général Bigarré*. Paris, 1893.

Bissainthe, Max. *Dictionnaire de Bibliographie Haïtienne*. Washington, D.C.: Scarecrow Press, 1951.

Bittremieux, Léo. *Mayombsch Idioticon*. 2 vols. Gent: Drukkerij Erasmus, 1922–1927.

Blackburn, Robin. *The Overthrow of Colonial Slavery*. London: Verso, 1988.

Blanchelande, Philibert-François Rouxel de. *Discours justificatif de Philibert-François Rouxel Blanchelande*. Paris, 1793.

------. *Mémoire de Blanchelande sur son administration. Supplément*. n.p., n.d.

Blassingame, John W. *The Slave Community: Plantation Life in the Antebellum South*. 1972. Reprint, New York: Oxford University Press, 1979.

Boisrond-Tonnerre, Louis Félix. *Mémoires pour servir à l'histoire d'Haïti*. 1806. Reprint, Port-au-Prince: Fardin, 1981.

Bolland, O. Nigel. *Slavery in Belize*. Belize City: Belize Institute for Social Research and Action Occasional Papers no. 7, 1979.

Bolt, Christine, and Seymour Drescher, eds. *Anti-slavery, Religion, and Reform: Essays in Memory of Roger Anstey*. Folkestone: Dawson Archon, 1980.

Bonnemain, Antoine. *La régénération des colonies*. Paris, 1792.

Bonniol, Jean-Luc. *La Couleur comme maléfice: Une illustration créole de la généalogie des "Blancs" et des "Noirs."* Paris: Albin Michel, 1992.

Boulle, Pierre. "In Defense of Slavery: Eighteenth Century Opposition to Abolition and the Origins of a Racist Ideology in France." In *History from Below,* ed. F. Krantz, 219–246. Oxford: Blackwell, 1988.

Bradley, Keith R. *Slavery and Rebellion in the Roman World, 140 B.C.–70 B.C.* Bloomington: Indiana University Press, 1989.

Brathwaite, Edward. *The Development of Creole Society in Jamaica, 1770–1820.* London: Oxford University Press, 1971.

Brette, A. "Les gens de couleur libres et leurs députés en 1789." *La Révolution Française* 29 (1895).

Brissot, Jacques-Pierre. *Discours de J.-P. Brissot . . . sur les causes des troubles de Saint-Domingue.* Paris, 1791.

Brito Figueroa, Federico. *Las insurecciones de esclavos en Venezuela.* Caracas: Cantaclaro, 1961.

Brutus, Edner. *Révolution dans Saint-Domingue.* 2 vols. Paris: Éditions du Panthéon, 1973.

Buckley, Roger. *Slaves in Red Coats.* New Haven: Yale University Press, 1979.

Buisseret, David, ed. *France in the New World: Proceedings of the 22nd Meeting of the French Colonial Historical Society.* East Lansing: Michigan State University Press, 1998.

Burdon, John. *The Archives of British Honduras.* 3 vols. London: Sifton Praed, 1931–1935.

Cabon, Adolphe. *Histoire d'Haïti.* 5 vols. Port-au-Prince: Ed. La Petite Revue, n.d.

———. "Les religieuses du Cap à Saint-Domingue." *Revue d'Histoire de l'Amérique Française* 3 (1949): 402–422.

Caiger, Stephen. *British Honduras, Past and Present.* London: George, Allen & Unwin, 1951.

Campbell, Mavis C. *The Maroons of Jamaica, 1655–1796: A History of Resistance, Collaboration and Betrayal.* Granby, Mass.: Bergin & Garvey, 1988.

Camus, Michel. "Une lettre du général Capoix." *Revue de la Société Haïtienne d'Histoire et de Géographie* 141 (1983): 69–72.

Carneiro, Edison. *O quilombo dos Palmares.* Rio de Janeiro: Civilizacão Brasileira, 1966.

Carnot, Hippolyte, ed., *Mémoires de Grégoire.* 2 vols. Paris, 1837.

Carteaux, Félix. *Soirées bermudiennes, ou entretiens sur les événemens qui ont opéré la ruine de la partie française de l'isle Saint-Domingue.* Bordeaux: Pellier-Lawalle, 1802.

Cartografía de Ultramar. 4 vols. in 8. Madrid: Servicio Geográfica e Histórica del Ejército, 1949–1957.

Cassidy, Frederic, and Robert Lepage. *Dictionary of Jamaican English.* 1967. Reprint, Cambridge: Cambridge University Press, 1980.

Castillero Calvo, Alfredo. *Conquista, evangelización y resistencia: Triunfo o fracaso de la política indigenista?* Panama: Mariano Arosemena, 1995.

Castonnet-Desfosses. *La Révolution de Saint-Domingue.* Paris, 1893.

Cauna, Jacques (de). *Au temps des isles à sucre: histoire d'une plantation de Saint-Domingue au XVIIIe siècle.* Paris: Karthala, 1987.

———. "Une habitation coloniale à la fin du XVIIIe siècle: la sucrerie Fleuriau de Bellevue." Thèse de 3me cycle, Université de Poitiers, 1983.

———. *Haïti: l'éternelle révolution.* Port-au-Prince: Deschamps, 1997.

———. "La Révolution à Port-au-Prince (1791–1792): Relation inédite du Négociant Lajard." *Revue de la Société Haïtienne d'Histoire et de Géographie* 152 (1986): 5–28.

Césaire, Aimé. *Toussaint Louverture: La Révolution française et le problème colonial.* Rev. ed. Paris: Présence Africaine, 1962.

Chanlatte jeune, Dubourg, Viart, and F. Ouvière. *Mémoire historique des dernières révolutions des provinces de l'Ouest et du Sud de la partie françoise de Saint-Domingue, publié par les commissaires des citoyens de couleur de Saint-Marc et de plusieurs paroisses de la colonie.* Paris, 1792.

Charles, Christophe Philippe. *Christophe Colomb, les Indiens et leurs survivances en Haïti.* Port-au-Prince: Editions Christophe, 1992.

Charlevoix, Pierre François Xavier de. *Histoire de l'isle espagnole ou de Saint Domingue.* 4 vols. Amsterdam: F. L'Honoré, 1733.

Charlier, Étienne. *Aperçu sur la formation historique de la nation haïtienne.* Port-au-Prince: Presses Libres, 1954.

Childs, Matt D. "'A Black French General Arrived to Conquer the Island': Images of the Haitian Revolution in Cuba's 1812 Aponte Rebellion." In *Impact of the Haitian Revolution in the Atlantic World,* ed. D. Geggus, 135–136. Columbia: University of South Carolina Press, 2001.

Clavier, Jean-Louis. "Toussaint-Louverture d'après le 'Mémoire abrégé des événements de l'île de Saint Domingue de l'année 1789 à celle de 1807.'" *Revue Française d'Histoire d'Outre-Mer* 62 (1975): 462–504.

Clavière, Étienne. *Adresse de la Société des Amis des Noirs à l'Assemblée Nationale.* 2nd ed. Paris, 1791.

Coatsworth, John. "American Trade with European Colonies in the Caribbean and South America, 1790–1812." *William and Mary Quarterly* 24 (1967): 243–266.

Cohen, William B. *The French Encounter with Africans.* Bloomington: Indiana University Press, 1980.

Cole, Hubert. *King Christophe of Haiti.* London: Eyre & Spottiswoode, 1967.

Columbus, Christopher. *The Diario of Christopher Columbus's First Voyages to America, 1492–1493.* Ed. Oliver Dunn and James E. Kelley. Norman: University of Oklahoma Press, 1989.

———. *The Four Voyages.* Trans. J. M. Cohen. Harmondsworth: Penguin Books, 1969.

Comhaire-Sylvain, Suzanne. "Les Contes haïtiens." 2 vols. Thèse: Université de Paris, 1937.

———. "Influences indiennes dans le folklore haïtien." In Pierre-Charles, *Problemas,* 155–57.

———. "Survivances africaines dans le vocabulaire religieux d'Haïti." *Études dahoméennes* 14 (1955): 5–20.

Commission des Colonies. *Débats entre les accusateurs et les accusés dans l'affaire des colonies.* 9 vols. Paris, 1795.

"Le concordat de Damiens." *Chemins Critiques* 2 (1992): 263–281.

Condorcet, Marquis de. *Au corps électoral contre l'esclavage des noirs.* Paris, 1789. In *Oeuvres complètes de Condorcet.* Brunswick, 1804.

Cordero Michel, Emilio. *La Revolución haitiana y Santo Domingo.* Santo Domingo: Editora nacional, 1968.

Córdova-Bello, Eleázar. *La independencia de Haití y su influencia en Hispanoamérica.* Caracas: Instituto Panamericano, 1967.

Corre, A. *Les papiers du Général A.-N. de La Salle (Saint-Domingue, 1792–1793).* Quimper, 1897.

Corvington, Georges. *Port-au-Prince au cours des ans: sous les assauts de la Révolution.* Port-au-Prince: Deschamps, 1972.

Courlander, Harold. *The Piece of Fire and Other Haitian Tales.* New York: Harcourt Brace, 1964.

Cournand, Antoine de. *Requête présentée à Nosseigneurs de l'Assemblée Nationale en faveur des gens de couleur de l'île de Saint Domingue.* Paris, 1789.

Cousin d'Avallon, C. *Histoire de Toussaint Louverture.* Paris, 1802.

Cox, Edward. *The Free Coloreds in the Slave Societies of St. Kitts and Grenada, 1763–1833.* Knoxville: University of Tennessee Press, 1984.

Craton, Michael. "The Passion to Exist: Slave Rebellions in the British West Indies." *Journal of Caribbean History* 13 (1980): 1–20.

———. "Proto-Peasant Revolts? The Late Slave Rebellions in the British West Indies, 1816–1832." *Past and Present* 85 (1979): 99–125.

———. *Searching for the Invisible Man: Slaves and Plantation Life in Jamaica.* Cambridge, Mass.: Harvard University Press, 1978.

———. "Slave Culture, Resistance and the Achievement of Emancipation in the British West Indies, 1783–1838." In *Slavery and British Society, 1774–1848,* ed. J. Walvin, 100–122. London: Macmillan, 1982.

———. *Testing the Chains: Resistance to Slavery in the British West Indies.* Ithaca: Cornell University Press, 1982.

Craton, Michael, ed. *Roots and Branches: Current Directions in Slave Studies.* Toronto: Pergamon, 1979.

Craton, Michael, James Walvin, and David Wright, eds. *Slavery, Abolition and Emancipation: Black Slaves and the British Empire, A Thematic Documentary.* London: Longman, 1976.

Dalencour, François. *Précis méthodique d'Histoire d'Haïti.* Port-au-Prince: Dalencour, 1935.

Dalmas, Antoine. *Histoire de la révolution de Saint-Domingue.* Paris, 1814.

Daney, Sidney. *Histoire de la Martinique depuis la colonisation jusqu'en 1846.* 6 vols. Fort Royal: 1846.

Davis, David B. *The Problem of Slavery in the Age of Revolution.* Ithaca: Cornell University Press, 1975.

———. *The Problem of Slavery in Western Culture.* Ithaca: Cornell University Press, 1966.

Davis, Thomas J. *A Rumor of Revolt: The "Great Negro Plot" in Colonial New York.* Amherst: University of Massachusetts Press, 1985.

Debbasch, Yvan. *Couleur et liberté: le jeu du critère ethnique dans l'ordre juridique esclavagiste.* Paris: Dalloz, 1967.

———. "Le marronnage: essai sur la désertion de l'esclave antillais." *Année Sociologique* 3 (1961): 1–112.

———. "Le marronnage: essai sur la désertion de l'esclave antillais." *Année Sociologique* 3 (1962): 117–195.

Debien, Gabriel. *Les colons de Saint-Domingue et la Révolution française: essai sur le Club Massiac.* Paris: A. Colin, 1953.

———. *Les esclaves aux Antilles françaises, XVIIe et XVIIIe siècles.* Basse-Terre: Société d'histoire de la Guadeloupe, 1974.

———. *Esprit colon et esprit d'autonomie.* Paris: Larose, 1954.

———. "Histoire de deux plantations à Saint-Domingue, 1781–1829 (Papiers Bongars-Broc)." *Revue de la Province du Maine* (1968): 305–20.

———. "Nouvelles de Saint-Domingue." *Notes d'Histoire Coloniale* 59 (1960): 1–35.

———. "Les travaux d'histoire sur Saint-Domingue (1938–1946): essai de mise au point." *Revue d'Histoire des Colonies* 34 (1947): 31–86.

Debien, Gabriel, Jean Fouchard, and Marie-Antoinette Menier. "Toussaint Louverture avant 1789: Légendes et Réalités." *Conjonction: Revue Franco-Haïtienne* 134 (1977): 67–80.

Debien, Gabriel, and Pierre Pluchon. "Un plan d'invasion de la Jamaïque." *Revue de la Société Haïtienne d'Histoire et de Géographie* 36 (1978): 3–72.

DeConde, Alexander. *The Quasi-War: The Politics and Diplomacy of the Undeclared War with France 1797–1801.* New York: Scribner, 1966.

Deerr, Noel. *History of Sugar.* 2 vols. London: Chapman and Hall, 1949–1950.

Degler, Carl. *Neither Black nor White: Slavery and Race Relations in Brazil and the United States.* New York: Macmillan, 1971.

Deive, Carlos Esteban. *Las emigraciones dominicanas a Cuba (1795–1808).* Santo Domingo: Fundación Cultural Dominicana, 1989.

———. *La esclavitud del negro en Santo Domingo (1492–1844).* 2 vols. Santo Domingo: Museo del Hombre, 1980.

———. *La Española y la Esclavitud del Indio.* Santo Domingo: Fundación García Arévalo, 1995.

———. *Los guerilleros negros: esclavos fugitivos y cimarrones en Santo Domingo.* Santo Domingo: Fundación Cultural Dominicana, 1989.

De Laet, Joanne. *Novus orbis, seu, descriptionis Indiae occidentalis.* Leyden, 1633.

Del Monte y Tejada, Antonio. *Historia de Santo Domingo.* 4 vols. Santo Domingo, 1890.

Delpêche, Bernard, ed. *Marronnage in the Caribbean: Myth and Reality.* Montreal: Centre International de Documentation et d'Information Haïtienne Caraïbéenne et Afro-Canadienne, 2002.

Denis, Lorimer, and François Duvalier. *Le problème des classes à travers l'histoire d'Haïti.* 2nd ed. Port-au-Prince: Au service de la Jeunesse, 1958.

Deren, Maya. *The Voodoo Gods.* 1953. Reprint, St. Alban's: Paladin, 1975.

Descourtilz, Michel Étienne. *Voyages d'un naturaliste et ses observations.* 3 vols. Paris, 1809.

Desrosiers, Toussaint. *Civilisation indienne et culture haïtienne.* Port-au-Prince: Imprimerie Rodríguez, n.d.

Dessalles, Pierre. *Historique des troubles survenus à la Martinique.* Ed. Léo Elisabeth. Fort de France, n.d.

Devas, Raymund. *The Island of Grenada, 1650–1950.* St. George's: n.p., 1964.

Diario de las sesiones de las Cortes generales y extraordinarias. 9 vols. Madrid, 1870–1874.

Diouf, Sylviane A. *Servants of Allah: African Muslims Enslaved in the Americas.* New York: New York University Press, 1998.

Dirks, Robert. *The Black Saturnalia: Conflict and Its Ritual Expression on British West Indian Slave Plantations.* Gainesville: University Presses of Florida, 1987.

Discours sur la nécessité d'établir à Paris une société pour concourir . . . à l'abolition de la traite et de l'esclavage des Nègres. Paris, 1788.

Dockès, Pierre. *Medieval Slavery and Liberation.* Chicago: University of Chicago Press, 1979.

Documentos relativos a la independencia de Norteamerica existentes en archivos españoles. Madrid: Ministerio de Asuntos Exteriores, 1981.

Dorigny, Marcel, ed. *Léger-Félicité Sonthonax, la première abolition de l'esclavage: la Révolution française et la Révolution de Saint-Domingue.* Paris: Société française d'Histoire d'Outre-mer, 1997.

Dorsainvil, Roger. *De Fatras Bâton à Toussaint Louverture*. Alger: Enal, 1983.

Douglass, Frederick. *The Life and Writings of Frederick Douglass*. 4 vols. Ed. Philip Foner. New York: International Publishers, 1955.

———. *Narrative of the Life of Frederick Douglass*. 1845. New York: Penguin, 1982.

Doyle, William. *Oxford History of the French Revolution*. Oxford: Oxford University Press, 1989.

Drescher, Seymour. "British Way, French Way: Opinion Building and Revolution in the Second French Slave Emancipation." *American Historical Review* 96 (1991): 709–734.

———. *Capitalism and Antislavery: British Mobilization in Comparative Perspective*. New York: Oxford University Press, 1986.

———. *Econocide: British Slavery in the Era of Abolition*. Pittsburgh: Pittsburgh University Press, 1977.

———. "Two Variants of Anti-Slavery." In *Anti-slavery, Religion, and Reform: Essays in Memory of Roger Anstey*, ed. C. Bolt and S. Drescher, 43–63. Folkestone: Dawson Archon, 1980.

Drolet, Patricia. "The Congo Ritual of Northeastern Panama: An Afro-American Expressive Structure of Cultural Adaptation." Ph.D. diss., University of Illinois, 1980.

Drouin de Bercy, Louis Marie César Auguste. *De Saint-Domingue, des ses guerres, de ses révolutions, de ses ressources*. Paris, 1814.

Dubois, Laurent. "A Colony of Citizens: Revolution and Slave Emancipation in the French Caribbean, 1789–1802." Ph.D. diss., University of Michigan, 1998.

Dubroca, Louis. *The Life of Toussaint Louverture*. London, 1802.

———. *La vie de Jean-Jacques Dessalines*. Paris, 1804.

———. *Vie de Toussaint-Louverture, chef des noirs insurgés de Saint-Domingue*. Paris, 1802.

Ducoeurjoly, S. *Manuel des habitants de Saint-Domingue*. Paris, 1802.

Duffy, Michael. "The Impact of the French Revolution on British Attitudes to the West Indian Colonies." In *A Turbulent Time: The French Revolution and the Greater Caribbean*, ed. D. B. Gaspar and D. P. Geggus, 78–101. Bloomington: Indiana University Press, 1997.

———. *Soldiers, Sugar, and Seapower: The British Expeditions to the West Indies and the War against Revolutionary France*. Oxford: Oxford University Press, 1987.

Duharte Jiménez, Rafael. "Cuba: Identidad cultural, mestizaje y racismo. Encuentros y desencuentros de la cultura cubana." *América Indígena* 52 (1992): 159–167.

———. *Rebeldía esclava en el Caribe*. Jalapa: Gobierno del Estado, 1992.

Dumesle, Hérard. *Voyage dans le nord d'Haïti ou révélations des lieux et des monuments historiques*. Les Cayes, 1824.

Duvalier, François (with Lorimer Denis). *Oeuvres essentielles du Dr. François Duvalier*. Port-au-Prince: Presses nationales d'Haïti, 1968.

D.V.A.E.P. *Historia de la Isla de Santo Domingo*. Madrid, 1806.

Edwards, Bryan. *An Historical Survey of the French Colony in the Island of St. Domingo*. London, 1797, 1801.

———. *History Civil and Commercial of the British West Indies*. 2 vols. London, 1793.

Egerton, Douglas R. *Gabriel's Rebellion: The Virginia Slave Conspiracies of 1800 and 1802*. Chapel Hill: University of North Carolina Press, 1993.

Élie, Louis. *Histoire d'Haïti*. 2 vols. Port-au-Prince: n.p., 1944–1945.

Elkins, Stanley. *Slavery: A Problem in American Institutional and Intellectual Life*. 3rd ed. Chicago: University of Chicago Press, 1976.

Eltis, David. *Economic Growth and the Ending of the Atlantic Slave Trade*. New York: Oxford University Press, 1987.

Eltis, David, Stephen Behrendt, David Richardson, and Herbert Klein. *The Transatlantic Slave Trade: A Database on CD-ROM*. Cambridge: Cambridge University Press, 1999.

Engerman, Stanley, and Robert Paquette, eds. *Parts beyond the Seas: The Lesser Antilles in the Age of European Expansion*. Gainesville: University of Florida Press, 1996.

Essai sur l'administration des colonies françoises. Antonina [Les Cayes]: n.p., 1788.

État détaillé des liquidations opérées par la commission . . . de l'indemnité de Saint-Domingue. 6 vols. Paris, 1828–1833.

Faine, Jules. *Philologie créole: Études historiques et étymologiques*. Port-au-Prince: Imprimerie de l'État, 1936.

Fennema, Meindert, and Troetje Loewenthal. *Construcción de raza y nación en la República Dominicana*. Santo Domingo: Editoria Universitaria, 1987.

Fernández de Oviedo y Valdés, Gonzalo. *Historia general y natural de las Indias*. 1535, 1549. Reprint, Ed. Juan Pérez de Tudela. 5 vols. Madrid: Ediciones Atlas, 1959.

Fernández Repetto, Francisco, and Genny Negroe Sierra. *Una población perdida en la memoria: los negros de Yucatán*. Mérida: Universidad Autónoma, 1995.

Fick, Carolyn. *The Making of Haiti: The Saint Domingue Revolution from Below*. Knoxville: University of Tennessee Press, 1990.

Finley, Moses I. *Ancient Slavery and Modern Ideology*. New York: Viking Press, 1980.

———. "A Peculiar Institution?" *Times Literary Supplement*, 2 July 1976.

———. "Revolution in Antiquity." In *Revolution in History*, ed. R. Porter and M. Teich, 47–60. Cambridge: Cambridge University Press, 1986.

Fleuriot de Langle, Paul. *Alexandrine Lucien-Bonaparte, princesse de Canino*. Paris: Plon, 1939.

Fogel, Robert W. *Without Consent or Contract: The Rise and Fall of American Slavery*. New York: Norton, 1989.

"Fondos del Archivo de la Nación: documentos de la época colonial, 1733–1795." *Boletín del Archivo General de la Nación* 38–39 (1945): 8–22.

Foster, Charles R., and Albert Valdman, eds. *Haiti—Today and Tomorrow*. Lanham: University Press of America, 1984.

Foubert, Bernard. *Les habitations Laborde à Saint-Domingue dans la seconde moitié du XVIIIe siècle: Contribution à l'histoire d'Haïti*. 2 vols. Lille: Université de Lille III, 1990.

———. "Le marronage sur les habitations Laborde à Saint-Domingue dans la seconde moitié du XVIIIe siècle." *Annales de Bretagne* 95 (1988): 277–310.

———. "Les volontaires nationaux de l'Aube et de la Seine Inférieure à Saint Domingue." *Bulletin de la Société d'Histoire de la Guadeloupe* 51 (1982): 3–56.

Fouchard, Jean. "Documents inédits: Thomas Madiou rend hommage à l'empereur." *Revue de la Société Haïtienne d'Histoire et de Géographie* 145 (1984): 5–12.

———. *The Haitian Maroons: Liberty or Death*. Trans. A. Faulkner Watts. New York: E. Blyden Press, 1981.

———. *Langue et littérature des aborigènes d'Ayti*. Paris: École, 1972.

———. *Les marrons de la liberté*. Paris: École, 1972.

———. *Les marrons du syllabaire*. Port-au-Prince: Deschamps, 1953.

———. *Plaisirs de Saint-Domingue: regards sur le temps passé*. 1955. Reprint, Port-au-Prince: Deschamps, 1988.

———. "Pourquoi Haïti? Où, quand et par qui fut choisi de redonner à notre patrie le nom indien d'Haïti." *Revue de la Société Haïtienne d'Histoire et de Géographie* 145 (1984): 13–17.

———. "Quand Haïti exportait la liberté." *Revue de la Société Haïtienne d'Histoire et de Géographie* 143 (1984): 42–45.

Franco, Franklin J. "Antihaitianismo e ideologia del Trujillato." In *Problemas dominico-haitianas y del Caribe,* ed. G. Pierre-Charles, et al., 83–109. Mexico City: Universidad Nacional Autónoma de México, 1973.

Franco, José Luciano. *Las conspiraciones de 1810 y 1811.* Havana: Editorial de Ciencias Sociales, 1977.

———. *Documentos para la historia de Haití en el Archivo Nacional.* Havana: Archivo Nacional, 1954.

———. *Revolución y conflictos en el Caribe, 1789–1854.* Vol. 2 of *La batalla por el dominio del Caribe y el Golfo de México.* Havana: Instituto de Historia, 1965.

Franklin, John Hope, and Loren Schweninger. *Runaway Slaves: Rebels on the Plantations.* New York: Oxford University Press, 1999.

Frostin, Charles. "L'Histoire de l'esprit autonomiste colon à Saint-Domingue aux XVIIe et XVIIIe siècles." 2 vols. Thèse de doctorat d'état, Université de Paris I, 1972.

———. *Les Révoltes blanches à Saint-Domingue aux XVIIe et XVIIIe siècles.* Paris: L'École, 1975.

García, José Gabriel. *Compendio de la historia de Santo Domingo.* 3 vols. Santo Domingo, 1867.

García Rodríguez, Gloria. *La esclavitud desde la esclavitud: la visión de los siervos.* Mexico: Centro Jorge Tamayo, 1996.

Garran-Coulon, Jean-Philippe. *Rapport sur les troubles de Saint-Domingue.* 4 vols. Paris, 1797–1799.

Garrett, Mitchell B. *The French Colonial Question, 1789–1791.* New York: Negro University Press, 1916.

Garrigus, John. "Between Servitude and Citizenship: Free Coloreds in Pre-Revolutionary Saint Domingue." Ph.D. diss., Johns Hopkins University, 1988.

———. "Blue and Brown: Contraband Indigo and the Rise of a Free Colored Planter Class in French Saint-Domingue." *The Americas* 50 (1993): 233–263.

———. "Catalyst or Catastrophe? Saint Domingue's Free Men of Color and the Battle of Savannah." *Revista/Review Interamericana* 22 (1992): 109–125.

———. "Colour, Class, and Identity on the Eve of the Haitian Revolution: Saint Domingue's Free Coloured Elite as *Colons Américains.*" *Slavery and Abolition* 17 (1996): 20–43.

———. "The Free Colored Elite of Pre-Revolutionary Saint Domingue: The Case of Julien Raimond." In *Brown Power in the Caribbean,* forthcoming from David B. Gaspar and Gad Heuman.

Gaspar, David Barry. *Bondmen and Rebels: Master-Slave Relations in Antigua.* Baltimore: Johns Hopkins University Press, 1985.

Gaspar, David Barry, and David Patrick Geggus, eds. *A Turbulent Time: The French Revolution and the Greater Caribbean.* Bloomington: Indiana University Press, 1997.

Gaspar, David Barry, and Gad Heuman, eds. *Brown Power in the Caribbean.* Durham: Duke University Press, forthcoming.

Gaspar, David Barry, and Darlene Clark Hine, eds. *More Than Chattel: Black Women and Slavery.* Bloomington: Indiana University Press, 1996.

Gastine, Civique de. *Histoire de la république d'Haïti ou Saint-Domingue, l'esclavage et les colons.* Paris, 1819.

Gatereau, Louis François Roger Armand. *Histoire des troubles de Saint-Domingue.* Paris, 1792.

Gaxotte, Pierre. *La Révolution Française.* New ed. 1928. Reprint, Paris: Fayard, 1975.

Geggus, David. "The Arming of Slaves in the Haitian Revolution." In *The Arming of Slaves: From Classical Times to the Modern Era,* ed. P. Morgan and C. Brown. Yale University Press, forthcoming.

——. "The British Government and the Saint Domingue Slave Revolt, 1791–1793." *English Historical Review* 96 (1981): 285–305.

——. "British Opinion and the Haitian Revolution, 1791–1805." In *Slavery and British Society, 1776–1848,* ed. J. Walvin, 123–149. London: Macmillan, 1982.

——. "The Caradeux and Colonial Memory." In *Impact of the Haitian Revolution in the Atlantic World,* ed. D. Geggus, 231–246. Columbia: University of South Carolina Press, 2001.

——. *The Caribbean Collection at the University of Florida: A Brief Description.* Gainesville: University of Florida Libraries, 1985.

——. "The Demographic Composition of the French Caribbean Slave Trade." In *Proceedings of the 13th and 14th Meetings of the FCHS* (Lanham, Md.: University Press of America, 1990), 14–30.

——. "Les derniers esclaves de Saint-Domingue: partie 1." *Revue de la Société Haïtienne d'Histoire et de Géographie* 161 (1988): 85–111.

——. "The Enigma of Jamaica in the 1790s: New Light on the Causation of Slave Rebellions." *William and Mary Quarterly* 44 (1987): 287–288.

——. "Les esclaves de la plaine du Nord à la veille de la Révolution." *Revue de la Société Haïtienne d'Histoire et de Géographie* 135 (1982): 85–107; 136 (1982): 5–32; 144 (1984): 24–36; 149 (1985): 16–52.

——. "Esclaves et gens de couleur libres de la Martinique pendant l'époque révolutionnaire et napoléonienne: trois moments de résistance." *Revue Historique* 295 (1996): 105–132.

——. "Une famille de La Rochelle et ses plantations de Saint-Domingue." In *France in the New World: Proceedings of the 22nd Meeting of the French Colonial Historical Society,* ed. D. Buisseret, 119–136. East Lansing: Michigan State University Press, 1998.

——. "The French and Haitian Revolutions, and Resistance to Slavery in the Americas." *Revue Française d'Histoire d'Outre-Mer* 232–233 (1989): 107–224.

——. "The French Slave Trade: An Overview." *William and Mary Quarterly* 58 (2001): 119–138.

——. "From His Most Catholic Majesty to the Godless République: The Volte-Face of Toussaint Louverture." *Revue Française d'Histoire d'Outre-Mer* 65 (1978): 481–499.

——. "Haiti and the Abolitionists, 1804–1838: Opinion, Propaganda and International Politics in Britain and France, 1804–1838." In *Abolition and Its Aftermath: The Historical Context, 1790–1916,* ed. D. Richardson, 113–140. London: Frank Cass, 1985.

——. "Haitian History in North American Archives." *Revista/Review Interamericana* 27 (1997): 151–179.

——. "The Haitian Maroons: Myth and History." In *Marronnage in the Caribbean: Myth and Reality,* ed. B. Delpêche. Montreal: Centre International de Documentation et d'Information Haïtienne Caraïbéenne et Afro-Canadienne, 2002.

———. "Haitian Voodoo in the Eighteenth Century: Language, Culture, Resistance." *Jahrbuch für Geschichte von Staat, Wirtschaft und Gesellschaft Lateinamerikas* 28 (1991): 21–51.

———. "Indigo and Slavery in Saint Domingue." *Plantation Society in the Americas* 5 (1998): 189–204.

———. "The Influence of the Haitian Revolution on Blacks in Latin America and the Caribbean." In *Blacks and National Identity in Nineteenth-Century Latin America*, ed. N. Naro. London: University of London, 2001.

———. "Jamaica and the Saint Domingue Slave Revolt, 1791–93." *The Americas* 38 (1981): 219–233.

———. "The Major Port Towns of Saint Domingue in the Late Eighteenth Century." In *Atlantic Port Cities: Economy, Culture, and Society*, ed. F. Knight and P. Liss, 87–116. Knoxville: University of Tennessee Press, 1991.

———. "On the Eve of the Haitian Revolution: Slave Runaways in Saint Domingue in 1790." In *From Out of the House of Bondage: Runaways, Resistance and Marronage in Africa and the New World*, ed. G. Heuman, 112–128. London: Frank Cass, 1986.

———. "Pélage-Marie Duboys, The Anonymous Author of the 'Précis Historique.'" *Archives Antillaises* 3 (1975): 5–10.

———. "Sex Ratio and Ethnicity: A Reply to Paul E. Lovejoy." *Journal of African History* 30 (1989): 395–397.

———. "Slave and Free Colored Women in Saint Domingue." In Gaspar and Hine, *More Than Chattel*, 259–278.

———. "Slave Resistance in the Spanish Caribbean in the 1790s." In *A Turbulent Time: The French Revolution and the Greater Caribbean*, ed. D. B. Gaspar and D. P. Geggus, 133–155. Bloomington: Indiana University Press, 1997.

———. *Slave Resistance Studies and the Saint Domingue Slave Revolt.* Miami: Florida International University, Occasional Papers Series, 1983.

———. *Slavery, War and Revolution: The British Occupation of Saint Domingue, 1793–1798.* Oxford: Oxford University Press, 1982.

———. "Slavery, War, and Revolution in the Greater Caribbean, 1789–1815." In *A Turbulent Time: The French Revolution and the Greater Caribbean*, ed. D. B. Gaspar and D. P. Geggus, 1–50. Bloomington: Indiana University Press, 1997.

———. "The Slaves and Free Coloreds of Martinique during the Age of the French and Haitian Revolutions: Three Moments of Resistance." In *Parts beyond the Seas: The Lesser Antilles in the Age of European Expansion*, ed. S. Engerman and R. Paquette, 300–321. Gainesville: University of Florida Press, 1996.

———. "The Slaves of British-Occupied Saint Domingue: An Analysis of the Workforces of 197 Absentee Plantations, 1796/97." *Caribbean Studies* 18 (1978): 5–41.

———. "Sugar and Coffee Cultivation in Saint Domingue and the Shaping of the Slave Labor Force." In *Cultivation and Culture: Labor and the Shaping of Afro-American Culture in the Americas*, ed. I. Berlin and P. Morgan, 73–98, 318–324. Charlottesville: University Press of Virginia, 1993.

———. "The Sugar Plantation Zones of Saint Domingue and the Revolution of 1791–1793." *Slavery and Abolition* 20 (1999): 31–46.

———. "Toussaint Louverture and the Slaves of the Bréda Plantations." *Journal of Caribbean History* 20 (1985–1986): 30–48.

———. "Toussaint Louverture et l'abolition de l'esclavage à Saint-Domingue." In *Les abolitions dans les Amériques: actes du colloque organisé par les Archives départementales dé la Martinique, 8–9 décembre 1998,* ed. L. Chauleau, 109–116. Fort de France: Société des Amis des Archives, 2001.

Geggus, David, ed. *The Impact of the Haitian Revolution in the Atlantic World.* Columbia: University of South Carolina Press, 2001.

Genovese, Eugene. *From Rebellion to Revolution: Afro-American Slave Revolts in the Making of the Modern World.* Baton Rouge: Louisiana State University Press, 1979.

———. *Roll, Jordan, Roll. The World the Slaves Made.* New York: Pantheon Books, 1974.

———. "Towards a Psychology of Slavery." In *Revisiting Blassingame's* The Slave Community, ed. Al-Tony Gilmore, 27–41. Westport, Conn.: Greenwood Press.

Gilmore, Al-Tony, ed. *Revisiting Blassingame's* The Slave Community. Westport, Conn.: Greenwood Press, 1978.

Girault, Christian, et al. *Atlas d'Haïti.* Talence: Université de Bordeaux, 1985.

Girod, F. *La vie quotidienne de la société créole.* Paris: Hachette, 1972.

Glissant, Edouard. *Le discours antillais.* Paris: Seuil, 1982.

Godechot, Jacques. *La Grande Nation.* Paris: Aubier, 1956.

Gonzalez, Nancie L. "New Evidence on the Origin of the Black Carib." *New West Indian Guide* 57 (1983): 143–172.

———. *Sojourners of the Caribbean: Ethnogenesis and Ethnohistory of the Garifuna.* Urbana: University of Illinois Press, 1988.

Goslinga, Cornelis. *The Dutch in the Caribbean and Surinam, 1791/95–1942.* Assen: Van Gorcum, 1991.

Gouges, Olympe de. *Réponse au champion Américain.* Paris, 1790.

Gough, Hugh. *The Newspaper Press in the French Revolution.* Chicago: Dorsey, 1988.

Gragnon-Lacoste, T. *Toussaint-Louverture.* Paris, 1877.

Grégoire, Henri. *De la littérature des nègres.* Paris, 1808.

———. *Lettre aux philanthropes sur . . . les réclamations des gens de couleur.* Paris, 1790.

———. *Mémoire en faveur des gens de couleur libres ou sang-mêlés de St.-Domingue.* Paris, 1789.

Grimouärd, Henri de. *L'amiral de Grimouärd au Port-au-Prince, d'après sa correspondance et son journal de bord (Mars 1791–Juillet 1792).* Paris: Larose, 1937.

Gros. *Isle Saint-Domingue, Province du Nord.* n.p., 1793.

Gurr, Ted Robert. *Why Men Rebel.* Princeton: Princeton University Press, 1970.

Handler, Jerome S. "Slave Medecine and Obeah in Barbados." *New West Indian Guide* 74 (2000): 57–90.

Hanotaux, Gabriel, and A. Martineau, eds. *Histoire des colonies françaises.* Paris: Plon, 1929.

Hardman, John. *French Revolution Documents.* Vol. 2. Oxford: Blackwell, 1973.

Harris, Joseph, ed. *Global Dimensions of the African Diaspora.* Washington, D.C.: Howard University Press, 1982.

Hart, Richard. *Black Jamaicans' Struggle against Slavery.* London: Community Education Trust, 1979.

———. *Slaves Who Abolished Slavery.* Vol. 2, *Blacks in Rebellion.* Kingston: Institute of Social and Economic Research, University of the West Indies, 1985.

Hayot, Émile. *Les gens de couleur libres du Fort-Royal, 1679–1823.* Paris: Société française d'histoire d'Outre-Mer, 1971.

Heinl, Robert D., and Nancy G. Heinl. *Written in Blood: The Story of the Haitian People, 1492–1995.* Rev. ed. by Michael Heinl. Lanham: University Press of America, 1996.

Helg, Aline. "A Fragmented Majority: Free 'of All Colors,' Indians, and Slaves in Caribbean Colombia during the Haitian Revolution." In *Impact of the Haitian Revolution in the Atlantic World*, ed. D. Geggus, 157–175. Columbia: University of South Carolina Press, 2001.

Henige, David. "On the Contact Population of Hispaniola: History as Higher Mathematics." *Hispanic American Historical Review* 58 (1978): 217–237.

Herrera, Antonio de. *Historia general de los hechos de los Castellanos en las islas y Tierrafirme del Mar Océano*. 17 vols. 1601. Reprint, Madrid: Tipografía de Archivos, 1934.

Heuman, Gad, ed. *From Out of the House of Bondage: Runaways, Resistance and Marronage in Africa and the New World*. London: Frank Cass, 1986.

———. *"The Killing Time": The Morant Bay Rebellion in Jamaica*. London: Macmillan, 1994.

Heusch, Luc de. "Kongo in Haiti: A New Approach to Religious Syncretism." *Man* 24 (1989): 290–303.

Higman, Barry. *Slave Population and Economy in Jamaica, 1807–1834*. Cambridge: Cambridge University Press, 1976.

———. *Slave Populations of the British Caribbean, 1807–1834*. Baltimore, Md.: Johns Hopkins University Press, 1984.

Hilliard d'Auberteuil, Michel-René. *Considérations sur l'état présent de la colonie française de Saint-Domingue*. 2 vols. Paris, 1776–1777.

Histoire des désastres de Saint-Domingue. Paris, 1795.

Hobsbawm, Eric. "Revolution." In *Revolution in History*, ed. R. Porter and M. Teich, 5–46. Cambridge: Cambridge University Press, 1986.

Hoffmann, Léon-François. "L'Élément indien dans la conscience collective des Haïtiens." *Etudes Créoles* 17 (1994): 11–38.

———. *Haïti: lettres et l'être*. Toronto: Éditions du GREF, 1992.

———. "Histoire, mythe et idéologie: la cérémonie du Bois-Caïman." *Études Créoles* 13 (1990): 9–34.

———. "Un mythe national: la cérémonie du Bois-Caïman." In *La république haïtienne: état des lieux et perspectives*, ed. G. Barthélemy and C. Girault, 434–448. Paris: Karthala, 1993.

———. "Un Négociant américain aux Gonaïves en 1806 et 1807." *Revue de la Société Haïtienne d'Histoire et de Géographie* 155 (1987): 1–18.

———. "Le vodou sous la colonie et pendant les guerres de l'indépendance." *Conjonction: Revue Franco-Haïtienne* 173 (1987): 109–135.

Houdaille, Jacques. "Les Français et les afrancesados en Amérique centrale, 1700–1810." *Revista de Historia de América* 44 (1957): 305–330.

———. "Negros Franceses en América Central a fines del siglo XVIII." *Antropología e historia de Guatemala* 6 (1954): 65–67.

———. "Negros Franceses en América Central a fines del siglo XVIII." *El Imparcial*, 13 March 1954, 11.

Houdaille, Jacques, Roger Massio, and Gabriel Debien. "Les origines des esclaves des Antilles." *Bulletin de l'Institut Français de l'Afrique Noire* 25 (1963): 215–265.

Hughes, H. B. L. "British Policy towards Haiti, 1801–1805." *Canadian Historical Review* 25 (1944): 397–408.

Hunt, Alfred. *Haiti's Influence on Antebellum America: Slumbering Volcano in the Caribbean*. Baton Rouge: Louisiana University Press, 1988.

Hurbon, Laënnec. *Le barbare imaginaire*. Paris: Ed. du Cerf, 1988.

———. *Comprendre Haïti: essai sur l'état, la nation, la culture*. Paris: Karthala, 1987.

——. *Voodoo: Search for the Spirit*. New York: Harry Abrams, 1995.

Hyppolite, Michelson P. *Héritage culturel et linguistique des Aytiens de la première civilisation de l'île d'Ayti*. Port-au-Prince: Imprimerie Nouvelle, 1989.

Hyslop, Beatrice F. *French Nationalism in 1789 According to the General Cahiers*. New York: Columbia University Press, 1934.

Incháustegui, Joaquín Marino. *Documentos para estudio: Marco de la época y problemas del tratado de Basilea de 1795*. 2 vols. Buenos Aires: Academia Dominicana de la Historia, 1957.

James, C. L. R. *The Black Jacobins: Toussaint L'Ouverture and the San Domingo Revolution*. 1938. 2nd. ed., New York: Vintage, 1963.

Janvier, Louis-Joseph. *Les constitutions d'Haïti*. Paris, 1886.

——. *Les Jacobins noirs*. Trans. Pierre Naville. Paris: Gallimard, 1949.

Janzen, John. *Lemba, 1650–1930: A Drum of Affliction*. New York: Garland, 1982.

Jaurès, Jean. *Histoire socialiste, 1789–1900*. 8 vols. Paris: Librairie de l'Humanité, 1922.

Jean-Baptiste, Saint-Victor. *Haïti: sa lutte pour l'indépendance*. Paris: Nef, 1957.

J.M.C. *Précis des gémissements des sang-mêlés dans les colonies françoises, par J.M.C. Américain, sang-mêlé*. Paris, 1789.

Joachim, Benoît. *Les racines du sous-développement en Haïti*. Port-au-Prince: Henri Deschamps, 1979.

Julien, Jean-Baptiste Emmanuel Francius. *La cérémonie du Bois Caïman*. n.p.: Éditions l'Ordre Nouveau, n.d.

Kápsoli Escudero, Wilfredo. *Sublevaciones de esclavos en el Perú*. Lima: Universidad Ricardo Palma, 1975.

Kennedy, Michael. *The Jacobin Clubs in the French Revolution*. Princeton: Princeton University Press, 1982.

Kerboull, Jean. *Le Vaudou: magie ou religion?* Paris: Laffont, 1973.

Kilson, Marion. "Towards Freedom: An Analysis of Slave Revolts in the United States." *Phylon* 25 (1964): 175–187.

King, Stewart. "Blue Coat or Lace Collar? Military and Civilian Free Coloreds in the Colonial Society of Saint-Domingue, 1776–1791." Ph.D. diss., Johns Hopkins University, 1997.

Klein, Herbert. *Slavery in the Americas: A Comparative Study of Virginia and Cuba*. Chicago: University of Chicago Press, 1967.

Knight, Franklin W. "The Haitian Revolution." *American Historical Review* 105 (2000): 103–115.

Knight, Franklin, and Peggy Liss, eds. *Atlantic Port Cities: Economy, Culture, and Society*. Knoxville: University of Tennessee Press, 1991.

Kolchin, Peter. *American Slavery, 1619–1877*. New York: Hill and Wang, 1993.

——. *Unfree Labor: American Slavery and Russian Serfdom*. Cambridge, Mass.: Belknap Press, 1987.

Korngold, Ralph. *Citizen Toussaint*. London: Gollancz, 1945.

Krantz, Frederick, ed. *History from Below: Studies in Popular Protest and Popular Ideology*. Oxford: Blackwell, 1988.

Kropotkine, Pierre. *La Grande Révolution, 1789–1793*. Paris: Stock, 1909.

Laborie, Pierre-Joseph. *Réflexions sommaires adressées à la France et à la colonie de Saint-Domingue*. Paris, 1789.

Lacroix, Pamphile de. *Mémoires pour servir à l'histoire de la Révolution de Saint-Domingue*. 2 vols. Paris, 1819.

Laguerre, M. "An Ecological Approach to Voodoo." *Freeing the Spirit* 3 (1974): 3–12.

———. *Voodoo and Politics in Haiti.* New York: St. Martin's Press, 1989.

Landers, Jane G. *Black Society in Spanish Florida.* Urbana: University of Illinois Press, 1999.

———. "Jorge Biassou: Black Chieftain." *El Escribano* 25 (1988): 87–100.

———. "Rebellion and Royalism in Spanish Florida." In *A Turbulent Time: The French Revolution and the Greater Caribbean,* ed. D. B. Gaspar and D. P. Geggus, 156–177. Bloomington: Indiana University Press, 1997.

La Rosa Corzo, Gabino. *Los palenques del Oriente de Cuba: resistencia y acoso.* Havana: Editorial academia, 1991.

Las Casas, Bartolomé de. *Historia General de las Indias.* 1877. Reprint, Ed. André St. Lu. Caracas: Fundación Biblioteca Ayacucho, 1986.

———. *Short Account of the Destruction of the Indies.* 1552. Reprint, London: Penguin Books, 1992.

Lattre, P. de. *Campagne des Français à Saint-Domingue.* Paris, 1805.

Laurent, Gérard M. *Documentation historique pour nos étudiants.* 2nd ed. Port-au-Prince: La Phalange, 1960.

———. *Quand les chaines volent en éclats.* Port-au-Prince: Deschamps, 1979.

———. *Toussaint Louverture à travers sa correspondance.* Madrid: G. Laurent, 1953.

———. *Trois mois aux archives d'Espagne.* Port-au-Prince: Les Presses Libres, 1956.

Laurent, Mentor. *Erreurs et vérités dans l'histoire d'Haïti.* Port-au-Prince: Telhomme, 1945.

Laveaux, Étienne. *Compte rendu par le Général Laveaux à ses concitoyens.* Paris, 1797.

Law, Robin. "On the African Background to the Slave Insurrection in Saint-Domingue (Haïti) in 1791: The Bois Caiman Ceremony and the Dahomian 'Blood Pact.'" Paper presented to the Harriet Tubman seminar, York University, Ontario, November 1999.

Lebeau, Auguste. *De la condition des gens de couleur libres sous l'Ancien Régime.* Poitiers: A. Masson, 1903.

Leiva Vivas, Rafael. *Tráfico de esclavos negros a Honduras.* Tegucigalpa: Guaymuras, 1982.

Lémery, Henry. *La Révolution française à la Martinique.* Paris: Larose, 1936.

Léon, Rulx. *Propos d'histoire.* 3 vols. Port-au-Prince: Imprimerie de l'État, 1945–1979.

Lepkowski, Tadeusz. *Haití.* 2 vols. Havana: Casa, 1968–1969.

Lettre à MM. les députés des trois ordres. Paris, 1789.

Lettres des diverses Sociétés des Amis de la Constitution qui réclament les droits de Citoyen actif en faveur des hommes de couleur des Colonies. Paris, 1791.

Levine, Laurence. *Black Slavery and Black Consciousness: Afro-American Folk Thought from Slavery to Freedom.* New York: Oxford University Press, 1977.

Leyburn, James. *The Haitian People.* 1941. Reprint, New Haven: Yale University Press, 1966.

Lincoln, Bruce. *Discourse and the Construction of Society.* New York: Oxford University Press, 1989.

Lincoln, Bruce, ed. *Religion, Rebellion, Revolution: An Interdisciplinary and Cross-Cultural Collection of Essays.* New York: St. Martin's, 1985.

Lipski, John M. *The Speech of the Negros Congos of Panama.* Amsterdam: Benjamins, 1989.

Logan, Rayford. *The Diplomatic Relations of the United States with Haiti, 1776–1891.* Chapel Hill: University of North Carolina Press, 1941.

Louverture, Isaac. *Notes diverses d'Isaac sur la vie de Toussaint-Louverture.* In *Histoire de l'expédition des Français à Saint-Domingue,* by Antoine Métral, 325–339. Paris, 1825.

Lovejoy, Paul. *Transformations in Slavery*. Cambridge: Cambridge University Press, 1983.

Loven, Sven. *Origins of the Tainan Culture of the West Indies*. Göteborg: Elanders Boktryckeri Aktiebolag, 1935.

Lowenthal, David. *Caribbean Societies*. London: Oxford University Press, 1972.

Madiou, Thomas. *Histoire d'Haïti*. 1847–1848. Rev. ed. 8 vols. Port-au-Prince: H. Deschamps, 1989–1991.

Malenfant, Charles. *Des colonies et particulièrement de celle de Saint-Domingue*. Paris, 1814.

Mangonès, Edmond. "L'Île d'Haïti: Une regrettable initiative de la U.S. Geographic Board." *Revue de la Société Haïtienne d'Histoire de Géographie et de la Géologie* 15 (1934): 1–63.

Manigat, Leslie F. "Relationship between Marronage and Slave Revolts and Revolution in St. Domingue–Haiti." *Annals of the New York Academy of Sciences* 292 (1977): 420–438.

Manning, Patrick. *Slavery, Colonialism, and Economic Growth in Dahomey*. Cambridge: Cambridge University Press, 1982.

Marchetti, Giovanni. *Cultura indígena e integración nacional: la "Historia antigua de México" de F. J. Clavijero*. Xalapa: Universidad Veracruzana, 1986.

Marion, Jean. "Un Nantais à Saint-Domingue (1756–1792)." *Bulletin de la Société d'Archéologie de Nantes* 78 (1938): 114–133.

Martir de Angleria, Pedro. *Décadas del Nuevo Mundo*. 1504–1530. 2 vols. Reprint, Santo Domingo: Sociedad Dominicana de Bibliófilos, 1989.

Mathelier, G. *Tousen Louveti*. Port-au-Prince: Deschamps, n.d.

Matthewson, Timothy. "George Washington's Policy towards the Haitian Revolution." *Diplomatic History* 3 (1979): 321–336.

———. "Jefferson and Haiti." *Journal of Southern History* 61 (1995): 209–248.

———. "Jefferson and the New Order of Things: The United States and the Haitian Slave Revolution." Unpublished ms.

Maurel, Blanche. *Le vent du large*. Paris: La Nef, 1952.

Maximilien, Louis. "Quelques apports indiens dans la vie haïtienne." In *Problemas dominico-haitianas y del Caribe*, ed. G. Pierre-Charles, 171–184. Mexico City: Universidad Nacional Autónoma de México, 1973.

———. *Le vodou haïtien*. Port-au-Prince: Imprimerie de l'État, 1945.

Mazères. *De l'utilité des colonies*. Paris, 1814.

McClellan, James. *Colonialism and Science: Saint Domingue in the Old Regime*. Baltimore: Johns Hopkins University Press, 1992.

Mejía Ricart, Adolfo. *Historia de Santo Domingo*. Ciudad Trujillo: Editores Pol Hermanos, 1948.

Méndez, Gabriel Jesús. "Mérida, Yucatán, and its Hinterland, 1780–1860." Ph.D. diss., Washington State University, 1994.

Menier, Marie-Antoinette. "Dépôt des papiers publics des colonies: Saint-Domingue, notariat." *Revue d'Histoire des Colonies* 35 (1951): 339–358.

———. "Saint-Domingue, abornements, recensements des biens domaniaux et urbains." *Revue Française d'Histoire d'Outre-Mer* 44 (1957): 223–50.

———. "Les sources de l'histoire de la partie française de l'ile de Saint-Domingue aux Archives Nationales de la France." *Conjonction* 140 (1978): 119–35.

———. "Les sources de l'histoire des Antilles dans les Archives nationales de la France." *Bulletin de la Société d'Histoire de la Guadeloupe* 36 (1978): 7–39.

Mennesson-Rigaud, Odette. "Le rôle du Vaudou dans l'indépendance d'Haïti." *Présence Africaine* 17–18 (1958): 43–67.

Mentor, Gaétan. *Histoire d'un crime politique: le Général Étienne Victor Mentor.* Port-au-Prince: Fondation Sogebank, 1999.

Meredith, John. *The Plantation Slaves of Trinidad, 1783–1816: A Mathematical and Demographic Enquiry.* Cambridge: Cambridge University Press, 1988.

Metcalf, Alida C. "Millenarian Slaves? The Santidade de Jaguaripe and Slave Resistance in the Americas." *American Historical Review* 104 (1999): 1531–1559.

Métral, Antoine. *Histoire de l'expédition des Français à Saint-Domingue.* Paris, 1825.

———. *Histoire de l'insurrection des esclaves dans le Nord de Saint-Domingue.* Paris, 1818.

Métraux, Alfred. *Haiti: Black Peasants and Their Religion.* London: Harrap's, 1960.

———. *Le vaudou haïtien.* Paris: Gallimard, 1958.

Mettas, Jean. *Répertoire des expéditions negrières françaises au XVIIIe siècle.* 2 vols. Ed. Serge Daget and Michelle Daget. Paris: Société française d'histoire d'Outre-Mer, 1978, 1984.

Michel, Antoine. *La Mission du Général Hédouville.* Port-au-Prince: n.p., n.d.

Middelanis, Carl Hermann, ed. *Schwarze Freiheit im Dialog: Saint-Domingue 1791–Haiti 1991.* Bielefeld: Hans Kock, 1991.

Miers, Suzanne, and Igor Kopytoff, eds. *Slavery in Africa: Historical and Anthropological Perspectives.* Madison: University of Wisconsin Press, 1977.

Miller, Joseph C. *Way of Death: Merchant Capitalism and the Angolan Slave Trade, 1730–1830.* Madison: University of Wisconsin Press, 1988.

Milscent, Claude-Louis-Michel. *Du régime colonial.* Paris, 1792.

———. *Sur les troubles de Saint-Domingue.* Paris, 1792.

Mintz, Sidney, and Richard Price. *An Anthropological Approach to the Afro-American Past.* 2nd. printing. Philadelphia: Institute for the Study of Human Issues, 1977.

Mirot, Sylvie. "Un document inédit sur le marronage en la Guyane française." *Revue d'Histoire des Colonies* (1954): 245–256.

Montejo, Esteban. *Autobiography of a Runaway Slave.* 1968. Trans. Jocasta Innes. Reprint, Ed. M. Barnet and A. Hennessy. London: Macmillan, 1993.

Monti, Laura V. *A Calendar of the Rochambeau Papers at the University of Florida Libraries.* Gainesville: University of Florida Libraries, 1972.

Montilus, Guérin C. "Africa in Diaspora: The Myth of Dahomey in Haiti." *Journal of Caribbean History* 2 (1981): 73–84.

———. "Guinea versus Congo Lands: Aspects of Collective Memory in Haiti." In *Global Dimensions of the African Diaspora,* ed. J. Harris, 163–169. Washington, D.C.: Howard University Press, 1982.

Moore, Barrington. *Injustice: The Social Bases of Obedience and Revolt.* New York: M. E. Sharpe, 1978.

Moreau de Saint-Méry, Médéric-Louis-Élie. *Description topographique, physique, civile, politique et historique de la partie française de l'isle Saint-Domingue.* 1797. Rev. ed. Ed. Blanche Maurel, Étienne Taillemite. 3 vols. Paris: Société de l'histoire des colonies françaises, 1958.

———. *Topographical and Political Description of the Spanish Part of Saint-Domingo.* 2 vols. Trans. William Cobbett. Philadelphia, 1796.

Moreno Fraginals, Manuel. *El ingenio: Complejo económico social cubano del azúcar.* 3 vols. Havana: Editorial de Ciencias Sociales, 1978.

———. *The Sugarmill: The Socioeconomic Complex of Sugar in Cuba.* New York: Monthly Review Press, 1976.

Morgan, Philip, and Chris Brown. *The Arming of Slaves in World History: From Classical Times to the Modern Age.* New Haven: Yale University Press, forthcoming.

Morrissey, Marietta. *Slave Women in the New World: Stratification in the Caribbean.* Lawrence: University of Kansas Press, 1989.

Mott, Luiz. "A revolução dos negros do Haiti e o Brasil." *Mensario do Arquivo Nacional* (Rio de Janeiro) 13 (1982): 3–10.

Mozard (Ravinet), Laurette-Aimée. *Mémoires d'une créole du Port-au-Prince (île Saint-Domingue).* Paris: Chez l'auteur, 1844.

Mulinda, Habi Buganza. "Le nkisi dans la tradition woyo du Bas-Zaïre." *Systèmes de Pensée en Afrique Noire* 8 (1985): 208–214.

Mullin, Gerald. *Flight and Rebellion: Slave Resistance in Eighteenth-Century Virginia.* New York: Oxford University Press, 1972.

Mullin, Michael. *Africa in America: Slave Acculturation and Resistance in the American South and the British Caribbean, 1736–1831.* Urbana: University of Illinois Press, 1992.

Najman, Charles. *Haïti, Dieu seul me voit.* Paris: Balland, 1995.

———. *Le Serment du Bois-Caïman* [film]. Paris, 1992.

Nardin, Jean-Claude. *La mise en valeur de l'île de Tabago (1763–1783).* Paris: Mouton, 1969.

Naro, Nancy, ed. *Blacks and National Identity in Nineteenth-Century Latin America.* London: University of London, 2002.

Nau, Émile. *Histoire des caciques d'Haïti.* 2 vols. 1854. Reprint, Port-au-Prince: Panorama, 1963.

Nemours, Alfred. *Histoire de la captivité et de la mort de Toussaint-Louverture: notre pélerinage au fort de Joux.* Paris: Berger-Levrault, 1929.

Nemours, Luc. "Pour quelles raisons Toussaint Louverture est-il passé des Espagnols aux Français?" *Annales Historiques de la Révolution Française* (1948): 166–171.

Nicholls, David. *From Dessalines to Duvalier: Race, Colour, and National Independence in Haiti.* Cambridge: Cambridge University Press, 1979.

———. "Pompée Valentin de Vastey." *Jahrbuch für Geschichte von Staat, Wirtschaft und Gesellschaft Lateinamerikas* 28 (1991): 107–123.

Ogé, Vincent. *Motion faite par M. Vincent Ogé, jeune à l'Assemblée des Colons.* Paris, 1789.

Ott, Thomas O. *The Haitian Revolution, 1789–1804.* Knoxville: University of Tennessee Press, 1972.

Page, Pierre-François. *Essais sur les causes et les effets de la Révolution.* Paris, 1795.

Palacios, Roberto. "Ansia de libertad." *Lanternú* (Curaçao) 1 (1983): 20–27.

Palmer, Robert R. *The Age of the Democratic Revolution.* 2 vols. Princeton: Princeton University Press, 1959, 1964.

Pané, Ramón. *Relación acerca de las antigüedades de los indios.* Santo Domingo: Fundación Corripio, 1988.

Paquette, Robert. *Sugar Is Made with Blood: The Conspiracy of La Escalera and the Conflict between Empires over Slavery in Cuba.* Middletown, Conn.: Wesleyan University Press, 1988.

A Particular Account of the Commencement and Progress of the Insurrection of the Negroes in St. Domingo. London, 1792.

Patterson, Orlando. *Slavery and Social Death: A Comparative Study.* Cambridge, Mass.: Harvard University Press, 1982.

———. *The Sociology of Slavery: An Analysis of the Origins, Development and Structure of Negro Slave Society in Jamaica.* London: MacGibbon & Kee, 1967.

Paul, Emmanuel C. *Panorama du folklore haïtien: présence africaine en Haïti.* Port-au-Prince: Imprimerie de l'État, 1962.

———. *Questions d'histoire (Études critiques).* Port-au-Prince: Imprimerie de l'État, 1956.

Pauléus Sannon, Horace. *Histoire de Toussaint-Louverture.* 3 vols. Port-au-Prince: Héraux, 1920–1933.

Pearson, Edward, *Designs against Charleston: The Trial Record of the Denmark Vesey Slave Conspiracy of 1822.* Chapel Hill: University of North Carolina Press, 1999.

Pérez de la Riva, Francisco. *El Café: Historia de su cultivo y explotación en Cuba.* Havana: J. Montero, 1944.

Pérotin-Dumon, Anne. "Les Jacobins des Antilles ou l'esprit de liberté dans les Îles-du-Vent." *Revue d'Histoire Moderne et Contemporaine* 35 (1988): 275–304.

Peyser, Joseph. "The Fate of the Fox Survivors." *Wisconsin Magazine of History* 73 (1989–1990): 83–110.

Peytraud, Lucien. *L'esclavage aux Antilles françaises avant 1789.* Paris, 1897.

Picquenard, Jean-Baptiste. *Zoflora ou la bonne négresse: Anecdote coloniale.* 2 vols. Paris, 1799.

Pierre-Charles, Gérard, et al. *Problemas dominico-haitianas y del Caribe.* Mexico City: Universidad Nacional Autónoma de México, 1973.

Pinto Vallejo, J. "Slave Resistance in Minas Gerais, 1700–1750." *Journal of Latin American Studies* (1985): 1–34.

Pluchon, Pierre. *Nègres et Juifs au XVIIIe siècle.* Paris: Tallandier, 1984.

———. *Toussaint Louverture: de l'esclavage au pouvoir.* Paris: L'École, 1979.

———. *Toussaint Louverture: un révolutionnaire noir d'Ancien régime.* Paris: Fayard, 1989.

———. *Vaudou, sorciers, empoisonneurs: de Saint-Domingue à Haïti.* Paris: Karthala, 1987.

Popovic, A. *La révolte des esclaves en Iraq au IIIe/IXe siècle.* Paris: Geuthner, 1976.

Porter, Roy, and M. Teich, eds. *Revolution in History.* Cambridge: Cambridge University Press, 1986.

Price, Richard, ed. *Maroon Societies.* New York: Anchor, 1973.

Price-Mars, Jean. *Ainsi Parla l'Oncle: essais d'éthnographie.* Port-au-Prince: Imprimerie de Compiègne, 1928.

———. "Toussaint Louverture." *Revue de la Société Haïtienne d'Histoire, de Géographie et de Géologie* 57 (1945): 7–17.

Raboteau, Albert. *Slave Religion: The "Invisible Institution" in the Antebellum South.* New York: Oxford University Press, 1978.

Rainsford, Marcus. *An Historical Account of the Black Empire of Hayti.* London, 1805.

Raymond, Julien. *Réflexions sur les véritables causes des troubles.* Paris, 1793.

Raynal, Abbé. *Histoire philosophique et politique des établissemens et de commerce des Européens dans les Deux Indes.* 1st ed. 7 vols. La Haye, 1774.

———. *Histoire philosophique et politique des établissemens et de commerce des Européens dans les Deux Indes.* 3rd ed. 10 vols. Geneva, 1780.

Reckord, Mary. "The Jamaican Slave Rebellion of 1831." *Past and Present* 40 (1968): 108–125.

Reis, João José. *Slave Rebellion in Brazil: The Muslim Uprising of 1835 in Bahia.* Trans. Arthur Brakel. Baltimore: Johns Hopkins University Press, 1993.

Richard, Robert. "Les minutes des notaires de Saint-Domingue." *Revue d'Histoire des Colonies* 35 (1951): 281–338.

Richardson, Alan. "Romantic Voodoo: Obeah and British Culture, 1797–1807." *Studies in Romanticism* 32 (1993): 3–28.

Richardson, David, ed. *Abolition and Its Aftermath: The Historical Context, 1790–1916.* London: Frank Cass, 1985.

———. "Slave Exports from West and West-Central Africa, 1700–1809: New Estimates of Volume and Distribution." *Journal of African History* 30 (1989): 1–22.

Rigaud, Milo. *La tradition voudoo et le voudoo haïtien.* Paris: Niclaus, 1953.

Roberts, John. *French Revolution Documents.* New York: Blackwell, 1966.

Robin, Guy. "La lettre de Saint-Domingue." *Genèse* [e-journal] 1 (April 2000) (http://www.agh.qc.ca/alaune.htm).

Rodríguez Demorizi, Emilio, ed. *Cesión de Santo Domingo a Francia.* Ciudad Trujillo: Impresora Dominicana, 1958.

———. *La era de Francia en Santo Domingo.* Ciudad Trujillo: Editora del Caribe, 1955.

———. *Invasiones haitianas de 1801, 1805 y 1822.* Ciudad Trujillo: Editora del Caribe, 1955.

Röhrig Assunção, Matthias. "Elite Politics and Popular Rebellion in the Construction of Post-colonial Order: The Case of Maranhão, Brazil (1820–41)." *Journal of Latin American Studies* 31 (1999): 1–38.

Roume, Philippe Rose. *Rapport de P.R. Roume sur sa mission à Saint-Domingue.* Paris, 1793.

Rubio Sánchez, Manuel. *Historia del puerto de Trujillo.* 3 vols. Tegucigalpa: Banco Central de Honduras, 1975.

Rudé, George. *The French Revolution after 200 Years.* New York: Weidenfeld and Nicholson, 1988.

Rüsch, Erwin. *Die Revolution von Saint Domingue.* Hamburg: Friedrichsen, De Gruyter, 1930.

Sagás, Ernesto. "A Case of Mistaken Identity: *Antihaitianismo* in Dominican Culture." *Latinamericanist* 29 (1993): 1–5.

Saintoyant Jules. *La colonisation française pendant la Révolution.* 2 vols. Paris: Renaissance du Livre, 1930.

Saint-Rémy, Joseph. *Mémoires du Général Toussaint L'Ouverture.* Paris, 1853.

———. *Pétion et Haïti.* 5 vols. in 1. 1854–1857. Reprint, Paris: Berger-Levrault, 1956.

———. *Vie de Toussaint L'Ouverture.* Paris, 1850.

Sánchez Valverde, Antonio. *Idea del valor de la isla Española.* 1785. Reprint, Ed. Cipriano de Utrera and Emilio Rodríguez Demorizi. Santo Domingo: Editora Nacional, 1971.

Sanz Tapia, Angel. *Los militares emigrados y prisonieros franceses en Venezuela durante la guerra contra la revolución.* Caracas: Instituto Panamericano, 1977.

Sauer, Carl Ortwin. *The Early Spanish Main.* Berkeley: University of California Press, 1966.

Schama, Simon. *Citizens: A Chronicle of the French Revolution.* New York: Knopf, 1989.

Schoelcher, Victor. *Colonies étrangères et Haïti.* 2 vols. Paris, 1842–1843.

———. *Vie de Toussaint-Louverture.* Paris, 1889.

Schuler, Monica. "Ethnic Slave Rebellions in the Caribbean." *Journal of Social History* 3 (1970): 374–385.

Schüller, Karin. *Die deutsche Rezeption haitianischer Geschichte in der ersten Hälfte des 19. Jahrhunderts.* Köln: Böhlau, 1992.

Schwartz, Stuart. "Brésil: le royaume noir des 'mocambos.'" *L'Histoire* 41 (1982): 38–48.

———. "Resistance and Accommodation in Eighteenth Century Brazil." *Hispanic American Historical Review* 57 (1977): 69–81.

———. *Sugar Plantations in the Formation of Brazilian Society: Bahia, 1550–1835.* Cambridge: Cambridge University Press, 1986.

Scott, James C. *Weapons of the Weak: Everyday Forms of Peasant Resistance.* New Haven: Yale University Press, 1985.

Scott, Julius. "The Common Wind: Currents of Afro-American Communication in the Era of the Haitian Revolution." Ph.D. diss., Duke University, 1986.

Sevilla Soler, Maria Rosario. *Santo Domingo, Tierra de Frontera (1750–1800)*. Seville: Escuela de Estudios Hispano-Americanos, 1980.

Sheller, Mimi B. "Democracy after Slavery: Black Publics and Peasant Rebellion in Postemancipation Haiti and Jamaica." Ph.D. diss., New School for Social Research, 1996.

Skocpol, Theda. *States and Social Revolution*. Cambridge: Cambridge University Press, 1979.

Smucker, Glenn R. "The Social Character of Religion in Rural Haiti." In *Haiti—Today and Tomorrow*, ed. C. Foster and A. Valdman, 35–36. Lanham, Md.: University Press of America, 1984.

Stampp, Kenneth. "Rebels and Sambos: The Search for the Negro's Personality in Slavery." *Journal of Southern History* 37 (1971): 367–392.

Stein, Robert. *The French Sugar Business*. Baton Rouge: Louisiana State University Press, 1988.

———. *Léger-Félicité Sonthonax: The Lost Sentinel of the Republic*. Rutherford, N.J.: Fairleigh Dickinson University Press, 1985.

Stern, Steve J., ed. *Resistance, Rebellion, and Consciousness in the Andean Peasant World, 18th to 20th Centuries*. Madison: University of Wisconsin Press, 1987.

Stoddard, Theodore L. *The French Revolution in San Domingo*. New York: Houghton Mifflin, 1914.

Sutherland, Donald G. M. *France, 1789–1815: Revolution and Counterrevolution*. New York: Oxford University Press, 1987.

Sylvain, Franck. *Le serment du Bois Caïman et la première Pentecôte*. Port-au-Prince: Deschamps, 1979.

Synnott, Anthony. "Slave Revolts in the Caribbean." Ph.D. thesis, University of London, 1976.

Tabari. *The Revolt of the Zanj*. Trans. David Waines. Albany: State University of New York Press, 1992.

Tannenbaum, Frank. *Slave and Citizen: The Negro in the Americas*. New York: Vintage Books, 1946.

Tarbé, Charles. *Rapport et projet de décret relatif au débarquement . . . par le capitaine Colmin*. Paris, 1792.

———. *Rapport sur les troubles de Saint-Domingue fait à l'Assemblée Nationale*. Paris, 1792.

Tarrade, Jean. *Le commerce colonial à la fin de l'Ancien Régime: l'évolution du régime de l'Exclusif de 1763 à 1789*. Paris: Presses Universitaires de France, 1972.

Tejera, Apolinar. "Quid de Quisqueya?" *Boletín del Archivo General de la Nación* (Santo Domingo) 8 (1945): 216–221.

Tejera, Emilio. *Indigenismos*. 2 vols. Santo Domingo: Editora de Santo Domingo, 1977.

Tella, Torcuato di. *La rebelión de esclavos de Haití*. Buenos Aires: Ides, 1984.

Thésée, Françoise. "Les assemblées paroissiales des Cayes à Saint-Domingue (1774–1793)." *Revue de la Société Haïtienne d'Histoire et de Géographie* 137 (1982): 5–212.

———. "Autour de la Société des Amis des Noirs." *Présence Africaine* 125 (1983): 3–82.

Thibau, Jacques. *Le temps de Saint-Domingue: l'esclavage et la Révolution Française*. Paris: J. C. Lattès, 1989.

Thornton, John. "African Soldiers in the Haitian Revolution." *Journal of Caribbean History* 25 (1993): 58–80.

———. "'I am the subject of the King of Congo': African Political Ideology and the Haitian Revolution." *Journal of World History* 4 (1993): 181–214.

———. "On the Trail of Voodoo: African Christianity in Africa and the Americas." *The Americas* 44 (1988): 261–278.

Tilly, Charles. *From Mobilization to Revolution.* Reading, Mass.: Addison-Wesley, 1978.

Tocqueville, Alexis de. *L'Ancien Régime et la Révolution.* Ed. G. W. Headlam. Oxford: Oxford University Press, 1904.

Torres Saillant, Silvio. "The Tribulations of Blackness: Stages in Dominican Racial Identity." *Latin American Perspectives* 25 (1998): 126–146.

Toumson, Roger, ed. *La période Révolutionnaire aux Antilles.* Schoelcher: Groupe de Recherche et d'Étude des Littératures et Civilisations de la Caraïbe et des Amériques Noires, 1989.

Trouillot, Hénock. *Introduction à une histoire du vaudou.* Port-au-Prince: Fardin, 1970.

———. *Les origines sociales de la littérature haïtienne.* 1962. Port-au-Prince: Fardin, 1986.

Trouillot, Michel-Rolph. Review of *Les marrons de la liberté* in *New West Indian Guide* 56 (1982): 180–182.

———. *Silencing the Past: Power and the Production of History.* Boston: Beacon Press, 1995.

———. *Ti dife boule sou istoua Ayiti.* New York: Lakansiel, 1977.

Turner, Mary. *Slaves and Missionaries: The Disintegration of Jamaican Slave Society, 1787–1834.* Urbana: University of Illinois Press, 1982.

Utrera, Cipriano de. *Polémica de Enriquillo.* Santo Domingo: Editora del Caribe, 1973.

Valente, Waldemar. *Sincretismo religioso afro-brasileiro.* Sao Paulo: Companhia Editora Nacional, 1977.

Vallejo, Antonio R. *Primer anuario estadístico.* Tegucigalpa: Tipografía nacional, 1893.

Vanhee, Hein. "Central African Popular Christianity and the Making of Haitian Vodou Religion." In *Central Africans and Cultural Transformations in the American Diaspora,* ed. Linda Heywood. Cambridge: Cambridge University Press, in press.

Vastey, Valentin Pompée de. *Essay on the Causes of the Revolution and Civil Wars of Hayti.* 1823. Reprint, New York: Negro Universities Press, 1969.

———. *Le système colonial dévoilé.* Cap Henry, 1814.

Venault de Charmilly, Pierre-François. *Lettre à M. Bryan Edwards.* London, 1797.

Verna, Paul. *Petión y Bolívar: Cuarenta años de relaciones haitiano-venezolanas.* Caracas: n.p., 1969.

Victoria Ojeda, Jorge, and Jorge Canto Alcocer. "Impulso y dispersión de los negros auxiliadores: El caso de San Fernando Aké, Yucatán." *Por Eso! Suplemento Cultural* (Mérida), 26 July 1998, 3–9.

Viotti da Costa, Emilia. *Crowns of Glory, Tears of Blood: The Demerara Slave Rebellion of 1823.* New York: Oxford University Press, 1994.

Voelz, Peter. *Slave and Soldier: The Military Impact of Blacks in the Colonial Americas.* New York: Garland, 1993.

Vogt, Joseph. *Ancient Slavery and the Ideal of Man.* Oxford: Oxford University Press, 1974.

Walne, Peter. *A Guide to the Manuscript Sources for the History of Latin America and the Caribbean in the British Isles.* London: Oxford University Press for the Institute of Latin American Studies, University of London, 1973.

Walvin, James, ed. *Slavery and British Society, 1774–1848.* London: Macmillan, 1982.

Ward, J. R. *British West Indian Slavery, 1750–1834: The Process of Amelioration.* Oxford: Oxford University Press, 1988.

Warner-Lewis, Maureen. *Guinea's Other Suns.* Dover, Mass.: Majority Press, 1991.

Watson, James L., ed. *Asian and African Systems of Slavery.* Berkeley: University of California Press, 1980.

Westergaard, W. "Account of the Negro Rebellion on St. Croix, Danish West Indies, in 1759." *Journal of Negro History* 11 (1926): 50–61.

———. *The Danish West Indies under Company Rule.* New York: Macmillan, 1917.

Wilberforce, Robert I., and Samuel Wilberforce. *Life of William Wilberforce.* 5 vols. London, 1838.

Wyatt-Brown, Bertram. "The Mask of Obedience: Male Slave Psychology in the Old South." *American Historical Review* 93 (1988): 1228–1252.

Yacou, Alain. "L'administration coloniale espagnole à Cuba et les débuts des révolutions française et haïtienne." *Bulletin de la Société d'Histoire de la Guadeloupe* 39 (1979): 47–52.

———. "La présence française dans la partie occidentale de l'île de Cuba au lendemain de la Révolution de Saint-Domingue." *Revue Française d'Histoire d'Outre-Mer* 84 (1987): 149–188.

———. "Le projet des révoltes serviles de l'île de Cuba dans la première moitié du XIXe siècle." *Revue du CERC* 1 (1984): 46–67.

Yonker, Dolores M. "From the Belly of Dan: Dahomey in Haiti." Paper presented at the Cultural Vibrations conference, University of Florida, Gainesville, 1996.

Záiter Mejía, Alba Josefina. *La Identidad social y nacional en Dominicana: Un análisis psico-social.* Santo Domingo: Taller, 1996.

Zeuske, Michael, and Clarence Munford. "Die 'Grosse Furcht' in der Karibik: Saint Domingue und Kuba (1789–1795)." *Zeitschrift fur Geschichtswissenschaft* 39 (1991): 41–60.

Index

David Patrick Geggus is Professor of History at the University of Florida, Gainesville. He is the author of *Slavery, War and Revolution: The British Occupation of Saint Domingue, 1793–1798,* editor of *The Impact of the Haitian Revolution in the Atlantic World,* and co-editor (with David Barry Gaspar) of *A Turbulent Time: The French Revolution and the Greater Caribbean* (Indiana University Press).